Sociology Full Circle

Sociology Full Circle

Contemporary Readings on Society

edited by
William Feigelman

Praeger Publishers
New York · Washington · London

PRAEGER PUBLISHERS
111 Fourth Avenue, New York, N.Y. 10003, U.S.A.
5, Cromwell Place, London SW7 2JL, England

Published in the United States of America in 1972
by Praeger Publishers, Inc.

Library of Congress Catalog Card Number: 72-75689

Printed in the United States of America

To My Parents

Contents

Preface

The object of this collection of essays, as of most anthologies in introductory sociology, is to give the student some notion of the scope and intellectual range of the discipline while presenting examinations in some depth of certain selected issues and topics generally explored in the introductory course. At the same time, the anthology, it is hoped, will make sociology real to the student by giving him a clearer idea of what the sociologist does, how sociological research is actually conducted, and how the sociologist applies seemingly abstract concepts to illuminate our understanding of social phenomena.

One bothersome problem I have noted in many anthologies is that they seem to take little account of the intellectual potentialities and interests of the beginning sociology student. Although the collection may be fairly representative in presenting what is being done and has been done by sociologists, most of what is offered seems to be directed toward professional sociologists rather than beginning students. The classroom performance can often create bridges of understanding across this chasm, but more frequently the student is left with a feeling that sociology consists of a great deal of verbal hocus-pocus overladen with statistics.

What I have attempted to do in this book is to select materials that are highly readable, straightforward, and inherently interesting to the beginner, including both the student who plans to specialize in the field and the student who does not expect to go beyond the introductory course. Moreover, these selections, it is hoped, will be comprehensible and appealing not only to undergraduates in a four-year college but to junior- and community-college students as well. Although several of the selections have been taken from such professional sociological journals as *The American Sociological Review*, *The American Journal of Sociology*, and *Social Problems*, several come from more popular sources such as *The New York Times Magazine*,

Trans-action, and *Natural History*. The authors represented are all outstanding sociologists and social scientists; a number of the works included are prizewinning social-science efforts.

In order to stimulate interest in, and appreciation of, the discipline, several areas of sociological inquiry are emphasized. Considerable attention has been devoted to the sociology of social problems, that is, examining contemporary and topical issues in a sociological way, sometimes in their own right and sometimes as part of larger or more basic social processes. In our increasingly complex world, we look more and more to the sociologist to provide answers to such social questions as alienation, the generation gap, youth culture, the crisis of overpopulation, black power, women's liberation, the growth of extremist politics, changing courtship and family patterns, and the like.

Another dimension highlighted here is the cross-cultural approach. Many of the selections either were written by anthropologists or concern preliterate peoples and their problems. If we want to develop a systematic understanding of human society, we must take its total variety and diversity into account. By studying the social institutions and cultural patterns of so-called primitives, we may be able to observe social forms in a purer, more elemental state, in a way that better illuminates their dynamics, than would be the case if we observed our own complex and heterogeneous social world. The cross-cultural perspective also enables us to develop and test hypotheses about the interrelatedness of social forms as we compare societies on various axes. From the data provided by cross-cultural research, we may one day derive a meaningful picture of the origins of society, its present situation, how it is changing, and how the transformations may affect our lives in the future.

Still another focus of this collection is what might be called the sociology of the absurd. A number of the essays deal with ostensibly off-beat or bizarre subjects–nudists, queueing up for football games, sending Christmas cards, popular song lyrics, and so forth. Sociological understanding can be obtained from a study of all human behavior, eccentric as well as conventional. Exploring seemingly absurd questions may enable us to clarify our understanding of important social forms and may give us insight into those workings of society that previously seemed obscured to us. Only by encouraging free-ranging curiosity can we acquire truly imaginative sociological insight.

The selections also represent the most important theoretical and methodological approaches to the study of society–functionalism, conflict theory, social-exchange theory, and symbolic interactionism. The styles of research represented include questionnaire and interview surveys, participant and direct-observation research, content analysis, census studies, intervention research, and socio-historical analysis–all of which involve a variety of sampling and statistical-analytical procedures.

In arranging this collection, we have made certain more or less arbitrary decisions regarding the particular chapters in which the articles appear. It should be understood, however, that many articles have ramifications for other topics as well. The introduction to each chapter indicates other articles in the book that might be assigned in connection with the subject under study. The instructor, of course, may wish to assign these essays in still another order.

It is hoped that these selections will convey to the student not only the range of subject matter and techniques of the professional sociologist but also some sense of the wonder and fascination sociologists experience as they study society and group behavior.

Sociology Full Circle

1. The Nature of Sociology

INTRODUCTION

What is sociology? What benefits can it provide for mankind? How does one conduct sociological research? What important moral, socio-political, and methodological problems are involved in being a sociologist? The selections in this opening chapter explore some of these questions related to the basic characteristics of sociology and ways of doing social research.

Sociology may be defined as the scientific study of human society. The sociologist's interest is in human relationships: how they arise, how they persist, how they change. Unlike the psychologist, who studies individual behavior, the sociologist is interested in human interaction. Groups, in all their myriad forms, represent the distinctive focus of sociology. The range of human relationships explored by the sociologist is limitless. The behavior of the most respected and the most despised members of society, of the most ordinary and the most extraordinary people—all fall within the province of the sociologist.

The assertion that sociology is "scientific" carries with it a number of implications. It means that one of the sociologist's primary goals is the identification of regularities in group behavior. The sociologist seeks to establish a systematic body of knowledge about human society in the form of logically interrelated sets of hypotheses and theories that are directly verifiable and capable of accurately predicting social action.

To obtain systematic knowledge about society, the sociologist uses the so-called scientific method. This involves adopting a speculative attitude; everything is open to doubt until it is proved, and nothing is taken for granted. Moreover, the regularities presumed by the social scientist must be capable of being substantiated empirically (directly observable) and thus capable of convincing any rational man. Furthermore, the scientist is obliged to suspend his prejudices and predilections and to examine questions about society impartially and dispassionately.

Among the most significant benefits of sociological knowledge is that, by helping people to see clearly what their society is and what it can become, it affords them the opportunity to pursue their goals in rational, intelligent, and effective ways. It also gives them a vision of the manifold consequences of their beliefs and actions and helps them to choose among them.

Moreover, a knowledge of sociology provides man with a viewpoint, a way of looking at his world, of examining his society critically. A sociological perspective prods him to peer behind the commonplace rituals, conventions, and traditions of his culture. A sociological perspective can thus be unsettling; nevertheless, it yields a broadening vista of human life and engenders an appreciation of the infinite variety of human potentialities.

Some of the many benefits of sociological inquiry are suggested in the late C. Wright Mills's essay "The Promise," an excerpt from his well-known book *The Sociological Imagination*. Mills contends that in the contemporary world—where urban-industrial man finds himself torn from his traditional moorings—a sociological imagination has become indispensable for individual well-being.

We can trace sociological analysis in Western history back as early as ancient Greece, specifically to the writings of the Sophists. However, it was not until 1839, in the work of Auguste Comte, that the term "sociology" was first used. Although Comte defined sociology much as it is conceived today, the major corpus of Comte's work was not in keeping with his view of the discipline; for the most part, it represented a social-philosophical, nonempirical approach.

The positivist furor of the late nineteenth century, with its devotion to science and its commitment to the notion of unremitting evolution toward progress, provided the take-off point for the development of sociology. The development has dramatically accelerated during this century. Notwithstanding several notable exceptions, much early sociological research was, like Comte's, of the "armchair theory" variety. However, sociological study during the twentieth century, particularly in America, has had a decidedly empirical orientation.

The idea of a value-free sociology is one of the legacies of its positivist roots. From the early days of sociology until fairly recently, almost all sociologists argued that in order to maintain scientific objectivity the social scientist must avoid advocacy. Many social scientists believed that any expression of value judgment would necessarily hamper the scientist's ability to study society impartially and would ultimately result in a kind of pseudosociological analysis representing narrow self-interest or political partisanship.

This doctrine has recently been subjected to considerable re-examination. In "Anti-Minotaur: The Myth of a Value-free Sociology," Alvin Gouldner argues that the value-free ideal has frequently been propounded to mask moral indifference, crass commercialism, and political conservatism. Gouldner suggests that expression of the social scientist's interests, beliefs, and values is both unavoidable and necessary. As the social scientist selects problems for study, he inevitably suggests his own biases and beliefs. Also, once a social-science product is presented to society, it is viewed as favoring the interests of some groups and disfavoring those of others. Gouldner argues that it is one thing for the scientist to suspend his moral judgment in the interest of scientific precision and objectivity; it is quite another for him to be indifferent to the ways in which his research bears on the human predicament and how it might be applied to human affairs. Accepting Mills's notion that the modern world has made a sociological imagination indispensable, Gouldner maintains that the sociologist has a public responsibility to address existing social problems, both by identifying their origins and by attempting to ameliorate them. Although most contemporary sociologists agree with the former objective, it should be noted that a sizable number of others do not share his advocacy of social amelioration.

Sociology, like the other behavioral sciences, involves several methodological problems not found in the physical sciences. These problems hinge on the central fact that the subject of sociological study is mankind. Unlike the laboratory scientist studying animals or inanimate things, the sociologist can never perfectly control his subject; no one will permit another to rearrange his life completely for a scientific experiment. Secondly, in studying society we are usually studying ourselves, our families, our intimate friends, and other groups of whom we may have formed very definite evaluations. Can we suspend our attitudes and moral judgments so that they do not distort our analysis? While studying ourselves, can we be scientifically objective? In "Body Ritual Among the Nacirema," Horace Miner suggests, in a most amusing and thoughtful manner, that transcending the precepts of our own culture, studying a group dispassionately on its own terms, may be an insurmountable task. He leads us to wonder whether the stranger has a distinct advantage over the native in social research. Because his moral investments in the culture are less great, he may be better able to suspend his judgment in the interest of scientific objectivity.

Social-science research involves, first, the selection of a problem for study and the formulation of hypotheses. In the next step, the scientist painstakingly observes and records data relevant to the hypotheses, possibly examining official records, collecting interviews, or directly observing his sample or group. The data are then organized or classified; at this point, statistical computations are performed if necessary. Then, the scientist generalizes from his findings, indicates whether they confirm or refute his original hypotheses, and determines whether they add anything to established theory or suggest its revision. Finally, he makes his work public; he puts his findings on record, complete with data and procedures, so that his work can be repeated by others, tested, and added to the cumulative fund of knowledge.

There are many ways in which sociologists study society, including direct observation, interviewing, questionnaire surveys, the study of official records, content analysis (inferring social trends from popular literature, films, songs, or other such cultural items), and correlation analysis (examining data to find whether change in the amount of one variable is accompanied by comparable change in the amount of another). A variety of research designs are employed, including case studies, sampling surveys, and applications and variations of the "classical" experimental design (observing differences between a group exposed to an experimental manipulation and a control group, similar in every respect with the exception of the experimental condition).

Sociological curiosity has led to the exploration of a broad and diverse range of problems and questions about human society. In the chapters that follow, we shall attempt to provide an overview of both the types of questions explored and the methods and techniques used in sociological research.

The Sociological Imagination

The Promise*

C. Wright Mills

Nowadays, men often feel that their private lives are a series of traps. They sense that, within their everyday worlds, they cannot overcome their troubles, and, in this feeling, they are often quite correct: What ordinary men are directly aware of and what they try to do are bounded by the private orbits in which they live; their visions and their powers are limited to the close-up scenes of job, family, neighborhood; in other milieux, they move vicariously and remain spectators. And the more aware they become, however vaguely, of ambitions and of threats, that transcend their immediate locales, the more trapped they seem to feel.

Underlying this sense of being trapped are seemingly impersonal changes in the very structure of continent-wide societies. The facts of contemporary

* From *The Sociological Imagination* by C. Wright Mills. Copyright © 1959 by Oxford University Press, Inc. Reprinted by permission.

history are also facts about the success and the failure of individual men and women. When a society is industrialized, a peasant becomes a worker; a feudal lord is liquidated or becomes a businessman. When classes rise or fall, a man is employed or unemployed; when the rate of investment goes up or down, a man takes new heart or goes broke. When wars happen, an insurance salesman becomes a rocket launcher; a store clerk, a radar man; a wife lives alone; a child grows up without a father. Neither the life of an individual nor the history of a society can be understood without understanding both.

Yet, men do not usually define the troubles they endure in terms of historical change and institutional contradiction. The well-being they enjoy, they do not usually impute to the big ups and downs of the societies in which they live. Seldom aware of the intricate connection between the patterns of their own lives and the course of world history, ordinary men do not usually know what this connection means for the kinds of men they are becoming and for the kinds of history-making in which they might take part. They do not possess the quality of mind essential to grasp the interplay of man and society, of biography and history, of self and world. They cannot cope with their personal troubles in such ways as to control the structural transformations that usually lie behind them.

Surely, it is no wonder. In what period have so many men been so totally exposed at so fast a pace to such earthquakes of change? That Americans have not known such catastrophic changes as have the men and women of other societies is due to historical facts that are now quickly becoming "merely history." The history that now affects every man is world history. Within this scene and this period, in the course of a single generation, one-sixth of mankind is transformed from all that is feudal and backward into all that is modern, advanced, and fearful. Political colonies are freed; new and less visible forms of imperialism, installed. Revolutions occur; men feel the intimate grip of new kinds of authority. Totalitarian societies rise, and are smashed to bits–or succeed fabulously. After two centuries of ascendancy, capitalism is shown up as only one way to make society into an industrial apparatus. After two centuries of hope, even formal democracy is restricted to a quite small portion of mankind. Everywhere in the underdeveloped world, ancient ways of life are broken up and vague expectations become urgent demands. Everywhere in the overdeveloped world, the means of authority and of violence become total in scope and bureaucratic in form. Humanity itself now lies before us, the supernation at either pole concentrating its most coordinated and massive efforts upon the preparation of World War III.

The very shaping of history now outpaces the ability of men to orient themselves in accordance with cherished values. And which values? Even when they do not panic, men often sense that older ways of feeling and thinking have collapsed, and that newer beginnings are ambiguous to the point of moral stasis. Is it any wonder that ordinary men feel they cannot cope with the larger worlds with which they are so suddenly confronted?

That they cannot understand the meaning of their epoch for their own lives? That—in defense of selfhood—they become morally insensible, trying to remain altogether private men? Is it any wonder that they come to be possessed by a sense of the trap?

It is not only information that they need—in this Age of Fact, information often dominates their attention and overwhelms their capacities to assimilate it. It is not only the skills of reason that they need—although their struggles to acquire these often exhaust their limited moral energy.

What they need, and what they feel they need, is a quality of mind that will help them to use information and to develop reason in order to achieve lucid summations of what is going on in the world and of what may be happening within themselves. It is this quality, I am going to contend, that journalists and scholars, artists and publics, scientists and editors are coming to expect of what may be called the sociological imagination.

The sociological imagination enables its possessor to understand the larger historical scene in terms of its meaning for the inner life and the external career of a variety of individuals. It enables him to take into account how individuals, in the welter of their daily experience, often become falsely conscious of their social positions. Within that welter, the framework of modern society is sought, and within that framework the psychologies of a variety of men and women are formulated. By such means, the personal uneasiness of individuals is focused upon explicit troubles, and the indifference of publics is transformed into involvement with public issues.

The first fruit of this imagination—and the first lesson of the social science that embodies it—is the idea that the individual can understand his own experience and gauge his own fate only by locating himself within his period, that he can know his own chances in life only by becoming aware of those of all individuals in his circumstances. In many ways, it is a terrible lesson; in many ways, a magnificent one. We do not know the limits of man's capacities for supreme effort or willing degradation, for agony or glee, for pleasurable brutality or the sweetness of reason. But in our time we have come to know that the limits of "human nature" are frighteningly broad. We have come to know that every individual lives, from one generation to the next, in some society; that he lives out a biography, and that he lives it out within some historical sequence. By the fact of his living he contributes, however minutely, to the shaping of this society and to the course of its history, even as he is made by society and by its historical push and shove.

The sociological imagination enables us to grasp history and biography and the relations between the two within society. That is its task and its promise. To recognize this task and this promise is the mark of the classic social analyst. It is characteristic of Herbert Spencer—turgid, polysyllabic, comprehensive; of E. A. Ross—graceful, muckraking, upright; of Auguste Comte and Emile Durkheim; of the intricate and subtle Karl Mannheim. It is the quality of all that is intellectually excellent in Karl Marx; it is the clue to Thorstein Veblen's brilliant and ironic insight, to Joseph Schumpeter's many-sided constructions of reality; it is the basis of the psychological sweep of W. E. H. Lecky no less than of the profundity and clarity of Max Weber. And it is the signal of what is best in contemporary studies of man and society.

No social study that does not come back to the problems of biography, of history, and of their intersections within a society has completed its intellectual journey. Whatever the specific problems of the classic social analysts, however limited or however broad the features of social reality they have examined, those who have been imaginatively aware of the promise of their work have consistently asked three sorts of questions:

1. What is the structure of this particular society as a whole? What are its essential components, and how are they related to one another? How does it differ from other varieties of social order? Within it, what is the meaning of any particular feature for its continuance and for its change?
2. Where does this society stand in human history? What are the mechanics by which it is changing? What is its place within, and its meaning for, the development of humanity as a whole? How does any particular feature we are examining affect, and how is it affected by, the historical period in which it moves? And this period—what are its essential features? How does it differ from other periods? What are its characteristic ways of history-making?
3. What varieties of men and women now prevail in this society and in this period? And what varieties are coming to prevail? In what ways are they selected and formed, liberated and repressed, made sensitive and blunted? What kinds of "human nature" are revealed in the conduct and character we observe in this society in this period? And what is the meaning for "human nature" of each and every feature of the society we are examining?

Whether the point of interest is a great power state or a minor literary mood, a family, a prison, a creed—these are the kinds of questions the best social analysts have asked. They are the intellectual pivots of classic studies of man in society—and they are the questions inevitably raised by any mind possessing the sociological imagination. For that imagination is the capacity to shift from one perspective to another—from the political to the psychological; from examination of a single family to comparative assessment of the national budgets of the world; from the theological school to the military establishment; from considerations of an oil industry to studies of contemporary poetry. It is the capacity to range from the most impersonal and remote transformations to the most intimate features of the human self—and to see the relations between the two. Back of its use, there is always the urge to know the social and historical meaning of the individual in the society and in the period in which he has his quality and his being.

That, in brief, is why it is by means of the sociological imagination that men now hope to grasp what is going on in the world, and to understand what is happening in themselves as minute points of the intersections of biography and history within society. In large part, contemporary man's self-conscious view of himself as at least an outsider, if not a permanent stranger, rests upon an absorbed realization of social relativity and of the transformative power of history. The sociological imagination is the most fruitful form of this self-consciousness. By its use, men whose mentalities have swept only a series of limited orbits often come to feel as if suddenly awakened in a house with which they had only supposed themselves to be familiar. Correctly or incorrectly, they often come to feel that they can now provide themselves with adequate summations, cohesive assessments, comprehensive orientations. Older decisions that once appeared sound now seem to them products of a mind unaccountably dense. Their capacity for astonishment is made lively again. They acquire a new way of thinking, they experience a transvaluation of values: In a word, by their reflection and by their sensibility, they realize the cultural meaning of the social sciences.

Perhaps the most fruitful distinction with which the sociological imagination works is between the "personal troubles of milieu" and the "public issues of social structure." This distinction is an essential tool of the sociological imagination and a feature of all classic work in social science.

Troubles occur within the character of the individual and within the range of his immediate relations with others; they have to do with his self and with those limited areas of social life of which he is directly and personally aware. Accordingly, the statement and the resolution of troubles properly lie within the individual as a biographical entity and within the scope of his immediate milieu—the social setting that is directly open to his personal experience and, to some extent, his willful activity. A trouble is a private matter: Values cherished by an individual are felt by him to be threatened.

Issues have to do with matters that transcend these local environments of the individual and the range of his inner life. They have to do with the organization of many such milieux into the institutions of a historical society as a whole, with the ways in which various milieux overlap and interpenetrate to form the larger structure of social and historical life. An issue is a public matter: Some value cherished by publics is felt to be threatened. Often, there is a debate about what that value really is and about what it is that really threatens it. This debate is often without focus, if only because it is the very nature of an issue, unlike even widespread trouble, that it cannot very well be defined in terms of the immediate and everyday environments of ordinary men. An issue, in fact, often involves a crisis in institutional arrangements, and often, too, it involves what Marxists call "contradictions" or "antagonisms."

In these terms, consider unemployment. When, in a city of 100,000, only one man is unemployed, that is his personal trouble, and for its relief we properly look to the character of the man, his skills, and his immediate opportunities. But when, in a nation of 50 million employees, 15 million men are unemployed, that is an issue, and we may not hope to find its solution within the range of opportunities open to any one individual. The very structure of opportunities has collapsed. Both the correct statement of the problem and the range of possible solutions require us to consider the economic and political institutions of the society, and not merely the personal situation and character of a scatter of individuals.

Consider war. The personal problem of war, when it occurs, may be how to survive it or how to die in it with honor; how to make money out of it; how to climb into the higher safety of the military apparatus; or how to contribute to the war's termination. In short, according to one's values, to find a set of milieux and within it to survive the war or make one's death in it meaningful. But the structural issues of war have to do with its causes; with what types of men it throws up into command; with its effects upon economic and political, family and religious institutions, with the unorganized irresponsibility of a world of nation-states.

Consider marriage. Inside a marriage, a man and a woman may experience personal troubles; but, when the divorce rate during the first four years of marriage is 250 out of every 1,000 attempts, this is an indication of a structural issue having to do with the institutions of marriage and the family and other institutions that bear upon them.

Or consider the metropolis—the horrible, beautiful, ugly, magnificent sprawl of the great city. For many upper-class people, the personal solution to the problem of the city is to have an apartment with private garage under it in the heart of the city, and, forty miles out, a house by Henry Hill, garden by Garrett Eckbo, on a hundred acres of private land. In these two controlled environments—with a small staff at each end and a private helicopter connection—most people could solve many of the problems of personal milieux caused by the facts of the city. But all this, however splendid, does not solve the public issues that the structural fact of the city poses. What should be done with this wonderful monstrosity? Break it all up into scattered units, combining residence and work? Refurbish it as it stands? Or, after evacuation, dynamite it and build new cities according to new plans in new places? What should those plans be? And who is to decide and to accomplish whatever choice is made? These are structural issues; to confront them and to solve them requires us to consider political and economic issues that affect innumerable milieux.

Insofar as an economy is so arranged that slumps occur, the problem of unemployment becomes incapable of personal solution. Insofar as war is inherent in the nation-state system and in the uneven industrialization of the world, the ordinary individual in his restricted milieu will be powerless —with or without psychiatric aid—to solve the troubles this system or lack of system imposes upon him. Insofar as the family as an institution turns women into darling little slaves and men into their chief providers and unweaned dependents, the problem of a satisfactory marriage remains incapable of purely private solution. Insofar as the overdeveloped megalopolis and the overdeveloped automobile are built-in features of the overdeveloped society, the issues of urban living will not be solved by personal ingenuity and private wealth.

What we experience in various and specific milieux, I have noted, is often caused by structural changes. Accordingly, to understand the changes of many personal milieux, we are required to look beyond them. And the number and variety of such structural changes increase as the institutions within which we live become more embracing and more intricately connected with one another. To be aware of the idea of social structure and to use it with sensibility is to be capable of tracing such linkages among a great variety of milieux. To be able to do that is to possess the sociological imagination.

What are the major issues for publics and the key troubles of private individuals in our time? To formulate issues and troubles, we must ask what values are cherished yet threatened, and what values are cherished and supported, by the characterizing trends of our period. In the case both of threat and of support, we must ask what salient contradictions of structure may be involved.

When people cherish some set of values and do not feel any threat to them, they experience *well-being*. When they cherish values but *do* feel them to be threatened, they experience a crisis—either as a personal trouble or as a public issue. And, if all their values seem involved, they feel the total threat of panic.

But suppose people are neither aware of any cherished values nor experience any threat? That is the experience of *indifference,* which, if it seems to involve all their values, becomes apathy. Suppose, finally, they are unaware of any cherished values, but still are very much aware of a threat? That is the experience of *uneasiness*, of anxiety, which, if it is total enough, becomes a deadly, unspecified malaise.

Ours is a time of uneasiness and indifference—not yet formulated in such ways as to permit the work of reason and the play of sensibility. Instead of troubles—defined in terms of values and threats—there is often the misery of vague uneasiness; instead of explicit issues, there is often merely the beat feeling that all is somehow not right. Neither the values threatened nor whatever threatens them has been stated; in short, they have not been carried to the point of-decision. Much less have they been formulated as problems of social science.

In the 1930's, there was little doubt—except among certain deluded business circles—that there was an economic issue that was also a pack of personal troubles. In these arguments about the "crisis of capitalism," the formulations of Marx and the many unacknowledged reformulations of his work probably set the leading terms of the issue, and some men came to understand their personal troubles in these terms. The values threatened were plain to see and cherished by all; the structural contradictions that threatened them also seemed plain. Both were widely and deeply experienced. It was a political age.

But the values threatened in the era after World War II are often neither widely acknowledged as values nor widely felt to be threatened. Much private uneasiness goes unformulated; much public malaise and many decisions of enormous structural relevance never become public issues. For those who accept such inherited values as reason and freedom, it is the uneasiness itself that is the trouble; it is the indifference itself that is the issue. And it is this condition, of uneasiness and indifference, that is the signal feature of our period.

All this is so striking that it is often interpreted by observers as a shift in the very kinds of problems that need now to be formulated. We are frequently told that the problems of our decade, or even the crises of our period, have shifted from the external realm of economics and now have to do with the quality of individual life–in fact, with the question of whether there is soon going to be anything that can properly be called individual life. Not child labor but comic books, not poverty but mass leisure, are at the center of concern. Many great public issues as well as many private troubles are described in terms of the "psychiatric"–often, it seems, in a pathetic attempt to avoid the large issues and problems of modern society. Often, this statement seems to rest upon a provincial narrowing of interest to the Western societies, or even to the United States–thus ignoring two-thirds of mankind; often, too, it arbitrarily divorces the individual life from the larger institutions within which that life is enacted, and which on occasion bear upon it more grievously than do the intimate environments of childhood.

Problems of leisure, for example, cannot even be stated without considering problems of work. Family troubles over comic books cannot be formulated as problems without considering the plight of the contemporary family in its new relations with the newer institutions of the social structure. Neither leisure nor its debilitating uses can be understood as problems without recognition of the extent to which malaise and indifference now form the social and personal climate of contemporary American society. In this climate, no problems of the "private life" can be stated and solved without recognition of the crisis of ambition that is part of the very career of men at work in the incorporated economy.

It is true, as psychoanalysts continually point out, that people do often have the "increasing sense of being moved by obscure forces within themselves that they are unable to define." But it is *not* true, as Ernest Jones asserted, that "man's chief enemy and danger is his own unruly nature and the dark forces pent up within him." On the contrary: "Man's chief danger" today lies in the unruly forces of contemporary society itself, with its alienating methods of production, its enveloping techniques of political domination, its international anarchy–in a word, its pervasive transformations of the very "nature" of man and the conditions and aims of his life.

It is now the social scientist's foremost political and intellectual task–for here the two coincide–to make clear the elements of contemporary uneasiness and indifference. It is the central demand made upon him by other cultural workmen–by physical scientists and artists, by the intellectual community in general. It is because of this task and these demands, I believe, that the social sciences are becoming the common denominator of our cultural period, and the sociological imagination, our most needed quality of mind.

* * *

Is Sociology Value-free?

Anti-Minotaur: The Myth of a Value-free Sociology*

Alvin W. Gouldner

This is an account of a myth created by and about a magnificent minotaur named Max–Max Weber, to be exact; his myth was that social science should and could be value-free. The lair of this minotaur, although reached only by a labyrinthian logic and visited only by a few who never return, is still regarded by many sociologists as a holy place. In particular, as sociologists grow older they seem impelled to make a pilgrimage to it and to pay their respects to the problem of the relations between values and social science.

Considering the perils of the visit, their motives are somewhat perplexing. Perhaps their quest is the first sign of professional senility; perhaps it is the last sigh of youthful yearnings. And perhaps a concern with the value problems is just a way of trying to take back something that was, in youthful enthusiasm, given too hastily.

In any event, the myth of a value-free sociology has been a conquering one. Today, all the powers of sociology, from Parsons to Lundberg, have entered into a tacit alliance to bind us to the dogma that "Thou shalt not commit a value judgment," especially as sociologists. Where is the introductory textbook, where the lecture course on principles, that does not affirm or imply this rule?

In the end, we cannot disprove the existence of minotaurs, who, after all, are thought to be sacred precisely because, being half-man and half-bull, they are so unlikely. The thing to see is that a belief in them is not so much untrue as it is absurd. Like Berkeley's argument for solipsism, Weber's brief for a value-free sociology is a tight one and, some say, logically unassail-

* From *Social Problems,* vol. 9, no. 3 (Winter, 1962). Reprinted by permission of The Society for the Study of Social Problems.

able; yet, it, too, is absurd. Both arguments appeal to reason but ignore experience.

I do not here wish to enter into an examination of the *logical* arguments involved, not because I regard them as incontrovertible, but because I find them less interesting to me as a sociologist. Instead, what I will do is to view the belief in a value-free sociology in the same manner that sociologists examine any element in the ideology of any group. This means that we will look upon the sociologist just as we would any other occupation, be it the taxicab driver, the nurse, the coal miner, or the physician. In short, I will look at the belief in a value-free sociology as part of the ideology of a working group and from the standpoint of the sociology of occupations.

The image of a value-free sociology is more than a neat intellectual theorem demanded as a sacrifice to reason; it is also a felt conception of a role and a set of more or less shared sentiments as to how sociologists should live. We may be sure that it became this not simply because it is true or logically elegant, but, also, because it is somehow useful to those who believe in it. Applauding the dancer for her grace is often the audience's way of concealing its lust.

That we are in the presence of a group myth, rather than a carefully formulated and well-validated belief appropriate to scientists, may be discerned if we ask, just what is it that is believed by those holding sociology to be a value-free discipline? Does the belief in a value-free sociology mean that, in point of fact, sociology is a discipline actually free of values, and that it successfully excludes all nonscientific assumptions in selecting, studying, and reporting on a problem? Or does it mean that sociology should do so? Clearly, the first is untrue, and I know of no one who even holds it possible for sociologists to exclude completely their nonscientific beliefs from their scientific work; and, if this is so, on what grounds can this impossible task be morally incumbent on sociologists?

Does the belief in a value-free sociology mean that sociologists cannot, do not, or should not make value judgments concerning things outside their sphere of technical competence? But what has technical competence to do with the making of value judgments? If technical competence does provide a warrant for making value judgments, then there is nothing to prohibit sociologists from making them within the area of their expertise. If, on the contrary, technical competence provides no warrant for making value judgments, then, at least, sociologists are as free to do so as anyone else; their value judgments are at least as good as anyone else's—say, a twelve-year-old child's. And, if technical competence provides no warrant for making value judgments, then what does?

I fear that there are many sociologists today who, in conceiving social science to be value-free, mean widely different things; that many hold these beliefs dogmatically without having examined seriously the grounds upon which they are credible; and that some few affirm a value-free sociology ritualistically without having any clear idea of what it might mean. Weber's own views on the relation between values and social science are scarcely identical with some held today. While Weber saw grave hazards in the sociologist's expression of value judgments, he also held that these might be voiced if caution were exercised to distinguish them from statements of fact. If Weber insisted on the need to maintain scientific objectivity, he also warned that this was altogether different from moral indifference.

Not only was the cautious expression of value judgments deemed permissible by Weber, but, he emphasized, these were positively mandatory under certain circumstances. Although Weber inveighed against the professorial "cult of personality," we might also remember that he was not against all value-imbued cults, and that he himself worshipped at the shrine of individual responsibility. A familiarity with Weber's work on these points would only be embarrassing to many who today affirm a value-free sociology in his name.

What, to Weber, was an agonizing expression of a highly personal faith, intensely felt and painstakingly argued, has today become a hollow catechism, a password, and a good excuse for no longer thinking seriously. It has become increasingly the trivial token of professional respectability, the caste mark of the decorous; it has become the gentleman's promise that boats will not be rocked. Rather than showing Weber's work the respect that it deserves, by carefully re-evaluating it in the light of our own generation's experience, we reflexively reiterate it even as we distort it to our own purposes. Ignorance of the gods is no excuse; but it can be convenient. For, if the worshipper never visits the altar of his god, then he can never learn whether the fire still burns there, or whether the priests, grown fat, are simply sifting the ashes.

The needs that the value-free conception of social science serves are both personal and institutional. Briefly, my contention will be that one of the main institutional forces facilitating the survival and spread of the value-free myth was its usefulness in maintaining both the cohesion and the autonomy of the modern university, in general, and the newer social science disciplines, in particular. There is little difficulty, at any rate, in demonstrating that these were among the motives originally inducing Max Weber to formulate the conception of a value-free sociology.

This issue might be opened at a seemingly peripheral and petty point; namely, when Weber abruptly mentions the problem of competition among professors for students. Weber notes that professors who do express a value stand are more likely to attract students than those who do not and are, therefore, likely to have undue career advantages. In effect, this is a complaint against a kind of unfair competition by professors who pander to student interests. Weber's hope seems to have been that the value-free principle would serve as a kind of "Fair Trades Act" to restrain such competition.

This suggests that one of the latent functions of the value-free doctrine is to bring peace to the academic house, by reducing competition for students, and, in turn, it directs us to some of the institutional peculiarities of German universities in Weber's time. Unlike the situation in the American university, career advancement in the German university was then felt to depend too largely on the professor's popularity as a teacher; indeed, at the lower ranks, the instructor's income was directly dependent on student enrollment. As a result, the competition for students was particularly keen, and it was felt that the system penalized good scholars and researchers in favor of attractive teaching. In contrast, of course, the American system has been commonly accused of overstressing scholarly publication, and the typical complaint is that good teaching goes unrewarded, and that you must "publish or perish." In the context of the German academic system, Weber was raising no trivial point when he intimated that the value-free doctrine would reduce academic competition. He was linking the doctrine to guild problems and anchoring this lofty question to academicians' earthy interests.

Weber also opposed the use of the lecture hall as an arena of value affirmation by arguing that it subjects the student to a pressure he is unable to evaluate or resist adequately. Given the comparatively exalted position of the professor in German society, and given the one-sided communication inherent in the lecture hall, Weber did have a point. His fears were, perhaps, all the more justified if we accept a view of the German "national character" as being authoritarian–in Nietzsche's terms, a combination of arrogance and servility. But these considerations do not hold with anything like equal cogency in more democratic cultures such as our own. For, here, not only are professors held in more modest esteem, but the specific ideology of education itself stresses the desirability of student initiative and participation, and there is more of a systematic solicitation of the student's "own" views in small "discussion" sections. There is little student servility to complement and encourage occasional professorial arrogance.

When Weber condemned the lecture hall as a forum for value affirmation, he had in mind most particularly the expression of political values. The point of Weber's polemic is not directed against all values with equal sharpness. It was not the expression of aesthetic or even religious values that Weber sees as most objectionable in the university but, primarily, those of politics. His promotion of the value-free doctrine may, then, be seen not so much as an effort to amoralize as to depoliticalize the university and to remove it from the political struggle. The political conflicts then echoing in the German university did not entail comparatively narrow differences, such as those now between Democrats and Republicans in the United States. Weber's proposal of the value-free doctrine was, in part, an effort to establish a *modus vivendi* among academicians whose political commitments were often intensely felt and in violent opposition.

Under these historical conditions, the value-free doctrine was a proposal for an academic truce. It said, in effect, if we all keep quiet about our political views, then we may all be able to get on with our work. But, if the value-free principle was suitable in Weber's Germany, because it served to restrain political passions, is it equally useful in America today, where not only is there pitiable little difference in politics, but men often have no politics at all? Perhaps the need of the American university today, as of American society more generally, is for more commitment to politics and for more diversity of political views. It would seem that now the national need is to take the lid off, not to screw it on more tightly.

Given the historically unique conditions of nuclear warfare, where the issue would not be decided in a long-drawn-out war requiring the sustained cohesion of mass populations, national consensus is no longer, I believe, as important a condition of national survival as it once was. But, if we no longer require the same degree of unanimity to fight a war, we do require a greater ferment of ideas and a radiating growth of political seriousness and variety within which alone we may find a way to prevent war. Important contributions to this have been made and may further be made by members of the academic community, perhaps especially by its social-science sector. The question arises, however, whether this group's political intelligence can ever be adequately mobilized for these purposes so long as it remains tranquilized by the value-free doctrine.

Throughout his work, Weber's strategy is to safeguard the integrity and freedom of action of both the state, as the instrument of German national policy, and the university, as the embodiment of a larger Western tradition of rationalism. He feared that the expression of political value judgments in the university would provoke the state into censoring the university and would imperil its autonomy. Indeed, Weber argues that professors are not entitled to freedom from state control in matters of values, since these do not rest on their specialized qualifications.

This view will seem curious only to those regarding Weber as a liberal in the Anglo-American sense: that is, as one who wishes to delimit the state's powers on behalf of the individual's liberties. Actually, however, Weber aimed not at curtailing but at strengthening the powers of the German state and making it a more effective instrument of German nationalism. It would seem, however, that an argument contrary to the one he advances is at least as consistent; namely, that professors are, like all others, entitled and perhaps obligated to express their values. In other words, professors have a right to profess. Rather than being made the objects of special suspicion and special control by the state, they are no less (and no more) entitled than others to the trust and protection of the state.

In a *Realpolitik* vein, Weber acknowledges that the most basic national questions cannot ordinarily be discussed with full freedom in government universities. Since the discussion there cannot be completely free and all-sided, he apparently concludes that it is fitting that there should be no discussion at all, rather than risk partisanship. But this is too pious by far. Even Socrates never insisted that all views must be at hand before the dialogue could begin. Here again, one might as reasonably argue to the contrary, that one limitation of freedom is no excuse for another. Granting the reality of efforts to inhibit unpopular views in the university, it seems odd to prescribe self-suppression as a way of avoiding external suppression. Suicide does not seem a reasonable way to avoid being murdered. It appears, however, that Weber was so intent on safeguarding the autonomy of the university and the autonomy of politics that he was willing to pay almost any price to do so, even if this led the university to detach itself from one of the basic intellectual traditions of the West—the dialectical exploration of the fundamental purposes of human life.

Insofar as the value-free doctrine is a mode of ensuring professional autonomy, it does not, as such, entail an interest peculiar to the social sciences. In this regard, as a substantial body of research in the sociology of occupations indicates, social scientists are kin to plumbers, house painters, or librarians. Most, if not all, occupations seek to elude control by outsiders and manifest a drive to maintain exclusive control over their practitioners.

Without doubt, the value-free principle did enhance the autonomy of sociology; it was one way in which our discipline pried itself loose—in some modest measure—from the clutch of its society, in Europe freer from political party influence, in the United States freer of ministerial influence. In both places, the value-free doctrine gave sociology a larger area of autonomy in which it could steadily pursue basic problems rather than journalistically react to passing events, and it gained more freedom to pursue questions uninteresting either to the respectable or to the rebellious. It made sociology freer—as Comte had wanted it to be—to pursue all its own theoretical implications. The value-free principle did, I think, contribute to the intellectual growth and emancipation of our enterprise.

There was another kind of freedom that the value-free doctrine also allowed: It enhanced a freedom from moral compulsiveness and permitted a partial escape from the parochial prescriptions of the sociologist's local or native culture. Above all, effective internationalization of the value-free principle has always encouraged at least a temporary suspension of the moralizing reflexes built into the sociologist by his own society. From one perspective, this, of course, has its dangers—a disorienting normlessness and moral indifference. From another standpoint, however, the value-free principle might also have provided a moral as well as an intellectual opportunity. Insofar as moral reactions are only suspended and not aborted, and insofar as this is done in the service of knowledge and intellectual discipline, then, in effect, the value-free principle strengthened Reason (or Ego) against the compulsive demands of a merely traditional morality. To this degree, the value-free discipline provided a foundation for the development of more reliable knowledge about men and, also, established a breathing space within which moral reactions could be less mechanical and in which morality could be reinvigorated.

The value-free doctrine thus had a paradoxical potentiality: It might enable men to make better value judgments rather than none at all. It could encourage a habit of mind that might help men in discriminating between their punitive drives and their ethical sentiments. Moralistic reflexes suspended, it was now more possible to sift conscience with the rod of reason and to cultivate moral judgments that expressed a man's total character as an adult person; he need not now live quite so much by his past parental programming but in terms of his more mature present.

The value-free doctrine could have meant an opportunity for a more authentic morality. It could and sometimes did aid men in transcending the morality of their "tribe" by opening themselves to the diverse moralities of unfamiliar groups and by seeing themselves and others from the standpoint of a wider range of significant cultures.

Doubtless, there were some who did use the opportunity thus presented; but there were also many who used the value-free postulate as an excuse for pursuing their private impulses to the neglect of their public responsibilities and who, far from becoming more morally sensitive, became morally jaded. Insofar as the value-free doctrine failed to realize its potentialities, it did so because its deepest impulses were—as we shall note later—dualistic; it invited men to stress the separation and not the mutual connectedness of facts and values; it had the vice of its virtues. In short, the conception of a value-free sociology has had diverse consequences, not all of them useful or flattering to the social sciences.

On the negative side, it may be noted that the value-free doctrine is useful both to those who want to escape from the world and to those who want to escape into it. It is useful to those young, or not so young, men who live off sociology rather than for it, and who think of sociology as a way of getting ahead in the world by providing them with neutral techniques that may be sold on the open market to any buyer. The belief that it is not the business of a sociologist to make value judgments is taken, by some, to mean that the market on which they can vend their skills is unlimited. From such a standpoint, there is no reason why one cannot sell one's knowledge to spread a disease just as freely as he can to fight it. Indeed, some sociologists have had no hesitation about doing market research designed to sell more cigarettes, although well aware of the implication of recent cancer research. In brief, the value-free doctrine of social science was sometimes used to justify the sale of one's talents to the highest bidder and is, far from new, a contemporary version of the most ancient sophistry.

In still other cases, the image of a value-free sociology is the armor of the alienated sociologist's self. Although C. Wright Mills may be right in saying this is the Age of Sociology, not a few sociologists, Mills included, have felt estranged and isolated from their society. They feel impotent to contribute usefully to the solution of its deepening problems, and, even when they can, they fear that the terms of such an involvement require them to submit to a commercial debasement or a narrow partisanship, rather than contributing to a truly public interest.

Many sociologists feel themselves cut off from the larger community of liberal intellectuals, in whose satire they see themselves as ridiculous caricatures. Estranged from the larger world, they cannot escape in fantasies of posthumous medals and by living huddled behind self-barricaded intellectual ghettoes. Self-doubt finds its anodyne in the image of a value-free sociology, because this transforms their alienation into an intellectual principle; it evokes the soothing illusion, among some sociologists, that their exclusion from the larger society is a self-imposed duty rather than an externally imposed constraint.

Once committed to the premise of a value-free sociology, such sociologists are bound to a policy that can only alienate them further from the surrounding world. Social science can never be fully accepted in a society, or by a part of it, without paying its way; this means it must manifest both its relevance and its concern for the contemporary human predicament. Unless the value relevance of sociological inquiry is made plainly evident, unless there are at least some bridges between it and larger human hopes and purposes, it must inevitably be scorned by laymen as pretentious word-mongering. But the manner in which some sociologists conceive the value-free doctrine disposes them to ignore current human problems and to huddle together like old men seeking mutual warmth. "This is not our job," they say, "and if it were we would not know enough to do it. Go away, come back when we're grown up," say these old men. The issue, however, is not whether we know enough; the real questions are whether we have the courage to say and use what we do know and whether anyone knows more.

* * *

The problem of a value-free sociology has its most poignant implications for the social scientist in his role as educator. If sociologists ought not to express their personal values in the academic setting, how, then, are students to be safeguarded against the unwitting influence of these values that shape the sociologist's selection of problems, his preferences for certain hypotheses or conceptual schemes, and his neglect of others? For these are unavoidable; and, in this sense, there is and can be no value-free sociology. The only choice is between an expression of one's values, as open and honest as it can be this side of the psychoanalytical couch, and a vain ritual of moral neutrality that, because it invites men to ignore the vulnerability of reason to bias, leaves it at the mercy of irrationality.

If truth is the vital thing, as Weber is reputed to have said on his deathbed, then it must be all the truth we have to give, as best we know it, being painfully aware, and making our students aware, that even as we offer it we may be engaged in unwitting concealment rather than revelation. If we would teach students how science is made, really made rather than as publicly reported, we cannot fail to expose them to the whole scientist by whom it is made, with all his gifts and blindnesses, with all his methods and his values as well. To do otherwise is to usher in an era of spiritless technicians who will be no less lacking in understanding than they are in passion, and who will be useful only because they can be used.

In the end, even these dull tools will build, through patient persistence and cumulation, a technology of social science strong enough to cripple us. Far as we are from a sociological atomic bomb, we already live in a world of the systematic brainwashing of prisoners of war and of housewives with their advertising-exacerbated compulsions; and the social-science technology of tomorrow can hardly fail to be more powerful than today's.

It would seem that social science's affinity for modeling itself after physical science might lead to instruction in matters other than research alone. Before Hiroshima, physicists also talked of a value-free science; they, too, vowed to make no value judgments. Today, many of them are not so sure. If, today, we concern ourselves exclusively with the technical proficiency of our students and reject all responsibility for their moral sense, or lack of it, then we may someday be compelled to accept responsibility for having trained a generation willing to serve in a future Auschwitz. Granted that science always has inherent in it both constructive and destructive potentialities, it does not follow that we should encourage our students to be oblivious to the difference. Nor does this in any degree detract from the indispensable norms of scientific objectivity; it merely insists that these differ radically from moral indifference.

* * *

Problems in Doing Sociological Research

Body Ritual Among the Nacirema*

Horace Miner

The anthropologist has become so familiar with the diversity of ways in which different peoples behave in similar situations that he is not apt to be surprised by even the most exotic customs. In fact, if all of the logically possible combinations of behavior have not been found somewhere in the world, he is apt to suspect that they must be present in some yet undescribed tribe. This point has, in fact, been expressed with respect to clan organization by Murdock (1949:71). In this light, the magical beliefs and practices of the Nacirema present such unusual aspects that it seems desirable to describe them as an example of the extremes to which human behavior can go.

Professor Linton first brought the ritual of the Nacirema to the attention of anthropologists twenty years ago (1936:326), but the culture of this people is still very poorly understood. They are a North American group living in the territory between the Canadian Cree, the Yaqui and Tarahumare of Mexico, and the Carib and Arawak of the Antilles. Little is known of their origin, although tradition states that they came from the east. Ac-

* Reproduced by permission of the American Anthropological Association from *American Anthropologist*, vol. 58, no. 3 (1956), pp. 503–7.

cording to Nacirema mythology, their nation was originated by a culture hero, Notgnihsaw, who is otherwise known for two great feats of strength—the throwing of a piece of wampum across the river Pa-To-Mac and the chopping down of a cherry tree in which the Spirit of Truth resided.

Nacirema culture is characterized by a highly developed market economy that has evolved in a rich natural habitat. While much of the people's time is devoted to economic pursuits, a large part of the fruits of these labors and a considerable portion of the day are spent in ritual activity. The focus of this activity is the human body, the appearance and health of which loom as a dominant concern in the ethos of the people. While such a concern is certainly not unusual, its ceremonial aspects and associated philosophy are unique.

The fundamental belief underlying the whole system appears to be that the human body is ugly, and that its natural tendency is to debility and disease. Incarcerated in such a body, man's only hope is to avert these characteristics through the use of the powerful influences of ritual and ceremony. Every household has one or more shrines devoted to this purpose. The more powerful individuals in the society have several shrines in their houses, and, in fact, the opulence of a house is often referred to in terms of the number of such ritual centers it possesses. Most houses are of wattle and daub construction, but the shrine rooms of the more wealthy are walled with stone. Poorer families imitate the rich by applying pottery plaques to their shrine walls.

While each family has at least one such shrine, the rituals associated with it are not family ceremonies but are private and secret. The rites are normally only discussed with children, and then only during the period when they are being initiated into these mysteries. I was able, however, to establish sufficient rapport with the natives to examine these shrines and to have the rituals described to me.

The focal point of the shrine is a box or chest, which is built into the wall. In this chest are kept the many charms and magical potions without which no native believes he could live. These preparations are secured from a variety of specialized practitioners. The most powerful of these are the medicine men, whose assistance must be rewarded with substantial gifts. However, the medicine men do not provide the curative potions for their clients but decide what the ingredients should be and then write them down in an ancient and secret language. This writing is understood only by the medicine men and by the herbalists who, for another gift, provide the required charm.

The charm is not disposed of after it has served its purpose but is placed in the charm-box of the household shrine. As these magical materials are specific for certain ills, and the real or imagined maladies of the people are many, the charm-box is usually full to overflowing. The magical packets are so numerous that people forget what their purposes were and fear to use them again. While the natives are very vague on this point, we can only assume that the idea in retaining all the old magical materials is that their presence in the charm-box, before which the body rituals are conducted, will in some way protect the worshipper.

Beneath the charm-box is a small font. Each day, every member of the family, in succession, enters the shrine room, bows his head before the charm-box, mingles different sorts of holy waters in the font, and proceeds with a brief rite of ablution. The holy waters are secured from the Water Temple of the community, where the priests conduct elaborate ceremonies to make the liquid ritually pure.

In the hierarchy of magical practitioners, and below the medicine men in prestige, are specialists whose designation is best translated "holy-mouth-men." The Nacirema have an almost pathological horror of, and fascination with, the mouth, the condition of which is believed to have a supernatural influence on all social relationships. Were it not for the rituals of the mouth, they believe that their teeth would fall out, their gums bleed, their jaws shrink, their friends desert them, and their lovers reject them. They also believe that a strong relationship exists between oral and moral characteristics. For example, there is a ritual ablution of the mouth for children that is supposed to improve their moral fiber.

The daily body ritual performed by everyone includes a mouth-rite. Despite the fact that these people are so punctilious about care of the mouth, this rite involves a practice that strikes the uninitiated stranger as revolting. It was reported to me that the ritual consists of inserting a small bundle of hog hairs into the mouth, along with certain magical powders, and then moving the bundle in a highly formalized series of gestures.

In addition to the private mouth-rite, the people seek out a holy-mouth-man once or twice a year. These practitioners have an impressive set of paraphernalia, consisting of a variety of augers, awls, probes, and prods. The use of these objects in the exorcism of the evils of the mouth involves almost unbelievable ritual torture of the client. The holy-mouth-man opens the client's mouth and, using the above-mentioned tools, enlarges any holes that decay may have created in the teeth. Magical materials are put into these holes. If there are no naturally occurring holes in the teeth, large sections of one or more teeth are gouged out so that the supernatural substance can be applied. In the client's view, the purpose of these ministrations is to arrest decay and to draw friends. The extremely sacred and traditional character of the rite is evident in the fact that the natives return to the holy-mouth-men year after year, despite the fact that their teeth continue to decay.

It is to be hoped that, when a thorough study of the Nacirema is made, there will be careful inquiry into the personality structure of these people. One has but to watch the gleam in the eye of a holy-mouth-man, as he jabs an awl into an exposed nerve, to suspect that a certain amount of sadism is involved. If this can be established, a very interesting pattern emerges, for most of the population shows definite masochistic tendencies. It was to these that Professor Linton referred in discussing a distinctive part of the daily body ritual that is performed only by men. This part of the rite involves scraping and lacerating the surface of the face with a sharp instrument. Special women's rites are performed only four times during each lunar month, but what they lack in frequency is made up in barbarity. As part of this ceremony, women bake their heads in small ovens for about an hour. The theoretically interesting point is that what seems to be a preponderantly masochistic people have developed sadistic specialists.

The medicine men have an imposing temple, or *latipso,* in every community of any size. The more elaborate ceremonies required to treat very sick patients can be performed only at this temple. These ceremonies involve not only the thaumaturge but a permanent group of vestal maidens who move sedately about the temple chambers in distinctive costume and headdress.

The *latipso* ceremonies are so harsh that it is phenomenal that a fair proportion of the really sick natives who enter the temple ever recover. Small children whose indoctrination is still incomplete have been known to resist attempts to take them to the temple, because "that is where you go to die." Despite this fact, sick adults are not only willing but eager to undergo the protracted ritual purification, if they can afford to do so. No matter how ill the supplicant or how grave the emergency, the guardians of many temples will not admit a client if he cannot give a rich gift to the custodian. Even after one has gained admission and survived the ceremonies, the guardians will not permit the neophyte to leave until he makes still another gift.

The supplicant entering the temple is first stripped of all his or her clothes. In everyday life, the Nacirema avoids exposure of his body and its natural functions. Bathing and excretory acts are performed only in the secrecy of the household shrine, where they are ritualized as part of the body-rites. Psychological shock results from the fact that body secrecy is suddenly lost upon entry into the *latipso*. A man whose own wife has never seen him in an excretory act suddenly finds himself naked and assisted by a vestal maiden while he performs his natural functions into a sacred vessel. This sort of ceremonial treatment is necessitated by the fact that the excreta are used by a diviner to ascertain the course and nature of the client's sickness. Female clients, on the other hand, find their naked bodies are subjected to the scrutiny, manipulation, and prodding of the medicine men.

Few supplicants in the temple are well enough to do anything but lie on their hard beds. The daily ceremonies, like the rites of the holy-mouth-men, involve discomfort and torture. With ritual precision, the vestals awaken their miserable charges each dawn and roll them about on their beds of pain while performing ablutions, in the formal movements of which the maidens are highly trained. At other times, they insert magic wands into the supplicant's mouth or force him to eat substances that are supposed to be healing. From time to time, the medicine men come to their clients and jab magically treated needles into their flesh. The fact that these temple ceremonies may not cure, and may even kill, the neophyte in no way decreases the people's faith in the medicine men.

There remains one other kind of practitioner, known as a "listener." This witch doctor has the power to exorcise the devils that lodge in the heads of people who have been bewitched. The Nacirema believe that parents bewitch their own children. Mothers are particularly suspected of putting a curse on children while teaching them the secret body rituals. The countermagic of the witch doctor is unusual in its lack of ritual. The patient simply tells the "listener" all his troubles and fears, beginning with the earliest difficulties he can remember. The memory displayed by the Nacirema in these exorcism sessions is truly remarkable. It is not uncommon for the patient to bemoan the rejection he felt upon being weaned as a babe, and a few individuals even see their troubles going back to the traumatic effects of their own birth.

In conclusion, mention must be made of certain practices that have their base in native esthetics, but which depend upon the pervasive aversion to the natural body and its functions. There are ritual fasts to make fat people thin and ceremonial feasts to make thin people fat. Still other rites are used to make women's breasts larger if they are small, and smaller if they are large. General dissatisfaction with breast shape is symbolized in the fact that the ideal form is virtually outside the range of human variation. A few women afflicted with almost inhuman hypermammary development are so idolized that they make a handsome living by simply going from village to village and permitting the natives to stare at them for a fee.

Reference has already been made to the fact that excretory functions are ritualized, routinized, and relegated to secrecy. Natural reproductive functions are similarly distorted. Intercourse is taboo as a topic and scheduled as an act. Efforts are made to avoid pregnancy by the use of magical materials or by limiting intercourse to certain phases of the moon. Conception is actually very infrequent. When pregnant, women dress so as to hide their condition. Parturition takes place in secret, without friends or relatives to assist, and the majority of women do not nurse their infants.

Our review of the ritual life of the Nacirema has certainly shown them to be a magic-ridden people. It is hard to understand how they have managed to exist so long under the burdens they have imposed upon themselves. But even such exotic customs as these take on real meaning when they are viewed with the insight provided by Malinowski when he wrote (1948:70):

> Looking from far and above, from our high places of safety in the developed civilization, it is easy to see all the crudity and irrelevance of magic. But without its power and guidance early man could not have mastered his practical difficulties as he has done, nor could man have advanced to the higher stages of civilization.

REFERENCES

LINTON, RALPH. *The Study of Man* (New York: D. Appleton-Century Co., 1936).

MALINOWSKI, BRONISLAW. *Magic, Science, and Religion* (Glencoe, Ill.: The Free Press, 1948).

MURDOCK, GEORGE P. *Social Structure* (New York: The Macmillan Co., 1949).

1. SUGGESTIONS FOR FURTHER READING

BATES, ALAN. *The Sociological Enterprise* (Boston: Houghton Mifflin, 1967).*
BENSMAN, JOSEPH, ARTHUR VIDICH, AND MAURICE STEIN (eds.). *Reflections on Community Studies* (New York: John Wiley & Sons, 1964).
BERGER, PETER. *Invitation to Sociology* (Garden City: Doubleday Anchor, 1963).*
CAMERON, WILLIAM. *Informal Sociology* (New York: Random House, 1961).*
DOUGLAS, JACK (ed.). *The Relevance of Sociology* (New York: Appleton, 1970).*
FESTINGER, LEON, AND DANIEL KATZ (eds.). *Research Methods in the Behavioral Sciences* (New York: Holt, Rinehart, 1953).
GOODE, W. J., AND P. K. HATT. *Methods of Social Research* (New York: McGraw Hill, 1952).
GOULDNER, ALVIN. *The Coming Crisis of Western Sociology* (New York: Basic Books, 1970).*
HAMMOND, PHILLIP (ed.). *Sociologists at Work* (New York: Basic Books, 1964).*
HINKLE, ROSCOE, AND GISELLA. *Development of Modern Sociology* (New York: Random House, 1954).*
HUGHES, H. STUART. *Consciousness and Society* (New York: Vintage, 1961).*
INKELES, ALEX. *What Is Sociology?* (Englewood Cliffs, N.J.: Prentice-Hall, 1964).*
KAPLAN, ABRAHAM. *The Conduct of Inquiry* (San Francisco: Chandler, 1964).*
MADGE, JOHN. *Origins of Scientific Sociology* (New York: The Free Press, 1962).*
MARTINDALE, DON. *The Nature and Types of Sociological Theory* (Boston: Houghton Mifflin, 1960).
MILLS, C. WRIGHT. *The Sociological Imagination* (New York: Oxford University Press, 1959).*
NISBET, ROBERT. *The Sociological Tradition* (New York: Basic Books, 1966).
PARSONS, TALCOTT, *et al.* (eds.). *Theories of Society* (New York: The Free Press, 1961).
SHOSTAK, ARTHUR (ed.). *Sociology in Action* (Homewood, Ill.: Dorsey Press, 1966).*
TIMASHEFF, NICHOLAS. *Sociological Theory: Its Nature and Growth* (New York: Random House, 1961).

* *Available in paperback.*

2. Culture

INTRODUCTION

Among laymen, culture is generally conceived of as the "finer things in life"—art, music, literature, philosophy. For the social scientist, however, the term has a much broader meaning. Anthropologist Clyde Kluckhohn states that it denotes the "distinctive way of life of a group of people" or a "design for living."[1] The classic definition of culture is Edward Tylor's: "Culture is that complex whole which includes knowledge, belief, art, morals, custom and other capabilities acquired by man as a member of society."[2]

Most definitions of culture include the following characteristics:

1. *Culture is socially shared.* Cultural patterns are socially transmitted by members of a group to one another, thus creating pressure toward uniformity of social behavior.
2. *Culture is learned.* Culture is not instinctive or inborn; it is not part of man's biological apparatus. All animals learn to some extent, but it is man's substantially greater learning ability that makes him the only animal able to acquire culture.
3. *Culture is transmitted from one generation to the next.* Man inherits a social tradition. Thus, culture is cumulative; it permits each new generation to build on the achievements of preceding generations.
4. *Culture enhances adaptation.* It serves to accommodate man to the demands of his biological nature and his physical environ-

[1] Clyde Kluckhohn, "The Study of Culture," in Daniel Lerner and Harold Lasswell (eds.), *The Policy Sciences* (Stanford, Calif.: Stanford University Press, 1951), p. 86.
[2] Edward Tylor, *The Origins of Culture* (New York: Harper & Row, 1958), p. 1.

ment. It is culture that furnishes man with the technical means to overcome the obstacles in his environment.

As Tylor has indicated, the components of culture are numerous and include knowledge, beliefs, technology, customs (the actual patterns of behavior shared by members of a group), norms (the ideal patterns for behavior, the rules that specify appropriate and inappropriate behavior), values, ideologies (systems of belief about the social world that are strongly rooted in specific sets of values and interests), and artifacts (everything man-made a people may possess, from primitive stone tools and pottery to electronic data-processing machines and television sets).

Norms may be classified in various ways. In his highly influential book *Folkways,* published in 1906, William Graham Sumner distinguished two main types of norms—folkways and mores. Folkways are norms that the members of a society do not regard as extremely important and that may be violated without severe punishment. For example, most rules of social etiquette are folkways; greeting another person without attempting to shake hands or using inappropriate eating utensils while dining might elicit social disapproval, but it is not likely to be intense.

Mores, on the other hand, are norms that are regarded as extremely important and that, if violated, will bring severe punishment. Many marriage rules are among the mores; the social rule of sexual fidelity in marriage, monogamy, and the taboos against incest are all mores.

Laws are distinguished from folkways and mores in that laws are institutionalized, maintained and enforced by specially designated agents of society; in contrast, folkways and mores are maintained and enforced by public sentiment. Laws vary in intensity from the weakly sanctioned codes governing the licensing of pets to the strongly sanctioned statutes concerned with the punishment for murder. There tends to be a general correspondence in society between the folkways and mores, on the one hand, and the laws, on the other. The most effective laws are grounded in the mores; for example, whether particular communities have antibigamy statutes is of less significance than the fact that injunctions against bigamy are firmly embedded in the mores. When the mores and the laws are discrepant, one or more of the following causes are indicated: rapid social change, group conflict or normative dissensus, totalitarian social control. The current controversy over the illegal status of marijuana possession and use reflects such a gap between the laws and the mores of a sizable group in society.

Many social scientists hold the view that the culture of a people is not simply an agglomeration of specific beliefs, values, customs, and the like but the integration of these components into some meaningful whole embodying a dominant set or direction, which may be called the ethos of a society. This should not be interpreted to mean that every culture possesses a similar degree of coherence around a central theme. Rather, the components of a culture are subject to a strain toward consistency, exhibiting varying degrees of integration.

The notion of a subculture (a subgroup whose patterns of thinking, feeling, and acting depart from those of the larger group) would appear to be antithetical to the conception of cultural integration. Yet, in many ways, all subcultures, no matter how insulated or alienated from the surrounding society they may be, find that their cultural patterns are influenced and shaped by the dominant culture. For example, in Martin Weinberg's "Sexual Modesty, Social Meanings, and the Nudist Camp," we learn that, although nudism is obviously at odds with the dominant morality, many of the specific norms governing nudist behavior appear to involve various puritanical elements. For the nudist, it seems, these social codes alleviate personal feelings of guilt and anxiety over nonconformity; thus, they represent an attempt to reconcile nudism with the values of the dominant, nonnudist society.

The study of culture invariably leads us to examine other cultures and to consider people whose way of life is different from our own. One's precepts, standards, and commitments to one's own social world are likely to affect the judgments one makes of others. The tendency to evaluate other cultures in terms of one's own, to consider one's own group superior to all others, is called ethnocentrism. For the anthropologist, ethnocentrism can have most adverse consequences, transforming attempts at analytic description into self-congratulatory moralism. Horace Miner's "Body Ritual Among the Nacirema," which appears in Chapter 1, shows very clearly how ethnocentrism can distort one's perceptions and thus entirely prevent scientific objectivity. In the realm of human relations, ethnocentrism tends to lead to resistance to social change, intolerance, misunderstanding, and group conflict.

Of enormous significance in attempts to understand other cultures is the viewpoint of cultural relativity (the principle that every culture must be judged on its own terms, that moral judgments are always relative to the standards of a given culture). This view, of course, is the converse of ethnocentrism. The fact that much of our own culture was formed by contact with other cultures over time supports the relativity approach. Ralph Linton's "One Hundred Per Cent American" indicates several of the sources of the so-called American way. His discussion raises the issue of the quantity of culture that is a result of innovation (additions to knowledge and the use of knowledge in novel forms) as compared with the amount that is due to diffusion (the process by which culture traits spread from one social unit to another). It appears that innovation accounts for a minor portion of the cultural whole, that the great bulk of culture is a product of diffusion. Linton estimates that no more than 10 per cent of the material objects used by any people represents its own inventions.

Diffusion is a two-way process. For example, the Anglo-American owes to the Indians of the Americas his knowledge of corn, potato, tomato, peanut, tobacco, chocolate, pineapple, and many other plant foods. Had the Indians not domesticated these plants, it is doubtful that Anglo-Americans would have done so, for they would probably have introduced the crops they were familiar with from Europe. From the Indians, Anglo-Americans also learned much about woodcraft, canoes, and rubber, among many other inventions, as well as the use of numerous medicinal plants, including quinine. In turn, the Indians owe to the Anglo-Americans their knowledge of metallurgy, the rifle, and countless other innovations. The process of assimilation, therefore, has reciprocal consequences. This point is well illustrated in Nelson Graburn's "The Eskimos and 'Airport Art,' " which suggests a most surprising and complex combination of influences in the development of Eskimo soapstone carving. Graburn's work should serve as an admonition to the student of culture to exercise extreme caution in attempting to identify cultural influences.

Culture influences, shapes and modifies the physiological functioning of the individual, as well as his use of material objects. Physiologist W. B. Cannon has argued that a person's conviction that he is the victim of witchcraft can cause so great a disturbance of autonomic functioning as to result in death. The experience of menstrual cramps or morning sickness during pregnancy may be a result of cultural beliefs; Margaret Mead, for example, reported that she could discover no instances of morning sickness among the Arapesh of New Guinea. Similarly, Ford and Beach have noted that, for the majority of men in our society, ejaculation occurs within two minutes after the beginning of intercourse, whereas, among the Marquesans, every man learns early in life to control his reflexes so as to permit maintenance of an erection and continuation of coitus for as long as desired.

Within our own society, we can observe the influence of culture on the biological functioning of subgroups. Mark Zborowski, in "Cultural Components in Responses to Pain," finds important differences among "WASP," Italian, and Jewish patients in their reactions to the pain caused, in most cases, by the same illnesses. On the basis of this research, we can observe the pervasive effects of culture, which influences virtually every aspect of our experience.

Sexual Modesty, Social Meanings, and the Nudist Camp*

Martin S. Weinberg

* * *

THE NUDIST CAMP

The ideology of the nudist camp provides a new definition of the situation regarding nudity, which, in effect, maintains that

1. Nudism and sexuality are unrelated
2. There is nothing shameful about exposing the human body
3. The abandonment of clothes can lead to a feeling of freedom and natural pleasure
4. Nude activities, especially full bodily exposure to the sun, leads to a feeling of physical, mental, and spiritual well-being

These definitions are sustained by nudists to a remarkable degree, illustrating the extent to which adult socialization can function in changing long-maintained meanings; in this case, regarding the exposure of one's nude body in heterosexual situations. The tremendous emphasis on covering the sexual areas, and the relation between nudism and sexuality that exists in the outside society, however, suggest that the nudist definition of the situation might, at times, be quite easily called into question. The results of the field work and formal interviews indicate how the social organization of the nudist camp has developed a system of norms that contributes to sustaining the official definition of the situation. Since the major concern of this paper is modesty, we will restrict our discussion to the first two declarations of nudist ideology (i.e., that nudism and sexuality are unrelated, and that there is nothing shameful about exposing the human body). These are also the elements that lead to the classification of nudists as deviant. The normative proscriptions that contribute to the maintenance of this definition of the situation will be described.

Organizational precautions. Organizational precautions are initially taken in the requirements for admission to a nudist camp. Most camps do not allow unmarried individuals, especially single men, or allow only a small

* From *Social Problems,* vol. 12, no. 3 (Winter, 1965), 314–18. Reprinted by permission of The Society for the Study of Social Problems.

quota of singles. Those camps that do allow male-singles may charge up to 35 per cent higher rates for the single's membership than is charged for the membership of an entire family. This is intended to discourage single memberships, but, since the cost is still relatively low in comparison to other resorts, this measure is not very effective. It seems to do little more than create resentment among the singles. By giving formal organizational backing to the definition that singles are not especially desirable, it also might be related to the social segregation of single and married members that is evident in nudist camps.

An overabundance of single men is recognized by the organization as threatening the definition of nudism that is maintained. The presence of singles at the camp is suspected to be for purposes other than the "nudist way of life" (e.g., to gape at the women). Such a view may call into question the denied relation between nudity and sexuality.

Certification by the camp owner is also required before anyone is admitted on the camp grounds. This is sometimes supplemented by three letters of recommendation in regard to the character of the applicant. This is a precaution against admitting those "social types" who might conceivably discredit the ideology of the movement.

A limit is sometimes set on the number of trial visits that can be made to the camp; that is, visits made without membership in some camp or intercamp organization. In addition, a limit is usually set on the length of time one is allowed to maintain oneself clothed. These rules function to weed out those guests whose sincere acceptance of the "nudist" definition of the situation is questionable.

Norms regarding interpersonal behavior. Norms regarding patterns of interpersonal behavior are also functional for the maintenance of the organization's system of meanings. The existence of these norms, however, should be recognized as formally acknowledging that the nudist definition of the situation could become problematic unless precautions were taken.

No staring. This rule functions to prevent any overt signs of "overinvolvement." In the words of a nonnudist who is involved in the publication of a nudist magazine, "They all look up to the heavens and never look below." This pattern of civil inattention[1] is most exaggerated among the females, who manage the impression that there is absolutely no concern or awareness that the male body is in an unclothed state. Women often recount how they expect everyone will look at them when they are nude, only to find that no one communicates any impression of concern when they finally do get up their nerve and undress. One woman told the writer: "I got so mad because my husband wanted me to undress in front of other men that I just pulled my clothes right off thinking everyone would look at me." She was amazed (and somewhat disappointed) when no one did. Thus, even though nudists are immodest in their behavior by "showing" their bodies, . . . "looking at" immodesty is controlled; external constraints prohibit staring.

[1] See Erving Goffman, *Behavior in Public Places* (New York: The Free Press, 1963), p. 84.

(Have you ever observed or heard about anyone staring at someone's body while at camp?)[2] I've heard stories—particularly about men that stare. Since I heard these stories, I tried not to, and even done away with my sunglasses after someone said, half-joking, that I hide behind sunglasses to stare. Toward the end of the summer, I stopped wearing sunglasses. And you know what? It was a child who told me this.

No sex talk. Sex talk, or telling "dirty" jokes, is not common in the nudist camp. The owner of one of the most widely known camps in the Midwest told the writer: "It is usually expected that members of a nudist camp will not talk about sex, politics, or religion." Or, in the words of one single-male: "It is taboo to make sexual remarks here." Verbal immodesty was not experienced by the writer during his period of field work. Interview respondents who mentioned that they had discussed or talked about sex qualified this by stating that such talk was restricted to close friends, was of a "scientific" nature, or, if a joke, was of a "cute" sort. Verbal immodesty . . . is not common to the nudist camp.

When respondents were asked what they would think of someone who breached this norm, they indicated that such behavior would cast doubt on the actor's acceptance of the nudist definition of the situation:

One would expect to hear less of that at camp than at other places. (Why's that?) Because you expect that the members are screened in their *attitude for nudism*—and this isn't one who prefers sexual jokes.

They probably don't belong there. They're there to see what they can find to observe. (What do you mean?) Well, their mind isn't on being a nudist, but to see so-and-so nude.

Body contact is taboo. Although the degree to which this rule is enforced varies among camps, there is at least some degree of informal enforcement. Nudists mention that one is particularly careful not to brush against anyone or have any body contact, because of the way it might be interpreted. The following quotation illustrates the interpersonal precautions taken: "I stay clear of the opposite sex. They're so sensitive, they imagine things." One respondent felt that this taboo was simply a common-sense form of modesty: "Suppose one had a desire to knock one off or feel his wife—modesty or a sense of protocol prohibits you from doing this." When asked to conceptualize a breakdown in this form of modesty, a common response was:

They are in the wrong place. (How's that?) That's not part of nudism. (Could you tell me some more about that?) I think they are there for some sort of sex thrill. They are certainly not there to enjoy the sun.

If any photographs are taken for publication in a nudist magazine, the subjects are allowed to have only limited body contact. As one female nudist said: "We don't want anyone to think we're immoral." Outsiders' interpretations of body contact among nudists would cast doubt on the

[2] Interview questions and probes have been placed in parentheses.

nudist definition of the situation or the characteristics set forth as the "nudist way of life."

A correlate of the body contact taboo is the prohibition of dancing in the nude. This is verbalized by nudist actors as a separate rule, and it is often the object of jest by members. This indication of "organizational strain" can be interpreted as an instance in which the existence of the rule itself brings into question the nudist definition of the situation; that is, that there is no relationship between nudism and sexuality. The following remark acknowledges this: "This reflects a contradiction in our beliefs. But it's self-protection. One incident and we'd be closed." Others define dancing in the nude as an erotic overture that would incite sexual arousal. Such rationalizations are common to the group. . . .

Alcoholic beverages are not allowed in American camps. This rule also functions in controlling any breakdown in inhibitions that could lead to "aggressive-erotic" overtures. Even those respondents who told the writer that they had "snuck a beer" before going to bed went on to say, however, that they fully favored the rule. The following quotation is representative of nudists' thoughts:

> Anyone who drinks in camp is jeopardizing their membership and they shouldn't. Anyone who drinks in camp could get reckless. (How's that?) Well, when guys and girls drink, they're a lot bolder—they might get fresh with someone else's girl. That's why it isn't permitted, I guess.

Rules regarding photography. Taking photographs in a nudist camp is a sensitive matter. Unless the individual is an official photographer (i.e., one photographing for the nudist magazines), the photographer's definition of the situation is sometimes suspect, especially when one hears such remarks as the following: "Do you think you could open your legs a little more?"

There may be a general restriction on the use of cameras, and, when cameras are allowed, it is expected that no pictures will be taken without the subject's permission. Members especially tend to blame the misuse of cameras on single men. As one nudist said: "You always see the singles poppin' around out of nowhere snappin' pictures." In general, however, control is maintained, and any infractions that might exist are not blatant or obvious. Any overindulgence in taking photographs would communicate an overinvolvement in the nude state of the alters and bring doubt on the denied connection between nudism and sexuality. This, like staring, . . . is controlled by the norms of the nudist camp.

The official photographers who are taking pictures for nudist magazines recognize the impression communicated by forms of immodesty other than nudity, that is, for the communication of sexuality. In regard to . . . erotic overtures . . . the following statement of an official photographer is relevant: "I never let a girl look straight at the camera. It looks too suggestive. I always have her look off to the side."

Accentuation of the body is suspect as being incongruent with the ideology of nudism. The internalization of the previously discussed principles of nudist ideology would be called into question by such accentuation. Thus, one woman who had shaved her pubic area was labeled as disgusting by those members who talked to the writer about it. Women who blatantly sit in an "unladylike" manner are similarly typed. In the words of one female nudist:

> It's no more nice to do than when you are dressed. I would assume they have a purpose. (What's that?) Maybe to draw someone's attention sexually. I'd think it's bad behavior, and it's one thing that shouldn't be done, especially in a nudist camp. (Why's that?) Because it could lead to trouble or some misfortune. (Could you tell me some more about that?) It could bring up some trouble or disturbance among those who noticed it. It would not be appreciated by "true nudists."

Unnatural attempts at covering any area of the body are similarly ridiculed, since they call into question the actor's acceptance of the definition that there is no shame in exposing any area of the human body. If such behavior occurs early in one's nudist career, however, it is responded to mostly with smiles. The actor is viewed as not yet able to get over the initial difficulty of disposing of "outsiders' " definitions.

Communal toilets are also related to the ideological view that there is nothing shameful about the human body or its bodily functions. Although all camps do not have communal toilets, the large camp at which the writer spent the majority of his time did have such a facility, which was labeled "Little Girls Room and Little Boys Too." The stalls were provided with three-quarter-length doors. The existence of this combined facility helped, however, to sustain the nudist definition of the situation by the element of consistency: If you are not ashamed of any part of your body, or of any of its natural body functions, why do you need separate toilets? Thus, even the physical ecology of the nudist camp is designed in a way that will be consistent with the organization's definition of modesty.

CONSEQUENCES OF A BREAKDOWN IN CLOTHING MODESTY

In the introductory section of this paper, it was stated that common-sense actors anticipate breakdowns in clothing modesty to result in rampant sexual interest, promiscuity, embarrassment, jealousy, and shame. The field work and interview data from this study, however, indicate that such occurrences are not common to the nudist camp. The social organization of the nudist camp provides a system of meanings and norms that negate these consequences.

CONCLUSIONS

Our results make possible some general conclusions regarding modesty: (1) Covering the body through the use of clothes is not a necessary condition for a pattern of modesty to exist, nor is it required for tension management and social control of latent sexual interests. Sexual interests are very adequately controlled in nudist camps; in fact, those who have visited nudist camps agree that sexual interests are controlled to a much greater extent than they are on the outside. Clothes are also not a sufficient condition for a pattern of modesty; the manipulation of clothes and fashion in stimulating sexual interest is widely recognized. (2) Except for clothing immodesty, . . . all . . . forms of modesty are maintained in a nudist camp (e.g., not looking, not saying, not communicating erotic overtures). This suggests that the latter proscriptions are entirely adequate in achieving the functions of modesty when definitions regarding the exposure of the body are changed. (3) When deviance from the institutionalized patterns of modesty is limited to one cell of our typology, (i.e., clothing is dispensed with), and the definition of the situation is changed, the typically expected consequence of such a breakdown in this normative pattern does not occur. Rampant sexual interest, promiscuity, embarrassment, jealousy, and shame were not found to be typical of the nudist camp.

Cultural Diffusion

· One Hundred Per Cent American*

Ralph Linton

* * *

Our solid American citizen awakens in a bed built on a pattern that originated in the Near East but that was modified in Northern Europe before it was transmitted to America. He throws back covers made from cotton, domesticated in India, or linen, domesticated in the Near East, or wool from sheep, also domesticated in the Near East, or silk, the use of which was discovered in China. All of these materials have been spun and woven by processes invented in the Near East. He slips into his moccasins, invented by the Indians of the Eastern woodlands, and goes to the bathroom, whose fixtures are a mixture of European and American inventions, both of recent date. He takes off his pajamas, a garment invented in India, and washes with soap, invented by the ancient Gauls. He then shaves—a masochistic rite that seems to have been derived from either Sumer or ancient Egypt.

Returning to the bedroom, he removes his clothes from a chair of southern European type and proceeds to dress. He puts on garments whose form

* From: *The Study of Man: An Introduction,* by Ralph Linton. Copyright 1936 by D. Appleton-Century Company, Inc. © 1964 by Meredith Corporation. Reprinted by permission of Appleton-Century-Crofts, Educational Division, Meredith Corporation.

originally derived from the skin clothing of the nomads of the Asiatic steppes, puts on shoes made from skins tanned by a process invented in ancient Egypt and cut to a pattern derived from the classical civilizations of the Mediterranean, and ties around his neck a strip of bright-colored cloth that is a vestigial survival of the shoulder shawls worn by the seventeenth-century Croatians. Before going out for breakfast, he glances through the window, made of glass invented in Egypt, and, if it is raining, puts on overshoes made of rubber discovered by the Central American Indians and takes an umbrella, invented in Southeastern Asia. Upon his head he puts a hat made of felt, a material invented in the Asiatic steppes.

On his way to breakfast, he stops to buy a paper, paying for it with coins, an ancient Lydian invention. At the restaurant, a whole new series of borrowed elements confronts him. His plate is made of a form of pottery invented in China. His knife is of steel, an alloy first made in southern India; his fork, a medieval Italian invention; and his spoon, a derivative of a Roman original. He begins breakfast with an orange, from the eastern Mediterranean, a canteloupe from Persia, or perhaps a piece of African watermelon. With this he has coffee, an Abyssinian plant, with cream and sugar. Both the domestication of cows and the idea of milking them originated in the Near East, while sugar was first made in India. After his fruit and first coffee, he goes on to waffles, cakes made by a Scandinavian technique from wheat domesticated in Asia Minor. Over these he pours maple syrup, invented by the Indians of the Eastern woodlands. As a side dish, he may have the egg of a species of bird domesticated in Indochina, or thin strips of the flesh of an animal domesticated in Eastern Asia that have been salted and smoked by a process developed in Northern Europe.

When our friend has finished eating, he settles back to smoke, an American Indian habit, consuming a plant domesticated in Brazil in either a pipe, derived from the Indians of Virginia, or a cigarette, derived from Mexico. If he is hardy enough, he may even attempt a cigar, transmitted to us from the Antilles by way of Spain. While smoking, he reads the news of the day, imprinted in characters invented by the ancient Semites upon a material invented in China by a process invented in Germany. As he absorbs the accounts of foreign troubles, he will, if he is a good, conservative citizen, thank a Hebrew deity in an Indo-European language that he is 100 per cent American.

* * *

· The Eskimos and "Airport Art"*

Nelson Graburn

The motion picture and the mobile are considerably more ancient art forms than Eskimo soapstone carving. Only in the last two decades have the Eskimos of the Eastern Canadian Arctic been producing these carvings, although they have already become commonplace in museums, arts-and-crafts stores, and the homes of middle-class North America. The short history of these carvings suggests certain worldwide acculturative processes and poses new problems about the relationship between art and culture.

Until very recently, these Eskimos produced little that we would call art. Occasionally, for the amusement of themselves and their children, they carved small models–usually in ivory but sometimes in soapstone–that are called *pinguak*. Literally, the word means "imitation of a thing," but it is usually translated as "toy," because that is how these models, an inch or two long, were used. There were amulets or charms made of lightly carved whale or bear teeth; shamans wore these in quantity, but most people wore one or two. Also, everyday utensils of wood, bone, or ivory were sometimes etched or scratched for decorative reasons. The Eskimos had no over-all concepts of art or aesthetics, but, of course, they knew what they liked. The word *takuminaktuk* means "It is good to look at, or beautiful," but it could be applied to a sledge or the northern lights or any other natural or manufactured phenomenon and not just to the "objets d'art" I have mentioned.

The arrival of the white man in the North meant a demand for souvenirs. During the first two centuries of regular contact, this demand was satisfied through trading in the normal manufacture of the Eskimos–parkas, harpoons, utensils, and so forth. Few carvings were offered, but, as long ago as the 1880's, anthropologists noted that such carvings were distinctly souvenirs. In return, the Eskimos received the manufactured objects of the white man–guns, nets, and steel harpoon tips, for instance–and generally thought they were getting a bargain. They could always make more of what they had offered in exchange.

CREATING AN ART FORM

It was not until 1949 that any concerted attempt was made to sell these objects other than by direct exchange. The year before, James Houston, a

* From *Trans-action,* vol. 4, no. 10 (October, 1967), 28–33.

Canadian artist, visited Port Harrison, Quebec, on the east coast of Hudson Bay. Houston collected a small number of ivory and soapstone figurines, which he took to a Montreal art exhibition, where they were admired and sold. The next year, he returned to encourage the Eskimos of Port Harrison and the nearby settlement of Povungnituk to produce more carvings for sale "down south."

Ivory from the fast-disappearing walrus was rare. Whatever was available was already being used. Soapstone is abundant. It is called "lamp material" (*qullisak*), because it was widely used in making ordinary utensils, such as lamps and dishes. The rarity of ivory also meant that the people of the area were less accustomed to, and less skillful in, working it.

The old Canadian Department of Northern Affairs and other agencies responsible for the welfare of the Eskimos were quick to see the chance to increase the cash income of the Eskimos through expansion of this venture. Since World War II, their economic position had been weak because of the poor prices paid for skins. Houston was prevailed upon to return north to encourage the production of figurines and spread the idea to other settlements. It is said that he even trained some carvers and persuaded the government to produce a do-it-yourself manual for others. In the summer of 1950, he brought back $3,000 worth of carvings. Sugluk and Cape Dorset on the Hudson Strait, about 450 miles north of Port Harrison, became important carving centers, and later other smaller settlements took it up. By the end of the 1950's, the annual production was being measured in hundreds of thousands of dollars. A system of marketing was established with the Hudson's Bay Company and the Canadian Handicrafts Guild.

In Povungnituk, an enterprising missionary started a Sculptors' Association. This unique organization was a guild in which the better carvers were to produce, price, and sell carvings of supposedly higher quality. It became a prestige group to which other carvers might aspire. Admission to the group was extended by the members on the basis of quality. The Hudson's Bay Company store continued to buy carvings from the rest of the population. This competition meant higher prices for all the carvers.

The carving boom was a response to the economic position of the Eskimos. They were caught between a rising total population and constant or declining natural resources. Wage employment was for the very few. Port Harrison, Povungnituk, Sugluk, and Cape Dorset greatly increased their production. By 1952, 20,000 carvings had been sold; by 1954, 30,000. The total income of Sugluk from all sources in 1956 was $66,000. Carvings alone accounted for half of it. Nearly all adults carved, and some were almost full-time specialists.

In 1957, the Hudson's Bay Company surveyed the market and its inventory and suddenly, without warning, stopped buying carvings. The Eskimos were distraught and often destitute. One man recalled: "We were so poor that it was like the old days; we could not even afford to have a cup of tea before going hunting in the morning!" The demand for welfare rose sharply, and the government began buying carvings. Later, when the demand picked up, the Company started buying again, although more selectively than before. Competition was the result, and carving has continued to be a major economic support, although never to the extent of the first years.

In the 1960's, the Sculptors' Association of Povungnituk began operating a full-blown cooperative store in competition with the Hudson's Bay Company. Similar arts-and-crafts cooperatives have been started with government support in most of the major settlements.

In 1959, the industrious James Houston introduced another "Eskimo" art form; Eskimo prints using soapstone lithography or sealskin stencils were made under his direction at Cape Dorset. Under the auspices of white agents, this technique has spread.

SOAPSTONE AND SUBJECT MATTER

Soapstone is found throughout the Eastern Arctic area in large veins, often near the coast. It is mined in the summer by Eskimos of the nearby settlements, who use axes and sometimes large saws. The blocks of stone are shared among the men of a family or camp, and each man usually has a supply in his household so that he may carve whenever there is little else to do. The blocks are roughly shaped with small metal axes, and the carvings are then perfected using chisels, awls, and drills, all of which are purchased at the settlement store. The final polishing may be done with sandpaper, and some carvings are then oiled to produce a particularly dark, shiny surface.

The commercial carvings of the modern era are incomparably larger than the traditional *pinguak* toys and may weigh 100 pounds. They are produced for an entirely different consumer and occupy a far greater place in the life of these Eskimos than any previous nonutilitarian manufacture. However, carving shares many characteristics with the "art" of a growing number of other contemporary "primitive" peoples.

The subject matter of the Eskimo works is usually confined to human and natural phenomena with which the carvers are familiar, such as animals, people, hunting, and camping. In Povungnituk and Cape Dorset, the Eskimos have been encouraged to add scenes and figures relating to their traditional mythology. The Eskimos themselves, however, have been devout Anglicans for many decades. From the great range of phenomena with which the Eskimos are now familiar–including much of the industrial culture of North America–there is considerable selection in favor of what is felt to be traditional.

Very little study has been given to the influence of the market on the content, much less the style, of these carvings. I do know that many carvings have proved unsalable, because the white man's market could not identify them as "Eskimo" or "primitive." One of the best carvers at Great Whale River was unable to sell an excellent sculpture of a human figure that had been inspired by the Steve Reeves movie *Atlas*. Edmund Carpenter reports that Eskimo inmates of a government tuberculosis sanatorium in Ontario did carvings of Edsels and kangaroos. These were destroyed by officials on the grounds that they were not authentic.

Still, many of the carvings reflect an Eskimo life that is not truly traditional–for instance, scenes of hunting with guns or fishing with nets. In some cases, most Eskimos and all whites are unaware that the subject matter is not traditional, as in carvings that show the parka with a peak.

In spite of the obvious pressures on them, the Eskimos do not seem to be bothered by these limitations on their subject matter. In fact, most seem to prefer to carve objects that they believe to be "Eskimo" and enjoy the identification with the past and the fact that the white man could hardly attempt to do the same.

One important consideration is that there is no special class of artists in this medium. (This is not true of the printmakers.) Soapstone carving tends to override even the traditional division of labor by age and sex. Young children have been encouraged by their parents in the hope of increasing the family income. Not only do most adults attempt carving, but they are usually successful–that is, the carvings sell.

While most carvings cannot be classified as great art, the vast majority are by no means mediocre. From our point of view, most Eskimos have a superior ability to carve in soapstone. Two factors seem to explain this: familiarity with the tools, materials, and subject matter; and an extremely well-developed series of mental and linguistic conceptions of space and form. The latter is probably related to the necessity of visualizing and communicating location and shape in a relatively featureless landscape. Carpenter gives a striking example of this skill:

> Of course, what appeared to me as a monotonous land was, to the Aivilik [an Eskimo group], varied, filled with meaningful reference points. When I travel by car, I can, with relative ease, pass through a complex and chaotic city, Detroit for example, by simply following a handful of highway markers. I begin with the assumption that the streets are laid out in a grid and the knowledge that certain signs mark my route. Apparently, the Aivilik have similar, though natural, reference points. By and large, these are not actual objects or points but relationships: relationships between, say, contour, type of snow, wind, salt air, ice crack.

One observer claimed that the Eskimos were completely unable to make good judgments about the quality of their own carvings, and that the Sculptors' Association was thus not pricing the pieces correctly. In the vast majority of the settlements, the white man is responsible for the pricing. To the Eskimos, the rewards of carving are financial rather than aesthetic. Most works are produced when there is nothing else to do–in bad weather, for instance. Carving is also done when money is needed and there is no other means of obtaining it.

Once, I was returning from a whale hunt in the Hudson Strait when we spotted a ship far off. One young Eskimo quickly took a piece of soapstone from a quantity that we had mined and carved a seal by the time we reached the ship. We went on board, and he immediately sold the carving for $2.50.

The rate of return on most carving, however, is about 15 to 50 cents an hour. When the opportunity arises for some more pleasurable occupation, a carving may be left on the floor, whatever its state. Many are broken or lost before they can be finished. I interviewed nearly all of the 90 adults of one settlement, and all but one said [they] disliked carving although it was necessary to earn a living. In another settlement, a long-time white resident fluent in Eskimo thought that only one carver really enjoyed his work or took pains to "get things right" for his own satisfaction.

It is often asserted by the retailers that no Eskimo ever carves two pieces alike or copies another's carvings. This is said to prove that all Eskimos are artists. This is not true. An individual "down south" rarely sees more than a small proportion of the output of any one man. I asked one old man in Ivujivik why he always produced "Man sitting on a walrus head." He replied that he did the carving well, and it was a good seller. The Canadian Government propaganda has made much of the great range of subject matter in order to help the market, but the government has recently admitted the repetitions, and now one may even order carvings by number.

There is a great deal of variety, however. Not all soapstone is of the same color or consistency. Often, the type of stone identifies a certain settlement's production. Furthermore, each settlement seems to develop its own style. Although the reasons for this have not been investigated, I can suggest that the nature of the stone available and conscious or unconscious copying of the more successful carvers may affect local styles.

ACCULTURATION AND ART

The place of carving in the economic side of acculturation is most clear. Carving is an occupation that the dominant white man rewards well, because he could produce the result himself only with great difficulty. No white man has ever been known to carve soapstone successfully. During the boom in the 1950's, "Eskimo soapstone carvings" were produced in the Orient, but they were obvious fakes to the trained eye. The Canadian Government put an end to the practice by registering a trademark for the genuine article. I do know of one Japanese-Canadian anthropologist who passed as an Eskimo and sold another's carving for $7 to the crew of a ship visiting a northern settlement.

Carving has fallen into place as a natural occupation alongside fox trapping and seal hunting. If carving had not developed, the Canadian Government would have been saddled with an even greater welfare burden because of the lack of a sound economic base. This is typical as a stage in worldwide acculturative processes where the original special economic relationship–for the Eskimos, fox trapping–is no longer adequately beneficial to either side. The controlling authorities find themselves in a situation where they no longer need the large indigenous population, and yet do not know what to do with it. The subordinate group is not ready for assimilation, even if the larger population would allow it. Yet, total neglect is impossible.

From the aesthetic point of view, both the white buyers and the Eskimo sellers admit the pleasing quality of the carvings. To the majority of buyers, the works are simply Eskimo or even "primitive" art. The Eskimos themselves still have no conception of art; they call the carvings *qullisangmik sanasimavanga*, "things made out of lamp material." A few talented individuals have an "artistic" approach to their work, but these are not necessarily those whose works sell best. An examination of both form and content cannot reveal whether the creator was trying to meet his own requirements or to make money, or both. In our own society, we depend on the special class of artists and art critics to tell us what is art and what is good art. This difficult task is rendered more difficult when the artists are in one culture and the critics in another.

If we are to judge the carvings on technical merit–control of material and technique–we must conclude that nearly all Eskimos are artists. We would probably come to the same conclusion about the Australian aborigines of Arnhem Land at Yirrkalla and Milingimbi, although their bark paintings are in a traditional technique. Carpenter asserts, however, that soapstone carving is "a new, delightful non-Eskimo art that has brought financial assistance to needy Eskimos and joy to many Western art connoisseurs." He bases this on the grounds that the idea and the market are the white man's, and that the form resembles white efforts more than it does the traditional Eskimo *pinguak*. However true this may be, the assertion that the carvings are non-Eskimo is untenable, because only Eskimos can produce them. Carpenter could answer, of course, that the producers are not "real Eskimos." Still, Charles A. Martijn, in his very fine summary on the subject (*Anthropos* 59, 1964), is much nearer the point when he says: ". . . carving is an Eskimo art, but one of directed acculturation."

There are a number of parallel cases of acculturation art, or "airport art," as it is sometimes called, such as that of Navajo silversmiths, Arnhem Land bark painters, and Kamba wood carvers of East Africa. Airport art has been little studied as such, however. In all cases, there has been considerable modification of style and even introduction of new materials in order to satisfy a market. The culturally embedded meanings of the productions have become tenuous, and, in many cases, "mass production" has been introduced as well. Eskimo prints are a particularly striking example. These phenomena are characteristic of the structural positions of the small-scale peoples with respect to the world's dominant socio-economic systems.

Acculturation art may also tell us much about social changes among its producers. In Great Whale River, for example, the Naskapi Indians living alongside the Eskimos abandoned their traditional wood carving in favor of soapstone. No doubt, they hoped to cash in on the demand. But their first efforts in soapstone, while technically proficient and aesthetically pleasing, still looked more like Naskapi wood carvings than Eskimo soapstone works.

Now, however, the difference between the two carving styles is disappearing. Indian and Eskimo pieces have begun to look very much the same. What is significant here for the relation between art and culture is the fact that this assimilation of art styles has been closely paralleled by assimilation of another sort: the fast-developing coalescence of Eskimos and Indians into an undifferentiated "native lower caste."

The Canadian Eskimos are producing an art form that is a good example of that long-neglected category of "transitional" or "acculturation" art. For a century or more, Western man has been excited by the exotic, and collections of "primitive" art are numerous. However, even today, when so little truly traditional art is being produced, many still consider it somehow impure to take a serious interest in the artistic production of those many peoples who have come in contact with civilization. Such an approach ignores artistic values. Just as people do not stop being people just because they are becoming assimilated, neither does their art cease to be art just because it is no longer traditional. The Eskimos have developed a new art form in response to demands from the outside, and they have successfully incorporated traditional themes into a style much admired by the market. They are using new (metal) tools with great skill on a material–soapstone–with which they were already familiar. Far from "degenerating" with the increasing influence of civilization, their present art, in many opinions, surpasses anything they have produced previously.

If we are seriously interested in art, rather than in the titillations of the exotic, the Eskimos should be considered artists first and members of an exotic culture second. The Canadian Government has taken a lead in encouraging the artistic abilities of its indigenous citizens, and this example might well be followed in many other countries where the potential of native groups is still untapped.

The Effect of Culture on the Individual

Cultural Components in Responses to Pain*

Mark Zborowski

This paper reports on one aspect of a larger study: that concerned with discovering the role of cultural patterns in attitudes toward, and reactions to, pain that is caused by disease and injury–in other words, responses to spontaneous pain. . . .

* * *

* From *The Journal of Social Issues,* vol. 8, no. 4 (1953), pp. 16–31. Reprinted by permission of The Society for the Psychological Study of Social Issues.

In setting up the research, we were interested not only in the purely theoretical aspects of the findings in terms of possible contribution to the understanding of the pain experience in general; we also had in mind the practical goal of a contribution to the field of medicine. In the relationship between the doctor and his patient, the respective attitudes toward pain may play a crucial role, especially when the doctor feels that the patient exaggerates his pain, while the patient feels that the doctor minimizes his suffering. The same may be true, for instance, in a hospital where the members of the medical and nursing staff may have attitudes toward pain different from those held by the patient, or when they expect a certain pattern of behavior according to their cultural background, while the patient may manifest a behavior pattern that is acceptable in his culture. These differences may play an important part in the evaluation of the individual pain experience, in dealing with pain at home and in the hospital, in administration of analgesics, etc. Moreover, we expected that this study of pain would offer opportunities to gain insight into related attitudes toward health, disease, medication, hospitalization, medicine in general, etc.

With these aims in mind, the project was set up at the Kingsbridge Veterans Hospital, Bronx, New York, where four ethnocultural groups were selected for an intensive study. These groups included patients of Jewish, Italian, Irish, and "Old American" stock. Three groups–Jews, Italians, and Irish–were selected because they were described by medical people as manifesting striking differences in their reaction to pain. Italians and Jews were described as tending to "exaggerate" their pain, while the Irish were often depicted as stoical individuals who are able to take a great deal of pain. The fourth group, the "Old Americans," were chosen because the values and attitudes of this group dominate in the country and are held by many members of the medical profession and by many descendants of the immigrants, who, in the process of Americanization, tend to adopt American patterns of behavior. The members of this group can be defined as White, native-born individuals, usually Protestant, whose grandparents, at least, were born in the United States, and who do not identify themselves with any foreign group, either nationally, socially, or culturally.

The Kingsbridge Veterans Hospital was chosen because its population represents roughly the ethnic composition of New York City, thus offering access to a fair sample of the four selected groups, and also because various age groups were represented among the hospitalized veterans of World War I, World War II, and the Korean War. In one major respect, this hospital was not adequate, namely, in not offering the opportunity to investigate sex differences in attitude toward pain. This aspect of research will be carried out in a hospital with a large female population.

In setting up this project, we were mainly interested in discovering certain regularities in reactions and attitudes toward pain characteristic of the four groups. Therefore, the study has a qualitative character, and the efforts of the researchers were not directed toward a collection of material suitable for quantitative analysis. The main techniques used in the collection of the material were interviews with patients of the selected groups, observation of their behavior when in pain, and discussion of the individual cases with doctors, nurses, and other people directly or indirectly involved in the pain experience of the individual. In addition to the interviews with patients, "healthy" members of the respective groups were interviewed on their attitudes toward pain; because, in terms of the original hypothesis, those attitudes and reactions that are displayed by the patients of the given cultural groups are held by all members of the group, regardless of whether or not they are in pain, although in pain these attitudes may come more sharply into focus. In certain cases, the researchers have interviewed a member of the patient's immediate family in order to check the report of the patient on his pain experience, and in order to find out what are the attitudes and reactions of the family toward the patient's experience.

These interviews, based on a series of open-ended questions, were focused upon the past and present pain experiences of the interviewee. However, many other areas were considered important for the understanding of this experience. For instance, it was felt that complaints of pain may play an important role in manipulating relationships in the family and the larger social environment. It was also felt that, in order to understand the specific reactive patterns in controlling pain, it is important to know certain aspects of child-rearing in the culture, relationships between parents and children, the role of infliction of pain in punishment, the attitudes of various members of the family toward specific expected, accepted pain experiences, and so on. The interviews were recorded on wire and transcribed verbatim for an ultimate detailed analysis. The interviews usually lasted for approximately two hours, the time being limited by the condition of the interviewee and by the amount and quality of his answers. When it was considered necessary, an interview was repeated. In most of the cases, the study of the interviewee was followed by informal conversations and by observation of his behavior in the hospital.

The information gathered from the interviews was discussed with members of the medical staff, especially in the areas related to the medical aspects of the problem, in order to get their evaluation of the pain experience of the patient. Information as to the personality of the patient was checked against results of psychological testing by members of the psychological staff of the hospital when these were available.

The discussion of the material presented in this paper is based on interviews with 103 respondents, including 87 hospital patients in pain and 16 healthy subjects. According to their ethno-cultural background, the respondents are distributed as follows: "Old Americans," 26; Italians, 24; Jews, 31; Irish, 11; and others, 11. In addition, there were the collateral interviews and conversations noted above with family members, doctors, nurses, and other members of the hospital staff.

With regard to the pathological causes of pain, the majority of the interviewees fall into the group of patients suffering from neurological diseases, mainly herniated discs and spinal lesions. The focusing upon a group of patients suffering from a similar pathology offered the opportunity to investigate reactions and attitudes toward spontaneous pain that is symptomatic of one group of diseases. Nevertheless, a number of patients suffering from other diseases were also interviewed.

This paper is based upon the material collected during the first stage of study. The generalizations are to a great extent tentative formulations on a descriptive level. There has been no attempt as yet to integrate the results with the value system and the cultural pattern of the group, although here and there there will be indications to the effect that they are part of the culture pattern. The discussions will be limited to main regularities within three groups, namely, the Italians, the Jews, and the "Old Americans." Factors related to variations within each group will be discussed after the main prevailing patterns have been presented.

PAIN AMONG PATIENTS OF JEWISH AND ITALIAN ORIGIN

As already mentioned, the Jews and Italians were selected mainly because interviews with medical experts suggested that they display similar reactions to pain. The investigation of this similarity provided the opportunity to check a rather popular assumption that similar reactions reflect similar attitudes. The differences between the Italian and Jewish cultures are great enough to suggest that, if the attitudes are related to cultural pattern, they will also be different, despite the apparent similarity in manifest behavior.

Members of both groups were described as being very emotional in their responses to pain. They were described as tending to exaggerate their pain experience and being very sensitive to pain. Some of the doctors stated that, in their opinion, Jews and Italians have a lower threshold of pain than members of other ethnic groups, especially members of the so-called Nordic group. This statement seems to indicate a certain confusion as to the concept of the threshold of pain. According to people who have studied the problem of the threshold of pain—for instance, Harold Wolff and his associates—the threshold of pain is more or less the same for all human beings regardless of nationality, sex, or age.

In the course of the investigation, the general impressions of doctors were confirmed to a great extent by the interview material and by the observation of the patients' behavior. However, even a superficial study of the interviews has revealed that, although reactions to pain appear to be similar, the underlying attitudes toward pain are different in the two groups. While the Italian patients seemed to be mainly concerned with the immediacy of the pain experience and were disturbed by the actual pain sensation that they experienced in a given situation, the concern of patients of Jewish origin was focused mainly upon the symptomatic meaning of pain and upon the significance of pain in relation to their health, welfare, and, eventually, for the welfare of the families. The Italian patient expressed, in his behavior and in his complaints, the discomfort caused by pain as such, and he manifested his emotions with regard to the effects of this pain experience upon his immediate situation in terms of occupation, economic situation, and so on; the Jewish patient expressed primarily his worries and anxieties as to the extent to which the pain indicated a threat to his health. In this connection, it is worth mentioning that one of the Jewish words to describe strong pain is *yessurim*, a word that is also used to describe worries and anxieties.

Attitudes of Italian and Jewish patients toward pain-relieving drugs can serve as an indication of their attitude toward pain. When in pain, the Italian calls for pain relief and is mainly concerned with the analgesic effects of the drugs that are administered to him. Once the pain is relieved, the Italian patient easily forgets his sufferings and manifests a happy and joyful disposition. The Jewish patient, however, often is reluctant to accept the drug, and he explains this reluctance in terms of concern about the effects of the drug upon his health in general. He is apprehensive about the habit-forming aspects of the analgesic. Moreover, he feels that the drug relieves his pain only temporarily and does not cure him of the disease that may cause the pain. Nurses and doctors have reported cases in which patients would hide the pill that was given to them to relieve their pain and would prefer to suffer. These reports were confirmed in the interviews with the patients. It was also observed that many Jewish patients, after being relieved from pain, often continued to display the same depressed and worried behavior, because they felt that, although the pain was currently absent, it may recur as long as the disease was not cured completely. From these observations, it appears that, when one deals with a Jewish and an Italian patient in pain, in the first case it is more important to relieve the anxieties with regard to the sources of pain, while in the second it is more important to relieve the actual pain.

Another indication as to the significance of pain for Jewish and Italian patients is their respective attitudes toward the doctor. The Italian patient seems to display a most confident attitude toward the doctor, which is usually reinforced after the doctor has succeeded in relieving pain; whereas the Jewish patient manifests a skeptical attitude, feeling that the fact that the doctor has relieved his pain by some drug does not mean at all that he is skillful enough to take care of the basic illness. Consequently, even when the pain is relieved, he tends to check the diagnosis and the treatment of one doctor against the opinions of other specialists in the field. Summarizing the difference between the Italian and Jewish attitudes, one can say that the Italian attitude is characterized by a present-oriented apprehension with regard to the actual sensation of pain, and the Jew tends to manifest a future-oriented anxiety as to the symptomatic and general meaning of the pain experience.

It has been stated that the Italians and Jews tend to manifest similar behavior in terms of their reactions to pain. As both cultures allow for free expression of feelings and emotions by words, sounds, and gestures, both the Italians and Jews feel free to talk about their pain, complain about it, and manifest their sufferings by groaning, moaning, crying, etc. They are not ashamed of this expression. They admit willingly that, when they are in pain, they do complain a great deal, call for help, and expect sympathy and assistance from other members of their immediate social environment, especially from members of their family. When in pain, they are reluctant to be alone and prefer the presence and attention of other people. This behavior, which is expected, accepted, and approved by the Italian and Jewish cultures, often conflicts with the patterns of behavior expected from a patient by American or Americanized medical people. Thus, they tend to describe the behavior of the Italian and Jewish patients as exaggerated and overemotional. The material suggests that they do tend to minimize the actual pain experiences of the Italian and Jewish patients, regardless of whether they have the objective criteria for evaluating the actual amount of pain that the patient experiences. It seems that the uninhibited display of reaction to pain as manifested by the Jewish and Italian patients provokes distrust in American culture instead of provoking sympathy.

Despite the close similarity between the manifest reactions among Jews and Italians, there seem to be differences in emphasis, especially with regard to what the patient achieves by these reactions and as to the specific manifestations of these reactions in the various social settings. For instance, they differ in their behavior at home and in the hospital. The Italian husband, who is aware of his role as an adult male, tends to avoid verbal complaining at home, leaving this type of behavior to the women. In the hospital, where he is less concerned with his role as a male, he tends to be more verbal and more emotional. The Jewish patient, on the contrary, seems to be more calm in the hospital than at home. Traditionally, the Jewish male does not emphasize his masculinity through such traits as stoicism, and he does not equate verbal complaints with weakness. Moreover, the Jewish culture allows the patient to be demanding and complaining. Therefore, he tends more to use his pain in order to control interpersonal relationships within the family. Although similar use of pain to manipulate the relationships between members of the family may be present also in some other cultures, it seems that, in the Jewish culture, this is not disapproved, while in others it is. In the hospital, one can also distinguish variations in the reactive patterns among Jews and Italians. Upon his admission to the hospital, and in the presence of the doctor, the Jewish patient tends to complain, ask for help, be emotional even to the point of crying. However, as soon as he feels that adequate care is given to him, he becomes more restrained. This suggests that the display of pain reaction serves less as an indication of the amount of pain experienced than as a means to create an atmosphere and setting in which the pathological causes of pain will be best taken care of. The Italian patient, on the other hand, seems to be less concerned with setting up a favorable situation for treatment. He takes for granted that adequate care will be given to him, and, in the presence of the doctor, he seems to be somewhat calmer than the Jewish patient. The mere presence of the doctor reassures the Italian patient, while the skepticism of the Jewish patient limits the reassuring role of the physician.

To summarize the description of the reaction patterns of the Jewish and Italian patients, the material suggests that, on a semiconscious level, the Jewish patient tends to provoke worry and concern in his social environment as to the state of his health and the symptomatic character of his pain, while the Italian tends to provoke sympathy toward his suffering. In one case, the function of the pain reaction will be the mobilization of the efforts of the family and the doctors toward a complete cure, while, in the second case, the function of the reaction will be focused upon the mobilization of effort toward relieving the pain sensation.

On the basis of the discussion of the Jewish and Italian material, two generalizations can be made: (1) *Similar reactions to pain manifested by members of different ethnocultural groups do not necessarily reflect similar attitudes to pain.* (2) *Reactive patterns similar in terms of their manifestations may have different functions and serve different purposes in various cultures.*

PAIN AMONG PATIENTS OF "OLD AMERICAN" ORIGIN

There is little emphasis on emotional complaining about pain among "Old American" patients. Their complaints about pain can best be described as reporting on pain. In describing his pain, the "Old American" patient tries to find the most appropriate ways of defining the quality of pain, its localization, duration, etc. When examined by the doctor, he gives the impression of trying to assume the detached role of an unemotional observer who gives the most efficient description of his state for a correct diagnosis and treatment. The interviewees repeatedly state that there is no point in complaining and groaning and moaning, etc., because "it won't help anybody." However, they readily admit that, when pain is unbearable, they may react strongly, even to the point of crying, but they tend to do it when they are alone. Withdrawal from society seems to be a frequent reaction to strong pain.

There seem to be different patterns in reacting to pain, depending on the situation. One pattern, manifested in the presence of members of the family, friends, etc., consists of attempts to minimize pain, to avoid complaining and provoking pity; when pain becomes too strong, there is a tendency to withdraw and express freely such reactions as groaning, moaning, etc. A different pattern is manifested in the presence of people who, on account of their profession, should know the character of the pain experience, because they are expected to make the appropriate diagnosis, advise the proper cure, and give the adequate help. The tendency to avoid deviation from certain expected patterns of behavior plays an important role in the reaction to pain. This is also controlled by the desire to seek approval on the part of the social environment, especially in the hospital, where the "Old American" patient tries to avoid being a "nuisance" in the ward. He seems to be, more than any other patient, aware of an ideal pattern of behavior that is identified as "American," and he tends to conform to it. This was characteristically expressed by a patient who answered the question how he reacts to pain by saying, "I react like a good American."

An important element in controlling the pain reaction is the wish of the patient to cooperate with those who are expected to take care of him. The situation is often viewed as a team composed of the patient, the doctor, the nurse, the attendant, etc., and, in this team, everybody has a function and is supposed to do his share in order to achieve the most successful result. Emotionality is seen as a purposeless and hindering factor in a situation that calls for knowledge, skill, training, and efficiency. It is important to note that this behavior is also expected by American or Americanized members of the medical or nursing staff, and the patients who do not fall into this pattern are viewed as deviants, hypochondriacs, and neurotics.

As in the case of the Jewish patients, the American attitude toward pain can be best defined as a future-oriented anxiety. The "Old American" patient is also concerned with the symtomatic significance of pain, which is correlated with a pronounced health-consciousness. It seems that the "Old American" is conscious of various threats to his health that are present in his environment and therefore feels vulnerable and is prone to interpret his pain sensation as a warning signal indicating that something is wrong with his health and therefore must be reported to the physician. With some exceptions, pain is considered bad and unnecessary and therefore must be immediately taken care of. In those situations where pain is expected and accepted, such as in the process of medical treatment or as a result of sports activities, there is less concern with the pain sensation. In general, however, there is a feeling that suffering pain is unnecessary when there are means of relieving it.

Although the attitudes of the Jewish and "Old American" patients can be defined as pain anxiety, they differ greatly. The future-oriented anxiety of the Jewish interviewee is characterized by pessimism or, at best, by skepticism, while the "Old American" patient is rather optimistic in his future-orientation. This attitude is fostered by the mechanistic approach to the body and its functions and by the confidence in the skill of the experts, which are so frequent in the American culture. The body is often viewed as a machine that has to be well taken care of, be periodically checked for disfunctioning, and, eventually, when out of order, be taken to an expert who will "fix" the defect. In the case of pain, the expert is the medical man who has the "know-how" because of his training and experience and therefore is entitled to full confidence. An important element in the optimistic outlook is faith in the progress of science. Patients with intractable pain often stated that, although at the present moment the doctors do not have the "drug," they will eventually discover it, and they will give the examples of sulfa, penicillin, etc.

The anxieties of a pain-experiencing "Old American" patient are greatly relieved when he feels that something is being done about it in terms of specific activities involved in the treatment. It seems that his security and confidence increase in direct proportion to the number of tests, X-rays, examinations, injections, etc., that are given to him. Accordingly, "Old American" patients seem to have a positive attitude toward hospitalization, because the hospital is the adequate institution that is equipped for the necessary treatment. While a Jewish and an Italian patient seem to be disturbed by the impersonal character of the hospital and by the necessity of being treated there instead of at home, the "Old American" patient, on the contrary, prefers the hospital treatment to the home treatment, and neither he nor his family seems to be disturbed by hospitalization.

To summarize the attitude of the "Old American" toward pain, he is disturbed by the symptomatic aspect of pain and is concerned with its incapacitating aspects, but he tends to view the future in rather optimistic colors, having confidence in the science and skill of the professional people who treat his condition.

SOME SOURCES OF INTRAGROUP VARIATION

In the description of the reactive patterns and attitudes toward pain among patients of Jewish and "Old American" origin, certain regularities have been observed for each particular group, regardless of individual differences and variations. This does not mean that each individual in each group manifests the same reactions and attitudes. Individual variations are often due to specific aspects of pain experience, to the character of the disease that causes the pain, or to elements in the personality of the patient. However, there are also other factors that are instrumental in provoking these differences, and that can still be traced back to the cultural backgrounds of the individual patients. Such variables as the degree of Americanization of the patient, his socio-economic background, education, and religiosity may play an important role in shaping individual variations in the reactive patterns. For instance, it was found that the patterns described are manifested most consistently among immigrants, while their descendants tend to differ in terms of adopting American forms of behavior and American attitudes toward the role of the medical expert, medical institutions, and equipment in controlling pain. It is safe to say that the further the individual is from the immigrant generation, the more American is his behavior. This is less true for the attitudes toward pain, which seem to persist to a great extent even among members of the third generation, and even though the reactive patterns are radically changed. A Jewish or Italian patient born in this country of American-born parents tends to *behave* like an "Old American" but often expresses *attitudes* similar to those that are expressed by the Jewish or Italian people. They try to appear unemotional and efficient in situations where the immigrant would be excited and disturbed. However, in the process of the interview, if a patient is of Jewish origin, he is likely to express attitudes of anxiety as to the meaning of his pain, and, if he is an Italian, he is likely to be rather unconcerned about the significance of his pain for his future.

The occupational factor plays an important role when pain affects a specific area of the body. For instance, manual workers with herniated discs are more disturbed by their pain than are professional or business people with a similar disease because of the immediate significance of this particular pain for their respective abilities to earn a living. It was also observed that headaches cause more concern among intellectuals than among manual workers.

The educational background of the patient also plays an important role in his attitude with regard to the symptomatic meaning of a pain sensation. The more educated patients are more health-conscious and more aware of pain as a possible symptom of a dangerous disease. However, this factor plays a less important role than might be expected. The less educated "Old American" or Jewish patient is still more health-conscious than the more educated Italian. On the other hand, the less educated Jew is as much worried about the significance of pain as the more educated one. The education of the patient seems to be an important factor in fostering specific reactive patterns. The more educated patient, who may have more anxiety with regard to illness, may be more reserved in specific reactions to pain than an unsophisticated individual, who feels free to express his feelings and emotions.

THE TRANSMISSION OF CULTURAL ATTITUDES TOWARD PAIN

In interpreting the differences that may be attributed to different socioeconomic and education backgrounds, there is enough evidence to conclude that these differences appear mainly on the manifest and behavioral level, whereas attitudinal patterns toward pain tend to be more uniform and to be common to most of the members of the group, regardless of their specific backgrounds.

These attitudes toward pain and the expected reactive patterns are acquired by the individual members of the society from the earliest childhood, along with other cultural attitudes and values that are learned from the parents, parent-substitutes, siblings, peer groups, etc. Each culture offers to its members an ideal pattern of attitudes and reactions, which may differ for various subcultures in a given society, and each individual is expected to conform to this ideal pattern. Here, the role of the family seems to be of primary importance. Directly and indirectly, the family environment affects the individual's ultimate response to pain. In each culture, the parents teach the child how to react to pain, and, by approval or disapproval, they promote specific forms of behavior. This conclusion is amply supported by the interviews. Thus, the Jewish and Italian respondents are unanimous in relating how their parents, especially mothers, manifested overprotective and overconcerned attitudes toward the child's health, participation in sports, games, fights, etc. In these families, the child is constantly reminded of the advisability of avoiding colds, injuries, fights, and other threatening situations. Crying in complaint is responded to by the parents with sympathy, concern, and help. By their overprotective and worried attitude, they foster complaining and tears. The child learns to pay attention to each painful experience and to look for help and sympathy, which are readily given to him. In Jewish families, where not only a slight sensation of pain but also each deviation from the child's normal behavior is looked upon as a sign of illness, the child is prone to acquire anxieties with regard to the meaning and significance of these manifestations. The Italian parents do not seem to be concerned with the symptomatic meaning of the child's pains and aches, but, instead, there is a great deal of verbal expression of emotions and feelings of sympathy toward the "poor child" who happens to be in discomfort because of illness or because of an injury in play. In these families, a child is praised when he avoids physical injuries and is scolded when he does not pay enough attention to bad weather, to drafts, or when he takes part in rough games and fights. The injury and pain are often interpreted to the child as punishment for the wrong behavior, and physical punishment is the usual consequence of misbehavior.

In the "Old American" family, the parental attitude is quite different. The child is told not to "run to mother with every little thing." He is told to take pain "like a man," not to be a "sissy," not to cry. The child's participation in physical sports and games is not only approved but is also strongly stimulated. Moreover, the child is taught to expect to be hurt in sports and games and is taught to fight back if he happens to be attacked by other boys. However, it seems that the American parents are conscious of the threats to the child's health, and they teach the child to take immediate care of any injury. When hurt, the right thing to do is not to cry and get emotional but to avoid unnecessary pain and prevent unpleasant consequences by applying the proper first-aid medicine and by calling a doctor.

Often, attitudes and behavior fostered in a family conflict with those patterns that are accepted by the larger social environment. This is especially true in the case of children of immigrants. The Italian or Jewish immigrant parents promote patterns that they consider correct, while the peer groups in the street and in the school criticize this behavior and foster a different one. In consequence, the child may acquire the attitudes that are part of his home-life but may also adopt behavior patterns that conform to those of his friends.

The direct promotion of certain behavior described as part of the child-rearing explains only in part the influence of the general family environment and the specific role of the parents in shaping responses to pain. They are also formed indirectly by observing the behavior of other members of the family and by imitating their responses to pain. Moreover, attitudes toward pain are also influenced by various aspects of parent-child relationship in a culture. The material suggests that differences in attitudes toward pain in Jewish, Italian, and "Old American" families are closely related to the role and image of the father in the respective cultures in terms of his authority and masculinity. Often, the father and mother assume different roles in promoting specific patterns of behavior and specific attitudes. For example, it seems that, in the "Old American" family, it is chiefly the mother who stimulates the child's ability to resist pain, thus emphasizing his masculinity. In the Italian family, it seems that the mother is the one who inspires the child's emotionality, while, in the Jewish family, both parents express attitudes of worry and concern that are transmitted to the children.

Specific deviations from expected reactive and attitudinal patterns can often be understood in terms of a particular structure of the family. This became especially clear from the interviews of two Italian patients and one Jewish patient. All three subjects revealed reactions and attitudes diametrically opposite to those that the investigator would expect on the basis of his experience. In the process of the interview, however, it appeared that one of the Italian patients was adopted into an Italian family, found out about his adoption at the age of fourteen, created a phantasy of being of Anglo-Saxon origin because of his physical appearance, and, accordingly, began to eradicate everything "Italian" in his personality and behavior. For instance, he denied knowledge of the Italian language, despite the fact that he always spoke Italian in the family, and even learned to abstain from smiling, because he felt that being happy and joyful is an indication of Italian origin. The other Italian patient lost his family at a very early age because of family disorganization and was brought up in an Irish foster home. The Jewish patient consciously adopted a "non-Jewish" pattern of behavior and attitude because of strong sibling rivalry. According to the respondent, his brother, a favored son in the immigrant Jewish family, always manifested "typical" Jewish reactions toward disease, and the patient, who strongly disliked the brother and was jealous of him, decided to be "completely different."

2. SUGGESTIONS FOR FURTHER READING

BARNOUW, VICTOR. *Culture and Personality* (Homewood, Ill.: Dorsey Press, 1963).

BECKER, HOWARD. *Outsiders* (New York: The Free Press, 1963).*

BENEDICT, RUTH. *Patterns of Culture* (Boston: Houghton Mifflin, 1961).*

CHILDE, V. GORDON. *Man Makes Himself* (New York: New American Library, 1951).*

GRABURN, NELSON. *Eskimos Without Igloos* (Boston: Little, Brown, 1969).*

HALL, EDWARD T. *The Silent Language* (New York: Doubleday, 1959).*

HAYS, H. R. *From Ape to Angel* (New York: Capricorn, 1964).*

HENRY, JULES. *Culture Against Man* (New York: Random House, 1963).*

HOEBEL, E. ADAMSON. *The Law of Primitive Man* (Cambridge, Mass.: Harvard University Press, 1954).*

HUNT, ROBERT (ed.). *Personalities and Cultures* (Garden City, N.Y.: Natural History Press, 1967).*

KLUCKHOHN, CLYDE. *Mirror For Man* (New York: McGraw Hill, 1949).*

LEWIS, OSCAR. *Children of Sanchez* (New York: Random House, 1961).*

———. *Tepoztlan* (New York: Holt, Rinehart, 1960).*

LINTON, RALPH. *The Study of Man* (New York: D. Appleton-Century, 1936).*
MALINOWSKI, BRONISLAW. *Argonauts of the Western Pacific* (New York: E. P. Dutton, 1961).*
MEAD, MARGARET (ed.). *Cultural Patterns and Technical Change* (Paris: UNESCO, 1953).*
———. *New Lives For Old* (New York: William Morrow, 1953).*
———. *Sex and Temperament in Three Primitive Societies* (New York: William Morrow, 1935).*
ROSENBERG, B., AND D. WHITE (eds.). *Mass Culture* (New York: The Free Press, 1957).*
RUESCH, HANS. *Top of the World* (New York: Pocket Books, 1951).*
SHAPIRO, HARRY (ed.). *Man, Culture and Society* (New York: Oxford University Press, 1960).*
SUMNER, WILLIAM G. *Folkways* (Boston: Ginn, 1906).*

* *Available in paperback.*

3. Social Organization

INTRODUCTION

Sociologists use the term "social structure" or "social organization" to refer to the orderly or patterned way in which individuals and groups of people relate to one another in society. In any given society, social organization involves the assignment of different functions to different people and the relation of these functions to one another and to the group purposes.

To illustrate social organization: Think of a metropolitan hospital that serves the health-care needs of thousands of patients daily. During an average day, the hospital receives many requests for admission. Some patients require ambulance service. The patient population requires a wide variety of medical ministrations, as well as food, bed changes, and the like. If the entire hospital staff had to deliberate as to who would do what and how every time a request for any of these services developed, it is doubtful whether many of the patients would receive much health care. The social organization of the hospital, by its differentiation and coordination of functions—admission personnel, ambulance drivers, physicians, nurses, dieticians, social workers, and so forth—stabilizes interaction between staff and patients in a manner that makes the provision of health care possible.

As we focus on the structure of groups and individuals within a society, we can discern a network of statuses (positions occupied by members of society) and roles (the functions these people are expected to perform according to the cultural norms shared by the members). For example, within the hospital society we find the status or position of nurse; this position has a variety of roles associated with it, such as taking patients' temperatures and administering medication.

Any individual may be said to have various statuses; for example, the same man may be professor, father, taxpayer, patient. As these examples suggest, status is always relational or reciprocal. Without its complement—professor-student, father-child—status would be meaningless. Role defines the rights, obligations, and privileges of a person who occupies a particular status. It tells a person what he ought to do in his positions of professor, father, and so forth; to whom he has obligations; and upon whom he has a rightful claim.

In the course of performing his many roles, a person is subject to conflicting pressures and strains that arise because different and inconsistent kinds of behavior are required by his different statuses. For example, a "working wife" has role obligations toward her family and toward her job. Should a member of her family become ill, she would feel the obligation to care for him and yet, at the same time, the obligation to perform her work role.

Often, role strains and conflicts are built into a single role. Consider, for example, the role of a military officer. Success in this role requires, on the one hand, a relationship of friendship and intimacy with his men, which can stimulate them to perform effectively; yet, at the same time, the role requires impersonal judgment and command, which discourage the development of friendship and personal loyalty. The individual subjected to role conflict is confronted with a dilemma: How should he behave? As people move in ever wider social circles, performing more roles than ever before, the likelihood of role strain and role conflict will inevitably increase.

It has been suggested that, without the interrelated system of roles and statuses of social organization, the number of decisions that social life requires would be totally overwhelming to the individual. Yet, social organization can conceivably become a straitjacket, impeding the individual from adapting to changing circumstances or conditions. Culture provides the script, and social organization casts the players in the ongoing, yet ever changing, drama of social life. To put this in another way, social organization coordinates the social relationships among persons and groups into a meaningful pattern, which, if the group or society is to persist, must respond to the changing needs of the group and to the changing pressures from the physical and social environment.

The transition from rural to urban society probably represents the single most sweeping and comprehensive reordering of social relationships that has taken place in the history of human society. It has been examined by a great number of sociologists from the nineteenth century to the present. Henry S. Maine called this change the transition from status to contract; Ferdinand Toennies saw it as a movement from *Gemeinschaft* (commune) to *Gesellschaft* (society); Émile Durkheim referred to it as a shift from mechanical solidarity to organic solidarity. Robert Redfield's essay on "The Folk Society" explores several dimensions of this movement from rural, or folk, to urban society.

In folk society, a man's family membership was a paramount factor in his social placement; in the wake of industrialization, his role in the process of production, his occupation, has now assumed the pivotal position. Where status in society was once ascriptive (based on given characteristics such as family, age, and sex), it is now predominantly achieved (based on the accomplishments of the individual).

Urban society is a social world in which many of our encounters are transitory, instrumental (merely a means to some other end), and nonintimate; in which group memberships are formal and secondary (relationships that are specialized, unemotional, and impersonal, involving a limited aspect of one's personality); and in which roles are delimited and segmented. The values of the urban, industrial world are oriented toward the future, highlight the rational and scientific, and are essentially secular.

Many critics of the modern world have argued that urban society exhibits severe social disorganization. They claim that the kind of behavior that prompted thirty-odd New Yorkers several years ago to "mind their own business" when Katherine Genovese, screaming for help within earshot of them, was assaulted and murdered is symptomatic of some of the social-disorganizational tendencies of urban society. Sociologists refer to this condition as anomie (normlessness), analogous to the notion of political deregulation—anarchy.

Yet, the urban scene may not be so disorganized as many people argue. Recently, sociologists have been devoting much attention to the normative order and social organization governing the urban scene. One result of this research is Leon Mann's "Queue Culture: The Waiting Line as a Social System," which demonstrates that, despite intense competition among avid soccer fans for the relatively few general-admission seats, there has evolved a rather elaborate, widely understood, and highly effective social system governing the distribution of tickets. This normative order is quite antithetical to the idea of anomie. More studies of the urban scene, particularly of public places, may lead to greater understanding of social rules and structures in our present-day experience.

Another significant aspect of the study of social organization is bureaucracy. Although bureaucratic organization in the layman's view generally refers to a government agency or "red tape" (administrative rigidity), the term has a different meaning for the sociologist. A bureaucracy, as defined by Max Weber, is any organization in which (1) the regular activities are distributed in a fixed way as official duties; (2) the arrangement of offices follows the principle of hierarchy; (3) operations are governed by a consistent system of abstract rules and represent the application of these rules to particular cases; (4) the ideal official conducts his office in a spirit of formalistic impersonality; and (5) employment is based on technical qualifications, is protected against arbitrary dismissal, and constitutes a career with promotions based on seniority or achievement.

When Weber studied bureaucracy, well over fifty years ago, he was convinced that its technical efficiency would lead to its increasing expansion. This prediction has so far proved accurate, despite the many dehumanizing features of bureaucracy, its discouragement of individual initiative, its susceptibility to rigidity, and its inability to cope with changing and unique conditions. Many social scientists argue that this continuing bureaucratic development has had an atomizing effect on human relationships, ushering in a prototototalitarian period in which most people experience feelings of powerlessness, insignificance, and alienation. Melvin Seeman, in "Antidote to Alienation: Learning to Belong," discusses this viewpoint and suggests a number of ways in which man might reassume his social involvement.

Social Organization in Folk and Urban Societies

The Folk Society*

Robert Redfield

* * *

"The conception of a 'primitive society' which we ought to form," wrote Sumner, "is that of small groups scattered over a territory."[1] The folk society is a small society. There are no more people in it than can come to know each other well, and they remain in long association with each other. Among the Western Shoshone, the individual parental family was the group, which went about, apart from other families, collecting food; a group of families would assemble and so remain for a few weeks, from time to time, to hunt together; during the winter months, such a group of families would form a single camp.[2] Such a temporary village included perhaps a hundred people. The hunting or food-collecting bands considered by Steward, representing many parts of the world, contained, in most cases, only a few score people.[3] A Southwestern pueblo contained no more than a few thousand persons.

[1] W. G. Sumner, *Folkways* (Boston: Ginn & Co., 1907), p. 12.

[2] Julian Steward, *Basin-Plateau Aboriginal Sociopolitical Groups* (Smithsonian Institution, Bureau of American Ethnology, Bull. 120 [Washington: Government Printing Office, 1938]), pp. 230–34.

[3] Julian Steward, "Economic and Social Basis of Primitive Bands," *Essays in Anthropology Presented to A. L. Kroeber* (Berkeley: University of California Press, 1936), pp. 341–42.

* From *American Journal of Sociology*, vol. 52, no. 4 (January, 1947), 293–308.

The folk society is an isolated society. Probably there is no real society whose members are in complete ignorance of the existence of people other than themselves; the Andamanese, although their islands were avoided by navigators for centuries, knew of outsiders and occasionally came in contact with Malay or Chinese visitors.[4] Nevertheless, the folk societies we know are made up of people who have little communication with outsiders, and we may conceive of the ideal folk society as composed of persons having communication with no outsider.

This isolation is one half of a whole of which the other half is intimate communication among the members of the society. A group of recent castaways is a small and isolated society, but it is not a folk society; and, if the castaways have come from different ships and different societies, there will have been no previous intimate communication among them, and the society will not be composed of people who are much alike.

May the isolation of the folk society be identified with the physical immobility of its members? In building this ideal type, we may conceive of the members of the society as remaining always within the small territory they occupy. There are some primitive peoples who have dwelt from time immemorial in the same small valley, and who rarely leave it.[5] Certain of the pueblos of the American Southwest have been occupied by the same people or their descendants for many generations. On the other hand, some of the food-collecting peoples, such as the Shoshone Indians and certain aborigines of Australia, move about within a territory of very considerable extent; and there are Asiatic folk groups that make regular seasonal migrations hundreds of miles in extent.

It is possible to conceive of the members of such a society as moving about physically without communicating with members of other groups than their own. Each of the Indian villages of the midwest highlands of Guatemala is a folk society distinguishable by its customs and even by the physical type of its members from neighboring villages; yet, the people are great travelers, and, in the case of one of the most distinct communities, Chichicastenango, most of the men travel far and spend much of their time away from home.[6] This does not result, however, in much intimate communication between those traveling villagers and other peoples. The gypsies have moved about among the various peoples of the earth for generations, and yet they retain many of the characteristics of a folk society.

Through books, the civilized people communicate with the minds of other people and other times, and an aspect of the isolation of the folk society is the absence of books. The folk communicate only by word of mouth; therefore, the communication upon which understanding is built is

[4] A. R. Radcliffe-Brown. *The Andaman Islanders* (Cambridge: At the University Press, 1933), pp. 6–9.

[5] A. L. Kroeber, *Handbook of Indians of California* (Smithsonian Institution, Bureau of American Ethnology, Bull. 78 [Washington: Government Printing Office, 1925]) p. 13.

[6] Robert Redfield, "Primitive Merchants of Guatemala," *Quarterly Journal of Inter-American Relations,* I, no. 4, 42–56.

only that which takes place among neighbors, within the little society itself. The folk has no access to the thought and experience of the past, whether of other peoples or of their own ancestors, such as books provide. Therefore, oral tradition has no check or competitor. Knowledge of what has gone before reaches no further back than memory and speech between old and young can make it go; behind "the time of our grandfathers," all is legendary and vague. With no form of belief established by written record, there can be no historical sense, such as civilized people have, no theology, and no basis for science in recorded experiment. The only form of accumulation of experience, except the tools and other enduring articles of manufacture, is the increase of wisdom that comes as the individual lives longer; therefore, the old, knowing more than the young can know until they, too, have lived that long, have prestige and authority.

The people who make up a folk society are much alike. Having lived in long intimacy with one another and with no others, they have come to form a single biological type. The somatic homogeneity of local, inbred populations has been noted and studied. Since the people communicate with one another and with no others, one man's learned ways of doing and thinking are the same as another's. Another way of putting this is to say that, in the ideal folk society, what one man knows and believes is the same as what all men know and believe. Habits are the same as customs. In real fact, of course, the differences among individuals in a primitive group and the different chances of experience prevent this ideal state of things from coming about. Nevertheless, it is near enough to the truth for the student of a real folk society to report it fairly well by learning what goes on in the minds of a few of its members, and a primitive group has been presented, although sketchily, as learned about from a single member. The similarity among the members is found also as one generation is compared with its successor. Old people find young people doing, as they grow up, what the old people did at the same age, and what they have come to think right and proper. This is another way of saying that, in such a society, there is little change.

The members of the folk society have a strong sense of belonging together. The group that an outsider might recognize as composed of similar persons different from members of other groups is also the group of people who see their own resemblances and feel correspondingly united. Communicating intimately with each other, each has a strong claim on the sympathies of the others. Moreover, against such knowledge as they have of societies other than their own, they emphasize their own mutual likeness and value themselves as compared with others. They say of themselves "we" as against all others, who are "they."[7]

Thus, we may characterize the folk society as small, isolated, nonliterate, and homogeneous, with a strong sense of group solidarity. Are we not soon to acknowledge the simplicity of the technology of the ideal folk society? Something should certainly be said about the tools and tool-making of this generalized primitive group, but it is not easy to assign a meaning to

[7] Sumner, *op. cit.*, pp. 13–15.

"simple," in connection with technology, that will do justice to the facts as known from the real folk societies. The preciseness with which each tool, in a large number of such tools, meets its needs in the case of the Eskimo, for example, makes one hesitate to use the word "simple." Some negative statements appear to be safe: Secondary and tertiary tools–tools to make tools–are relatively few as compared with primary tools; there is no making of artifacts by multiple, rapid, machine manufacture; there is little or no use of natural power.

There is not much division of labor in the folk society: What one person does is what another does. In the ideal folk society, all the tools and ways of production are shared by everybody. The "everybody" must mean "every adult man" or "every adult woman," for the obvious exception to the homogeneity of the folk society lies in the differences between what men do and know and what women do and know. These differences are clear and unexceptional (as compared with our modern urban society, where they are less so). "Within the local group there is no such thing as a division of labor save as between the sexes," writes Radcliffe-Brown about the Andaman Islanders. ". . . Every man is expected to be able to hunt pig, to harpoon turtle and to catch fish, and also to cut a canoe, to make bows and arrows and all the other objects that are made by men."[8] So, all men share the same interests and have, in general, the same experience of life.

We may conceive, also, of the ideal folk society as a group economically independent of all others: The people produce what they consume and consume what they produce. Few, if any, real societies are completely in this situation; some Eskimo groups, perhaps, most closely approach it. Although each little Andamanese band could get along without getting anything from any other, exchange of goods occurred between bands by a sort of periodic gift-giving.

The foregoing characterizations amount, roughly, to saying that the folk society is a little world off by itself, a world in which the recurrent problems of life are met by all its members in much the same way. This statement, while correct enough, fails to emphasize an important, perhaps the important, aspect of the folk society. The ways in which the members of the society meet the recurrent problems of life are conventionalized ways; they are the results of long intercommunication within the group in the face of these problems; and these conventionalized ways have become interrelated within one another so that they constitute a coherent and self-consistent system. Such a system is what we mean in saying that the folk society is characterized by a "culture." A culture is an organization or integration of conventional understandings. It is, as well, the acts and the objects, insofar as they represent the type characteristic of that society, that express and maintain these understandings. In the folk society, this integrated whole, this system, provides for all the recurrent needs of the individual from birth to death and of the society through the seasons and the years. The society is

[8] Radcliffe-Brown, *op. cit.*, p. 43.

to be described, and distinguished from others, largely by presenting this system.

This is not the same as saying, as was said early in this paper, that, in the folk society, what one man does is the same as what another man does. What one man does in a mob is the same as what another man does, but a mob is not a folk society. It is, so far as culture is concerned, its very antithesis.[9] The members of a mob (which is a kind of "mass") each do the same thing, it is true, but it is a very immediate and particular thing, and it is done without much reference to tradition. It does not depend upon and express a great many conventional understandings related to one another. A mob has no culture. The folk society exhibits culture to the greatest conceivable degree. A mob is an aggregation of people doing the same simple thing simultaneously. A folk society is an organization of people doing many different things successively as well as simultaneously. The members of a mob act with reference to the same object of attention. The members of a folk society are guided in acting by previously established comprehensive and interdependent conventional understandings; at any one time, they do many different things, which are complexly related to one another, to express collective sentiments and conceptions. When the turn comes for the boy to do what a man does, he does what a man does; thus, although in the end the experiences of all individuals of the same sex are alike, the activities of the society, seen at a moment of time, are diverse, while interdependent and consistent.

The Papago Indians, a few hundred of them, constituted a folk society in southern Arizona. Among these Indians, a war party was not so simple a thing as a number of men going out together to kill the enemy. It was a complex activity involving everybody in the society, before, during, and after the expedition, and dramatizing the religious and moral ideas fundamental to Papago life.[10] Preparation for the expedition involved many practical or ritual acts on the part of the immediate participants, their wives and children, previously successful warriors, and many others. While the party was away, the various relatives of the warriors had many things to do or not to do—prayer, fasting, preparation of ritual paraphernalia, etc. These were specialized activities, each appropriate to just that kind of relative or other category of person. So, the war was waged by everybody. These activities, different and special as they were, interlocked, so to speak, with each other to make a large whole, the society-during-a-war-expedition. And all these specialized activities obeyed fundamental principles, understood by all and expressed and reaffirmed in the very forms of the acts—the gestures of the rituals, the words of songs, the implied or expressed explanations and admonitions of the elders to the younger people. All understood that the end in view was the acquisition by the group of the supernatural

[9] Herbert Blumer, "Mass Behavior and the Motion Picture," *Publications of the American Sociological Society,* XXIX, no. 3 (August, 1935), 115–27.

[10] Ruth Underhill, *The Autobiography of a Papago Woman* ("American Anthropological Association, Memoirs," no. 46 [1936]).

power of the slain enemy. This power, potentially of great positive value, was dangerous, and the practices and rituals had as their purposes, first, the success of the war party and, then, the draining off of the supernatural power acquired by the slaying into a safe and "usable" form.

We may say, then, that, in the folk society, conventional behavior is strongly patterned: It tends to conform to a type or a norm. These patterns are interrelated in thought and in action with one another, so that one tends to evoke others and to be consistent with the others. Every customary act among the Papago when the successful warriors return is consistent with and is a special form of the general conceptions held as to supernatural power. We may still further say that the patterns of what people think should be done are closely consistent with what they believe is done, and that there is one way, or a very few conventional ways, in which everybody has some understanding, and some share, of meeting each need that arises.[11] The culture of a folk society is, therefore, one of those wholes that is greater than its parts. Gaining a livelihood takes support from religion, and the relations of men to men are justified in the conceptions held of the supernatural world or in some other aspect of the culture. Life, for the member of the folk society, is not one activity and then another and different one; it is one large activity out of which one part may not be separated without affecting the rest.

A related characteristic of the folk society was implied when it was declared that the specialized activities incident to the Papago war party obeyed fundamental principles understood by all. These "principles" had to do with the ends of living, as conceived by the Papago. A near-ultimate good for the Papago was the acquisition of supernatural power. This end was not questioned; it was a sort of axiom in terms of which many lesser activities were understood. This suggests that we may say of the folk society that its ends are taken as given. The activities incident to the war party may be regarded as merely complementarily useful acts–aspects of the division of labor. They may also, and more significantly, be seen as expressions of unquestioned common ends. The folk society exists not so much in the exchange of useful functions as in common understandings as to the ends given. The ends are not stated as matters of doctrine but are implied by the many acts that make up the living that goes on in the society. Therefore, the morale of a folk society–its power to act consistently over periods of time and to meet crises effectively–is dependent not upon discipline exerted by force or upon devotion to some single principle of action but to the concurrence and consistency of many or all of the actions and conceptions that make up the whole round of life. In the trite phrase, the folk society is a "design for living."

What is done in the ideal folk society is done not because somebody or some people decided, at once, that it should be done but because it seems "necessarily" to flow from the very nature of things. There is, moreover,

[11] Ralph Linton, *The Study of Man* (New York: D. Appleton–Century Co., 1936), chap. 16, esp. p. 283.

no disposition to reflect upon traditional acts and consider them objectively and critically. In short, behavior in the folk society is traditional, spontaneous, and uncritical. In any real folk society, of course, many things are done as a result of decision as to that particular action, but as to that class of actions tradition is the sufficient authority. The Indians decide now to go on a hunt; but it is not a matter of debate whether or not one should, from time to time, hunt.

The folkways are the ways that grow up out of long and intimate association of men with each other; in the society of our conception, all the ways are folkways. Men act with reference to each other by understandings that are tacit and traditional. There are no formal contracts or other agreements. The rights and obligations of the individual do not come about by special arrangement; they are, chiefly, aspects of the position of the individual as a person of one sex or the other, one age group or another, one occupational group or another, and as one occupying just that position in a system of relationships that are traditional in the society. The individual's status is thus, in large part, fixed at birth; it changes as he lives, but it changes in ways that were "foreordained" by the nature of his particular society. The institutions of the folk society are of the sort that has been called "crescive"; they are not of the sort that is created deliberately for special purposes, as was the juvenile court. So, too, law is made up of the traditional conceptions of rights and obligations and the customary procedures whereby these rights and obligations are assured; legislation has no part in it.

If legislation has no part in the law of the ideal folk society, neither has codification, still less jurisprudence. Radin has collected material suggesting the limited extent to which real primitive people do question custom and do systematize their knoweldge.[12] In the known folk societies, they do these things only to a limited extent. In the ideal folk society, there is no objectivity and no systematization of knowledge as guided by what seems to be its "internal" order. The member of this mentally constructed society does not stand off from his customary conduct and subject it to scrutiny apart from its meaning for him as that meaning is defined in culture. Nor is there any habitual exercise of classification, experiment, and abstraction for its own sake, least of all for the sake of intellectual ends. There is common practical knowledge, but there is no science.

Behavior in the folk society is highly conventional, custom fixes the rights and duties of individuals, and knowledge is not critically examined or objectively and systematically formulated; but it must not be supposed that primitive man is a sort of automaton in which custom is the mainspring. It would be as mistaken to think of primitive man as strongly aware that he is constrained by custom. Within the limits set by custom, there is invitation to excel in performance. There is lively competition, a sense of opportunity, and a feeling that what the culture moves one to do is well worth doing. "There is no drabness in such a life. It has about it all the allurements of

[12] Paul Radin, *Primitive Man as Philosopher* (New York: D. Appleton–Century Co., 1927).

personal experience, very much one's own, of competitive skill, of things well done."[13] The interrelations and high degree of consistency among the elements of custom that are presented to the individual declare to him the importance of making his endeavors in the directions indicated by tradition. The culture sets goals that stimulate action by giving great meaning to it.[14]

It has been said that the folk society is small, and that its members have lived in long and intimate association with one another. It has also been said that, in such societies, there is little critical or abstract thinking. These characteristics are related to yet another characteristic of the folk society: Behavior is personal, not impersonal. A "person" may be defined as that social object which I feel to respond to situations as I do, with all the sentiments and interests that I feel to be my own; a person is myself in another form, his qualities and values are inherent within him, and his significance for me is not merely one of utility. A "thing," on the other hand, is a social object that has no claim upon my sympathies, that responds to me, as I conceive it, mechanically; its value for me exists insofar as it serves my end. In the folk society, all human beings admitted to the society are treated as persons; one does not deal impersonally ("thing-fashion") with any other participant in the little world of that society. Moreover, in the folk society much besides human beings is treated personally. The pattern of behavior that is first suggested by the inner experience of the individual—his wishes, fears, sensitivenesses, and interests of all sorts—is projected into all objects with which he comes into contact. Thus, nature, too, is treated personally: The elements, the features of the landscape, the animals, and especially anything in the environment that, by its appearance or behavior, suggests that it has the attributes of mankind—to all these are attributed qualities of the human person.[15]

In short, the personal and intimate life of the child in the family is extended, in the folk society, into the social world of the adult and even into inanimate objects. It is not merely that relations in such a society are personal; it is also that they are familial. The first contacts made as the infant becomes a person are with other persons; moreover, each of these first persons, he comes to learn, has a particular kind of relation to him that is associated with that one's genealogical position. The individual finds himself fixed within a constellation of familial relationships. The kinship connections provide a pattern in terms of which, in the ideal folk society, all personal relations are conventionalized and categorized. All relations are personal. But relations are not, in content of specific behavior, the same for everyone. As a mother is different from a father, and a grandson from a nephew, so are these classes of personal relationship, originating in genealogical connection, extended outward into all relationships whatever. In this sense, the folk society is a familial society. Lowie[16] has demonstrated the

[13] A. A. Goldenweiser, "Individual, Pattern and Involution," *Essays in Honor of A. L. Kroeber* (Berkeley: University of California Press, 1936), p. 102.

[14] Ruth Benedict, *Patterns of Culture* (Boston: Houghton Mifflin, 1934).

[15] Ruth Benedict, "Animism," *Encyclopaedia of the Social Sciences*.

[16] Robert H. Lowie, *The Origin of the State* (New York: Harcourt, Brace, 1927), pp. 51–73.

qualification that is to be introduced into the statement of Maine[17] that the primitive society is organized in terms of kinship rather than territory. It is true that the fact that men are neighbors contributes to their sense of belonging together. But the point to be emphasized in understanding the folk society is that, whether mere contiguity or relationship as brother or as son is the circumstance uniting men into the society, the result is a group of people among whom prevail the personal and categorized relationships that characterize families as we know them, and in which the patterns of kinship tend to be extended outward from the group of genealogically connected individuals into the whole society. The kin are the type persons for all experience.

This general conception may be resolved into component or related conceptions. In the folk society, family relationships are clearly distinguished from one another. Very special sorts of behavior may be expected by a mother's brother of his sister's son, and this behavior will be different from that expected by a father's brother of his brother's son. Among certain Australian tribes, animals killed by a hunter must be divided so that nine or ten certain parts must be given to nine or ten corresponding relatives of the successful hunter–the right ribs to the father's brother, a piece of the flank to the mother's brother, and so on.[18] The tendency to extend kinship outward takes many special forms. In many primitive societies, kinship terms and kinship behavior (in reduced degree) are extended to persons not known to be genealogically related at all, but who are nevertheless regarded as kin. Among the central Australians, terms of relationship are extended "so as to embrace all persons who come into social contact with one another. . . . In this way the whole society forms a body of relatives."[19] In the folk society, groupings that do not arise out of genealogical connection are few, and those that do exist tend to take on the attributes of kinship. Ritual kinship is common in primitive and peasant societies in the forms of blood brotherhood, godparental relationships, and other ceremonial sponsorships.[20] These multiply kinship connections; in these cases, the particular individuals to be united depend upon choice. Furthermore, there is frequently a recognizedly fictitious or metaphorical use of kinship terms to designate more casual relationships, as between host and guest or between worshipper and deity.[21]

The real primitive and peasant societies differ very greatly as to the forms assumed by kinship. Nevertheless, it is possible to recognize two main types. In one of these, the connection between husband and wife is emphasized, while neither one of the lineages, matrilineal or patrilineal, is singled out as

[17] Henry Maine, *Ancient Law* (London: J. Murray, 1861).

[18] A. W. Howitt, *The Native Tribes of Southeastern Australia* (New York: Macmillan, 1904), p. 759.

[19] A. R. Radcliffe-Brown, "Three Tribes of Western Australia," *Journal of the Royal Anthropological Institute,* XLIII, 150–51.

[20] Benjamin Paul, "Ritual Kinship: With Special Reference to Godparenthood in Middle America" (Ph.D. thesis, University of Chicago, 1942).

[21] E. C. Parsons, *Notes on Zuni,* Part II ("American Anthropological Association Memoirs," IV, no. 4 [1917]).

contrasted with the other. In such a folk society, the individual parental family is the social unit, and connections with relatives outside this family are of secondary importance. Such family organization is common where the population is small, the means of livelihood are by precarious collection of wild food, and larger units cannot permanently remain together because the natural resources will not allow it. But, where a somewhat larger population remains together, either in a village or in a migratory band, there often, although by no means always, is found an emphasis upon one line of consanguine connection rather than the other with subordination of the conjugal connection.[22] There results a segmentation of the society into equivalent kinship units. These may take the form of extended domestic groups or joint families (as in China) or may include many households of persons related in part through recognized genealogical connection and in part through the sharing of the same name or other symbolic designation (in the latter case, we speak of the groups as clans). Even in societies where the individual parental family is an independent economic unit, as in the case of the eastern Eskimo, husband and wife never become a new social and economic unit with the completeness that is characteristic of our own society. When a marriage in primitive society comes to an end, the kinsmen of the dead spouse assert upon his property a claim they have never given up.[23] On the whole, we may think of the family among folk peoples as made up of persons consanguinely connected. Marriage is, in comparison with what we in our society directly experience, an incident in the life of the individual who is born, brought up, and dies with his blood kinsmen. In such a society, romantic love can hardly be elevated to a major principle.

Insofar as the consanguine lines are well defined (and, in some cases, both lines may be of importance to the individual),[24] the folk society may be thought of as composed of families rather than of individuals. It is the familial groups that act and are acted upon. There is strong solidarity within the kinship group, and the individual is responsible to all his kin as they are responsible to him. "The clan is a natural mutual aid society. . . . A member belongs to the clan, he is not his own; if he is wrong, they will right him; if he does wrong, the responsibility is shared by them."[25] Thus, in folk societies wherein the tendency to maintain consanguine connection has resulted in joint families or clans, it is usual to find that injuries done by an individual are regarded as injuries against his kinship group, and the group takes the steps to right the wrong. The step may be revenge regulated by custom or a property settlement. A considerable part of primitive law exists in the regulation of claims by one body of kin against another. The fact that

[22] Ralph Linton, *The Study of Man* (New York: D. Appleton-Century, 1936), p. 159.

[23] Ruth Benedict, "Marital Property Rights in Bilateral Societies," *American Anthropologist,* XXXVIII, no. 3 (July–September, 1936), 368–73.

[24] Peter Murdock, "Double Descent," *American Anthropologist,* XLII (new ser.), no. 4, pt. 1 (October–December, 1940), 555–61.

[25] Edwin W. Smith and Andrew Murray Dale, *The Ila-Speaking Peoples of Northern Rhodesia* (London: Macmillan, 1920), I, 296.

the folk society is an organization of families rather than an aggregation of individuals is further expressed in many of those forms of marriage in which a certain kind of relative is the approved spouse. The customs by which, in many primitive societies, a man is expected to marry his deceased brother's widow or a woman to marry her deceased sister's husband express the view of marriage as an undertaking between kinship groups. One of the spouses having failed by death, the undertaking is to be carried on by some other representative of the family group. Indeed, in the arrangements for marriage —the selection of spouses by the relatives, in bride-price, dowry, and in many forms of familial negotiations leading to a marriage—the nature of marriage as a connubial form of social relations between kindreds finds expression.

It has been said in foregoing paragraphs that behavior in the folk society is traditional, spontaneous, and uncritical, that what one man does is much the same as what another man does, and that the patterns of conduct are clear and remain constant throughout the generations. It has also been suggested that the congruence of all parts of conventional behavior and social institutions with each other contributes to the sense of rightness that the member of the folk society feels to inhere in his traditional ways of action. In the well-known language of Sumner, the ways of life are folkways; furthermore, the folkways tend to be also mores—ways of doing or thinking to which attach notions of moral worth. The value of every traditional act or object or institution is, thus, something that the members of the society are not disposed to call into question; and, should the value be called into question, the doing so is resented. This characteristic of the folk society may be briefly referred to by saying that it is a sacred society. In the folk society, one may not, without calling into effect negative social sanctions, challenge as valueless what has come to be traditional in that society.

Presumably, the sacredness of social objects has its source, in part at least, in the mere fact of habituation; probably the individual organism becomes early adjusted to certain habits, motor and mental, and to certain associations between one activity and another or between certain sense experiences and certain activities, and it is almost physiologically uncomfortable to change or even to entertain the idea of change. There arises "a feeling of impropriety of certain forms, of a particular social or religious value, or a superstitious fear of change."[26] Probably the sacredness of social objects in the folk society is related also to the fact that, in such well-organized cultures, acts and objects suggest the traditions, beliefs, and conceptions that all share. There is reason to suppose that, when what is traditionally done becomes less meaningful because people no longer know what the acts stand for, life becomes more secular.[27] In the repetitious character of conventional action (aside from technical action), we have ritual; in its expressive character, we have ceremony; in the folk society, ritual tends also

[26] Franz Boas, *Primitive Art* (Oslo, 1927), p. 150.

[27] Robert Redfield, *The Folk Culture of Yucatan* (Chicago: University of Chicago Press, 1941), p. 364.

to be ceremonious, and ritual-ceremony tends to be sacred, not secular.

The sacredness of social objects is apparent in the ways in which, in the folk society, such an object is hedged around with restraints and protections that keep it away from the commonplace and the matter-of-fact.[28] In the sacred, there is alternatively, or in combination, holiness and dangerousness. When the Papago Indian returned from a successful war expedition, bringing the scalp of a slain Apache, the head-hairs of the enemy were treated as loaded with a tremendous "charge" of supernatural power; only old men, already successful warriors and purified through religious ritual, could touch the object and make it safe for incorporation into the home of the slayer. Made into the doll-like form of an Apache Indian, it was, at last, after much ceremonial preparation, held for an instant by the members of the slayer's family, addressed in respect and awe by kinship terms, and placed in the house, there to give off protective power.[29] The Indians of San Pedro de la Laguna, Guatemala, recognize an officer, serving for life, whose function it is to keep custody of ten or a dozen Latin breviaries printed in the eighteenth century and to read prayers from one or another of these books on certain occasions. No one but this custodian may handle the books, save his assistants on ceremonial occasions, with his permission. Should anyone else touch a book, he would go mad or be stricken with blindness. Incense and candles are burnt before the chest containing the books, yet the books are not gods —they are objects of sacredness.[30]

In the folk society, this disposition to regard objects as sacred extends, characteristically, even into the foodstuffs of the people. Often, the foodstuffs are personified as well as sacred. " 'My granduncle used to say to me,' explained a Navajo Indian, ' "if you are walking along a trail and see a kernel of corn, pick it up. It is like a child lost and starving." According to the legends, corn is just the same as a human being, only it is holier. . . . When a man goes into a cornfield, he feels that he is in a holy place, that he is walking among Holy People. . . . Agriculture is a holy occupation. Even before you plant you sing songs. You continue this during the whole time your crops are growing. You cannot help but feel that you are in a holy place when you go through your fields and they are doing well.' "[31] In the folk society, ideally conceived, nothing is solely a means to an immediate practical end. All activities, even the means of production, are ends in themselves, activities expressive of the ultimate values of the society.

[28] Émile Durkheim, *The Elementary Forms of the Religious Life* (London: Allen & Unwin, 1926).

[29] Underhill, *op. cit.,* p. 18.

[30] Benjamin Paul, unpublished MS.

[31] W. W. Hill, *The Agricultural and Hunting Methods of the Navaho Indians* ("Yale University Publications in Anthropology," no. 18 [New Haven: Yale University Press, 1938]), p. 53.

* * *

Queue Culture: The Waiting Line as a Social System*

Leon Mann

* * *

THE STUDY

Every Saturday afternoon in the month of September, over 100,000 spectators crowd into a stadium in Melbourne, Australia, to watch the "world series" of Australian rules football.

On August 15, 1967, approximately 10,000 people formed twenty-two queues outside the Melbourne Football Stadium to buy 14,000 sets of tickets for the four games. It was the last opportunity to get tickets, because mail applications for the bulk of the tickets had been oversubscribed weeks before. A great many of the 10,000 faced disappointment, because most queuers usually buy the full allotment of two adult and two children's tickets.

From 6 A.M. until 8 A.M., when the selling windows opened, a team of nine research assistants, male psychology majors from the University of Melbourne, conducted short, standard interviews with 216 people in ten of the twenty-two queues. Each interviewer was randomly assigned a queue. Starting with the first person in line, the procedure was to approach every tenth person. The request was brief and informal: "I am from the University, and we are doing a study of how people feel about the queues. Would you care to answer a few questions?" Only two refusals were encountered; with the exception of one queue, all interviews were completed by 8 A.M., when the lines began to move. Questions covered attitudes toward the system of queueing, evidence of pushing in and place keeping, arrangements to make the task of queueing more pleasant, as well as estimates of position in line and chances of getting a ticket. Interviewers also made notes on their observations of the physical shape of the queues and on their impressions of the mood and morale of the people in them. Data from the Melbourne stadium are the main source of evidence cited in this paper.

Members of the research team also conducted interviews and made observations in the club queues at suburban Collingwood, Carlton, and Richmond, each of which had allocations of 1,000 tickets for club members.

* From *American Journal of Sociology,* vol. 74, no. 3 (November, 1969), 340–54.

Data gathered from the club queues provide additional evidence presented in this paper.

THE QUEUE TRADITION

The system of selling seat bookings for the football finals several weeks before the start of the series was first introduced in 1956. Before 1956, people queued outside the stadium on the day of the game, and "first in" took the best seats. Over the years, because of the large increase in the number of football followers, the queue system became accepted as the only workable method for selling tickets. Although there were complaints from the public, the great overnight queues became a regular event at the end of a Melbourne winter. And, as the queues took on an institutional character, increasing numbers of veterans began to regard them as a kind of cherished tradition or ritual. For example, even during the regular season, although it was possible to get choice seats two hours before the commencement of most Saturday games, long queues formed outside stadiums on Friday, perhaps to train for the big one in August.

The queue of 1965 was perhaps the most remarkable, for in that year 25,000 people waited for 12,500 tickets, some of them for over a week, in mud and drizzling rain. Queuers erected a shantytown of tents and caravans outside the stadium, and conditions, according to the Melbourne town clerk, rapidly became "squalid and unhygienic." In 1966, to prevent a recurrence of the shantytown, the Melbourne City Council banned tents and camping equipment from the queues and prohibited the lighting of fires. Also, queues or assemblies were not allowed outside the stadium until twenty hours before ticket sales started. The city council regulations made the wait for tickets colder, but much shorter, and accordingly, it was decided to retain them the following year.

In the 1967 queues, our interviewers noted that people improvised tents by tying tarpaulins to the side of barricades and brought stretchers, sleeping bags, and supplies of liquor to make themselves comfortable during the wait. Even after a cold night in the open, 26 per cent of the respondents claimed they were happy with the queue system. Only the aged and those who had to go straight to work felt very unhappy about their night out. In 1966, when a sample of 122 queuers were interviewed on a mild afternoon before the ticket windows opened, 47 per cent reported satisfaction with this method of selling tickets.

At Collingwood, the Melbourne City Council regulations did not apply, and accommodations in the first part of the queue resembled a refugee camp. The first three families in line, numbering approximately thirty men, women, and children, pitched a bedouin tent on the sidewalk fronting the ticket box and settled down to a six-day wait around a blazing camp fire. Some enthusiasts moved out of their homes and took up formal residence in the queue. Five days before tickets went on sale, the general secretary of Collingwood, Gordon Carlyon, received a letter addressed to "Mr. Alfred McDougall, c/o Queue outside Collingwood Football Ground, Collingwood,

3066." The *Melbourne Herald* of August 8, 1967, reported that Mr. Carlyon threaded his way through beds and tents on the sidewalk outside the stadium to deliver the letter. Melbournians had not only started to tolerate queues but actually seemed to be enjoying them. One woman outside the Melbourne stadium was heard to remark: "People are always knocking queues; what I would like to know is what people like myself would do without them" (*Melbourne Age,* August 16, 1967).

It seems that the means behavior, that is, lining up to get tickets for the event, almost becomes an end in itself, with its own intrinsic rewards and satisfactions. What does queueing mean, and why has it become an important occasion in the lives of these people? The answer lies partly in the publicity and recognition given to the queuers and partly in the challenge and excitement. For several days in August, the attention of Melbourne and its mass media is focused on the brave queues outside its stadium. To be able to claim, in football-mad Melbourne, that one has stood through the night and obtained tickets earns the kind of kudos and respect that must have been given to those who fought at Agincourt. And there are other pleasures. Outside the stadium, something of a carnival atmosphere prevails. The devotees sing, sip warm drinks, play cards, and huddle together around the big charcoal braziers. If he has come as part of a large group, or a cheer squad, the aficionado enjoys a brief taste of communal living and the chance to discuss and debate endlessly the fine points of the game. Above all, football fans regard the great queue as an adventure, an unusual and yet traditional diversion at the end of a Melbourne winter, as the football season approaches its exciting climax.

PROFILE OF THE QUEUER

The typical queuer is male, not yet twenty-five years of age, lives in a working-class suburb, and probably has absented himself from work to wait in line. Together with three friends, he has waited for at least fifteen hours to get tickets to watch his club play in the finals. He cannot explain why he likes football, but he has followed his team faithfully since childhood. He claims he would still be queueing even if his team were not playing, but the scarcity of supporters of nonfinals teams in the queue indicates that this is not likely. He has not counted the number of people ahead of him and has no real idea of the number of tickets for sale to the queue. He is fairly confident that he will get tickets, and he does not seem very unhappy about the queue system.

THE PROFESSIONAL QUEUER

When demand exceeds supply, it is inevitable that ticket speculators move into the queue in search of supplies for the flourishing market in hard-to-get tickets.

The Australian football queue contains two kinds of speculators: groups of highly organized people, hired at a fee to wait and buy tickets for large business concerns; and small-time operators, who resell their two tickets to the highest bidder. Often, the speculators are university students, whose earnings help to pay tuition fees. Two days before ticket sales opened at the Melbourne stadium, twenty students flew from Tasmania to the mainland to join the queue. The airline company, which hired them to buy the tickets, also provided free return flights, accommodation at a leading hotel, and taxis during their stay (*Melbourne Herald,* August 12, 1967). An advertising agency engaged Melbourne University students to stand in line for one dollar an hour each, the tickets to be given away as prizes. Other students, operating as free-lance scalpers, asked an outraged public fifty dollars for $5.60 tickets, and had no difficulty getting their price.[1]

It is difficult to estimate the number of speculators in the football queues, as most people would be reluctant to admit to this kind of activity, but it was apparent from the number of advertisements for tickets in the "Wanted to Sell" columns of the Melbourne newspapers that a large proportion of queuers turned professional in the week following the ticket sales.

In the Melbourne stadium lines, very few people actually counted their position, perhaps because they believed there was no point in it, since there was no accurate information available about the number of tickets available to each line (Mann and Taylor, 1969). In club queues, however, a different set of conditions obtained. There was usually a single mammoth queue (at Richmond it included over 3,000 people and ringed the perimeter of the stadium). Most important, the number of tickets on sale was well publicized, and, therefore, it was possible to make a fairly accurate estimate of the chances of getting tickets, if the person had accurate information about his position in line. Accordingly, the estimates of position in the club queues were somewhat more accurate than at the stadium, because people either had taken the trouble to count the number ahead or had consulted with a queue "counter." Queue counters are boys who count the queue at regular intervals if it is long and winding. Queue counters, like ticket speculators, "invent" businesses to go along with what began simply as a necessary social act. At Carlton, a group of boys went backward and forward during the night, counting the queue, and, at Richmond, the counters turned professional and, for a fee (ten cents), gave each customer up-to-date information on the number of people ahead and behind, as well as topical news and gossip.

THE PRE-QUEUE

A queue is a line of persons waiting in turn to be served, according to order of arrival. But the act of queueing involves more than the acquisition of a right to prior service because of early arrival. To validate this priority, the person must also spend time in the queue, not only to show late-comers that he occupies a given position but also to demonstrate that his right to

[1] Speculation in the physical position itself is not found in Australian queues, as it is in waiting lines for Broadway hit shows. At smash hits, it is not unusual for people to make a business of getting in line early in order to sell their advanced positions to late-comers for a large fee (*Life,* September 24, 1956).

priority is confirmed by an unquestionable willingness to undergo further suffering to get the commodity.

If all that is required to reserve a place in a queue is the act of registering order of arrival, everyone would make an effort to be present at the time of queue formation. This would lead either to uncontrolled competition and hostility at the time of registration or, more probably, the formation of pre-queues to establish recognition of the right to priority in the official queue.

The pre-queue is an unofficial line that forms spontaneously before the official, recognized queue is allowed to form. The Melbourne football queues were not allowed to form until 3 P.M. of the afternoon before the sale of tickets. To enforce this regulation, police erected a perimeter of barricades around the wall of the stadium. Nevertheless, hundreds of people gathered in the park hours before queueing was officially allowed to start and, without police direction or intervention, spontaneously formed lines outside the barricades. At 3 P.M., when the barricades were removed, they folded their chairs and, keeping the lines intact, filed in perfect order to the ticket windows to commence the official seventeen-hour wait. The formation of a pre-queue, in this instance, almost certainly functioned to prevent an explosive situation, which could have occurred had people failed to sort themselves into some kind of recognized order before the official line started. The lack of competition for positions among the early-comers can be explained in terms of the reward-cost structure in the first part of the line. There is little to be gained from being first, rather than twentieth or fiftieth (all are virtually guaranteed a ticket), but there is much to be lost if aggressive competition leads to physical damage and general disorder.

SERVING TIME IN QUEUES

There is a curious dilemma in the overnight queue. If there is a unanimous willingness to respect the order of arrival, it is pointless to require everyone to spend an uncomfortable night in the open. But, if large numbers absent themselves, those remaining to protect the queue from outsiders will feel that their greater inputs of time and suffering now outweigh the merits of early arrival and entitle them to priority of service. Also, they will feel no responsibility for minding the places of people who, by their absence, are in no position to offer reciprocal place-minding services. In recognition of the conflicting considerations of unnecessary suffering caused by continuous occupancy, and the necessity to validate one's position by spending some time in residence, various arrangements are made that function to lessen the ordeal while protecting the rights of early-comers. Usually, the arrangements represent a compromise that allows the queuer to take brief leaves of absence while retaining undisputed rights of re-entry.

In Australian football lines, "time-out" is accomplished by two informal arrangements. Early-comers, who usually come in groups of four or five, often organize a "shift system," in which members spend one hour on with four hours off. One person can hold up to four places until the relief reports back to take over as group custodian. In our survey, an average of 39 per cent of respondents in the first 100 of every queue reported that they had organized a shift system; in the latter part of the queue, only 24 per cent reported participation in a shift system. Sometimes, the system involves a large group of people who share not only place-keeping duties but also facilities for eating, sleeping, and entertainment. The *Melbourne Herald* of August 15, 1967, described a seventeen-year-old girl, one of twelve people who took turns to leave the queue to eat and sleep in one of the few trailers found outside the Melbourne stadium. The same newspaper carried a story of a young scalper who combined business with pleasure: "I was one of a group of 20 students who stood together all night in the queue outside the ground. We were well organized. A couple of us kept our positions, and the others went out on the town" (*Melbourne Herald,* August 22, 1967).

It is rare for queuers at the head of the line to come alone; 94 per cent of the respondents questioned in the first 100 of every line reported that they had come with others. However, a large minority toward the end of each line came alone; while their need for time-outs was less pressing, they also made arrangements to cover brief absences, if necessary. It is an accepted practice to "stake a claim" in a queue by leaving some item of personal property. One can keep a place in a line with a labeled box, folding chair, haversack, or sleeping bag for quite long periods. The object stands for the person and his place, symbolism reminiscent of burial customs of the ancient Egyptians.[2] During the early hours of waiting, when many people were enjoying a carefree game of football in the surrounding park, the queues often consisted of one part people to two parts inanimate objects. The norm in leaving position markers is that one must not be absent for periods longer than two to three hours. In the Collingwood queue of 1966, irate late-comers, who noticed that many people in the middle of the queue had not made an appearance for most of the day, spontaneously seized their boxes and burnt them. The late-comers were protesting the violation of the principle of serving time to earn occupancy of a position. In the ensuing melee, scores of people made significant advances in their positions. Because arrangements for absence from the football queue are of necessity extremely informal, inefficiency and abuse often occur. To ensure protection of their valued positions, some do not trust the shift or marker systems but prefer to keep a constant vigil, which lasts the entire life of the queue.

First come, first served, the fundamental concept of queueing, is a basic principle of the behavior referred to as distributive justice (Homans 1961). There is a direct correspondence between inputs (time spent waiting) and outcomes (preferential service). Generally, if a person is willing to invest large amounts of time and suffering in an activity, people who believe there should be an appropriate fit between effort and reward will respect his right to priority. We have seen, however, that the principle of distributive justice

[2] Markers such as notebooks, coats, newspapers, and umbrellas are often used to defend a "reserved" space in public places, such as a crowded cafeteria or study hall (Sommer, 1969).

is elaborated to encompass the need for leaves of absence in marathon queues. In recognition of the fact that continuous residence in the line imposes great hardship, members come to an agreement on the minimum inputs of time necessary to validate occupancy of a position. It is reasonable to claim that rules regulating time spent in and out of the line are the essential core of the queue culture.[3]

QUEUE JUMPING

Place-keeping and pushing in violate the principle of first come, first served. When people at the end of a queue feel certain that the violation does not jeopardize their own chances of obtaining the commodity, there is likely to be some irritation but no attempt to eject the offender. Stronger measures are likely, however, if people at the tail end believe that the lengthening of the line worsens their prospects of receiving service.

Since there is a great deal at stake, football queuers are especially annoyed by any attempt to jump the queue, and they adopt a variety of physical and social techniques to keep people in line. At certain times in the life of the queue when police supervision was minimal, queuers had to devise their own constraints. The most extreme constraint was physical force. During the early hours of August 15, five men were taken to hospitals after four separate brawls broke out in the ticket lines (*Melbourne Herald,* August 15, 1967). The strategic placement of barriers acts as a constraint against would-be infiltrators. It was observed that people in the middle of the queue worked together to erect barricades from material left in the park. Keeping close interperson distance also serves to maintain the "territory" in the face of would-be intruders. At times of maximum danger, and in the hour before the ticket windows opened, there was a visible bunching together, or shrinkage, in the physical length of the queue, literally a closing of the ranks. The exercise of effective social constraints depends on the capacity for cohesive action on the part of the queuers. At the stadium, whenever outsiders approached the head of the queue, they were intimidated by vociferous catcalls and jeering. Ordinarily, this mode of protecting the queue was successful during daylight, the pressure of concerted disapproval inhibiting all but the boldest. During the hours of darkness, social pressure proved less effective; the knowledge that one cannot be seen easily undermines social pressure and shaming as a technique.

Despite these constraints, many late-comers attempted to push in, and it was apparent that some succeeded. Letters to the newspapers by disappointed queuers testified to the activity of queue jumpers. One man who

[3] Queue systems with inbuilt guarantees of distributive justice are to be found in both the United States and the U.S.S.R. At the weekly line for tickets to the Metropolitan Opera in New York, an unofficial "keeper of the list" registers applicants in order of arrival, assigns numbers, and checks names when the queuers appear for roll call every three hours (*New Yorker,* January 14, 1967). In Moscow, when scarce goods go on sale, a series of queue custodians take turns "standing guard" and list the names of interested customers as they arrive throughout the night (Levine, 1959, pp. 338–39).

missed out in the Carlton queue claimed that he had been dislodged from 185th to 375th place in the span of two hours. When asked "Has anyone tried to push in?" respondents in every part of each queue reported that they had witnessed attempts to jump the queue, but only in a minority of cases had the intruder been ejected. According to the reports of our respondents, the act of intrusion was usually met with passivity rather than a physically hostile response, especially toward the end of the line, where people came alone and were not organized for dealing with intruders. Yet, when asked what they would do if someone tried to crash the queue immediately in front of them, respondents were almost unanimous in claiming that they would resort to physical force.

According to our respondents' reports, pushing in occurred most often near the tail of the queue. This seems puzzling at first, for, if someone is going to risk pushing in, it seems sensible to try at the front, where there is a greater certainty of getting tickets. However, we must bear in mind the more effective policing at the front, as well as the decreased risk toward the rear of the queue, where, in absolute numbers, fewer people are put out by the violation and, hence, there is less likelihood of concerted action. In brief, opposition to a queue jumper decreases as a function of the number of people whose chances of getting tickets are affected by the intrusion; at the end of the line, there are very few such people. Ironically, however, it is these people, regardless of where pushing in occurs, who stand to lose most by the infraction, because their chances of getting tickets are put in even greater jeopardy.

Why does the queue fail to act in unison to dismiss the queue jumper? To some extent, the varying interests of people in different parts of the queue provide an answer. People at the front of the queue do not care particularly about pushing in that occurs behind them, because they do not suffer from the intrusion. Of course, if queue jumping becomes widespread, the early-comers show concern, because their positions may be threatened by late-comers who realize that the entire line is vulnerable. But, usually, they have nothing to gain and much to lose from becoming involved in policing the queue. It is surprising, however, that people after the point of intrusion do not act together to expel the violator, since they all suffer equally by the loss of a place. It seems that responsibility for evicting a trespasser falls squarely on the shoulders of the person who is the immediate victim of the violation, that is, the person directly behind the violator. Those farther back may jeer and catcall, but the immediate victim is expected to take the initiative in ejecting the queue jumper. The reasoning seems to be that the victim, either through his passive looks or careless surveillance of his territory, must have given some encouragement to the queue jumper, so he is now obliged to handle the situation without causing unpleasantness for other people.

The reluctance of queuers to exert physical action against queue jumpers may also be related to the nature of informal versus formal organization of the queue. In any informal queue, there are many signs of organizational control, role prerogatives, and orderly behavior, which are almost exactly the same as those in well-organized queues, where there is real policing and monitoring of the line. Therefore, people will assume that the informal queue will function in much the same way as the organized queue. When acts of pushing in and disorder occur, members of the queue realize they were mistaken and jeer spontaneously, exert informal pressure, and make threats to preserve their positions. If verbal constraints fail, physical violence emerges as a last resort. At this point, there is a reluctance to pursue the matter further, because more may be lost from physical action than from a small loss in position. The person who jumps the queue could be desperate, and the immediate victim anticipates the possibility that a struggle could cause injury and damage. If the police action is unsuccessful, the person is made to look foolish in the eyes of the onlookers. It is also possible that, if the struggle sets off a widespread melee, he stands to lose more than face and position. Therefore, if verbal censure fails, members of the queue fall back on a conspiracy of silence to ignore minor violations. Resorting to physical violence seems to represent a kind of public acknowledgment that the queue is no longer organized and under control. Once this happens, a grave danger exists that people in less favorable positions, as well as outsiders, will take advantage of what is then recognized to be a helpless, unorganized queue. To prevent this, occasional minor infractions, if they are not met successfully by verbal threats and jeering, are seldom handled by physical threats and violence. The use of physical methods, especially if they prove unsuccessful, are a signal to others that the queue organization is about to disintegrate completely, and this may actually serve to encourage an epidemic of queue jumping.

One reason for the prevalence of pushing in, and the failure to exert effective action against it, is the confusion that exists between illegal acts of entry and the somewhat more acceptable act of place-keeping. Because place-keeping occurs fairly frequently, it is not always clear whether an individual who moves boldly into a line is attempting to crash the queue or is merely joining his group. Therefore, many are reluctant to challenge the entry of outsiders during the early hours of the queue. Although the custom of place-keeping is a cause of friction, only informal rules have been formulated to regulate its practice. Of the respondents, 29 per cent believed that it is permissible to keep a place for someone, and that people behind would not care. However, only a handful of queuers admitted to actually keeping a place for someone. People do not admit freely to place-keeping, because the newcomer usually makes his appearance only in the last hour before tickets go on sale, and people already in line are likely to be very resentful.

THE QUEUE AS A SOCIAL SYSTEM

The queue, although made up of numerous groups of strangers gathered together temporarily, emerges as an embryonic social system with a set of norms for controlling conflict.

Parsons (1951) maintains that social systems develop spontaneously whenever two or more people come into some stabilized, patterned mode of interaction. He lists three properties of any social system: (1) two or more actors occupying differentiated statuses or positions and performing differentiated roles; (2) some organized pattern governing the relationships of the members, describing their rights and obligations with respect to one another; and (3) some set of common norms and values, together with various types of shared cultural objects and symbols.

The long, overnight queue has all three characteristics of a social system. While the queue may not directly allocate different statuses or roles to its members, the members themselves assume different roles. In and around every queue there is a host of people–professional and hired speculators, queue counters, custodians, vigilantes, people, and officials–performing a variety of queue-related tasks.

The other two properties of a social system–an organized pattern of relationships and a set of common norms–are readily identifiable in the queue. Order of arrival governs the relationship among members, while the shift system and the practice of time-outs controls the network of rights and obligations. Moreover, there are shared norms about the desirability of distributive justice, as reflected in the set of rules regulating place-keeping and pushing in.

Interactive systems, such as the queue, develop within the matrix of a long-established sociocultural system that defines roles, normative standards, and goals. When a large number of people gather together and priority of service has value, a line is formed. All members bring to the new queue a host of ideas about the roles they should play, and develop firm notions about the way in which deviant behavior should be punished. Roles in the queue are drawn from, and are molded by, the institutional system of the larger society. The precise form of social organizations, the sharing and division of labor inherent in the shift system, the preferred modes of policing the queue, the development of businesses and ticket speculation, the notion that one must earn one's place in line by spending time in it, even the very reason for queueing itself, reflects the character of the surrounding society.

The culture of the queue also draws upon, and incorporates elements in, the broader culture. The importance of time as a value in Western society is reflected in the emphasis placed on serving time, and restrictions on time-outs. The way in which people orient themselves toward a scarce commodity, their preference for cooperation, the entrepreneurial zeal they display in scalping tickets and charging fees for counting the queue, is a function of broad-culture patterns, as well as the way society has taught them to behave.

The queue, moreover, is subject to sanctioning pressure from outside officials and onlookers, who try to bring it into conformity with societal expectations. Ultimately, of course, each queue has to work out its own final set of mutual adjustments, in which socially prescribed rules about queueing are modified and embellished in various ways. A prime example of these adjustments is to be found in the various interpretations of the rules governing leaves of absence from the line.

While the queue system is embedded in a larger social matrix, it is also composed of many subsystems–groups, cliques, and coacting individuals–whose physical presence reinforces the very idea or concept of a line.

According to Parsons and Smelser (1957), there are four functional problems, or imperatives, faced by every social system: goal attainment, adaptation, integration, and latency. The queue, even though it is a relatively minor, short-lived social system, must confront these four problems.

The problem of goal attainment is to keep the system moving steadily toward the collective goal of its members–in this case, the purchase of tickets in an orderly manner, with a minimum of unpleasantness. Before the system can move toward this goal, however, a host of instrumental and technical problems must be solved. Many of the problems are external to the queue, in the sense that they are not under the control of its members; for example, the seller (not the customer) must decide when and where people should be allowed to queue, how many lines should be formed, how many tickets will be made available, what limitation will be placed on the number of tickets sold to each customer, and so on. But the question of how to begin the queue, especially if people have gathered before the official starting time, is a problem left to the members themselves. As we have seen, the football fans solved this difficulty by forming a prequeue, which became the officially recognized queue when the barriers to the ticket boxes were lowered.

Adaptation is the problem of bringing facilities and resources to the system that enable it to come to terms with the environment. One aspect of adaptation is the active manipulation of the environment. Thus, queuers formed their line along concrete paths, constructed barriers out of material found in the park, erected shelters by tying tarpaulins to the barriers, built fires, and even brought in trailers, to make their temporary living quarters as comfortable as possible.

Manipulation of the system itself to blend with the environment is another aspect of adaptation. For the most part, the queue, rather than a single file of people, consisted of numerous knots of people, two and three abreast, who sat side by side to facilitate efficient communication and social interaction.

The integrative problem, perhaps the most distinctive in any social system, is concerned with the maintenance of appropriate emotional and social ties among members of the system. In order to achieve its goals, the system must establish and maintain a high degree of solidarity and cohesion. In the queue, cohesion is achieved by establishing informal rules, which are kept sufficiently general to allow individual members to adjust to the normative pattern. Those who stay out too long, and therefore are unable to make the line viable, are sanctioned, or lose their place. In a sense, this represents a form of turn taking; if the queue structure is to be preserved, only some members can be permitted to take leaves of absence at any one time.

The group or clique, by means of the shift system, regulates turn taking for its members, and this ensures continuity of the line. The group, since it is the carrier of queue culture, brings a high level of solidarity to the line.

At the head of the line, the group takes on the characteristics of a community. Large family groups share eating, rest, and recreational facilities, and time spent together serves to strengthen the feelings of community. It is likely that the major factor underlying the effective policing of the head and middle regions of the line is the presence of large, coordinated groups. The breakdown of defense against intruders in the end part of every line can be attributed primarily to the fragmented, isolated nature of the membership.

But, even in parts of the line where organized groups are less prominent, individuals trade on a mutual trust that allows them to ask one another to "mind my place" and feel confident that they will be vouched for when they return from a brief leave of absence. The latency function is reflected in two related but different problems–pattern maintenance and tension management.

Pattern maintenance is the problem faced by an individual in reconciling the conflicting norms and demands imposed by his participation in the queue. Many members experience role conflicts arising out of their obligations to the queue and to their family or work roles. As we have seen, some queuers solve the problem by moving their entire family into the line. Others are faced with a different kind of dilemma: whether or not to keep a place for friends. The member who fails to commit himself to the queue norms is subject to considerable social pressure. If rules governing leaves of absence are not observed, the member is likely to find himself no longer part of the queue.

Tension management is the related problem of maintaining a level of commitment sufficient to perform the required role. To cope with tension and fatigue, members introduce a variety of entertainments in and around the line, such as pick-up games, story and joke telling, and beer parties. Time-out from the queue is, however, the major mode of tension management.

The queue system is mostly concerned with the problem of pattern maintenance and tension management because these are the most significant from the viewpoint of continuous participation and control. Of course, at critical times in the life of the queue, the other three functional problems require attention. Indeed, all four must be solved if the system is to continue in the state of equilibrium necessary for control and order.

* * *

CONCLUSION

This paper described how patterned regularities in behavior and attitudes emerge to regulate life in an overnight football queue. Although arrangements made to control behavior in the queue are informal, they are clearly identifiable, and it is appropriate to regard them as constituting a kind of culture. The queue, which possesses the characteristics of a social system, attempts to solve the set of functional problems confronted by every social system.

Our major findings were: (1) the growth of a queue tradition in which large numbers of people return annually to share the experience of waiting for tickets overnight in the open; (2) an increasing professionalization of the queue, marked by an influx of speculators and middlemen who profit by the increased demand for tickets; (3) the formation of unofficial prequeues to recognize the priority of people who arrived before the start of the official queue; (4) elaboration of the principle of first come, first served to control the amount of time spent in and out of the queue ("shift" and "marker" systems, which control "time-outs," were developed to regulate leaves of absence from the line); and (5) social constraints, and less often physical constraints, used to control queue jumping and to govern the practice of place-keeping.

It is appropriate to conclude that queueing behavior, a neglected area of social research, could be a rich source of ideas for students of crowd behavior, judgmental processes, cross-national differences, and the influence of cultural values on public behavior.

REFERENCES

HALL, E. T. *The Hidden Dimension* (New York: Doubleday, 1964).

———. *The Silent Language* (New York: Doubleday, 1959).

HOMANS, G. C. *Social Behavior: Its Elementary Forms* (New York: Harcourt, Brace, 1961).

LEVINE, I. R. *Main Street, U.S.S.R.* (New York: Doubleday, 1959).

MANN, L., AND K. F. TAYLOR. "Queue Counting: The Effect of Motives Upon Estimates of Numbers in Waiting Lines," *Journal of Personality and Social Psychology,* XII (1969), 95-103.

PARSONS, T. *The Social System* (New York: The Free Press, 1951).

PARSONS, T., AND NEIL J. SMELSER. *Economy and Society* (New York: The Free Press, 1957).

SOMMER, R. *Personal Space* (Englewood Cliffs, N.J.: Prentice-Hall, 1969).

Social-Organizational Problems in Modern Society

Antidote to Alienation: Learning to Belong*

Melvin Seeman

Most of us in the United States now live in the great, faceless conglomerates of population—the large metropolitan areas with their strung-out suburban

* From *Trans-action,* vol. 3, no. 5 (May–June, 1966), 34–39. Copyright © 1966 by Trans-action, Inc., New Brunswick, New Jersey.

belts–where who one's neighbors are is largely a matter of accident, and it usually doesn't pay to get closely involved with them, because they keep changing. Parents and children are close–perhaps even closer than before–as long as they live in the same house; but older generations and other relatives drift away, take jobs in other cities, go to retirement homes, have their own interests and associates. Often, it seems painful but realistic to conclude that, in the last analysis, you and your family are alone, and the only ones you can really count on for help and support are yourselves. No one else cares.

The American legend has it that not much more than a generation ago it used to be very different. Our fathers lived, mostly, in a golden age of belonging, in the traditional tree-shaded small town or closely-knit neighborhood (complete with the *Saturday Evening Post* version of a colonial-style church at the end of the block). Everyone was friendly and solicitous, and, in the case of need, neighbors by the tens and cousins by the dozens would come running.

For most of us, this dream, to the extent that it ever was real, is dead.

It is the dominant theme of "mass theory" in social psychology that such social and personal ties cannot be cut or seriously weakened without major damage–both to us and to the democratic process. Torn loose from so many of our emotional supports and roots–from the guidelines that remind us who we are and what we are worth–we must, so the theme goes, become prey increasingly to feelings of isolation, helplessness, and alienation.

But a theme is not yet a theory. It becomes a theory by being specific about processes–by describing the step-by-step development from cause to effect. How do the feelings of isolation, helplessness, and alienation come about, and what is their consequence? Mass theory becomes useful when it combines (1) history and social structure with (2) a description of the psychological effects of that structure, those alienative effects that, in turn, lead to (3) predicted behavior. *Alienation* is the center and the key to mass theory–it is produced by the structure of society, and it produces distinctive behavior.

To describe this process in greater detail:

- *Historically* and *structurally,* the old roots and close relationships have practically disappeared and have been replaced by anonymity and impersonality in social and personal life and by bureaucracy and mechanization at work.
- *Psychologically,* this must result in *alienation.* Alienation can take a number of forms: feelings of powerlessness, rootlessness, lack of standards and beliefs, and "self-estrangement" (having no clear idea of your personality or place, not even "belonging" to yourself).
- Alienation, in turn, results in *alienated behavior,* such as political passivity, racial and religious prejudice, taking part in movements that promise to usher in the millenium (but have little immediate or practical effect), and the like.

SUCCESS AND FAILURE

Since personal alienation is the key element, psychological theory is crucial to its understanding. In trying to understand and explain these psychological processes, I have found the social-learning theory of Julian B. Rotter very helpful (*Social Learning and Clinical Psychology,* Prentice-Hall, 1954). Rotter's principal contention is that human behavior depends on (1) the degree to which a person *expects* that the behavior will have a successful outcome, and (2) the *value* of that success to the person trying to achieve it. If these factors are powerful, separately or together, the behavior is most likely to occur. Specifically, if a person expects that learning something will help him achieve some goal, or he values that goal, he is more likely to learn.

Rotter's theory helps clarify the different meanings of alienation. Let us concentrate on what is probably the most important aspect of alienation in mass society–feelings of *powerlessness,* a person's belief that there is little he can do to bring about what he wants. People conceive of success and failure as being not only due to *external* factors–those that work on a man essentially from the outside and are usually considered beyond his control (luck, fate, "city hall," or "they")–but also *internal* factors, coming from within, which often do give him some control (skills, motives, determination, work).

Rotter and his co-workers argue that most experimental studies in learning usually unwittingly emphasize *external* control–the experimenter himself controls most of the pressures and conditions of the situation, and the subject is really not independent at all. If the subject could feel that he had some personal control over the learning, could relate it to his own needs and self-respect, then the patterns and amounts of learning might be very different.

A number of recent studies have supported this principle. These studies show that, when the same learning task is performed in two separate ways, with two sets of instructions–one, for instance, emphasizing the skill and energy required from the learner, and the other stressing the luck or chance aspect of the task (*internal* versus *external* control)–there are striking differences in learning and retention. A person will definitely learn *less* from experiences he conceives to be dominated by others, or by chance, which he feels he cannot influence.

This finding parallels the argument of the followers of mass theory that the isolated individual in "the lonely crowd," subordinated to, and intimidated by, bureaucracy, becomes convinced of his powerlessness and gives up learning about those things that might affect his future. As a specific example, he becomes apathetic and indifferent to politics–"You can't fight city hall."

Thus, mass-society theory and Rotter's social-learning theory agree that those persons with greater feelings of powerlessness will not learn as much or as well as those who feel they exercise some control over the factors that influence their lives.

UNIVERSAL ALIENATION

The statement that feelings of powerlessness inhibit knowledge is a basic conclusion about human beings. If true, it should be true not only of a few people but of many; not only of those in our country but in other nations as well. It should be true not only about one type of learning but throughout a wide spectrum of learning situations. Providing always, of course, that the learning is *relevant to control*—that it seems to the learner to be giving him a tool he can use to change his condition. Thus, an unemployed man learning how and where best to apply for a job is acquiring *control-relevant* information—while one learning baseball batting averages is not. The alienated can presumably learn escapist and irrelevant information as quickly as anyone—perhaps more quickly.

To test the hypothesis that the connection between feelings of powerlessness and inhibition of learning was generally true of mankind, we conducted several studies on powerlessness and alienation:

- in different institutions (a hospital and a reformatory);
- with different degrees of belonging to a work organization (unorganized versus unionized workers in Columbus, Ohio);
- and in different nations (Sweden and the United States).

Although specific items used in the several studies (hospital, reformatory, Columbus, and Sweden) varied somewhat, in all cases the person was offered a choice between an expression of mastery and one of powerlessness. For example:

- "Many times I feel that I have little influence over the things that happen to me," or, "I do not believe that chance and luck are very important in my life";
- "Becoming a success is a matter of hard work; luck has little or nothing to do with it," or, "Getting a job depends mainly on being in the right place at the right time."

The study of the hospital, published by John W. Evans and myself in the *American Sociological Review* (1962), and of the reformatory in *American Journal of Sociology* (1963), may be considered as a pair. They were both done in the United States. They sought to find out how feelings of powerlessness are related to lack of knowledge and information, in places where knowledge and information might give the individual some understanding and control of his fate. The hospital study dealt with tuberculosis patients; we found that those with the strongest feelings of powerlessness knew less about health matters than those not so alienated. In the reformatory study, inmates with greater feelings of helplessness learned relatively little when given information about parole, even though it might have helped shorten their confinement.

A third American study with Arthur G. Neal (*American Sociological Review,* 1964), was designed to test whether, as predicted, members of a formal occupational organization, such as a union or professional association, would feel less powerless than nonmembers. In form and feeling (if not always in fact) joining a vocational association apparently dedicated to a common goal should give a member some feeling of control over his job destiny and perhaps over broader socio-economic matters as well. Mass theory postulates that the great centers of power–government and the major corporations–are rapidly increasing in size and impersonality. At the same time, and as a consequence, jobs are becoming more specialized, more interchangeable, and the workers are moving more and more from job to job and city to city. This breakdown of personal identification with his work is supposed to make the worker feel more insignificant, expendable, and isolated ("just another cog"). The labor organizations that mediate between him and the great bureaucracies should therefore become more and more important to him, especially as a means of providing him with some sense of control.

ORGANIZED FOR POWER

We picked at random about 800 adult male names from the Columbus, Ohio, city directory, and mailed questionnaires to them designed to explore this relationship between union membership and feelings of powerlessness. About 57 per cent answered–245 manual workers and 216 nonmanuals.

The results of the Columbus study were definite. When factors such as age, income, education, and type of job are equal, unorganized workers *do* feel more powerless. This was true of both manual and nonmanual workers. (The powerlessness was a little greater for workers who changed jobs most often.) Further, these results were *specific* to powerlessness; that is, a test of the workers' generalized unhappiness (anomie) showed that the unorganized do not feel significantly more despairing about everything (or even most things) than the organized–it is apparently a rather specific sense of *mastery,* but not of well-being in general, that organization membership provides.

On the basis of the Columbus study, we could state that feelings of powerlessness do arise among unorganized workers in the United States. But a further demonstration seemed necessary, one that could combine all three elements–organization, powerlessness, and knowledge–into a single study; that could show whether these findings were peculiar to America; and that could concentrate on a broader field than health or corrections–the field of politics and international affairs.

Accordingly, a study was designed for Sweden to fulfill these needs and was carried out by interview (in Swedish) with a sample of the male work force in Malmo. (Malmo is Sweden's third largest city, population about 240,000, with a heavy concentration of commercial and seaport occupations.) A random sample of males aged twenty to seventy-nine was drawn from the official register maintained by government authorities. A total of 558 workers were interviewed.

The interview contained questions on three major variables:

- *Feelings of powerlessness*: (The individual's expectations of control), proferring the usual choice between items expressing mastery and powerlessness.
- *Organization membership*: Apart from simple membership in a union or other work organization, evidence was gathered on (1) the person's *degree* of participation and (2) his *involvement* in organizations outside of work.
- *Political knowledge*: A sixteen-item information test dealt with both Swedish politics and international affairs.

When the Swedish data had been collected, checked, and evaluated, the differences were found to be consistently and significantly as predicted: *High feelings of powerlessness and low political knowledge were found together among the unorganized workers.* Second, there was a relatively small but predictable difference between those who were officials and those who were simply members of unions.

MASTER OF THE POLITICAL SHIP

These results are clearly consistent with the learning- and mass-society theses. But, before they can be accepted without question, other complicating factors must be eliminated. What about education? Could differences in education be the real underlying cause of the differences in feelings of powerlessness? What about other factors, such as age or job prestige? A close examination of the data, correcting for education and other elements, makes the result even more emphatic. In Sweden, as in the United States, neither education nor other differences obliterated the trend. High powerlessness among the workers appeared to flow from lack of union membership and was intimately related to low political knowledge.

The officers of unions were shown to have the lowest feelings of powerlessness and to be highest in political knowledge. But was this due to the fact that they were *officers* and, therefore, a special kind of member (and also, perhaps, a special breed of cat with different personality characteristics); or was it primarily because they were more involved—"more engaged"—in the affairs of the union and, therefore, more capable of exerting control? Would other "more engaged" members (who were nonofficers) also be less alienated and have greater capacity for learning control-relevant information?

"Engaged" members, we decided, would be those who attended meetings regularly, considered the union to be important in their lives, and thought individual members were important and influential in the union. Pitting the scores of such rank-and-file members against the "less engaged," we found a parallel with the over-all comparison of organized versus unorganized workers. The relationship is modest but consistent: The greater the personal involvement in union meetings and affairs, the less the feelings of powerlessness; and, for the manual workers (who would generally tend to have less education), involvement and amount of political knowledge go together as well. (This picture calls to mind the old socialist ideal of the politically wise proletarian who spent much time in study and discussion of the political and economic factors that controlled his life and then organized to do something about them.)

We found, too, that the person's *interest* in political affairs is part of the same picture. Of course, those with more interest in politics have greater knowledge of it; but more important here is the fact that strong feelings of powerlessness go along with low interest. Those who do not feel mastery do not develop interest and do not learn.

This interest, or lack of it, is directly related to union membership–to belonging to an organization that could exert job control. Organized workers were significantly more interested in political affairs than the nonunion workers. And this interest, again, was *specific* to what we call *control-relevant* information. The unorganized were *not* totally withdrawn or apathetic; they were just as interested as the organized workers in personal and local affairs and in discussing their work. But the unorganized felt powerless to control their larger destinies–and politics and international affairs represented these larger destinies.

So far, these conclusions agree with both learning theory and mass theory. Men with little hope for success feel powerless; lose interest in, and have difficulty learning, control-relevant information.

However, it must be recalled that Rotter's learning theory made a distinction between a person's *expectation* that he can achieve a goal and the *value* he places on that goal. Theoretically, at least, a person will not try very earnestly for a goal he does not value, no matter how sure he is he can get it; contrariwise, he may try very hard, even with little hope of achievement, if he wants the goal badly enough.

In the American reformatory study, knowledge that might have helped the inmate have some control over his future (parole information) and noncontrol knowledge (descriptive information about the institution) were both offered to the inmates tested. We split the subjects into two groups–those who tended to conform to what prison authorities wanted of them, who seemed to value the officially approved goals and behavior set for them (working hard, obeying regulations, making no trouble, trying to meet parole requirements), and those who would not conform. We reasoned that, if the inmate did not value parole (as part of the prison system) very highly, then whether or not he believed he could achieve it was not very important in determining whether he would learn parole information; however, if he did value parole, his expectation (or lack of it) that he could determine his own life should affect how much he would study and learn about parole. The results were consistent with this view: Generally, those inmates who valued the conventional standards of how to get ahead in the reformatory world, who "conformed," learned more of the parole information than did the "unconventionals." But even in this conforming group, those who felt powerless learned less. We may conclude, then, that both the *value* of the goal and the *expectation* of achieving it will be reflected in how much learning a man will acquire that relates to the goal.

RISING EXPECTATIONS

Summarizing the over-all conclusions of all four studies:

- *Powerlessness and organization*: A person's feelings of self-reliance and power are tied up with whether he belongs to an organization that has some control over his occupational destiny. If he does belong to such an organization—union, business, or professional association—his further feelings of mastery are directly tied up with how actively he works in it—whether he has some control over *its* destiny.
- *Powerlessness and learning*: The ability to learn and retain knowledge that has some connection with control over an individual's future (politics, parole, or health information) is also directly affected by belonging to a union or other relevant organization, and to a person's alienation. To the extent that he feels powerless to affect his future, he will not learn as well what he needs to know to affect it. And he will not be as interested in it—he may even reject it.

To the degree that he *expects* to achieve his goal, he will attend to the associated learning; to the degree that he *values* the goal, he will also be oriented to learn.

- The connection between organization membership and powerlessness holds true from nation to nation—it is as true in Sweden, for example, as in the United States.
- The connection between powerlessness and learning holds true through many different kinds of organizations (reformatories, hospitals, unions) and many different kinds of control information (parole and health information, politics, international affairs).

These studies are perhaps more important for what they promise than for what they presently accomplish. The promise is that controlled studies of this kind, carried out in various cultures and settings, can establish the validity of arguments and theories about contemporary life that depend upon the idea of alienation. There is much literature of this kind, both inside and outside of social science; and it deals with a wide range of subjects—for example, mass movements, intergroup prejudice, mass communication, and politics. It is a literature that touches a powerful array of basic human values: normlessness and trust, meaninglessness and understanding, self-estrangement and integrity.

The promise is that we can concern ourselves with such large questions about the individual in modern society and test long-held theories that have highly practical consequences—learning what it really means, under various circumstances, to exert control, to sink roots, to find understanding, or even to be oneself.

3. SUGGESTIONS FOR FURTHER READING

BERNE, ERIC. *Games People Play* (New York: Grove Press, 1964).*

BLAU, PETER. *Bureaucracy in Modern Society* (New York: Random House, 1971).*

———. *Exchange and Power in Social Life* (New York: John Wiley & Sons, 1964).

DURKHEIM, ÉMILE. *Division of Labor in Society* (New York: The Free Press, 1957).*

———. *Suicide* (New York: The Free Press, 1951).*

ETZIONI, AMITAI. *Modern Organizations* (Englewood Cliffs, N.J.: Prentice-Hall, 1964).*

FARB, PETER. *Man's Rise to Civilization, etc.* (New York: Avon Books, 1969).*

GERTH, H. H., AND C. WRIGHT MILLS (eds.). *From Max Weber* (New York: Oxford University Press, 1946).*

GOFFMAN, ERVING. *Behavior in Public Places* (New York: The Free Press, 1963).*

———. *Presentation of Self in Everyday Life* (Garden City, N.Y.: Doubleday, 1959).*

GREER, SCOTT. *Social Organization* (New York: Random House, 1955).*

JOSEPHSON, E., AND M. (eds.). *Man Alone: Alienation in Modern Society* (New York: Dell, 1962).*

MERTON, ROBERT. *Social Theory and Social Structure* (New York: The Free Press, 1957).

MURDOCK, GEORGE P. *Social Structure* (New York: The Free Press, 1949).*

OLMSTEAD, MICHAEL. *The Small Group* (New York: Random House, 1959).*

REDFIELD, ROBERT. *The Folk Culture of Yucatan* (Chicago: University of Chicago Press, 1941).

SERVICE, ELMAN. *Primitive Social Organization* (New York: Random House, 1962).*

STEIN, M., A. VIDICH, AND D. WHITE (eds.). *Identity and Anxiety* (New York: The Free Press, 1960).*

WHYTE, WILLIAM F. *Street Corner Society* (Chicago: University of Chicago Press, 1943).*

WHYTE, WILLIAM H., JR. *Organization Man* (New York: Simon & Schuster, 1956).*

WOLFF, KURT (ed.). *The Sociology of George Simmel* (New York: The Free Press, 1950).

* *Available in paperback.*

4. Socialization

INTRODUCTION

Socialization is the process by which an individual learns how to become a functioning member of his society by internalizing appropriate behavior patterns, values, and attitudes as well as acquiring necessary skills and information.

Socialization begins at birth. In due course, the child learns to take part in group life and to embody to some degree the values of his society and of groups within it. Socialization also continues into adult life. In response to his ever changing web of group affiliations and his inexorable movement through the life cycle, the individual inevitably participates in new social forms and institutions, learns new disciplines, and develops new values.

Many theories have been conceived to explain the process by which socialization occurs. Some have been derived from the observation of normal children in our society; others, from study of the emotionally disturbed; others, from laboratory experiments with children and animals; and still others, from the study of preliterate peoples. Piecing together the various theories may yield a broader, more comprehensive understanding of the nature of socialization.

Personality is an important concept in many theories of socialization. It is defined as a relatively organized and enduring structure of habits, feelings, attitudes, and predispositions to behave. The individual's personality is very much a product of the social and cultural forces impinging on him as well as of his biological inheritance.

Sigmund Freud's psychoanalytic theory, derived from the clinical study of emotionally disturbed individuals, has had enormously far-reaching effects on contemporary views of socialization. Freud was among the first to highlight the importance of the irrational, morbid, and emotional side of man's nature. He emphasized the cruciality of early childhood experiences in shaping the individual's later behavior and responses. Freud conceived of the psychosexual development of personality as a series of progressive resolutions of conflicts associated with the oral, anal, and genital areas of the body and related to weaning, toilet training, and the acquisition of socially accepted patterns for the expression of sexual drives.

Freud thought of the personality as divided into three segments; the id (unconscious, instinctual drives and wishes), the ego (the rational, conscious part of personality), and the superego (conscience, the person's conception of morality). Freud's theory, especially as it developed in his later years, held that the ego acted as mediator between the demands made by the id and the restrictions dictated by the superego. While contemporary psychoanalysts have modified many facets of Freudian theory, most acknowledge its fundamental insights into man's perennial dilemma—the conflict between his basic wants and his sense of right. David Elkind's essay on "Erik Erikson's Eight Ages of Man" suggests many parallels between Freud's psychoanalytic theory and that of a distinguished post-Freudian psychoanalyst. However, Erikson feels that personality development continues throughout the whole life cycle. He also believes that the personality is shaped at different stages of life by important resolutions the individual makes about how to orient himself to the world. To Freud, parents exerted the most important influence on the personality of the child. Erikson expands the influencing forces to include spouses, friends, peers, and others.

In sharp contrast to psychoanalysis, behaviorism focuses on the individual organism and its capacity to learn. The basic precepts of behaviorism are straightforward: (1) Overt behavior is the main, if not the exclusive, interest of the behavioral scientist; attitudes and subjective experience are ignored or given low priority. (2) Behavior is conceived in terms of stimulus and response; the learning process involves conditioning (attaching the desired responses to various stimuli through a system of reward and punishment), which is effective because, in general, the human organism seeks to maximize pleasure and minimize pain. (3) Aside from essential physiological needs, such as those for food, water, and sleep, the newborn infant exhibits considerable plasticity; he can learn almost anything.

Since it has developed mainly through laboratory work, behaviorist research is ordinarily more precise and controlled than psychoanalysis. For example, it is often possible to measure the extent of a drive or to regulate the strength of a stimulus. Behaviorism—or operant conditioning, as many of its contemporary adherents call it—has been best illuminated by research with animals and young children or with adults when the situations are relatively simple. Consider, for example, the rather impressive results obtained by Robert Hamblin and his associates in their behavior-modification research. "Changing the Game from 'Get the Teacher' to 'Learn' " strongly suggests that it may be totally unwarranted to apply a "hopeless" prognosis to many hyperaggressive, infantile, and autistic children. However, behaviorism's critics take issue with the behaviorist's dismissal of subjective phenomena as things to be ignored because they cannot be measured quantitatively. Behaviorism has also been faulted for its inability to explain successfully social situations involving self-judgment, ambivalent feelings, and complex motivations. But, whatever its shortcomings, behaviorism has encouraged social scientists to formulate operational definitions (definitions whose meaning inheres in a set of operations or objective measurements) and to test their hypotheses in ways that can be replicated by other scientists.

Still another perspective on the socialization process is offered by the social-role theory, developed by George Herbert Mead. Social-role theory highlights social interaction and role-playing in the development of the adult person. The focal point of socialization concerns the acquisition of a self (the aspect of the individual's personality that consists of his awareness and feelings about his own personal and social identity). Mead divided the self into two parts: the "I" and the "me." The "I" represents the spontaneous, active, expressive part of the person—the unique, natural, and innovative part. The "me" represents the reflexive, subjective, and conventional part of the person; it represents the internalized demands of society and the individual's awareness of these demands. The "I" appears first; the "me" develops later, after the individual has learned the rules and expectations of his society. The "me" acts as a censor of the "I"; it is based originally on the demands and expectations of parents and subsequently on the rules and expectations of society. Mead's conceptions of the "I" and the "me" are directly comparable to Freud's notions of the id and the superego.

According to Mead, the self develops in three distinct stages. In the first, or "preparatory," stage, the child does not have the ability to perceive his own behavior; he imitates specific actions. When his action comes close to social expectations, adults reward the behavior, thus encouraging the child to repeat this pattern.

In the second, or "play," stage, the child plays at specific roles: He links together specific behaviors that are identified with a given position and its expectations. For example, the girl plays at being a mother; she strokes her doll, attempts to feed it, puts it to bed, reprimands it for crying, etc.

In the third, or "game," stage, the child acquires the ability to respond to several people at the same time. In baseball, for example, the player does not act out a highly specific individual role; he must continually adapt his behavior to the needs of the team as a whole, to the specific situations that arise in the game, while bearing in mind the rules of the game. At this point, Mead would say that the individual is responding to the "generalized other," the organized community or group that gives the person his unity of self. By slow degrees, the child learns to take the point of view not only of his parents and friends but of the organized society as a whole.

Mead's theory is highly abstract and, therefore, does not lend itself readily to empirical verification. However, from the study by Miyamoto and Dornbusch, we see that social-role theory can be quantified and empirically tested. From this lead, perhaps future research will be able to explore other aspects of the theory, further extending our knowledge of the socialization process.

Throughout the world, the family is the most significant socializing agent for most people. Without doubt, in our own society the parent-child relationship is the most critical for the formation of individual personality and character. As industrialization has developed in the Western world, it has reduced to a certain extent the importance of the role the family enacts in the socialization process. Many skills that were once transmitted in the home are now conveyed at the university, school, office, or plant. But, although educational and economic institutions have eclipsed the family in the occupational and status preparation of the individual, the family is still supreme in the moral training of the person, for character development.

Nevertheless, the family exerts an all-pervasive influence on the behavior of the individual. Mark Zborowski's study in Chapter 2 suggests the importance of the family in shaping responses to pain. In Chapter 7, the reader will find more discussion of this question along with an examination of the family as a basic social institution in its own right.

After World War II, hundreds of thousands of American families began migrating from the overcrowded cities to the suburbs, on the theory that suburban life was "better for the children." Now, twenty-five years later, with a second generation of suburbia-reared children well under way, some social scientists are wondering whether it has been so successful. Urie Bronfenbrenner does not seem to think so. His article on "The Split-Level American Family" suggests that the American suburbia-reared child has been abandoned to his peer group, deprived of interaction with adults—his parents, in particular—and over-exposed to television. He suggests that this shift in the sources of socialization may lie behind the great increases in delinquency, drug use, and the development of the youth counterculture.

· Erik Erikson's Eight Ages of Man*

David Elkind

At a recent faculty reception, I happened to join a small group in which a young mother was talking about her "identity crisis." She and her husband, she said, had decided not to have any more children, and she was depressed at the thought of being past the child-bearing stage. It was as if, she continued, she had been robbed of some part of herself and now needed to find a new function to replace the old one.

When I remarked that her story sounded like a case history from a book by Erik Erikson, she replied, "Who's Erikson?" It is a reflection on the intellectual modesty and literary decorum of Erik H. Erikson, psychoanalyst and professor of developmental psychology at Harvard, that so few of the many people who today talk about the "identity crisis" know anything of the man who pointed out its pervasiveness as a problem in contemporary society two decades ago.

Erikson has, however, contributed more to social science than his delineation of identity problems in modern man. His descriptions of the stages of the life cycle, for example, have advanced psychoanalytic theory to the point where it can now describe the development of the healthy personality on its own terms and not merely as the opposite of a sick one. Likewise, Erikson's emphasis upon the problems unique to adolescents and adults living in today's society has helped to rectify the one-sided emphasis on childhood as the beginning and end of personality development.

Finally, in his biographical studies, such as "Young Man Luther" and "Gandhi's Truth" (which has just won a National Book Award in philosophy and religion), Erikson emphasizes the inherent strengths of the human personality by showing how individuals can use their neurotic symptoms and conflicts for creative and constructive social purposes while healing themselves in the process.

It is important to emphasize that Erikson's contributions are genuine advances in psychoanalysis, in the sense that Erikson accepts and builds upon many of the basic tenets of Freudian theory. In this regard, Erikson differs from Freud's early co-workers, such as Jung and Adler, who, when they broke with Freud, rejected his theories and substituted their own.

* From the *New York Times Magazine,* April 5, 1970, pp. 25–27, 83–92, 110–14.

Likewise, Erikson also differs from the so-called neo-Freudians, such as Horney, Kardiner, and Sullivan, who (mistakenly, as it turned out) assumed that Freudian theory had nothing to say about man's relation to reality and to his culture. While it is true that Freud emphasized, even mythologized, sexuality, he did so to counteract the rigid sexual taboos of his time, which, at that point in history, were frequently the cause of neuroses. In his later writings, however, Freud began to concern himself with the executive agency of the personality, namely, the ego, which is also the repository of the individual's attitudes and concepts about himself and his world.

It is with the psychosocial development of the ego that Erikson's observations and theoretical constructions are primarily concerned. Erikson has thus been able to introduce innovations into psychoanalytic theory without either rejecting or ignoring Freud's monumental contribution.

* * *

. . . Erikson set forth the implications of his clinical observations in "Childhood and Society." In that book, the summation and integration of fifteen years of research, he made three major contributions to the study of the human ego. He posited (1) that, side by side with the stages of psychosexual development described by Freud (the oral, anal, phallic, genital, Oedipal, and pubertal), were psychosocial stages of ego development, in which the individual had to establish new basic orientations to himself and his social world; (2) that personality development continued throughout the whole life cycle; and (3) that each stage had a positive *as well as* a negative component.

Much about these contributions—and about Erikson's way of thinking—can be understood by looking at his scheme of life stages. Erikson identifies eight stages in the human life cycle, in each of which a new dimension of "social interaction" becomes possible—that is, a new dimension in a person's interaction with himself and with his social environment.

TRUST VS. MISTRUST

The first stage corresponds to the oral stage in classical psychoanalytic theory and usually extends through the first year of life. In Erikson's view, the new dimension of social interaction that emerges during this period involves basic *trust* at the one extreme and *mistrust* at the other. The degree to which the child comes to trust the world, other people, and himself depends to a considerable extent upon the quality of the care that he receives. The infant whose needs are met when they arise, whose discomforts are quickly removed, who is cuddled, fondled, played with, and talked to, develops a sense of the world as a safe place to be and of people as helpful and dependable. When, however, the care is inconsistent, inadequate, and rejecting, it fosters a basic mistrust, an attitude of fear and suspicion on the part of the infant toward the world in general and people in particular that will carry through to later stages of development.

It should be said at this point that the problem of basic trust-versus-mistrust (as is true for all the later dimensions) is not resolved once and for all during the first year of life; it arises again at each successive stage of development. There is both hope and danger in this. The child who enters school with a sense of mistrust may come to trust a particular teacher who has taken the trouble to make herself trustworthy; with this second chance, he overcomes his early mistrust. On the other hand, the child who comes through infancy with a vital sense of trust can still have his sense of mistrust activated at a later stage if, say, his parents are divorced and separated under acrimonious circumstances.

This point was brought home to me in a very direct way by a four-year-old patient I saw in a court clinic. He was being seen at the court clinic because his adoptive parents, who had had him for six months, now wanted to give him back to the agency. They claimed that he was cold and unloving, took things, and could not be trusted. He was, indeed, a cold and apathetic boy, but with good reason. About a year after his illegitimate birth, he was taken away from his mother, who had a drinking problem, and was shunted back and forth among several foster homes. Initially, he had tried to relate to the persons in the foster homes, but the relationships never had a chance to develop, because he was moved at just the wrong times. In the end, he gave up trying to reach out to others, because the inevitable separations hurt too much.

Like the burned child who dreads the flame, this emotionally burned child shunned the pain of emotional involvement. He had trusted his mother, but now he trusted no one. Only years of devoted care and patience could now undo the damage that had been done to this child's sense of trust.

AUTONOMY VS. DOUBT

Stage Two spans the second and third years of life, the period that Freudian theory calls the anal stage. Erikson sees here the emergence of *autonomy*. This autonomy dimension builds upon the child's new motor and mental abilities. At this stage, the child can not only walk but also climb, open and close, drop, push and pull, hold and let go. The child takes pride in these new accomplishments and wants to do everything himself, whether it be pulling the wrapper off a piece of candy, selecting the vitamin out of the bottle, or flushing the toilet. If parents recognize the young child's need to do what he is capable of doing at his own pace and in his own time, then he develops a sense that he is able to control his muscles, his impulses, himself, and, not insignificantly, his environment—the sense of autonomy.

When, however, his caretakers are impatient and do for him what he is capable of doing himself, they reinforce a sense of shame and doubt. To be sure, every parent has rushed a child at times, and children are hardy enough to endure such lapses. It is only when caretaking is consistently overprotective and criticism of "accidents" (whether these be wetting, soiling, spilling, or breaking things) is harsh and unthinking that the child develops an excessive sense of shame with respect to other people and an excessive sense of doubt about [his] own abilities to control his world and himself.

If the child leaves this stage with less autonomy than shame or doubt, he will be handicapped in his attempts to achieve autonomy in adolescence and adulthood. Contrariwise, the child who moves through this stage with his sense of autonomy buoyantly outbalancing his feelings of shame and doubt is well prepared to be autonomous at later phases in the life cycle. Again, however, the balance of autonomy to shame and doubt set up during this period can be changed in either positive or negative directions by later events.

It might be well to note, in addition, that too much autonomy can be as harmful as too little. I have in mind a patient of seven who had a heart condition. He had learned very quickly how terrified his parents were of any signs in him of cardiac difficulty. With the psychological acuity given to children, he soon ruled the household. The family could not go shopping, or for a drive, or on a holiday if he did not approve. On those rare occasions when the parents had had enough and defied him, he would get angry and his purple hue and gagging would frighten them into submission.

Actually, this boy was frightened of this power (as all children would be) and was really eager to give it up. When the parents and the boy came to realize this, and to recognize that a little shame and doubt were a healthy counterpoise to an inflated sense of autonomy, the three of them could once again assume their normal roles.

INITIATIVE VS. GUILT

In this stage (the genital stage of classical psychoanalysis), the child, age four to five, is pretty much master of his body and can ride a tricycle, run, cut, and hit. He can thus initiate motor activities of various sorts on his own and no longer merely responds to or imitates the actions of other children. The same holds true for his language and fantasy activities. Accordingly, Erikson argues that the social dimension that appears at this stage has *initiative* at one of its poles and *guilt* at the other.

Whether the child will leave this stage with his sense of initiative far outbalancing his sense of guilt depends to a considerable extent upon how parents respond to his self-initiated activities. Children who are given much freedom and opportunity to initiate motor play such as running, bike riding, sliding, skating, tussling, and wrestling have their sense of initiative reinforced. Initiative is also reinforced when parents answer their children's questions (intellectual initiative) and do not deride or inhibit fantasy or play activity. On the other hand, if the child is made to feel that his motor activity is bad, that his questions are a nuisance, and that his play is silly and stupid, then he may develop a sense of guilt over self-initiated activities in general that will persist through later life stages.

INDUSTRY VS. INFERIORITY

Stage Four is the age period from six to eleven, the elementary-school years (described by classical psychoanalysis as the *latency phase*). It is a time during which the child's love for the parent of the opposite sex and rivalry with the same-sexed parent (elements in the so-called family romance) are quiescent. It is also a period during which the child becomes capable of deductive reasoning and of playing and learning by rules. It is not until this period, for example, that children can really play marbles, checkers, and other "take turn" games that require obedience to rules. Erikson argues that the psychosocial dimension that emerges during this period has a sense of *industry* at one extreme and a sense of *inferiority* at the other.

The term industry nicely captures a dominant theme of this period, during which the concern with how things are made, how they work, and what they do predominates. It is the Robinson Crusoe age, in the sense that the enthusiasm and minute detail with which Crusoe describes his activities appeals to the child's own budding sense of industry. When children are encouraged in their efforts to make, do, or build practical things (whether it be to construct creepy crawlers, tree houses, or airplane models–or to cook, bake, or sew), are allowed to finish their products, and are praised and rewarded for the results, then the sense of industry is enhanced. But parents who see their children's efforts at making and doing as "mischief," and as simply "making a mess," help to encourage in children a sense of inferiority.

During these elementary-school years, however, the child's world includes more than the home. Now social institutions other than the family come to play a central role in the developmental crisis of the individual. (Here Erikson introduced still another advance in psychoanalytic theory, which heretofore concerned itself only with the effects of the parents' behavior upon the child's development.)

A child's school experiences affect his industry-inferiority balance. The child, for example, with an I.Q. of 80 to 90 has a particularly traumatic school experience, even when his sense of industry is rewarded and encouraged at home. He is "too bright" to be in special classes, but "too slow" to compete with children of average ability. Consequently, he experiences constant failures in his academic efforts that reinforce a sense of inferiority.

On the other hand, the child who had his sense of industry derogated at home can have it revitalized at school through the offices of a sensitive and committed teacher. Whether the child develops a sense of industry or inferiority, therefore, no longer depends solely on the caretaking efforts of the parents but on the actions and offices of other adults as well.

IDENTITY VS. ROLE CONFUSION

When the child moves into adolescence (Stage Five–roughly, the ages twelve to eighteen), he encounters, according to traditional psychoanalytic theory, a reawakening of the family-romance problem of early childhood.

His means of resolving the problem is to seek and find a romantic partner of his own generation. While Erikson does not deny this aspect of adolescence, he points out that there are other problems as well. The adolescent matures mentally as well as physiologically, and, in addition to the new feelings, sensations, and desires he experiences as a result of changes in his body, he develops a multitude of new ways of looking at and thinking about the world. Among other things, those in adolescence can now think about other people's thinking and wonder about what other people think of them. They can also conceive of ideal families, religions, and societies, which they then compare with the imperfect families, religions, and societies of their own experience. Finally, adolescents become capable of constructing theories and philosophies designed to bring all the varied and conflicting aspects of society into a working, harmonious, and peaceful whole. The adolescent, in a word, is an impatient idealist who believes that it is as easy to realize an ideal as it is to imagine it.

Erikson believes that the new, interpersonal dimension that emerges during this period has to do with a sense of *ego identity* at the positive end and a sense of *role confusion* at the negative end. That is to say, given the adolescent's newfound integrative abilities, his task is to bring together all of the things he has learned about himself as a son, student, athlete, friend, Scout, newspaper boy, and so on, and integrate these different images of himself into a whole that makes sense and that shows continuity with the past while preparing for the future. To the extent that the young person succeeds in this endeavor, he arrives at a sense of psychosocial identity, a sense of who he is, where he has been, and where he is going.

In contrast to the earlier stages, where parents play a more or less direct role in the determination of the result of the developmental crises, the influence of parents during this stage is much more indirect. If the young person reaches adolescence with, thanks to his parents, a vital sense of trust, autonomy, initiative, and industry, then his chances of arriving at a meaningful sense of ego identity are much enhanced. The reverse, of course, holds true for the young person who enters adolescence with considerable mistrust, shame, doubt, guilt, and inferiority. Preparation for a successful adolescence, and the attainment of an integrated psychosocial identity, must, therefore, begin in the cradle.

Over and above what the individual brings with him from his childhood, the attainment of a sense of personal identity depends upon the social milieu in which he or she grows up. For example, in a society where women are to some extent second-class citizens, it may be harder for females to arrive at a sense of psychosocial identity. Likewise, at times, such as the present, when rapid social and technological change breaks down many traditional values, it may be more difficult for young people to find continuity between what they learned and experienced as children and what they learn and experience as adolescents. At such times, young people often seek causes that give their lives meaning and direction. The activism of the current generation of young people may well stem, in part at least, from this search.

When the young person cannot attain a sense of personal identity, because of either an unfortunate childhood or difficult social circumstances, he shows a certain amount of *role confusion*—a sense of not knowing what he is, where he belongs, or whom he belongs to. Such confusion is a frequent symptom in delinquent young people. Promiscuous adolescent girls, for example, often seem to have a fragmented sense of ego identity. Some young people seek a "negative identity," an identity opposite to the one prescribed for them by their family and friends. Having an identity as a "delinquent," or as a "hippie," or even as an "acid head," may sometimes be preferable to having no identity at all.

In some cases, young people do not seek a negative identity so much as they have it thrust upon them. I remember another court case in which the defendant was an attractive sixteen-year-old girl who had been found "tricking it" in a trailer located just outside the grounds of an Air Force base. From about the age of twelve, her mother had encouraged her to dress seductively and to go out with boys. When she returned from dates, her sexually frustrated mother demanded a kiss-by-kiss, caress-by-caress description of the evening's activities. After the mother had vicariously satisfied her sexual needs, she proceeded to call her daughter a "whore" and a "dirty tramp." As the girl told me, "Hell, I have the name, so I might as well play the role."

Failure to establish a clear sense of personal identity at adolescence does not guarantee perpetual failure. And the person who attains a working sense of ego identity in adolescence will of necessity encounter challenges and threats to that identity as he moves through life. Erikson, perhaps more than any other personality theorist, has emphasized that life is constant change, and that confronting problems at one stage in life is not a guarantee against the reappearance of these problems at later stages or against the finding of new solutions to them.

INTIMACY VS. ISOLATION

Stage Six in the life cycle is young adulthood—roughly, the period of courtship and early family life that extends from late adolescence till early middle age. For this stage, and the stages described hereafter, classical psychoanalysis has nothing new or major to say. For Erikson, however, the previous attainment of a sense of personal identity and the engagement in productive work that marks this period give rise to a new interpersonal dimension of *intimacy* at the one extreme and *isolation* at the other.

When Erikson speaks of intimacy, he means much more than lovemaking alone; he means the ability to share with, and care about, another person without fear of losing oneself in the process. In the case of intimacy, as in the case of identity, success or failure no longer depends directly upon the parents but only indirectly as they have contributed to the individual's success or failure at the earlier stages. Here, too, as in the case of identity, social conditions may help or hinder the establishment of a sense of intimacy. Likewise, intimacy need not involve sexuality; it includes the relationship between friends. Soldiers who have served together under the most dangerous circumstances often develop a sense of commitment to one another that exemplifies intimacy in its broadest sense. If a sense of intimacy is not established with friends or a marriage partner, the result, in Erikson's view, is a sense of isolation–of being alone without anyone to share with or care for.

GENERATIVITY VS. SELF-ABSORPTION

This stage–middle age–brings with it what Erikson speaks of as either *generativity* or *self-absorption,* and stagnation. What Erikson means by generativity is that the person begins to be concerned with others beyond his immediate family, with future generations and the nature of the society and world in which those generations will live. Generativity does not reside only in parents; it can be found in any individual who actively concerns himself with the welfare of young people and with making the world a better place for them to live and to work [in].

Those who fail to establish a sense of generativity fall into a state of self-absorption, in which their personal needs and comforts are of predominant concern. A fictional case of self-absorption is Dickens's Scrooge in "A Christmas Carol." In his one-sided concern with money and in his disregard for the interests and welfare of his young employe, Bob Cratchit, Scrooge exemplifies the self-absorbed, embittered (the two often go together) old man. Dickens also illustrated, however, what Erikson points out: namely, that unhappy solutions to life's crises are not irreversible. Scrooge, at the end of the tale, manifested a sense both of generativity and of intimacy that he had not experienced before.

INTEGRITY VS. DESPAIR

Stage Eight in the Eriksonian scheme corresponds roughly to the period when the individual's major efforts are nearing completion, and when there is time for reflection–and for the enjoyment of grandchildren, if any. The psychosocial dimension that comes into prominence now has *integrity* on [the] one hand and *despair* on the other.

The sense of integrity arises from the individual's ability to look back on his life with satisfaction. At the other extreme is the individual who looks back upon his life as a series of missed opportunities and missed directions; now, in the twilight years, he realizes that it is too late to start again. For such a person, the inevitable result is a sense of despair at what might have been.

These, then, are the major stages in the life cycle as described by Erikson. Their presentation, for one thing, frees the clinician to treat adult emotional problems as failures (in part at least) to solve genuinely adult personality crises and not, as heretofore, as mere residuals of infantile frustrations and conflicts. This view of personality growth, moreover, takes some of the onus off parents and takes account of the role that society and the person himself play in the formation of an individual personality. Finally, Erikson has offered hope for us all by demonstrating that each phase of growth has its strengths as well as its weaknesses, and that failures at one stage of development can be rectified by successes at later stages.

The reason that these ideas, which sound so agreeable to "common sense," are, in fact, so revolutionary has a lot to do with the state of psychoanalysis in America. As formulated by Freud, psychoanalysis encompassed a theory of personality development, a method of studying the human mind, and, finally, procedures for treating troubled and unhappy people. Freud viewed this system as a scientific one, open to revision as new facts and observations accumulated.

The system was, however, so vehemently attacked that Freud's followers were constantly in the position of having to defend Freud's views. Perhaps because of this situation, Freud's system became, in the hands of some of his followers and defenders, a dogma upon which all theoretical innovation, clinical observation, and therapeutic practice had to be grounded. That this attitude persists is evidenced in the recent remark by a psychoanalyst that he believed psychotic patients could not be treated by psychoanalysis because "Freud said so." Such attitudes, in which Freud's authority rather than observation and data is the basis of deciding what is true and what is false, has contributed to the disrepute in which psychoanalysis is widely held today.

Erik Erikson has broken out of this scholasticism and has had the courage to say that Freud's discoveries and practices were the start and not the end of the study and treatment of the human personality. In addition to advocating the modifications of psychoanalytic theory outlined above, Erikson has also suggested modifications in therapeutic practice, particularly in the treatment of young patients. "Young people in severe trouble are not fit for the couch," he writes. "They want to face you, and they want you to face them, not as a facsimile of a parent, or wearing the mask of a professional helper, but as a kind of over-all individual a young person can live with or despair of."

Erikson has had the boldness to remark on some of the negative effects that distorted notions of psychoanalysis have had on society at large. Psychoanalysis, he says, has contributed to a widespread fatalism—"even as we were trying to devise, with scientific determinism, a therapy for the few, we were led to promote an ethical disease among the many."

* * *

There is now more and more teaching of Erikson's concepts in psychiatry, psychology, education, and social work in America and in other parts of the world. His description of the stages of the life cycle are summarized in major textbooks in all of these fields, and clinicians are increasingly looking at their cases in Eriksonian terms.

Research investigators have, however, found Erikson's formulations somewhat difficult to test. This is not surprising, inasmuch as Erikson's conceptions, like Freud's, take into account the infinite complexity of the human personality. Current research methodologies are, by and large, still not able to deal with these complexities at their own level, and distortions are inevitable when such concepts as "identity" come to be defined in terms of responses to a questionnaire.

Likewise, although Erikson's life stages have an intuitive "rightness" about them, not everyone agrees with his formulations. Douvan and Adelson, in their book *The Adolescent Experience,* argue that, while his identity theory may hold true for boys, it doesn't for girls. This argument is based on findings that suggest that girls postpone identity consolidation until after marriage (and intimacy) have been established. Such postponement occurs, say Douvan and Adelson, because a woman's identity is partially defined by the identity of the man whom she marries. This view does not really contradict Erikson's, since he recognizes that later events, such as marriage, can help to resolve both current and past developmental crises. For the woman, but not for the man, the problems of identity and intimacy may be solved concurrently.

Objections to Erikson's formulations have come from other directions as well. Robert W. White, Erikson's good friend and colleague at Harvard, has a long-standing (and warm-hearted) debate with Erikson over his life stages. White believes that his own theory of "competence motivation," a theory that has received wide recognition, can account for the phenomenon of ego development much more economically than can Erikson's stages. Erikson has, however, little interest in debating the validity of the stages he has described. As an artist, he recognizes that there are many different ways to view one and the same phenomenon and that a perspective that is congenial to one person will be repugnant to another. He offers his stage-wise description of the life cycle for those who find such perspectives congenial and not as a world view that everyone should adopt.

* * *

· Changing the Game from "Get the Teacher" to "Learn"*

Robert L. Hamblin, David Buckholdt, Donald Bushell, Desmond Ellis, and Daniel Ferritor

Almost any educator of experience will assure you that it is next to impossible—and often actually impossible—to teach normal classroom subjects to

* From *Trans-action,* vol. 6, no. 3 (January, 1969). Copyright © January, 1969, by Trans-action, Inc., New Brunswick, New Jersey.

children who have extreme behavior problems, or who are "too young." Yet, at four experimental classrooms of the Central Midwestern Regional Educational Laboratories (CEMREL), we have been bringing about striking changes in the behavior and learning progress of just such children.

In the eighteen months of using new exchange systems and working with different types of problem children, we have seen these results:

- Extraordinarily aggressive boys, who had not previously responded to therapy, have been tamed.
- Two-year-olds have learned to read about as fast and as well as their five-year-old classmates.
- Four ghetto children, too shy, too withdrawn to talk, have become better than average talkers.
- Several autistic children, who were either mute or could only parrot sounds, have developed functional speech, have lost their bizarre and disruptive behavior patterns, and their relationships with parents and other children have improved. All of these children are on the road to normality.

Our system is deceptively simple. Superficially, in fact, it may not even seem new—although, in detail, it has never been tried in precisely this form in the classroom before. In essence, we simply reinforce "good" behavior and nonpunitively discourage "bad" behavior. We structure a social exchange so that as the child progresses, we reinforce this behavior—give him something that he values, something that shows our approval. Therefore, he becomes strongly motivated to continue his progress. To terminate bizarre, disruptive, or explosive patterns, we stop whatever has been reinforcing that undesirable behavior—actions or attention that teachers or parents have unwittingly been giving him in exchange, often in the belief that they were punishing and thus discouraging him. Study after study has shown that, whenever a child persists in behaving badly, some adult has, perhaps inadvertently, been rewarding him for it.

"Socialization" is the term that sociologists use to describe the process of transforming babies—who can do little but cry, eat, and sleep—into adults who can communicate and function rather effectively in their society. Socialization varies from culture to culture, and, while it is going on all around us, we are seldom aware of it. But when normal socialization breaks down, "problems" occur—autism, nonverbal or hyperaggressive behavior, retardation, delinquency, crime, and so on.

The authors, after years of often interesting but, by and large, frustrating research, realized that the more common theories of child development (Freudian, neo-Freudian, the developmental theories of Gesell and Piaget, and a number of others) simply do not satisfactorily explain the socialization process in children. Consequently, in desperation we began to move toward the learning theories and then toward the related exchange theories of social structure. Since then, working with problem children, our view has gradually been amplified and refined. Each experimental classroom has given us a different looking glass. In each, we can see the child in different conditions, and can alter the conditions that hinder his socialization into a civilized, productive adult capable of happiness.

By the time they become students, most children love to play with one another, to do art work, to cut and paste, to play with Playdoh, to climb and swing on the playground, and so on. Most preschools also serve juice and cookie snacks and some have television sets or movies. There is, consequently, no dearth of prizes for us to reward the children [with] for good behavior. The problem is not in finding reinforcers but in managing them.

THE BASIC SYSTEM: TOKEN EXCHANGE

One of the simplest and most effective ways, we found, was to develop a token-exchange system. The tokens we use are plastic discs that children can earn. A child who completes his arithmetic or reading may earn a dozen tokens, given one by one as he proceeds through the lessons. And at the end of the lesson period comes the reward.

Often it is a movie. The price varies. For four tokens, a student can watch while sitting on the floor; for eight, he gets a chair; for twelve, he can watch while sitting on the table. Perhaps the view is better from the table–anyway, the children almost always buy it, if they have enough tokens. But, if they dawdled so much that they earned fewer than four, they are "timed out" into the hall while the others see the movie. Throughout the morning, therefore, the children earn, then spend, then earn, then spend.

This token-exchange system is very powerful. It can create beneficial changes in a child's behavior, his emotional reactions, and, ultimately, even his approach to life. But it is not easy to set up, nor simple to maintain.

At the beginning, the tokens are meaningless to the children; so, to make them meaningful, we pair them with M&M candies or something similar. As the child engages in the desired behavior (or a reasonable facsimile), the teacher gives him a "Thank you," an M&M, and a token. At first, the children are motivated by the M&M's and have to be urged to hold on to the tokens; but then they find that the tokens can be used to buy admission to the movie, Playdoh, or other good things. The teacher tells them the price and asks them to count out the tokens. Increasingly, the teacher "forgets" the M&M's. In two or three days, the children get no candy, just the approval and the tokens. By then, they have learned.

There are problems in maintaining a token exchange. Children become disinterested in certain reinforcers if they are used too frequently and, therefore, in the tokens that buy them. For instance, young children will work very hard to save up tokens to play with Playdoh once a week; if they are offered Playdoh every day, the charm quickly fades. Some activities–snacks, movies, walks outdoors–are powerful enough to be used every day.

As noted, the children we worked with had different behavior problems, reflecting various kinds of breakdowns in the socialization process. Each experiment we conducted concentrated on a particular type of maladjustment or a particular group of maladjusted children to see how a properly structured exchange system might help them. Let us look at each experiment, to see how each problem was affected.

AGGRESSION

Unfortunately, our world reinforces and rewards aggressive behavior. Some cultures and some families are open and brazen about it—they systematically and consciously teach their young that it is desirable, and even virtuous, to attack certain other individuals or groups. The child who can beat up the other kids on the playground is sometimes respected by his peers and perhaps by his parents; the soldier achieves glory in combat. The status, the booty, or the bargaining advantages that come to the aggressor can become reinforcement to continue and escalate his aggressions.

In more civilized cultures, the young are taught not to use aggression, and we try to substitute less harmful patterns. But, even so, aggression is sometimes reinforced unintentionally—and the consequences, predictably, are the same as if the teaching [was] deliberate.

In the long run, civilized cultures are not kind to hyperaggressive children. A recent survey in England, for instance, found that the great majority of teachers felt that aggressive behavior by students disturbed more classrooms than anything else and caused the most anxiety among teachers. At least partly as a result, the dropout rates for the hyperaggressives was two and a half times as great as for "normals," and disproportionate numbers of hyperaggressives turned up in mental clinics.

The traditional treatment for aggressive juveniles is punishment—often harsh punishment. This is not only of dubious moral value, but generally it does not work.

We took seriously—perhaps for the first time—the theory that aggression is a type of exchange behavior. Boys become aggressive because they get something for it; they continue to be aggressive because the rewards are continuing. To change an aggressive pattern in our experimental class at Washington University, therefore, we had to restructure appropriately the exchange system in which the boys were involved.

As subjects, we (Ellis and Hamblin) found five extraordinarily aggressive four-year-old boys, all referred to us by local psychiatrists and social workers who had been able to do very little with them. Next, we hired a trained teacher. We told her about the boys and the general nature of the experiment—then gave her her head. That is, she was allowed to use her previous training during the first period—and this would provide a baseline comparison with what followed after. We hoped she would act like the "typical teacher." We suspect that she did.

LET'S PLAY "GET THE TEACHER"

The teacher was, variously, a strict disciplinarian, wise counselor, clever arbitrator, and sweet peacemaker. Each role failed miserably. After the eighth day, the average of the children was 150 sequences of aggression per day! Here is what a mere four minutes of those sequences were like:

Mike, John, and Dan are seated together, playing with pieces of Playdoh. Barry, some distance from the others, is seated and also is playing with Playdoh. The children, except Barry, are talking about what they are making. Time is 9:10 A.M. Miss Sally, the teacher, turns toward the children and says, "It's time for a lesson. Put your Playdoh away." Mike says "Not me." John says "Not me." Dan says "Not me." Miss Sally moves toward Mike. Mike throws some Playdoh in Miss Sally's face. Miss Sally jerks back, then moves forward rapidly and snatches Playdoh from Mike. Puts Playdoh in her pocket. Mike screams for Playdoh, says he wants to play with it. Mike moves toward Miss Sally and attempts to snatch the Playdoh from Miss Sally's pocket. Miss Sally pushes him away. Mike kicks Miss Sally on the leg. Kicks her again and demands the return of his Playdoh. Kicks Miss Sally again. Picks up a small steel chair and throws it at Miss Sally. Miss Sally jumps out of the way. Mike picks up another chair and throws it more violently. Miss Sally cannot move in time. Chair strikes her foot. Miss Sally pushes Mike down on the floor. Mike starts up. Pulls over one chair. Now another [and] another. Stops a moment. Miss Sally is picking up chairs, Mike looks at Miss Sally. Miss Sally moves toward Mike. Mike runs away.

John wants his Playdoh. Miss Sally says "No." He joins Mike in pulling over chairs and attempts to grab Playdoh from Miss Sally's pocket. Miss Sally pushes him away roughly. John is screaming that he wants to play with his Playdoh. Moves toward phonograph. Pulls it off the table; lets it crash onto the floor. Mike has his coat on. Says he is going home. Miss Sally asks Dan to bolt the door. Dan gets to the door at the same time as Mike. Mike hits Dan in the face. Dan's nose is bleeding. Miss Sally walks over to Dan, turns to the others, and says that she is taking Dan to the washroom, and that, while she is away, they may play with the Playdoh. Returns Playdoh from pocket to Mike and John. Time: 9:14 A.M.

Wild? Very. These were barbarous little boys who enjoyed battle. Miss Sally did her best, but they were just more clever than she, and they *always* won. Whether Miss Sally wanted to or not, they could always drag her into the fray and just go at it harder and harder until she capitulated. She was finally driven to their level, trading a kick for a kick and a spit in the face for a spit in the face.

What Miss Sally did not realize [was] that she had inadvertently structured an exchange where she consistently reinforced aggression. First, as noted, whenever she fought with them, she *always lost.* Second, more subtly, she reinforced their aggressive pattern by giving it serious attention—by looking, talking, scolding, cajoling, becoming angry, even striking back. These boys were playing a teasing game called "Get the Teacher." The more she showed that she was bothered by their behavior, the better they liked it, and the further they went.

These interpretations may seem farfetched, but they are borne out dramatically by what happened later. On the twelfth day, we changed the conditions. First, we set up the usual token exchange to reinforce cooperative behavior. This was to develop or strengthen behavior that would replace aggression. Any strong pattern of behavior serves some function for the individual, so the first step in getting rid of a strong, disruptive pattern is substituting another one that is more useful and causes fewer problems. Not only therapy, but simple humanity dictates this.

First, the teacher had to be instructed in how *not to reinforce* aggression. Contrary to all her experience, she was asked to turn her back on the aggressor and, at the same time, to reinforce others' cooperation with tokens. Once we were able to coach her and give her immediate feedback over a wireless-communication system, she structured the exchanges almost perfectly. The data show the crucial changes: a gradual increase in cooperation from about 56 to about 115 sequences per day, and a corresponding decrease in aggression from 150 to about 60 sequences!

These results should have been satisfactory, but we were new at this kind of experimentation and nervous. We wanted to reduce the frequency of aggression to a "normal" level, to about 15 sequences a day. So we restructured the exchange system. We simply made sure that aggression would always be punished. The teacher was told to *charge* tokens for any aggression.

To our surprise, the frequency of cooperation remained stable, about 115 sequences per day; but aggression *increased* to about 110 sequences per day! Evidently, the boys were still playing "Get the Teacher," and the fines were enough reinforcement to increase aggression.

So, instead of fining the children, the teacher was again told to ignore aggression by turning her back and giving attention and tokens only for cooperation. The frequency of aggression went down to a nearly "normal" level–about 16 sequences per day–and cooperation increased to about 140 sequences.

Then, as originally planned, the conditions were again reversed. The boys were given enough tokens at the beginning of the morning to buy their usual supply of movies, toys, and snacks, and these were not used as reinforcers. The teacher was told to do the best she could. She was not instructed to return to her old pattern, but, without the tokens and without our coaching, she did–and with the same results. Aggression increased to about 120 sequences per day, and cooperation decreased to about 90. While this was an improvement over [the situation] before the boys had ever been exposed to the token exchange, it was not good. The mixture of aggression and cooperation was strange, even weird, to watch.

When the token exchange was restructured and the aggression no longer reinforced, the expected changes recurred–with a bang. Aggression decreased to seven sequences on the last day, and cooperation rose to about 181 sequences. In "normal" nursery schools, our observations have shown that five boys can be expected to have 15 aggression sequences and 60 cooperation sequences per day. Thus, from extremely aggressive and uncooperative, our boys had become less aggressive and far more cooperative than "normal" boys.

Here is an example of their new behavior patterns, taken from a rest period—precisely the time when the most aggressive acts had occurred in the past:

All of the children are sitting around the table, drinking their milk; John, as usual, has finished first. Takes his plastic mug and returns it to the table. Miss Martha, the assistant teacher, gives him a token. John goes to cupboard, takes out his mat, spreads it out by the blackboard, and lies down. Miss Martha gives him a token. Meanwhile, Mike, Barry, and Jack have spread their mats on the carpet. Dan is lying on the carpet itself, since he hasn't a mat. Each of them gets a token. Mike asks if he can sleep by the wall. Miss Sally says "Yes." John asks if he can put out the light. Miss Sally says to wait until Barry has his mat spread properly. Dan asks Mike if he can share his mat with him. Mike says "No." Dan then asks Jack. Jack says "Yes," but, before he can move over, Mike says "Yes." Dan joins Mike. Both Jack and Mike get tokens. Mike and Jack get up to put their tokens in their cans. Return to their mats. Miss Sally asks John to put out the light. John does so. Miss Martha gives him a token. All quiet now. Four minutes later—all quiet. Quiet still, three minutes later. Time: 10:23 A.M. Rest period ends.

The hyperaggressive boys actually had, and were, double problems; they were not only extremely disruptive, but they were also washouts as students. Before the token system, they paid attention to their teacher only about 8 per cent of the lesson time. The teacher's system of scolding the youngsters for inattention and taking their attention for granted with faint approval, if any, did not work at all. To the pupils, the "Get the Teacher" game was much more satisfying.

After the token exchange was started, it took a long, long time before there was any appreciable effect. The teacher was being trained from scratch, and our methods were then not very good. However, after we set up a wireless-communication system that allowed us to coach the teacher from behind a one-way mirror and to give her immediate feedback, the children's attention began to increase. Toward the end, it leveled off at about 75 per cent—from 8 per cent! After the token exchange was taken out, attention went down to level off at 23 per cent; put back in, it shot back up to a plateau of about 93 per cent. Like a roller coaster: 8 per cent without, to 75 with, to 23 without, to 93 with.

NORMAL CHILDREN

These results occurred with chronic, apparently hopeless hyperaggressive boys. Would token exchange also help "normal," relatively bright upper-middle-class children? Sixteen youngsters of that description—nine boys and seven girls, ranging from two years nine months to four years nine months—

were put through an experimental series by Bushell, Hamblin, and Denis Stoddard in an experimental preschool at Webster College. All had about a month's earlier experience with the token-exchange system.

At first, the study hour was broken up into 15-minute periods, alternating between the work that received tokens and the play or reward that the tokens could be used for. Probably because the children were already familiar with token exchange, no great increase in learning took place. On the twenty-second day, we decided to try to increase the learning period, perhaps for the whole hour. The time spent in studying went up rapidly and dramatically–almost doubling–from 27 to level off at 42 minutes.

[Then] the token exchange was taken out completely. The teachers still gave encouragement and prepared interesting lessons as before. The rewards –the nature walks, snacks, movies, and so on–were retained. But, as in a usual classroom, they were given to the children free instead of being sold. The children continued at about the same rate as before for a few days. But, after a week, attention dropped off slowly, then sharply. On the last day, it was down to about 15 minutes–one-third the level of the end of the token period.

[Finally], the token exchange was reinstituted. In only three days, attention snapped back from an average of 15 minutes to 45 minutes. However, by the end of [this period], the students paid attention an average of 50 of the available 60 minutes.

A comparison of the record of these normals with the record of the hyperaggressive boys is interesting. The increase in attention brought by the token exchange, from about 15 minutes to 50, is approximately threefold for the normal children; but for the hyperaggressive boys–who are disobedient and easily distracted–it is about elevenfold, from 8 per cent to 93 per cent of the time. Not only was the increase greater, but the absolute level achieved was higher. This indicates strongly, therefore, that the more problematic the child, the greater may be the effect of token exchange on his behavior.

The high rates of attention were not due to the fact that each teacher had fewer children to work with. Individualized lessons were not enough. Without the token exchange, even three teachers could not hold the interest of 16 children two to four years old–at least not in reading, writing, and arithmetic.

Praise and approval were not enough as rewards. The teachers, throughout the experiment, used praise and approval to encourage attention; they patted heads and said things like "Good," "You're doing fine," and "Keep it up"; yet, when the token exchange was removed, this attention nevertheless ultimately declined by two-thirds. Social approval is important but not nearly so powerful as material reinforcers.

Finally, it is obvious that, if the reinforcers (movies, snacks, toys, or whatever) do not seem directly connected to the work, they will not sustain a high level of study. To be effective with young children, rewards must occur in a structured exchange in which they are given promptly as recompense and thus are directly connected to the work performed.

THE VERY YOUNG CHILD

According to accepted educational theory, a child must be about six and a half before he can comfortably learn to read. But is this really true, or is it merely a convenience for the traditional educational system? After all, by the time a normal child is two and a half, he has learned a foreign language—the one spoken by his parents and family; and he has learned it without special instruction or coaching. He has even developed a feel for the rules of grammar, which, by and large, he uses correctly. It is a rare college student who becomes fluent in a foreign language with only two and a half years of formal training—and our college students are supposed to be the brightest of our breed. Paul Goodman has suggested that, if children learn to *speak* by the same methods that they learn to *read,* there might well be as many nonspeakers now as illiterates.

What if the problem is really one of motivation? If we structured an exchange that rewarded them, in ways they could appreciate, for learning to read, couldn't they learn as readily as five-year-olds?

We decided that, for beginners, the number of words a child can read is the best test of reading ability. In an experiment designed by Hamblin, Carol Pfeiffer, Dennis Shea, and June Hamblin, and administered at our Washington University preschool, the token-exchange system was used to reward children for the number of words each learned. The two-year-olds did about as well as the five-year-olds; their sight vocabularies were almost as large.

There was an interesting side effect: At the end of the school year, all but one of these children tested at the "genius" level. On Stanford-Binet individual tests, their I.Q. scores increased as much as 36 points. It was impossible to compute an average gain only because three of the children "topped out" —made something in excess of 149, the maximum score possible.

In general, the lower the measured I.Q. at the start, the greater the gain—apparently as a result of the educational experience.

THE NONVERBAL CHILD

What happens when ghetto children are introduced into a token-exchange system? At our Mullanphy Street preschool, 22 Afro-American children—aged three to five—attend regularly. All live in or near the notorious Pruitt-Igoe Housing Project and most come from broken homes. When the school began, the teachers were unenthusiastic about a token exchange, so we let them proceed as they wished. The result was pandemonium. About half of the children chased one another around the room, engaged in violent arguments, and fought. The others withdrew; some would not even communicate.

After the third day, the teachers asked for help. As in the other experimental schools, we (Buckholdt and Hamblin) instructed them to ignore aggressive-disruptive behavior and to reward attention and cooperation with social approval and the plastic tokens, later to be exchanged for such things as milk, cookies, admission to the movies, and toys. The children quickly caught on, the disruptions diminished, and cooperation increased. Within three weeks of such consistent treatment, most of the children took part in the lessons, and disruptive behavior had become only an occasional problem. All of this, remember, without punishment.

Our attention was then focused upon the children with verbal problems. These children seldom started conversations with teachers or other students, but they would sometimes answer questions with a word or perhaps two. This pattern may be unusual in the middle classes but is quite common among ghetto children. Our research has shown that children so afflicted are usually uneducable.

As we investigated, we became convinced that their problem was not that they were unable to talk as much as that they were too shy to talk to strangers–that is, to nonfamily. In their homes, we overheard most of them talking brokenly but in sentences. Consequently, we set up a token exchange for them designed specifically to develop a pattern of talking with outsiders, especially teachers and school children.

As it happened, we were able to complete the experiment with only four children. During the baseline period (before the tokens were used), the four children spoke only in about 8 per cent of the 15-second sampling periods. In [the next phase], the teachers gave social approval and tokens *only* for speaking; nonverbalisms, like pointing or headshaking, would not be recognized or reinforced. . . .

[Then] we reversed the conditions by using a teacher new to the school. The rate of talking dropped off immediately, then increased unevenly until it occurred in about 23 per cent of the sample periods.

[Then] the new teacher reintroduced the token exchange for talking, and once more there was a dramatic rise: The speaking increased much more rapidly than the first time, ending up at about 60 per cent. (This more rapid increase is known as the Contrast Effect. It occurs in part, perhaps, because the children value the token exchange more after it has been taken away.)

In the final test, we again took out the token exchange and introduced yet another new teacher. This time the drop was small, to 47 per cent.

We followed the children for three months after the end of the experiment. Their speech level remained at 48 per cent, with little drop-off. This compares with the 40 per cent talking rate for our other ghetto children and the 42 per cent rate for upper-middle-class children at the Washington University preschool.

Frequency of speech, however, was not the only important finding. . . . By the end of [the experiment] they spoke in sentences, used better syntax, and frequently started conversations.

Mothers, teachers, and neighbors all reported that the children were much more friendly and assertive. But some claimed that the children now talked too much! This could reflect individual bias; but there was little doubt that at least one child, Ben, had become an almost compulsive talker.

He was given to saying hello to everyone he met and shaking their hands. So, we terminated the experiment—what would have happened to Ben had we started *another* exchange?

This experiment shows that token exchange can bring on permanent behavior change, but that the culture must reinforce the new behavior. Talking is important in our culture, and so is reading; therefore, they are reinforced. But other subjects—such as mathematics beyond simple arithmetic—are not for most people. For behavior to change permanently, it must be reinforced at least intermittently.

AUTISM

The problems of autistic children usually dwarf those of all other children. To the casual observer, autistic children never sustain eye contact with others but appear to be self-contained—sealed off in a world of their own. The most severe cases never learn how to talk, although they sometimes echo or parrot. They remain dependent upon mother and become more and more demanding. They develop increasingly destructive and bizarre behavior problems. Finally, between five and ten years old, autistic children ordinarily become unbearable to their families, and, at that point, they are almost invariably institutionalized. Until recently, at least, this meant a rear ward to vegetate in until they died.

The breakthrough in therapy for autism came in 1964, when Dr. Ivar Lovaas and Dr. Montrose Wolfe, and a graduate student, now Dr. Todd Risley, simultaneously developed therapy systems using well-established principles of operant conditioning. They were particularly successful with those children who randomly echoed or imitated words or sentences (this is called echolalia).

The therapy systems we have designed, developed, and tested, though similar in some ways to those developed by Lovaas, Wolfe, and Risley, are quite different in others. First, we do not use punishment or other negative stimuli. We simply terminate exchanges that reinforce the autistic patterns and set up exchanges that reinforce normal patterns. Second, our children are not institutionalized; they live at home and are brought to the laboratory for 20 minutes to three hours of therapy per day. Third, as soon as possible —usually within months—we get the children into classrooms where a therapist works with four or five at a time. Fourth, we train the mother to be an assistant therapist—mostly in the home but also in the laboratory. These changes were introduced for several reasons but primarily in the hope of getting a better, more permanent cure for autism.

THE ETIOLOGY OF AUTISM

Is autism hereditary, as many believe? Our studies indicate that this is not the important question. Many mental faculties, including I.Q., have some physiological base. But the real issue is how much physiologically based potential is socially realized, for good or bad. As far as we can tell, the exchanges that intensify autism get structured inadvertently, often by accident; but, once started, a vicious cycle develops that relentlessly drives the child further into autism.

When autism starts, the mother often reacts by babying the child, trying to anticipate his every need before he signals. Thus, normal communication is not reinforced, and the child never learns to work his environment properly. But, even if he doesn't know how to get what he wants through talking, he does learn, through association, that his oversolicitous and anxious mother will always respond if he acts up violently or bizarrely enough. And she must, if only to punish. He thus learns to play "Get mother's attention"; and this soon develops into "Get mother exasperated but stop just short of the point where she punishes and really hurts." Here is an example (observed by Ferritor in the first of a series of experiments by the Laboratory's staff, not reported here):

Larry is allowed to pick out his favorite book. His mother then atttempts to read it to him; but he keeps turning the pages, so she can't. He gets up and walks away from the table. The mother then yells at him to come back. He *smiles* (a sign of pleasure usually, but not always, accompanies reinforcement). Mother continues to talk to the child to try to get him back for the story. Finally, he comes over to the table and takes the book away from her. She lets him and goes back to the bookcase for another book. He then sits down, and she begins to read. He tries to get up, but his mother pulls him back. Again. Again. She holds him there. He gets away and starts walking around the room. Goes to the toy cabinet. Mother gets up to go over and take a toy away from him. He sits on the floor. The mother comes over and sits down by him. He gets up and goes over by the door and opens it and tries to run out. She tells him he has to stay. He *smiles.* She resumes reading. He gets up and starts walking around the table. She grabs him as he comes by. He *smiles.*

A clinical psychologist who had tested Larry did not diagnose him as autistic but as an educable mental retardate with an I.Q. of perhaps 30. Yet, he had gaze aversion, and we suspected that Larry, like other autistics, was feigning inability as a way of getting what he wanted from his mother and then from other adults. He began to respond to the attractive exchanges that we structured for him, and, as we did, he began to tip his hand. For example, at one point when his mother was being trained to be an assistant therapist, the following incident occurred:

Mrs. C. told Larry that, as soon as he strung some beads, he could have gum from the gum machine that was across the room. For about 10 minutes, he fumbled, he whined—all the time crying—saying "I can't." Finally, he threw the beads at his mother. Eventually, the mother had the good sense to leave the room, saying, "As soon as you string those beads, you can have your gum." With his mother out of the room, according to our observers, he sat right down and, in less than 30 seconds, filled a string with beads with no apparent trouble.

Just two weeks later, after the mother had been through our ten-day training program, they again had a "story time." The mother begins by immediately asking Larry questions about this book (the same book used a few weeks before). He responds to every question. She gives approval for every correct answer. Then she tries to get him to say "That is a duck." He will not say it intelligibly but wants to turn the page. Mother says, "As soon as you say 'duck,' you may turn the page." Larry says "Duck" and turns the page. He *smiles*.

After seven minutes, Larry is still sitting down. They have finished one book and are beginning a second.

Most autistic children play the game "Look at me, I'm stupid" or "Look at me, I'm bizarre." These are simply attention-getting games that most adults repeatedly reinforce. Man is not a simple machine; he learns, and, as he develops his abilities, he develops stronger and stronger habits. Thus, once these inadvertent exchanges get established, the child becomes more and more dependent, more and more disruptive, more and more bizarre, more and more alienated from the positive exchanges that are structured in his environment. What is sad is that the parents and the others in the child's life sense that something is terribly wrong, but the more they do, the worse the situation becomes.

It seems to those of us who have been involved in these experiments from the beginning that the exchange techniques and theories we have used have without question demonstrated their effectiveness in treating and educating problem children. Watching these children as they go peacefully and productively about their lessons toward the end of each experimental series is both an exhilarating and a humbling experience. It is almost impossible to believe that so many had been written off as "uneducable" by professionals, that without this therapy and training–or something similar–most would have had dark and hopeless futures.

But it is not inevitable that so many hyperaggressive or environmentally retarded ghetto children become dropouts or delinquents; it is not inevitable that so many autistic children, saddest of all, must vegetate and die mutely in the back wards of mental hospitals.

· A Test of Interactionist Hypotheses of Self-Conception*

S. Frank Miyamoto and Sanford M. Dornbusch

George Herbert Mead constitutes something of a paradox for modern sociology. His works have been widely acclaimed for their fundamental importance to social-psychological and sociological theory. On the other hand, Mead's admirers have often encountered considerable difficulty in formulating research problems within the framework of his views. True, during the last decade initial advances have been made in the empirical study of roles, role-taking, and role conflicts; however, the notions of self and self-conception—two additional key concepts in his system and the system of Cooley and others within this tradition—remain among the neglected problems of social psychology. . . .

The aim of this paper is an empirical study of certain basic assumptions in the interactionist view of the self and self-conception. Essentially dynamic, the interactionist theory of the self is not easily translated into research operations. This paper does not study the ongoing process but concentrates, instead, on static consequences that can reasonably be deduced from Mead. The method here employed is too crude for investigating subtle aspects of Mead's theory, but improvements and refinements of the method are possible. Moreover, many interesting lines of inquiry into the self can be pursued with the method, such as it is.

Our concern is three problems suggested by the interactionist view of the self. First, a basic contribution of Mead and Cooley to the understanding of the self and self-conception lay in their emphasis upon the influence of the responses of others in shaping self-definitions. This principle, once recognized, may appear so self-evident as not to require empirical confirmation. However, it seems of interest to consider any empirical test that will confirm or deny the generalization.

Second, although it is Mead's habit to speak of "the response of the other" as providing the key to the definition of the self,[1] the phrase is somewhat ambiguous, for a distinction may be drawn between (1) the actual

[1] G. H. Mead, *Mind, Self and Society* (Chicago: University of Chicago Press, 1934), pp. 144–49.

* From *American Journal of Sociology,* vol. 61, no. 5 (March, 1956), 399–403.

response of the other and (2) the subject's perception of the response of the other. Mead often does not distinguish between these two; but it is consistent with his view that the perception of the other's response is the critical aspect. Will an empirical test support this assumption?

Finally, one of Mead's most illuminating analyses is his account of how the self may take the role of the generalized other. The "generalized other" refers to the individual's conception of the organized social process of which he is a part.[2] This organized social process is composed of numerous specialized roles, and the individual identifies his own role in it and so fulfils his part as to enable the organized process to continue. On the other hand, individuals often enter into social relations wherein the organization of roles is obscure or minimal. In such a case, the individual cannot take the role of the generalized other in Mead's sense; yet, for the individual to act in the situation, some conception of the generalized other may be necessary. What kind of conception of self and others may be employed under these circumstances?

In our research, we used social groups whose members were, at best, loosely joined by friendship and had no definite organized group activity within which to identify their respective roles. They were engaged as individuals, at the moment, in making emphatic judgments about one another. It seemed reasonable to assume that the individual might be able to define—and would, in fact, use—a self-conception based on the *typical* attitudes of others toward him. Hence, the third problem concerns the relation of self-conceptions to the perception of the typical attitudes of others toward one's self.

METHOD

Index of self-conception. In recent years, due mainly to the renewed interest of psychologists in the study of the self, a number of methods have been developed for getting self-evaluations from experimental subjects. In one, subjects are requested to give self-characterizations by means of one of the following devices: checking appropriate words on an adjective check list of self-descriptive terms,[3] responding to a standard personality inventory or to some other form of questionnaire that yields self-revealing responses,[4] or writing out self-evaluative autobiographical sketches.[5] These techniques are designed to reveal the content of individual self-conceptions.

A second method requires subjects to indicate their expected score on some test prior to taking the test—usually an aptitude or attitude scale—thus

[2] *Ibid.,* pp. 152–64.

[3] Theodore R. Sarbin, "Role Theory," in *Handbook of Social Psychology,* ed. Gardner Lindzey (Reading, Mass.: Addison-Wesley, 1954), I, 244.

[4] Ely S. Chertok, work in progress for Ph.D. dissertation in Department of Sociology, University of Washington.

[5] For an interesting variation on the autobiographical method, see the W-A-Y technique of J. F. T. Bugental and S. L. Zelen, "Investigation into the Self-Concept," *Journal of Personality,* XVIII (1950), 483–98.

providing a picture of how an individual evaluates himself.[6] Here the unique feature is the objective measure of performance or attitude against which the individual's expectation (self-conception) may be compared.

A third approach that combines features of the previous two requires subjects in a group of limited size to rate themselves on specified personal characteristics, relative to the others. For example, in a study by Calvin and Holtzman, members of fraternity groups (about twenty members each) ranked all group members, including themselves, on characteristics such as leadership, adjustment, tolerance, drive, and so on.[7] Not only was it possible to use the individuals' self-rankings as a measure of self-concept, but, because each member was rated by all others in the group, it was also possible to derive an average of the others' ratings against which the self-concept could be compared.

For the purpose of investigating interactionist hypotheses of the self, the latter provides the most satisfactory method. In the present study, the index of self-conception was derived in the course of investigating a different problem, namely, the measuring of empathic ability, by means of an adaptation of a method developed by Rosalind Dymond and Leonard Cottrell.[8] The Dymond-Cottrell method requires subjects in a group to give self-ratings as well as ratings on every other group member on a short list of specified personal characteristics.

Source of data. Our data were gathered from 195 subjects in ten groups ranging in size from eight to forty-eight persons. Four groups, totaling 63 subjects, consisted of volunteering members of two fraternities and two sororities. Each member had lived in his own club's house for at least three months. The other six groups, totaling 132 subjects, were classes in sociology, almost all class members of which participated in the study.

Definition of variables. For convenience in identifying the four variables in this study, labels have been adopted and given specific meanings. Our terminology implies no more than is stated in our definitions.

1. "Self-conception": Each subject was asked to rate himself on a five-point scale for each of the following four characteristics: intelligence, self-confidence, physical attractiveness, and likableness. Subjects were told that the middle of the scale should be regarded as "average for *this* group." The analysis for each characteristic is separate, no summing operations being performed in the four ratings.

2. "Actual response of others": Each member of a group rated every other member of the group on the same four characteristics, using the five-

[6] E. Paul Torrance, "Rationalizations about Test Performance as a Function of Self-Concepts," *Journal of Social Psychology,* XXXIX (1954), 211–17; see also Theodore M. Newcomb, *Personality and Social Change* (New York: Dryden Press, 1943).

[7] A. D. Calvin and Wayne H. Holtzman, "Adjustment and the Discrepancy between Self-concept and the Inferred Self," *Journal of Consulting Psychology,* XVII (1953), pp. 39–44.

[8] Rosalind F. Dymond, "A Scale for the Measurement of Empathic Ability," *Journal of Consulting Psychology,* XIII (1949), pp. 127–33.

point scale. The mean response to each subject was computed for each of the four characteristics.

The response of others as here defined does not correspond exactly with Mead's meaning of the term; he obviously refers to responses made in direct interpersonal relations, while our reference is to responses on a paper-and-pencil rating scale. It seems reasonable to assume, however, that the rating-scale response would tend to be a condensed symbolic version of real-life responses, and that the two would correspond sufficiently for the purposes of this investigation. Mead himself often spoke of "the attitude of the other" interchangeably with the term "the role of the other."

3. "Perceived response of others": Each member of a group predicted how every other member would rate him on the scale. The mean prediction of each subject was found for each of the four characteristics.

4. "The generalized other": Each subject was asked to state, using the same scale, how he perceived *most* persons as viewing him. The specific question was: "How intelligent (self-confident, physically attractive, likable) do most people think you are?"

Method of analysis. As in most studies of personal perception, good sampling was not easily achieved. Our sample was larger and more varied than those in most studies of this type, but our findings may not be reliable. Furthermore, data obtained as ours were not sufficiently sensitive to allow refined analyses. Because of these limitations in the design, we set restrictions upon our analysis.

First, since the groups are not a random sample from any known universe, statistical tests of significance are not employed, and the data are examined only for consistent tendencies from group to group. Second, we rely for our test upon inspection of gross differences. For each group, on each of the four characteristics, we determine whether the data support or do not support a specific hypothesis. Thus, the ten groups and four characteristics yield forty results. If a hypothesis is supported forty times in the forty possible tests, we regard it as receiving perfect support; if the score is only twenty supporting tests out of the possible forty, the hypothesis is regarded as having no more than chance success.

THE FINDINGS

Hypothesis 1. According to the interactionist view, the self-conceptions of most persons are likely to be determined by internalization of the behavior of others toward them. If so, those accorded high esteem by others should reflect a higher self-esteem than those poorly regarded. Stating this in the form of a testable hypothesis: *The mean of the actual responses of others to the subject will be higher for those persons with a high self-rating than for those with a low self-rating.* Sorting each group into high and low self-raters and comparing the means of the "actual responses of others" toward the subjects in each subclass, we get the results given in Table 1.

TABLE 1

Characteristic	Hypothesis supported	Hypothesis not supported	Tie
Intelligence	9	0	1
Self-confidence	8	2	0
Physical attractiveness	9	1	0
Likableness	9	1	0
Total	35	4	1

Analysis of the ten groups for all characteristics taken together shows that the hypothesis is supported ten out of ten times.

Hypothesis 2. Earlier, it was suggested that it is of interest to evaluate separately the effect on self-conception of the "actual response of other" and the "perceived response of others." As a first step in this analysis, the same procedure applied in the previous test to the "actual responses" may be applied to the "perceived responses." Again, after the high and low self-raters have been sorted, the hypothesis now reads: *The mean of the perceived responses of others will be higher for those persons with a high self-rating than for those with a low self-rating.* The results are shown in Table 2. Ten out of ten groups showed differences in the expected direction.

TABLE 2

Characteristic	Hypothesis supported	Hypothesis not supported	Tie
Intelligence	10	0	0
Self-confidence	10	0	0
Physical attractiveness	10	0	0
Likableness	10	0	0
Total	40	0	0

Hypothesis 3. The next question is the relative effect on self-conception of the perceived response of others as compared to the effect of their actual responses. Social-psychological theory leads us to believe that the perceived behavior of others toward the self has a more direct influence than their actual behavior. Hence the hypothesis: *Self-conception tends to be closer to the mean perceived response of others to the subject than to the mean actual response of others.* The findings are summarized in Table 3.

TABLE 3

Characteristic	Hypothesis supported	Hypothesis not supported	Tie
Intelligence	8	2	0
Self-confidence	9	0	1
Physical attractiveness	10	0	0
Likableness	7	3	0
Total	34	5	1

Of the ten groups, nine showed a tendency to support the hypothesis, with one class of eleven persons indeterminate, confirming the hypothesis for two characteristics and not confirming for the other two.

Hypothesis 4. It will be remembered that the index of the generalized other was determined by asking each subject, "How intelligent (etc.) do most people think you are?" In effect, the question that was used in testing Hypothesis 2, with respect to specific individuals in a specific group, was broadened to include all other social contacts of our subjects. Hence, it is reasonable to assume that the line of thinking employed in developing the earlier hypothesis should apply here. Again using high and low self-raters to provide subclasses with differential self-conception, the following hypothesis is investigated: *Those persons who have high self-ratings on a characteristic will have a higher mean perception of the generalized other than will those with low self-ratings* (Table 4). Once again, all ten groups showed differences as anticipated.

TABLE 4

Characteristic	Hypothesis supported	Hypothesis not supported	Tie
Intelligence	9	0	1
Self-confidence	9	1	0
Physical attractiveness	10	0	0
Likableness	10	0	0
Total	38	1	1

Hypothesis 5. In rating the "perceived responses of others," the subjects considered only those other persons present in the test group. However, self-conception emerges from interaction in divergent groups. Therefore, it should more closely reflect the way most persons are perceived as viewing the subject than the perception of the responses of any particular group of individuals to the subject. *Accordingly, self-conception should correspond more closely with the generalized other than with the mean of the perceived responses of others.* The results are shown in Table 5.

TABLE 5

Characteristic	Hypothesis supported	Hypothesis not supported	Tie
Intelligence	10	0	0
Self-confidence	5	4	1
Physical attractiveness	10	0	0
Likableness	10	0	0
Total	35	4	1

The hypothesis is confirmed for thirty-five out of forty comparisons. Only for self-confidence is there any tendency to show marked deviations from the expected direction. Analysis of the ten groups shows all ten tending to confirm the hypothesis. A deficiency of the test of Hypothesis 5 is that both self-conception and generalized other are discrete variables, while mean perception is continuous. Essentially, the results show that self-conception and generalized other are usually given the identical rating.

SUMMARY

The results of this research lend empirical support to the symbolic interactionist view of self-conception. Our findings indicate that the response, or at least the attitude, of others is related to self-conception; but they also indicate that the subject's perception of that response is even more closely related. We also find that an individual's self-conception is more closely related to his estimate of the generalized attitude toward him than to the perceived attitude of response of members of a particular group.

These empirical findings do little more than reinforce fundamental notions contained in the interactionist theory of self-conception. Beyond that, however, they suggest possibilities in studying self-conception within the symbolic interactionist framework.

Recent Trends in American Socialization Patterns

The Split-Level American Family*

Urie Bronfenbrenner

Children used to be brought up by their parents.

It may seem presumptuous to put that statement in the past tense. Yet it belongs to the past. Why? Because *de facto* responsibility for upbringing has shifted away from the family to other settings in the society, where the task is not always recognized or accepted. While the family still has the primary moral and legal responsibility for developing character in children, the power or opportunity to do the job is often lacking in the home, primarily because parents and children no longer spend enough time together in those situations in which such training is possible. This is not because parents don't want to spend time with their children. It is simply that conditions of life have changed.

To begin with, families used to be bigger—not in terms of more children so much as more adults—grandparents, uncles, aunts, cousins. Those relatives who didn't live with you lived nearby. You often went to their houses. They came as often to yours, and stayed for dinner. You knew them all—the old folks, the middle-aged, the older cousins. And they knew you. This had its good side and its bad side.

On the good side, some of these relatives were interesting people, or so you thought at the time. Uncle Charlie had been to China. Aunt Sue made the best penuche fudge on the block. Cousin Bill could read people's minds (according to him). And all these relatives gave you Christmas presents.

But there was the other side. You had to give Christmas presents to all your relatives. And they all minded your business throughout the years. They wanted to know where you had been, where you were going, and why. If they didn't like your answers, they said so (particularly if you had told them the truth).

Not just your relatives minded your business. Everybody in the neighborhood did. Again, this had its two sides.

If you walked on the railroad trestle, the phone would ring at your house. Your parents would know what you had done before you got back home. People on the street would tell you to button your jacket, and ask why you weren't in church last Sunday.

But you also had the run of the neighborhood. You were allowed to play in the park. You could go into any store, whether you bought anything or not. They would let you go back of the store to watch them unpack the cartons and to hope that a carton would break. At the lumber yard, they let you pick up good scraps of wood. At the newspaper office, you could punch the linotype and burn your hand on the slugs of hot lead. And, at the railroad station (they had railroad stations then), you could press the telegraph key and know that the telegraphers heard your dit-dah-dah all the way to Chicago.

These memories of a gone boyhood have been documented systematically in the research of Professor Herbert Wright and his associates at the University of Kansas. The Midwestern investigators have compared the daily life of children growing up in a small town with the lives of children living in a modern city or suburb. The contrast is sobering. Children in a small town get to know well a substantially greater number of adults in different walks of life and, in contrast to their urban and suburban agemates, are more likely to be active participants in the adult settings that they enter.

As the stable world of the small town has become absorbed into an ever shifting suburbia, children are growing up in a different kind of environment. Urbanization has reduced the extended family to a nuclear one with only two adults, and the functioning neighborhood—where it has not decayed into an urban or rural slum—has withered to a small circle of friends, most of them accessible only by motor car or telephone. Whereas the world in which the child lived before consisted of a diversity of people in a diversity of settings, now, for millions of American children, the neighborhood is nothing but row upon row of buildings inhabited by strangers. One house, or apartment, is much like another, and so are the people. They all have about the same income and the same way of life. And the child doesn't even see much of that, for all the adults in the neighborhood do is come home, have a drink, eat dinner, mow the lawn, watch TV, and sleep. Increasingly often, today's housing projects have no stores, no shops, no services, no adults at work or play. This is the sterile world in which many of our children grow, the "urban renewal" we offer to the families we would rescue from the slums.

Neighborhood experiences available to children are extremely limited nowadays. To do anything at all—go to a movie, get an ice cream cone, go swimming, or play ball—they have to travel by bus or private car. Rarely can a child watch adults working at their trades. Mechanics, tailors, or shopkeepers are either out of sight or unapproachable. A child cannot listen to gossip at the post office as he once did. And there are no abandoned houses, barns, or attics to break into. From a young point of view, it's a dull world.

Hardly any of this really matters, for children aren't home much, anyway. A child leaves the house early in the day, on a schoolbound bus, and it's almost suppertime when he gets back. There may not be anybody home when he gets there. If his mother isn't working, at least part-time (more than a third of all mothers are), she's out a lot—because of social obligations, not just friends—doing things for the community. The child's father leaves home in the morning before the child does. It takes the father an hour and a half to get to work. He's often away weekends, not to mention absences during the week.

If a child is not with his parents or other adults, with whom does he spend his time? With other kids, of course—in school, after school, over weekends, on holidays. In these relationships, he is further restricted to children of his own age and the same socio-economic background. The pattern was set when the old neighborhood school was abandoned as inefficient. Consolidated schools brought homogeneous grouping by age, and the homogenizing process more recently has been extended to segregate children by levels of ability; consequently, from the preschool years onward the child is dealing principally with replicas of the stamp of his own environment. Whereas social invitations used to be extended to entire families on a neighborhood basis, the cocktail party of nowadays has its segregated equivalent for every age group down to the toddlers.

It doesn't take the children very long to learn the lesson adults teach: Latch onto your peers. But, to latch, he must contend with a practical problem. He must hitch a ride. Anyone going in the right direction can take him. But, if no one is going in that direction just then, the child can't get there.

The child who can't go somewhere else stays home and does what everybody else does at home: He watches TV. Studies indicate that American youngsters see more TV than children in any other country do. By the late 1950's, the TV-watching figure had risen to two hours a day for the average five-year-old, three hours a day during the watching peak age period of twelve to fourteen years.

In short, whereas American children used to spend much of their time with parents and other grownups, more and more waking hours are now lived in the world of peers and of the television screen.

What do we know about the influence of the peer group, or of television, on the lives of young children? Not much.

The prevailing view in American society (indeed, in the West generally) holds that the child's psychological development, to the extent that it is susceptible to environmental influence, is determined almost entirely by the parents and within the first six years of life. Scientific investigators–who are, of course, products of their own culture, imbued with its tacit assumptions about human nature–have acted accordingly. Western studies of influences on personality development in childhood overwhelmingly take the form of research on parent-child relations, with the peer group, or other extraparental influences, scarcely being considered.

In other cultures, this is not always so. A year ago, at the International Congress of Psychology in Moscow, it was my privilege to chair a symposium on "Social Factors in Personality Development." Of a score of papers presented, about half were from the West (mostly American) and half from the Socialist countries (mostly Russian). Virtually without exception, the Western reports dealt with parent-child relationships; those from the Soviet Union and other East European countries focused equally exclusively on the influence of the peer group or, as they call it, the children's collective.

Some relevant studies have been carried out in our own society. For example, I, with others, have done research on a sample of American adolescents from middle-class families. We have found that children who reported their parents away from home for long periods of time rated significantly lower on such characteristics as responsibility and leadership. Perhaps because it was more pronounced, absence of the father was more critical than that of the mother, particularly in its effect on boys. Similar results have been reported in studies of the effects of father-absence among soldiers' families during World War II, in homes of Norwegian sailors and whalers, and in Negro households with missing fathers, both in the West Indies and in the United States. In general, father absence contributes to low motivation for achievement, inability to defer immediate for later gratification, low self-esteem, susceptibility to group influence, and juvenile delinquency. All of these effects are much more marked for boys than for girls.

The fact that father-absence increases susceptibility to group influence leads us directly to the question of the impact of the peer group on the child's attitudes and behavior. The first–and, as yet, the only–comprehensive research on this question was carried out by two University of North Carolina sociologists, Charles Bowerman and John Kinch, in 1959. Working with a sample of several hundred students from the fourth to the tenth grades in the Seattle school system, these investigators studied age trends in the tendency of children to turn to parents versus peers for opinion, advice, or company in various activities. In general, there was a turning point at about the seventh grade. Before that, the majority looked mainly to their parents as models, companions, and guides to behavior; thereafter, the children's peers had equal or greater influence.

Although I can cite no documentation from similar investigators since then, I suspect the shift comes earlier now and is more pronounced.

In the early 1960's, the power of the peer group was documented even more dramatically by James Coleman in his book *The Adolescent Society*. Coleman investigated the values and behaviors of teen-agers in eight large American high schools. He reported that the aspirations and actions of American adolescents were primarily determined by the "leading crowd" in the school society. For boys in this leading crowd, the hallmark of success was glory in athletics; for girls, it was the popular date.

Intellectual achievement was, at best, a secondary value. The most intellectually able students were not those getting the best grades. The classroom wasn't where the action was. The students who did well were "not really those of highest intelligence, but only the ones who were willing to work hard at a relatively unrewarded activity."

The most comprehensive study relevant to the subject of our concern here was completed only a year ago by the same James Coleman. The data were obtained from more than 600,000 children in grades one to twelve in 4,000 schools carefully selected as representative of public education in the United States. An attempt was made to assess the relative contribution to the child's intellectual development (as measured by standardized intelligence and achievement tests) of the following factors: (1) family background (e.g., parents' education, family size, presence in the home of reading materials, records, etc.); (2) school characteristics (e.g., per pupil expenditure, classroom size, laboratory and library facilities, etc.); (3) teacher characteristics (e.g., background, training, years of experience, verbal skills, etc.); and (4) characteristics of other children in the same school (e.g., their background, academic achievement, career plans, etc.).

Of the many findings of the study, two were particularly impressive; the first was entirely expected, the second somewhat surprising. The expected finding was that home background was the most important element in determining how well the child did at school, more important than any of all aspects of the school that the child attended. This generalization, while especially true for Northern whites, applied to a lesser degree to Southern whites and Northern Negroes, and was actually reversed for Southern Negroes, for whom the characteristics of the school were more important than those of the home. The child apparently drew sustenance from wherever sustenance was most available. Where the home had most to offer, the home was the most determining; but where the school could provide more stimulation than the home, the school was the more influential factor.

The second major conclusion concerned the aspects of the school environment that contributed most to the child's intellectual achievement. Surprisingly enough, such items as per pupil expenditure, number of children per class, laboratory space, number of volumes in the school library, and the presence or absence of ability grouping were of negligible significance.

Teacher qualifications accounted for some of the child's achievement. But by far the most important factor was the pattern of characteristics of the other children attending the same school. Specifically, if a lower-class child had schoolmates who came from advantaged homes, he did reasonably well; but, if all the other children also came from deprived backgrounds, he did poorly.

What about the other side of the story? What happens to a middle-class child in a predominantly lower-class school? Is he pulled down by his classmates? According to Coleman's data, the answer is no; the performance of the advantaged children remains unaffected. It is as though good home background had immunized them against the possibility of contagion.

This is the picture so far as academic achievement is concerned. How about other aspects of psychological development? Specifically, how about social behavior—such qualities as responsibility, consideration for others, or, at the opposite pole, aggressiveness or delinquent behavior? How are these affected by the child's peer group?

The Coleman study obtained no data on this score. Some light has been shed on the problem, however, by an experiment that my Cornell colleagues and I recently carried out with school children in the United States and in the Soviet Union. Working with a sample of more than 150 sixth-graders (from six classrooms) in each country, we placed the children in situations in which we could test their readiness to engage in morally disapproved behavior, such as cheating on a test, denying responsibility for property damage, etc. The results indicated that American children were far more ready to take part in such actions.

The effect of the peer group (friends in school) was quite different in the two societies. When told that their friends would know of their actions, American children were even more willing to engage in misconduct. Soviet youngsters showed just the opposite tendency. In their case, the peer group operated to support the values of the adult society, at least at their age level.

We believe these contrasting results are explained, in part, by the differing role of the peer group in the two societies. In the Soviet Union, *vospitanie,* or character development, is regarded as an integral part of the process of education, and its principal agent—even more important than the family—is the child's collective in school and out. A major goal of the Soviet educational process, beginning in the nursery, is "to forge a healthy, self-sufficient collective" that, in turn, has the task of developing the child into a responsible, altruistic, and loyal member of a socialist society. In contrast, in the United States, the peer group is often an autonomous agent relatively free from adult control and uncommitted—if not outrightly opposed—to the values and codes of conduct approved by society at large. Witness the new phenomenon of American middle-class vandalism and juvenile delinquency, with crime rates increasing rapidly not only for teen-agers but for younger children as well.

How early in life are children susceptible to the effects of contagion? Professor Albert Bandura and his colleagues at Stanford University have conducted some experiments that suggest that the process is well developed at the preschool level. The basic experimental design involves the following elements. The child finds himself in a familiar playroom. As if by chance, in another corner of the room a person is playing with toys. Sometimes this person is an adult (teacher), sometimes another child. This other person behaves very aggressively. He strikes a large Bobo doll (a bouncing, inflated figure), throws objects, and mutilates dolls and animal toys, with appropriate language to match. Later on, the experimental subject (i.e., the child who "accidentally" observed the aggressive behavior) is tested by being allowed to play in a room containing a variety of toys, including some similar to those employed by the aggressive model. With no provocation, perfectly normal, well-adjusted preschoolers engage in aggressive acts, not only repeating what they observed but elaborating on it. Moreover, the words and gestures accompanying the actions leave no doubt that the child is living through an emotional experience of aggressive expression.

It is inconvenient to use a live model every time. Thus, it occurred to Bandura to make a film. In fact, he made two, one with a live model and a second film of a cartoon cat that said and did everything the live model had said and done. The films were presented on a TV set left on in a corner of the room, as if by accident. When the children were tested, the TV film turned out to be just as effective as real people. The cat aroused as much aggression as the human model.

As soon as Bandura's work was published, the television industry issued a statement calling his conclusions into question on the interesting ground that the children had been studied "in a highly artificial situation," since no parents were present either when the TV was on or when the aggressive behavior was observed. "What a child will do under normal conditions cannot be projected from his behavior when he is carefully isolated from normal conditions and the influences of society," the statement declared. Bandura was also criticized for using a Bobo doll (which, the TV people said, is "made to be struck") and for failing to follow up his subjects after they left the laboratory. Since then, Bandura has shown that only a ten-minute exposure to an aggressive model still differentiates children in the experimental group from their controls (children not subjected to the experiment) six months later.

Evidence for the relevance of Bandura's laboratory findings to "real life" comes from a subsequent field study by Dr. Leonard Eron, now at the University of Iowa. In a sample of more than 600 third-graders, Dr. Eron found that the children who were rated most aggressive by their classmates were those who watched TV programs involving a high degree of violence.

At what age do people become immune from contagion to violence on the screen? Professor Richard Walters, of Waterloo University in Canada, and his associate, Dr. Llewellyn Thomas, showed two movie films to a group of thirty-four-year-old hospital attendants. Half of these adults were shown a knife fight between two teen-agers from the picture *Rebel Without a Cause*; the other half saw a film depicting adolescents engaged in art work. Subsequently, all the attendants were asked to assist in carrying out an experiment on the effects of punishment in learning.

In the experiment, the attendants gave an unseen subject an electric shock every time the subject made an error. The lever for giving shocks had settings from zero to ten. To be sure the assistant understood what the shocks were like, he was given several, not exceeding the level of four, before the experiment. Since nothing was said about the level of shocks to be administered, each assistant was left to make his own choice. The hospital attendants who had seen the knife-fight film gave significantly more severe shocks than those who had seen the art-work film. The same experiment was repeated with a group of twenty-year-old females. This time, the sound track was turned off, so that only visual cues were present. But neither the silence nor the difference in sex weakened the effect. The young women who had seen the aggressive film administered more painful shocks.

These results led designers of the experiment to wonder what would happen if no film were shown and no other deliberate incitement were introduced in the immediate setting of the experiment. Would the continuing emotional pressures of the everyday environment of adolescents—who see more movies and more TV and are called on to display virility through aggressive acts in teen-age gangs—provoke latent brutality comparable to that exhibited by the older people under direct stimulation of the movie of the knife fight?

Fifteen-year-old high school boys were used to test the answer to this question. Without the suggestive power of the aggressive film to step up their feelings, they pulled the shock lever to its highest intensities (levels eight to ten). A few of the boys made such remarks as "I bet I made that fellow jump."

Finally, utilizing a similar technique in a variant of what has come to be known as the "Eichmann experiment," Professor Stanley Milgram, then at Yale University, set up a situation in which the level of shock to be administered was determined by the lowest level proposed by any one of three "assistants," two of whom were confederates of Milgram and were instructed to call for increasingly higher shocks. Even though the true subjects (all adult males) could have kept the intensity to a minimum simply by stipulating mild shocks, they responded to the confederates' needling and increased the degree of pain they administered.

All of these experiments point to one conclusion: At all age levels, pressure from peers to engage in aggressive behavior is extremely difficult to resist, at least in American society.

Now, if the peer group can propel its members into antisocial acts, what about the opposite possibility? Can peers also be a force for inducing constructive behavior?

Evidence on this point is not so plentiful, but some relevant data exist. To begin with, experiments on conformity to group pressure have shown that the presence of a single dissenter—for example, one "assistant" who refuses to give a severe shock—can be enough to break the spell, so that the subject no longer follows the majority. But the only research explicitly directed at producing moral conduct as a function of group experience is a study conducted by Muzafer Sherif and his colleagues at the University of Oklahoma and known as the "Robber's Cave Experiment." In the words of Elton B. McNeil:

> War was declared at Robber's Cave, Oklahoma, in the summer of 1954 (Sherif *et al.,* 1961). Of course, if you have seen one war you have seen them all, but this was an interesting war, as wars go, because only the observers knew what the fighting was about. How, then, did this war differ from any other war? This one was caused, conducted, and concluded by behavioral scientists. After years of religious, political, and economic wars, this was, perhaps, the first scientific war. It wasn't the kind of war that an adventurer could join just for the thrill of it. To be eligible, ideally, you had to be an eleven-year-old, middle-class, American, Protestant, well-adjusted boy who was willing to go to an experimental camp.

Sherif and his associates wanted to demonstrate that, within the space of a few weeks, they could produce two contrasting patterns of behavior in this group of normal children. First, they could bring the group to a state of intense hostility, and then completely reverse the process by inducing a spirit of warm friendship and active cooperation. The success of their efforts can be gauged by the following two excerpts describing the behavior of the boys after each stage had been reached. After the first experimental treatment of the situation was introduced,

> good feeling soon evaporated. The members of each group began to call their rivals "stinkers," "sneaks," and "cheaters." They refused to have anything more to do with individuals in the opposing group. The boys . . . turned against buddies whom they had chosen as "best friends" when they first arrived at the camp. A large proportion of the boys in each group gave negative ratings to all the boys in the other. The rival groups made threatening posters and planned raids, collecting secret hoards of green apples for ammunition. To the Robber's Cave came the Eagles, after a defeat in a tournament game, and burned a banner left behind by the Rattlers; the next morning, the Rattlers seized the Eagles' flag when they arrived on the athletic field. From that time on, name-calling, scuffles, and raids were the rule of the day.
>
> . . . In the dining-hall line, they shoved each other aside, and the group that lost the contest for the head of the line shouted "Ladies first!" at the winner. They threw paper, food, and vile names at each other at the tables. An Eagle bumped by a Rattler was admonished by his fellow Eagles to brush "the dirt" off his clothes.
>
> But, after the second experimental treatment,
>
> . . . The members of the two groups began to feel more friendly to each other. For example, a Rattler whom the Eagles disliked for his

sharp tongue and skill in defeating them became a "good egg." The boys stopped shoving in the meal line. They no longer called each other names and sat together at the table. New friendships developed between individuals in the two groups.

In the end, the groups were actively seeking opportunities to mingle, to entertain and "treat" each other. They decided to hold a joint campfire. They took turns presenting skits and songs. Members of both groups requested that they go home together on the same bus, rather than on the separate buses in which they had come. On the way, the bus stopped for refreshments. One group still had $5, which they had won as a prize in a contest. They decided to spend this sum on refreshments. On their own initiative, they had invited their former rivals to be their guests for malted milks.

How were each of these effects achieved? Treatment One has a familiar ring:

> . . . To produce friction between the groups of boys, we arranged a tournament of games: baseball, touch football, a tug-of-war, a treasure hunt, and so on. The tournament started in a spirit of good sportsmanship. But, as the play progressed, good feeling soon evaporated.

How does one turn hatred into harmony? Before undertaking this task, Sherif wanted to demonstrate that, contrary to the views of some students of human conflict, mere interaction–pleasant social contact between antagonists–would not reduce hostility.

> . . . we brought the hostile Rattlers and Eagles together for social events: going to the movies, eating in the same dining room, and so on. But, far from reducing conflict, these situations only served as opportunities for the rival groups to berate and attack each other.

How was conflict finally dispelled? By a series of stratagems, of which the following is an example:

> . . . Water came to our camp in pipes from a tank about a mile away. We arranged to interrupt it and then called the boys together to inform them of the crisis. Both groups promptly volunteered to search the water line for trouble. They worked together harmoniously, and, before the end of the afternoon, they had located and corrected the difficulty.

On another occasion, just when everyone was hungry and the camp truck was about to go to town for food, it developed that the engine wouldn't start, and the boys had to pull together to get the vehicle going.

To move from practice to principle, the critical element for achieving harmony in human relations, according to Sherif, is joint activity in behalf of a *superordinate goal.* "Hostility gives way when groups pull together to achieve overriding goals which are real and compelling for all concerned."

Here, then, is the solution for the problems posed by autonomous peer groups and rising rates of juvenile delinquency. Confront the youngsters with some superordinate goals, and everything will turn out fine.

What superordinate goals can we suggest? Washing dishes and emptying wastebaskets? Isn't it true that meaningful opportunities for children no longer exist?

This writer disagrees. Challenging activities for children can still be found; but their discovery requires breaking down the prevailing patterns of segregation identified earlier in this essay–segregation not merely by race (although this is part of the story) but, to an almost equal degree, by age, class, and ability. I am arguing for greater involvement of adults in the lives of children and, conversely, for greater involvement of children in the problems and tasks of the larger society.

We must begin by desegregating age groups, ability groups, social classes, and, once again, engaging children and adults in common activities. Here, as in Negro-white relations, integration is not enough. In line with Sherif's findings, contact between children and adults, or between advantaged and disadvantaged, will not of itself reduce hostility and evoke mutual affection and respect. What is needed, in addition, is involvement in a superordinate goal, common participation in a challenging job to be done.

Where is a job to be found that can involve children and adults across the dividing lines of race, ability, and social class?

Here is one possibility: Urbanization and industrialization have not done away with the need to care for the very young. To be sure, "progress" has brought us to the point where we seem to believe that only a person with a master's degree is truly qualified to care for young children. An exception is made for parents, and for babysitters, but these are concessions to practicality; we all know that professionals could do it better.

It is a strange doctrine. For, if present-day knowledge of child development tells us anything at all, it tells us that the child develops psychologically as a function of reciprocal interaction with those who love him. This reciprocal interaction need be only of the most ordinary kind–caresses, looks, sounds, talking, singing, playing, reading stories–the things that parents, and everybody else, have done with children for generation after generation.

Contrary to the impression of many, our task in helping disadvantaged children through such programs as Head Start is not to have a "specialist" working with each child but to enable the child's parents, brothers, sisters, and all those around him to provide the kinds of stimulations that families ordinarily give children but that can fail to develop in the chaotic conditions of life in poverty. It is for this reason that Project Head Start places such heavy emphasis on the involvement of parents, not only in decision-making but in direct interaction with the children themselves, both at the center and (especially) at home. Not only parents but teen-agers and older children are viewed as especially significant in work with the very young; for, in certain respects, older siblings can function more effectively than adults. The latter, no matter how warm and helpful they may be, are, in an important sense, in a world apart; their abilities, skills, and standards are so clearly superior to those of the child as to appear beyond childish grasp.

Here, then, is a context in which adults and children can pursue together a superordinate goal, for there is nothing so "real and compelling to all concerned" as the need of a young child for the care and attention of his elders. The difficulty is that we have not yet provided the opportunities–the institutional settings–that would make possible the recognition and pursuit of this superordinate goal.

The beginning of such an opportunity structure, however, already exist in our society. As I have indicated, they are to be found in the poverty program, particularly those aspects of it dealing with children: Head Start, which involves parents, older children, and the whole community in the care of the very young; Follow Through, which extends Head Start into the elementary grades, thus breaking down the destructive wall between the school, on the one hand, and parents in the local community, on the other; Parent and Child Centers, which provide a neighborhood center where all generations can meet to engage in common activities in behalf of children, etc.

The need for such programs is not restricted to the nation's poor. So far as alienation of children is concerned, the world of the disadvantaged simply reflects in more severe form a social disease that has infected the entire society. The cure for the society as a whole is the same as that for its sickest segment. Head Start, Follow Through, Parent and Child Centers are all needed by the middle class as much as by the economically less favored. Again, contrary to popular impression, the principal purpose of these programs is not remedial education but the giving to both children and their families of a sense of dignity, purpose, and meaningful activity, without which children cannot develop capacities in any sphere of activity, including the intellectual.

Service to the very young is not the only superordinate goal potentially available to children in our society. The very old also need to be saved. In segregating them in their own housing projects and, indeed, in whole communities, we have deprived both them and the younger generations of an essential human experience. We need to find ways in which children once again can assist and comfort old people and, in return, gain insight to character development that occurs through such experiences.

Participation in constructive activities on behalf of others will also reduce the growing tendency to aggressive and antisocial behavior in the young, if only by diversion from such actions and from the stimuli that instigate them. But, so long as these stimuli continue to dominate the TV screen, those exposed to TV can be expected to react to the influence. Nor, as we have seen, is it likely that the TV industry will be responsive to the findings of research or the arguments of concerned parents and professionals. The only measure that is likely to be effective is pressure where it hurts most. The sponsor must be informed that his product will be boycotted until programing is changed.

My proposals for child rearing in the future may appear to some as a pipe dream, but they need not be a dream. For, just as autonomy and aggression have their roots in the American tradition, so have neighborliness, civic concern, and devotion to the young. By re-exploring these last, we can rediscover our moral identity as a society and as a nation.

4. SUGGESTIONS FOR FURTHER READING

BANDURA, A., AND R. WALTERS. *Social Learning and Personality Development* (New York: Holt, Rinehart, 1963).

BECKER, HOWARD, *et al. Boys in White* (Chicago: University of Chicago Press, 1961).

BERKOWITZ, LEONARD. *Aggression: A Social Psychological Study* (New York: McGraw-Hill, 1962).

BRIM, O., AND S. WHEELER. *Socialization After Childhood* (New York: John Wiley & Sons, 1966).*

BRONFENBRENNER, URIE. *Two Worlds of Childhood: U.S. and U.S.S.R.* (New York: Russell Sage, 1970).

COLEMAN, JAMES. *The Adolescent Society* (New York: The Free Press, 1961).*

ELKIN, FREDERICK. *The Child and Society* (New York: Random House, 1960).*

ERIKSON, ERIK. *Childhood and Society* (New York: W. W. Norton, 1950).*

FREUD, SIGMUND. *Civilization and Its Discontents* (Garden City, N.Y.: Doubleday, 1958).*

GOFFMAN, ERVING. *Asylums* (Garden City, N.Y.: Doubleday, 1961).*

HALL, CALVIN. *A Primer of Freudian Psychology* (New York: The New American Library, 1954).*

HOLLINGSHEAD, AUGUST. *Elmtown's Youth* (New York: John Wiley & Sons, 1949).*

MEAD, MARGARET. *Coming of Age in Samoa* (New York: William Morrow, 1928).*

MILLER, D., AND G. SWANSON. *Inner Conflict and Defense* (New York: Schocken Books, 1966).*

NEILL, A. S. *Summerhill* (New York: Hart, 1960).*

PIAGET, JEAN. *The Moral Judgment of the Child* (London: Kegan, Paul, 1932).*

RIESMAN, DAVID, *et al. The Lonely Crowd* (New Haven, Conn.: Yale University Press, 1950).*

SKINNER, B. F. *Beyond Freedom and Dignity* (New York: Alfred A. Knopf, 1971).

SPIRO, MELFORD. *Children of the Kibbutz* (New York: Schocken Books, 1965).*

STRAUSS, ANSELM (ed.). *The Social Psychology of George Herbert Mead* (Chicago: University of Chicago Press, 1934).*

* *Available in paperback.*

5. Social Stratification

INTRODUCTION

An important aspect of the social organization of society involves social stratification—the hierarchical ranking of positions in the social order according to unequal shares of socially valued rewards. Every society has some degree of social stratification. Even in the smallest, simplest, most primitive societies, there is some social ranking according to sex, age, and kinship differences, or differences in hunting or fishing proficiency. Evidence confirming rudimentary social stratification in very primitive societies can be found in the essay on the Nambikuara bands of Brazil's northwestern Mato Grosso in Chapter 9, "Political Sociology." The author, Claude Levi-Strauss, suggests that the Nambikuara chief's privilege of having several wives, which is denied to all other members of the group, may be an essential inducement to perform necessary leadership tasks. Differentially distributed rewards, in this manner, can contribute to social maintenance. In their functional theory of stratification,[1] Davis and Moore advance a very similar view with more formal theoretical precision. As societies grow in complexity, and as they acquire some economic surplus, they inevitably develop a relatively stable, enduring, and heritable system of social ranks.

Once a society arrives at the high degree of social-organizational complexity characteristic of the mass, urban-industrial social order, this hierarchy of social ranks becomes so deeply embedded that it seems impossible to eliminate it. From T. B. Bottomore's discussion of "Classes in Modern Society," it appears that, notwithstanding the efforts of the Soviets—and of some in the capitalistic West—to elimi-

[1] K. Davis and W. Moore, "Some Principles of Stratification," *American Sociological Review*, vol. 10 (April, 1945), pp. 242–49.

nate class distinctions, they continue to exist. Furthermore, stratification systems are very similar throughout modern industrial society. Perhaps the best that can be hoped for is movement in the direction of narrowing the gap between the haves and the have-nots.

Sociologists generally distinguish three main types of stratification systems: caste, estate, and class societies. A caste system consists of an array of closed social groups that exhibit a fixed order of superiority and inferiority. Intimate association, mobility, and intermarriage between castes are forbidden. The system is sanctioned by religion and the mores. One's caste position is based on ascription (birth). India best exemplifies a caste society.

An estate system of social stratification is based on hereditary relationships to land. Each estate constitutes a distinct stratum (a group of individuals and families who share similar social rank), whose rights and obligations are defined and sanctioned by law. Although mobility is possible, changes in status are unusual. The best-known example of an estate system is that of medieval Europe.

A class system, by contrast, is based primarily upon differences in wealth and income. There are no legal restraints on the movement of individuals and families from one class to another, although such movement may be difficult. Social classes are not closed social groups; they are aggregates of persons with similar amounts of income and property and similar sources of income. Positions in the class order, ideally, are based on achievement. The class system of stratification is found in most modern industrial societies.

These definitions suggest the possibility of social mobility in class society and its diminished likelihood in the caste order. However, some mobility actually occurs in caste societies as a result of changes in science and technology, in economic structures, in educational arrangements, in ideologies, or in the structure of authority and power; some castes may move up in status, others down. For example, a shoemaker subcaste, consisting of a group of highly skilled craftsmen, could experience a loss in status with the importation of mass-produced, low-cost shoes. Or a local subcaste may be able to accumulate sufficient wealth to buy land, thus entering a more highly valued occupation than the one it was in. Mobility in caste society, when it occurs, generally involves group mobility. Geographical mobility is also likely to affect social mobility in a caste system. A person who leaves his local village subcaste, moves to a city, and enters a secular occupation may find that his old social rank has a higher evaluation in his new community; the anonymity of the city facilitates social mobility.

In presumably open class societies, on the other hand, many, if not most, social ranks are passed from one generation to the next. The son of a railway porter is considerably less likely to become socially prominent than the kin of a Rockefeller or a Roosevelt. Within actual societies, there are both caste and class elements; societies can be conceived of as situated along a continuum exhibiting varying degrees of class or caste features. The estate society represents a type situated between these extremes but decidedly closer to the caste end of the continuum.

A social class is defined as a group of people who share a more or less similar rank and some similarity of behavior and values. Most laymen believe that income or wealth is the best indicator of social position. In fact, the best index of social rank depends, in part, on the phenomena being studied. If we were studying political attitudes, a subjective index of social class (the class a person thinks he belongs to) might be most useful in determining how he will vote. On the other hand, if differences in family size are being investigated, an objective method (class measured by education, occupation, or income) might yield the best results. If we had to commit ourselves to a single best indicator of social rank, however, the choice would be occupation. Occupation suggests a person's wealth or income, the degree of his authority and control over others, his education and specialized training, and who his close associates and friends are likely to be—all of which factors come much closer to indicating his total life-style and life chances than a merely economic criterion.

Studies of occupational rank over time indicate that the prestige of various occupations remains relatively stable in industrial society. The National Opinion Research Corporation conducted two studies, in 1947 and 1963, to find out the prestige granted to various occupational positions. A sample of nearly 3,000 Americans was asked to rate 90 occupations as having excellent, good, average, somewhat below average, or poor general standing. The answers were weighted so as to yield a score from 1 to 100 for each occupation. In 1963, Supreme Court justice received 94, the highest ranking; physician, 93; college professor, 90; trained machinist, 75; mail carrier, 66; filling-station attendant, 51; and the lowest category, shoeshiner, 34. These were substantially the same as the findings in 1947. Moreover, these studies found considerable agreement among respondents on the relative standings of various occupational categories. Cross-national comparisons, including data from several underdeveloped nations, also show little variation in the prestige ranking of occupations. These findings strongly suggest that there is a relatively fixed hierarchy of prestige associated with the positions and institutions of industrial society.

Belonging to a particular social class has dramatic consequences for one's life chances. Greater likelihood of infant mortality, shorter life expectancy, more physical and mental illness, malnutrition, and less adequate health care are characteristic of the lower social classes. The higher in the class scale we go, the taller, healthier, and heavier are the members and the higher their scores on IQ tests. Those lower on the social scale are more likely to be arrested and convicted for crimes and less likely to receive the degree of justice and legal protection accorded to those at the top. And they have much more limited educational opportunities than those available to the rich. The study by Schafer, Olexa, and Polk shows how the poor are sorted out of the high school world and shuttled into the more limited horizons of vocational programs.

The net effect of these and other life-chance differences among the classes ultimately reduces social mobility from one generation to the next. The children of the lower classes are encouraged to assume positions at the lower social levels; the uppers, at the top.

Class membership affects almost everything a person does, thinks, and believes. What his politics is, how actively he promotes it, where and how he lives, what he does in his leisure time, who his associates and friends are, what he reads, his religious participation, his organizational memberships, the size of his family—these are only a few of an infinity of matters affected by class membership. We note in Sheila Johnson's "Sociology of Christmas Cards" that even so trivial and seemingly unimportant a matter as selecting and sending Christmas cards is affected by social class. Johnson's work suggests that, by assuming the life-styles of their social superiors, individuals hope to encourage their own social mobility. What one does is not only an indicator of where one is located in the status hierarchy; it also indicates where one expects to be heading.

One of the results of cross-national social-stratification studies has been the development of the concept of a culture of poverty. Although there is much controversy concerning its existence and components, according to one of its advocates, the late Oscar Lewis, the subculture of poverty consists of a distinctive and remarkably stable and persistent way of life, passed down from generation to generation and involving a sense of alienation, lack of effective participation in the institutions of society, antipathy and cynicism toward the caretakers of society (i.e., the police, government officials, the church), precarious family relationships, early initiation into sex, a trend toward mother-centered families, and a privatized, helpless, dependent, and hedonistic outlook. Lewis argues, in "The Culture of Poverty," that these characteristics are accompaniments of the processes of urbanization and industrialization, and that they are associated with capitalistic society. Although the culture of poverty exists on a small scale in the United States and other highly urbanized and industrialized nations, it is widespread among transitional societies.

Classes in Modern Society*

T. B. Bottomore

The division of society into classes or strata, which are ranged in a hierarchy of wealth, prestige and power, is a prominent and almost universal feature of social structure that has always attracted the attention of social theorists and philosophers. During the greater part of human history, this inequality among men has been generally accepted as an unalterable fact. Ancient and medieval writers, when they touched upon the subject of the social hierarchy, always tended to provide a rationalization and justification of the established order, very often in terms of a religious doctrine concerning the origin of social ranks. This is most apparent, perhaps, in the Hindu religious myths about the formation of the caste system. On the other side, the sporadic rebellions of the poor and oppressed were usually revolts against particularly irksome conditions rather than against the whole system of ranks, and they did not give rise to any clear conceptions of an alternative form of society.

Only in modern times, and particularly since the American and French Revolutions, has social class, as a stark embodiment of the principle of inequality, become an object of scientific study, and, at the same time, of widespread condemnation in terms of new social doctrines. The revolutionary ideal of equality, however variously it was interpreted by nineteenth-century thinkers, at least implied an opposition to hereditary privileges and and to an immutable hierarchy of ranks. The revolutions of the late eighteenth century and the early nineteenth century, directed against the legal and political privileges that survived from the system of feudal estates, brought about an extension of civil and political rights and a greater degree of equality of opportunity. But, at the same time, they created a new social hierarchy, based directly upon the possession of wealth, and this in turn came to be attacked during the nineteenth century by socialist thinkers who believed that the ideal of equality ultimately implied a "classless society."

During the past hundred years, great changes have taken place in the social structure of the advanced industrial countries. The history of this period can be seen, in part, as a record of the growth of equality in new spheres of social life or, as some writers have expressed it, of the growth of citizenship.[1] *Laissez-faire* capitalism—and especially the doctrine of *laissez*

[1] See especially T. H. Marshall, *Citizenship and Social Class* (London, 1950).

* From T. B. Bottomore, *Classes in Modern Society* (New York: Pantheon, 1966), pp. 3–8.

faire, which was far more extreme than the practice—has more or less vanished; and in all the industrial countries there is some degree of central economic planning, some attempt to regulate the distribution of wealth and income, and a more or less elaborate public provision of a wide range of social services. But there are important differences between the two principal types of industrial societies—the Western capitalist societies[2] and the Soviet-type societies of Eastern Europe. In the former, there has been a gradual and limited movement toward "classlessness," which is usually held to be especially marked in the past two decades—the era of the welfare state—and which has resulted from changes in the relative earnings of different occupational groups and in rates of taxation, improvements in education and social services, increasing opportunities for individual social mobility, and, perhaps most of all, from the recent rapid growth in total national income. These changes . . . [however] do not amount to an abolition of social classes. The Western societies are still capitalist, in the sense that their economic systems are dominated by privately owned industrial enterprises, and that very pronounced social differences exist between the group of industrial property-owners and the group of wage-earners.

In the Soviet-type societies, on the other hand, the claim is made that social classes, or at least the hierarchical class structure, have disappeared with the abolition of private ownership of the means of production; and that the construction of a classless, socialist society is under way. This claim was not, at first, very closely examined, even by the critics of Soviet society, who concentrated their attention, during the Stalinist period, upon more blatant features of the social system—the repression of personal freedom and the prevalence of coercion and terror. Indeed, it seems to have been quite widely held at one time that the political dictatorship itself could be explained—in terms of an antithesis between liberty and equality—as a consequence of the attempt to enforce an unnatural equality of condition upon the members of society. But this was seen to be implausible when it was realized that there were great social inequalities in the Soviet-type societies; and, in more recent studies, the discussion has centered upon the emergence of a "new ruling class" in these societies and upon comparisons between the characteristics of elite groups in the Western and Soviet societies.

* * *

The inequalities of social class should not be regarded as identical with human inequality in general. There are other forms of inequality, other kinds

[2] I use the terms "capitalism" and "capitalist society" as they are habitually used by economic historians and sociologists, to refer to an economic and social system existing during a particular historical period, which is characterized principally by freedom of the market, free labor (i.e., individuals who are legally free and economically compelled to sell their labor power on the market), and private ownership of the means of production by industrial enterprises. These, together with secondary characteristics, make it possible to distinguish with reasonable clarity between capitalism and other types of society, such as feudalism or socialist society. This is not to say, however, that actual capitalist societies have remained unchanged since their origins, that there are not subtypes of capitalism, or that mixed and transitional forms of society cannot occur.

of privilege and domination, besides those that arise from difference of social class. Within particular societies, there may be inequalities originating in differences of race, language, or religion; and, between societies, there exist inequalities, such as those so evident today between rich and poor nations, that are the outcome of conquest, of differences in size and natural resources, and of specific historical opportunities and failures. Nor are political rights always determined by class membership, as Marxists sometimes assert. Political power itself may create new social classes, new property rights, new privileges.

It remains true, nonetheless, that the division of society into distinct social classes is one of the most striking manifestations of inequality in the modern world, that it has often been the source of other kinds of inequality, and that the economic dominance of a particular class has very often been the basis for its political rule. Class, therefore, is deeply involved in many of the most vital questions of modern politics and social policy.

Social Class and Life Chances

Programmed for Social Class: Tracking in High School*

Walter E. Schafer, Carol Olexa, and Kenneth Polk

If, as folklore would have it, America is the land of opportunity, offering anyone the chance to raise himself purely on the basis of his or her ability, then education is the key to self-betterment. The spectacular increase in those of us who attend school is often cited as proof of the great scope of opportunity that our society offers: 94 per cent of the high school age population was attending school in 1967, as compared to 7 per cent in 1890.

Similarly, our educational system is frequently called more democratic than European systems, for instance, which rigidly segregate students by ability early in their lives, often on the basis of nationally administered examinations, such as England's "11-plus." The United States, of course, has no official national policy of educational segregation. Our students, too, are tested and retested throughout their lives and put into faster or slower classes or programs on the basis of their presumed ability, but this procedure is carried out in a decentralized fashion that varies between each city or state.

However, many critics of the American practice claim that, no matter

* From *Trans-action,* vol. 7, no. 2 (October, 1970), 39–46.

how it is carried out, it does not meet the needs of the brighter and duller groups, so much as it solidifies and widens the differences between them. One such critic, the eminent educator Kenneth B. Clark, speculates: "It is conceivable that the detrimental effects of segregation based upon intellect are similar to the known detrimental effects of schools segregated on the basis of class, nationality, or race."

Patricia Cayo Sexton notes that school grouping based on presumed ability often reinforces already existing social divisions:

> Children from higher social strata usually enter the "higher quality" groups and those from lower strata the "lower" ones. School decisions about a child's ability will greatly influence the kind and quality of education he receives, as well as his future life, including whether he goes to college, the job he will get, and his feelings about himself and others.

And Arthur Pearl puts it bluntly:

> . . . "special ability classes," "basic track," or "slow learner classes" are various names for another means of systematically denying the poor adequate access to education.

In this article, we will examine some evidence bearing on this vital question of whether current educational practices tend to reinforce existing social class divisions. We will also offer an alternative aimed at making our public schools more effective institutions for keeping open the opportunities for social mobility.

EDUCATION EXPLOSION

Since the turn of the century, a number of trends have converged to increase enormously the pressure on American adolescents to graduate from high school: declining opportunity in jobs, the upgrading of educational requirements for job entry, and the diminishing needs for teen-agers to contribute to family income. While some school systems, especially in the large cities, have adapted to this vast increase in enrollment by creating separate high schools for students with different interests, abilities, or occupational goals, most communities have developed comprehensive high schools serving all the youngsters within a neighborhood or community.

In about half the high schools in the United States today, the method for handling these large and varied student populations is through some form of tracking system. Under this arrangement, the entire student body is divided into two or more relatively distinct career lines, or tracks, with such titles as college preparatory, vocational, technical, industrial, business, general, basic, and remedial. While students on different tracks may take some courses together in the same classroom, they are usually separated into entirely different courses or different sections of the same course.

School men offer several different justifications for tracking systems. Common to most, however, is the notion that college-bound students are academically more able, learn more rapidly, should not be deterred in their progress by slower, noncollege-bound students, and need courses for college preparation that noncollege-bound students do not need. By the same token, it is thought that noncollege-bound students are less bright, learn more slowly, should not be expected to progress as fast or learn as much as college-bound students, and need only a general education or work-oriented training to prepare themselves for immediate entry into the world of work or a business or vocational school.

In reply, the numerous critics of tracking usually contend that, while the college-bound are often encouraged by the tracking system to improve their performance, noncollege-bound students, largely as a result of being placed in a lower-rated track, are discouraged from living up to their potential or from showing an interest in academic values. What makes the system especially pernicious, these critics say, is that noncollege-bound students more often come from low-income and minority group families. As a result, high schools, through the tracking system, inadvertently close off opportunities for large numbers of students from lower social strata, and thereby contribute to the low achievement, lack of interest, delinquency, and rebellion that school men frequently deplore in their noncollege-track students.

If these critics are correct, the American comprehensive high school, which is popularly assumed to be the very model of an open and democratic institution, may not really be open and democratic at all. In fact, rather than facilitating equality of educational opportunity, our schools may be subtly denying it and, in the process, widening and hardening existing social divisions.

TRACKS AND WHO GETS PUT ON THEM

During the summer of 1964, we collected data from official school transcripts of the recently graduated senior classes of two Midwestern three-year high schools. The larger school, located in a predominantly middle-class, academic community of about 70,000, had a graduating class that year of 753 students. The smaller school, with a graduating class of 404, was located in a predominantly working-class, industrial community of about 20,000.

Both schools placed their students into either a college prep or a general track. We determined the positions of every student in our sample by whether he took tenth-grade English in the college prep or the general section. If he was enrolled in the college-prep section, he almost always took other college-prep sections or courses, such as advanced mathematics or foreign languages, in which almost all enrollees were also college prep.

Just how students in the two schools were assigned to—or chose—tracks is somewhat of a mystery. When we interviewed people both in the high schools and in their feeder junior highs, we were told that whether a student went into one track or another depended on various factors, such as his own desires and aspirations, teacher advice, achievement test scores, grades, pressure from parents, and counselor assessment of academic promise. One is hard put to say which of these weighs most heavily, but we must note that one team of researchers, Cicourel and Kitsuse, showed in their study of *The Educational Decision-Makers* that assumptions made by counselors about the character, adjustment, and potential of incoming students are vitally important in track assignment.

Whatever the precise dynamics of this decision, the outcome was clear in the schools we studied: socio-economic and racial background had an effect on which track a student took, quite apart from either his achievement in junior high or his ability as measured by I.Q. scores. In the smaller, working-class school, 58 per cent of the incoming students were assigned to the college-prep track; in the larger, middle-class school, 71 per cent were placed in the college-prep track. And, taking the two schools together, whereas 83 per cent of students from white-collar homes were assigned to the college-prep track, this was the case with only 48 per cent of students from blue-collar homes. The relationship of race to track assignment was even stronger: 71 per cent of the whites and only 30 per cent of the blacks were assigned to the college-prep track. In the two schools studied, the evidence is plain: Children from low-income and minority-group families more often found themselves in low-ability groups and noncollege-bound tracks than in high-ability groups or college-bound tracks.

Furthermore, this decision-point early in the students' high school careers was of great significance for their futures, since it was virtually irreversible. Only 7 per cent of those who began on the college-prep track moved down to the noncollege-prep track, while only 7 per cent of those assigned to the lower, noncollege track moved up. Clearly, these small figures indicate a high degree of rigid segregation within each of the two schools. In fact, greater mobility between levels has been reported in English secondary modern schools, where streaming–the British term for tracking–is usually thought to be more rigid and fixed than tracking in this country. (It must be remembered, of course, that, in England, the more rigid break is between secondary modern and grammar schools.)

DIFFERENCES BETWEEN TRACKS

As might be expected from the schoolmen's justification for placing students in separate tracks in the first place, track position is noticeably related to academic performance. Thirty-seven per cent of the college-prep students graduated in the top quarter of their class (measured by grade-point average throughout high school), while a mere 2 per cent of the noncollege group achieved the top quarter. By contrast, half of the noncollege-prep students fell in the lowest quarter, as opposed to only 12 per cent of the college prep.

Track position is also strikingly related to whether a student's academic performance improves or deteriorates during high school. The grade-point average of all sample students in their ninth year–that is, prior to their being assigned to tracks–was compared with their grade-point averages over the next three years. While there was a slight difference in the ninth year between those who would subsequently enter the college and noncollege tracks, this difference had increased by the senior year. This widening gap in academic performance resulted from the fact that a higher percentage of students subsequently placed in the college-prep track improved their grade-point average by the senior year, while a higher percentage of noncollege prep experienced a decline in grade-point average by the time they reached the senior year.

Track position is also related strongly to dropout rate. Four per cent of the college-prep students dropped out of high school prior to graduation, as opposed to 36 per cent of the noncollege group.

Track position is also a good indication of how deeply involved a student will be in school, as measured by participation in extracurricular activities. Out of the 753 seniors in the larger school, a comparatively small number of college-prep students–21 per cent–did not participate in any activities, while 44 per cent took part in three or more such activities. By contrast, 58 per cent, or more than half, of the noncollege group took part in no extracurricular activities at all, and only 11 per cent of this group took part in three or more activities.

Finally, track position is strikingly related to delinquency, both in and out of school. Out of the entire school body of the larger school during the 1963–64 school year–that is, out of 2,565 boys and girls–just over one-third of the college-bound, as opposed to more than half of the noncollege-bound, committed one or more violations of school rules. Nineteen per cent of the college-bound, compared with 70 per cent of the noncollege-bound, committed three or more such violations. During this year, just over one-third of all the college-bound students were suspended for infractions of school rules, while more than half of all the noncollege-bound group were suspended.

Furthermore, using juvenile court records, we find that, out of the 1964 graduating class in the larger school, 6 per cent of the college-prep and 16 per cent of the noncollege-bound groups were delinquent while in high school. Even though 5 per cent of those on the noncollege track had already entered high school with court records, opposed to only 1 per cent of the college-prep track, still more noncollege-bound students became delinquent during high school than did college-prep students (11 per cent compared with 5 per cent). So, the relation between track position and delinquency is further supported.

We have seen, then, that, when compared with college-prep students, noncollege-prep students show lower achievement, great deterioration of achievement, less participation in extracurricular activities, a greater tendency to drop out, more misbehavior in school, and more delinquency outside of school. Since students are assigned to different tracks largely on the basis of presumed differences in intellectual ability and inclination for further study, the crucial question is whether assignment to different tracks helped to meet the needs of groups of students who were already different, as many educators would claim, or actually contributed to, and reinforced, such differences, as critics like Sexton and Pearl contend.

The simplest way to explain the differences we have just seen is to attribute them to characteristics already inherent in the individual students, or —at a more sophisticated level—to students' cultural and educational backgrounds.

It can be argued, for example, that the difference in academic achievement between the college and noncollege groups can be explained by the fact that college-prep students are simply brighter; after all, this is one of the reasons they were taken into college-prep courses. Others would argue that noncollege-bound students do less well in school work because of family background: They more often come from blue-collar homes, where less value is placed on grades and college, where books and help in schoolwork are less readily available, and [where] verbal expression [is] limited. Still others would contend that lower-track students get lower grades because they performed less well in elementary and junior high, have fallen behind, and probably try less hard.

Fortunately, it was possible with our data to separate out the influence of track position from the other suggested factors of social-class background (measured by father's occupation), intelligence (measured by I.Q.—admittedly not a perfectly acceptable measure), and previous academic performance (measured by grade-point average for the last semester of the ninth year). Through use of a weighted percentage technique known as test factor standardization, we found that, even when the effects of I.Q., social class, and previous performance are ruled out, there is still a sizable difference in grade-point average between the two tracks. With the influence of the first three factors eliminated, we nevertheless find that 30 per cent of the college prep, as opposed to a mere 4 per cent of the noncollege group, attained the top quarter of their class; and that only 12 per cent of the college prep, as opposed to 35 per cent of the noncollege group, fell into the bottom quarter. These figures, which are similar for boys and girls, further show that track position has an independent effect on academic achievement that is greater than the effect of each of the other three factors—social class, I.Q., and past performance. In particular, assignment to the noncollege track has a strong negative influence on a student's grades.

Looking at dropout rate, and again controlling for social-class background, I.Q., and past performance, we find that track position in itself has an independent influence that is higher than the effect of any of the other three factors. In other words, even when we rule out the effect of these three factors, noncollege-bound students still dropped out in considerably greater proportion than college-bound students (19 per cent vs. 4 per cent).

WHEN FORECASTERS MAKE THE WEATHER

So our evidence points to the conclusion that the superior academic performance of the college-bound students, and the inferior performance of the noncollege students, is partly caused by the tracking system. Our data do not explain how this happens, but several studies of similar educational arrangements, as well as basic principles of social psychology, do provide a number of probable explanations. The first point has to do with the pupil's self-image.

Stigma. Assignment to the lower track in the schools we studied carried with it a strong stigma. As David Mallory was told by an American boy, "Around here you are *nothing* if you're not college prep." A noncollege-prep girl in one of the schools we studied told me that she always carried her "general"-track books upside down because of the humiliation she felt at being seen with them as she walked through the halls.

The corroding effect of such stigmatizing is well known. As Patricia Sexton has put it, "He [the low track student] is bright enough to catch on very quickly to the fact that he is not considered very bright. He comes to accept this unflattering appraisal because, after all, the school should know."

One ex-delinquent in Washington, D.C., told one of us how the stigma from this low track affected him.

> It really don't have to be the tests, but, after the tests, there shouldn't be no separation in the classes. Because, as I say again, I felt good when I was with my class, but when they went and separated us–that changed us. That changed our ideas, our thinking, the way we thought about each other, and turned us to enemies toward each other –because they said I was dumb and they were smart.
>
> When you first go to junior high school you do feel something inside–it's like ego. You have been from elementary, to junior high, you feel great inside. You say, well daggone, I'm going to deal with the *people* here now, I am in junior high school. You get this shirt that says Brown Junior High, or whatever the name is, and you are proud of that shirt. But then you go up there and the teacher says– "Well, so-and-so, you're in the basic section, you can't go with the other kids." The devil with the whole thing–you lose–something in you–like it just goes out of you.
>
> *Did you think the other guys were smarter than you?*
>
> Not at first–I used to think I was just as smart as anybody in the school–I knew I was smart. I knew some people were smarter, and I *wanted* to go to school, I wanted to get a diploma and go to college and help people and everything. I stepped into there in junior high –I felt like a fool going to school–I really felt like a fool.
>
> *Why?*
>
> Because I felt like I wasn't a part of the school. I couldn't get on special patrols, because I wasn't qualified.
>
> *What happened between the seventh and ninth grades?*
>
> I started losing faith in myself–after the teachers kept downing me. You hear "a guy's in basic section, he's dumb," and all this. Each year–"you're ignorant–you're stupid."

Considerable research shows that such erosion of self-esteem greatly increases the chances of academic failure, as well as dropping out and causing "trouble" both inside and outside of school.

Moreover, this lowered self-image is reinforced by the expectations that others have toward a person in the noncollege group.

The self-fulfilling prophecy. A related explanation rich in implications comes from David Hargreaves' *Social Relations in a Secondary School,* a study of the psychological, behavioral, and educational consequences of the student's position in the streaming system of an English secondary modern school. In "Lumley School," the students (all boys) were assigned to one of five streams on the basis of ability and achievement, with the score on the "11-plus" examination playing the major role.

Like the schools we studied, students in the different streams were publicly recognized as high or low in status and were fairly rigidly segregated, both formally in different classes and informally in friendship groups. It is quite probable, then, that Hargreaves' explanations for the greater anti-school attitudes, animosity toward teachers, academic failure, disruptive behavior, and delinquency among the low-stream boys apply to the noncollege-prep students we studied as well. In fact, the negative effects of the tracking system on noncollege-bound students may be even stronger in our two high schools, since the Lumley streaming system was much more open and flexible, with students moving from one stream to another several times during their four-year careers.

STREAMED SCHOOLS

As we noted, a popular explanation for the greater failure and misbehavior among low-stream or noncollege-bound students is that they come from homes that fail to provide the same skills, ambition, or conforming attitude as higher-stream or college-bound students. Hargreaves demonstrates that there is some validity to this position: In his study, low-stream boys more often came from homes that provided less encouragement for academic achievement and higher-level occupations, and that were less oriented to the other values of the school and teachers. Similar differences may have existed among the students we studied, although their effects have been markedly reduced by our control for father's occupation, I.Q., and previous achievement.

But Hargreaves provides a convincing case for the position that, whatever the differences in skills, ambition, self-esteem, or education commitment that the students brought to school, they were magnified by what happened to them in school, largely because low-stream boys were the victims of a self-fulfilling prophecy in their relations with teachers, with respect to both academic performance and classroom behavior. Teachers of higher-stream boys expected higher performance and got it. Similarly, boys who wore the label of stream "C" or "D" were more likely to be seen by teachers as limited in ability and troublemakers and were treated accordingly.

> In a streamed school, the teacher categorizes the pupils not only in terms of the inferences he makes of the child's classroom behavior but also from the child's stream level. It is for this reason that the teacher can rebuke an "A" stream boy for being like a "D" stream boy. The teacher has learned to *expect* certain kinds of behavior from members of different streams. . . . It would be hardly surprising if "good" pupils thus became "better," and the "bad" pupils become "worse." It is, in short, an example of a self-fulfilling prophecy. The negative expectations of the teacher reinforce the negative behavioral tendencies.

A recent study by Rosenthal and Jacobson in an American elementary school lends further evidence to the position that teacher expectations influence student's performance. In this study, the influence is a positive one. Teachers of children randomly assigned to experimental groups were told at the beginning of the year to expect "unusual intellectual" gains, while teachers of the control group children were told nothing. After eight months, and again after two years, the experimental group children, the "intellectual spurters," showed significantly greater gains in I.Q. and grades. Further, they were rated by the teachers as being significantly more curious, interesting, and happy and more likely to succeed in the future. Such findings are consistent with theories of interpersonal influence and with the interactional or labeling view of deviant behavior.

If, as often claimed, American teachers underestimate the learning potential of low-track students and expect more negative attitudes and greater trouble from them, it may well be that they partially cause the very failure, alienation, lack of involvement, dropping out and, rebellion they are seeking to prevent. As Hargreaves says of Lumley, "It is important to stress that, if this effect of categorization is real, it is entirely unintended by the teachers. They do not wish to make low streams more difficult than they are!" Yet, the negative self-fulfilling prophecy was probably real, if unintended and unrecognized, in our two schools as well as in Lumley.

Two further consequences of the expectation that students in the noncollege group will learn less well are differences in grading policies and in teacher effectiveness.

Grading policies. In the two schools we studied, our interviews strongly hint at the existence of grade ceilings for noncollege-prep students and grade floors for college-bound students. That is, by virtue of being located in a college preparatory section or course, college-prep students could seldom receive any grade lower than "B" or "C," while students in noncollege-bound sections or courses found it difficult to gain any grade higher than "C," even though their objective performance may have been equivalent to a college-prep "B." Several teachers explicitly called our attention to this practice, the rationale being that noncollege-prep students do not deserve the same objective grade rewards as college-prep students, since they "clearly" are less bright and perform less well. To the extent that grade ceilings do operate for noncollege-bound students, the lower grades that result from this policy, almost by definition, can hardly have a beneficial effect on motivation and commitment.

Teaching effectiveness. Finally, numerous investigations of ability grouping, as well as the English study by Hargreaves, have reported that teachers of higher ability groups are likely to teach in a more interesting and effective manner than teachers of lower ability groups. Such a difference is predictable from what we know about the effects of reciprocal interaction between teacher and class. Even when the same individual teaches both types of classes in the course of the day, as was the case for most teachers in the two schools in this study, he is likely to be "up" for college-prep classes and "down" for noncollege-prep classes–and to bring out the same reaction from his students.

A final, and crucial, factor that contributes to the poorer performance and lower interest in school of noncollege-bound students is the relation between school work and the adult career after school.

Future payoff. Noncollege-bound students often develop progressively more negative attitudes toward school, especially formal academic work, because they see grades–and, indeed, school itself–as having little future relevance or payoff. This is not the case for college-prep students. For them, grades are a means toward the identifiable and meaningful end of qualifying for college, while among the noncollege-bound grades are seen as far less important for entry into an occupation or a vocational school. This difference in the practical importance of grades is magnified by the perception among noncollege-bound students that it is pointless to put much effort into school work, since it will be unrelated to the later world of work anyway. In a study of *Rebellion in a High School* in this country, Arthur Stinchcombe describes the alienation of noncollege-bound high school students:

> The major practical conclusion of the analysis above is that rebellious behavior is largely a reaction to the school itself and to its promises, not a failure of the family or community. High school students can be motivated to conform by paying them in the realistic coin of future advantage. Except perhaps for pathological cases, any student can be motivated to conform if the school can realistically promise something valuable to him as a reward for working hard. But for a large part of the population, especially the adolescent who will enter the male working class or the female candidates for early marriage, the school has nothing to offer. . . . In order to secure conformity from students, a high school must articulate academic work with careers of students.

Being on the lower track has other negative consequences for the student that go beyond the depressing influence on his academic performance and motivation. We can use the principles just discussed to explain our findings with regard to different rates of participation in school activities and acts of misbehavior.

For example, the explanations having to do with self-image and the expectations of others suggest that assignment to the noncollege-bound track has a dampening effect on commitment to school in general, since it is the school that originally categorized these students as inferior. Thus, assignment to the lower track may be seen as independently contributing to resentment, frustration, and hostility in school, leading to lack of involvement in all school activities, and finally ending in active withdrawal. The self-exclusion of the noncollege group from the mainstream of college student life is probably enhanced by intentional or unintentional exclusion by other students and teachers.

Using the same type of reasons, while we cannot prove a definite causal linkage between track position and misbehavior, it seems highly likely that assignment to the noncollege-prep track often leads to resentment, declining commitment to school, and rebellion against it, expressed in lack of respect for the school's authority or acts of disobedience against it. As Albert Cohen argued over a decade ago in *Delinquent Boys,* delinquency may well be largely a rebellion against the school and its standards by teen-agers who feel they cannot get anywhere by attempting to adhere to such standards. Our analysis suggests that a key factor in such rebellion is noncollege-prep status in the school's tracking system, with the vicious cycle of low achievement and inferior self-image that go along with it.

This conclusion is further supported by Hargreaves' findings on the effect of streaming at Lumley:

> There is a real sense in which the school can be regarded as a generator of delinquency. Although the aims and efforts of the teachers are directed toward deleting such tendencies, the organization of the school and its influence on subcultural development unintentionally foster delinquent values. . . . For low stream boys . . . , school simultaneously exposes them to these values and deprives them of status in these terms. It is at this point they may begin to reject the values because they cannot succeed in them. The school provides a mechanism through the streaming system whereby their failure is effected and institutionalized, and also provides a situation in which they can congregate together in low streams.

Hargreaves' last point suggests a very important explanation for the greater degree of deviant behavior among the noncollege-bound.

The student subculture. Assignment to a lower stream at Lumley meant a boy was immediately immersed in a student subculture that stressed and rewarded antagonistic attitudes and behavior toward teachers and all they stood for. If a boy was assigned to the "A" stream, he was drawn toward the values of teachers not only by the higher expectations and more positive rewards from the teachers themselves but from other students as well. The converse was true of lower-stream boys, who accorded each other high status for doing the opposite of what teachers wanted. Because of class scheduling, little opportunity developed for interaction and friendship across streams. The result was a progressive polarization and hardening of the high- and low-stream subcultures between first and fourth years and a progressively greater negative attitude across stream lines, with quite predictable consequences.

> The informal pressures within the low streams tend to work directly against the assumption of the teachers that boys will regard promotion into a higher stream as a desirable goal. The boys from the low streams were very reluctant to ascend to higher streams because their stereotypes of "A" and "B" stream boys were defined in terms of values alien to their own and because promotion would involve rejection by their low stream friends. The teachers were not fully aware that this unwillingness to be promoted to a higher stream led the high informal status boys to depress their performance in examinations. This fear of promotion adds to our list of factors leading to the formation of anti-academic attitudes among low stream boys.

Observations and interviews in the two American schools we studied confirmed a similar polarization and reluctance by noncollege-prep students to pursue the academic goals rewarded by teachers and college-prep students. Teachers, however, seldom saw the antischool attitudes of noncollege-prep students as arising out of the tracking system—or anything else about the school—but out of adverse home influences, limited intelligence, or psychological problems.

Implications. These, then, are some of the ways the schools we studied contributed to the greater rates of failure, academic decline, uninvolvement in school activities, misbehavior, and delinquency among noncollege-bound students. We can only speculate, of course, about the generalization of these findings to other schools. However, there is little reason to think the two schools we studied were unusual or unrepresentative, and, despite differences in size and social-class composition, the findings are virtually identical in both. To the extent that findings are valid and general, they strongly suggest that, through their tracking system, the schools are partly causing many of the very problems they are trying to solve and are posing an important barrier to equal educational opportunity to lower-income and black students, who are disproportionately assigned to the noncollege-prep track.

The notion that schools help cause low achievement, deterioration of educational commitment and involvement, the dropout problem, misbehavior, and delinquency is foreign and repulsive to many teachers, administrators, and parents. Yet, our evidence is entirely consistent with Kai Erikson's observation that "deviant forms of conduct often seem to derive nourishment from the very agencies devised to inhibit them."

What, then, are the implications of this study? Some might argue that, despite the negative side effects we have shown, tracking systems are essential for effective teaching, especially for students with high ability, as well as for adjusting students early in their careers to the status levels they will occupy in the adult occupational system. We contend that, however reasonable this may sound, the negative effects demonstrated here offset and call into serious question any presumed gains from tracking.

Others might contend that the negative outcomes we have documented can be eliminated by raising teachers' expectations of noncollege-track students, making concerted efforts to reduce the stigma attached to noncollege classes, assigning good teachers to noncollege-track classes, rewarding them for doing an effective job at turning on their students, and developing fair and equitable grading practices in both college-prep and noncollege-prep classes.

Attractive as they may appear, efforts like these will be fruitless so long as tracking systems, and indeed schools as we now know them, remain unchanged. What is needed [is] wholly new, experimental environments of teaching-learning-living, even outside today's public schools, if necessary. Such schools of the future must address themselves to two sets of problems highlighted by our findings: ensuring equality of opportunity for students now "locked out" by tracking, and offering–to all students–a far more fulfilling and satisfying learning process.

One approach to building greater equality of opportunity, as well as fulfillment, into existing or new secondary schools is the New Careers model. This model, which provides for fundamentally different ways of linking up educational and occupational careers, is based on the recognition that present options for entering the world of work are narrowly limited: One acquires a high school diploma and goes to work, or he first goes to college and perhaps then to a graduate or professional school. (Along the way, of course, young men must cope with the draft.)

The New Careers model provides for new options. Here, the youth who does not want to attend college, or would not qualify according to usual criteria, is given the opportunity to attend high school part time while working in a lower-level position in an expanded professional career hierarchy (including such new positions as teacher aide and teacher associate in education). Such a person would then have the options of moving up through progressively more demanding educational and work stages, and moving back and forth between the work place, the high school, and then the college. As ideally conceived, this model would allow able and aspiring persons ultimately to progress to the level of the fully certified teacher, nurse, librarian, social worker, or public administrator. While the New Careers model has been developed and tried primarily in the human-service sector of the economy, we have pointed out elsewhere that it is applicable to the industrial and business sector as well.

This alternative means of linking education with work has a number of advantages: Students can try different occupations while still in school; they can earn while studying; they can spend more time outside the four walls of the school, learning what can best be learned in the work place; less stigma will accrue to those not immediately college bound, since they, too, will have a future; studying and learning will be inherently more relevant, because it will relate to a career in which they are actively involved; teachers of such students will be less likely to develop lower expectations, because these youth, too, will have an unlimited, open-ended future; and antischool subcultures will be less likely to develop, since education will not be as negative, frustrating, or stigmatizing.

Changes of this kind imply changes in the economy as well and, therefore, are highly complicated and far-reaching. Because of this, they will not occur overnight. But they are possible, through persistent, creative, and rigorously evaluated educational, economic, and social experimentation.

Whatever the future, we hope teachers, administrators, and school boards will take one important message from our findings: What they do to students makes a difference. Through the kind of teaching-learning process they create, the schools can screen out and discourage large numbers of youth, or they can develop new means for serving the interests and futures of the full range of their students.

Social Class and Life-Style

Sociology of Christmas Cards*

Sheila K. Johnson

Anyone who has ever composed a Christmas card list has pondered the inclusion and exclusion of names on the basis of a variety of fairly explicit considerations. Shall I send so-and-so a card this year, since he didn't send me one last year? Or, I *must* send so-and-so a card this year, even though he probably won't send me one, because I want to be remembered by him. Like the decisions we make about whom to vote for, we like to think of these choices as purely individual, rational matters. Nevertheless, sociologists have demonstrated that, regardless of how and why we choose a candidate, voting behavior can be analyzed as a function of one's socio-economic status, mobility aspirations, ethnicity, and religious affiliation. Similarly, it seems likely that the patterns in which people send and receive Christmas cards can also be explained in terms of certain social characteristics, especially their social status and mobility aspirations.

This proposition first occurred to me several years ago, as I was opening some Christmas cards and noticed that there was a strange disjunction between the cards we were receiving and the ones we had sent out. About half of the cards we received were from people to whom we had also sent cards, but the other half came from people to whom we had not sent cards and to

* From *Trans-action,* vol. 8, no. 3 (January, 1971), 40–45. Copyright © January, 1971, by Trans-action, Inc., New Brunswick, New Jersey.

whom we had had no intention of sending cards, and we ourselves had sent half of our cards to people from whom we had not expected to receive (and did not receive) a card in return. When I studied the names that fell into each of these three categories, it dawned on me that the people with whom we had exchanged cards reciprocally were either relatives or people with whom we were on an equal social footing–professional friends of my husband or personal friends in different but nevertheless comparable occupations. The cards we had sent but to which we had received no reply, I discovered, went invariably to individuals whom *we* wanted to cultivate–people with regard to whom we were, in sociological terms, "upwardly mobile," such as professional acquaintances who might someday prove useful or important or social acquaintances whom we wished we knew better. By the same token, the cards we received and to which we did not reply came from individuals who wanted to cultivate us–some of my husband's graduate students and office employees, the liquor store, the hairdresser, and foreign scholars who obviously expected to visit the United States at some time in the future.

In order to test out my theory, I telephoned several friends shortly after Christmas and asked them to sort the cards they had received into two piles –reciprocals and those to whom they had not sent cards–and also to count up the number of cards they had sent "upward." (Some of the incensed replies to this request would indicate that the nature of Christmas card sending is a very touchy subject indeed.) Those of my friends who continued to speak to me and who complied with my request corroborated my theory. Several couples in their late thirties or early forties who, though of different professions, were rather similar to ourselves in their mobility aspirations and in the number of people they knew who were upwardly mobile with regard to them found that their Christmas cards could be grouped into equal thirds (one-third sent and not received, one-third sent and received, and one-third received but not sent). However, a young graduate student reported that about 70 per cent of his cards were reciprocal, with 30 per cent sent upward and none received from people who were trying to curry favor with him. This is clearly the pattern for those with their foot on the bottom rung of the status ladder. At the other end, several retired people reported that 90 per cent of their cards were reciprocal, with only 5 per cent sent upward and 5 per cent received from people who still regarded them as important. A man who had retired but taken a second job, however, reported that 70 per cent of his cards were reciprocal but that 10 per cent had been sent upward and 20 per cent had come from people trying to cultivate him.

While the percentages of cards an individual sends and receives tell us a good deal about his mobility aspirations, the fact that he sends Christmas cards at all places him rather firmly in the middle class. Members of the upper class–particularly a closed upper class to which one gains admission by birth rather than through the acquisition of wealth–have no need to send cards upward, and sending cards to other members of the upper class is a formality that many are dispensing with. In England, for example, it is increasingly common for upper-class families to place an ad in the personal columns of the London *Times* stating that Lord and Lady So-and-So send warm greetings to all their friends for Christmas and the New Year, as they will not be sending cards. (Several years ago, an upper-class English wit poked fun at these ads by placing one asking *his* friends to send him Christmas cards, as he would not be able to read the *Times* columns during December.) In the United States, because the upper class is more fluid than in England, and because the country is simply too large for all one's upper-class friends to read the same daily newspaper, the custom of sending cards among upper-class individuals has not died out. One would predict, however, that most of the private card sending of the upper class is reciprocal, and that only its business Christmas cards are sent upward, since there is always room for upward mobility in the business world.

Lower-class and working-class individuals also send few or no Christmas cards, but for entirely different reasons. Sociologists have demonstrated that lower- and working-class individuals tend to rely upon tightly knit family networks and neighbors for their friendships, and that they are less geographically mobile than the middle class. Thus, a skilled union man will probably have a large number of relatives living in the same town or same general area as he does, and he will be on friendly terms with many of his neighbors. There is no need to send these people Christmas cards, however, since he sees them nearly every day. He may be upwardly mobile in terms of his job, but this is handled by the union, and a Christmas card to the front office is not likely to do the trick. Only if he is upwardly mobile to the extent of trying to leave his stratum and become a white-collar worker may he take to sending Christmas cards to people who can help him. In that case, he may adopt other middle-class behavior patterns, such as joining various clubs and lodges, in which he will make a broader range of friends to whom he will also want to send cards at Christmas.

SENDERS AND RECIPIENTS

It is the middle class—particularly the upper middle class, consisting of high managerial and professional people—who are the Christmas card senders par excellence. These are the people who are both geographically and socially mobile—growing up in one place, going to college somewhere else, and then moving about as success in one's firm or profession seems to dictate. Kinship ties tend to be far-flung and tenuous, since it would not be advantageous to be tied down to a given area by one's aging parents or embarrassed by the sudden appearance of a lower-class cousin. Friendships are formed among social equals—at school, at work, in professional or social organizations—but these, too, change as one moves up the ladder of success or to a different section of the country. Such are the ideal conditions for the exchange of Christmas cards. Friends and relatives are scattered widely, but one wants to keep "in touch," and there are vast sources of upward mobility to be tapped.

I realize that some people will object strenuously to this analysis of their Christmas card sending and receiving. While I was attempting to collect data on the subject, several of my friends declined to cooperate on the grounds that they did not fit into the pattern I had just described to them. "Really," one of them said self-righteously, "I keep an up-to-date Christmas list, and the only people I send cards to are people who send me cards. There is no upward sending or downward receiving in our family: it's strictly reciprocal." This is pure propaganda, nurtured by the myth of absolute social equality that exists in this country. Everyone can think of some acquaintances to whom he simply *has* to send cards, regardless of whether he gets one in return. The obligatory nature of the act is the real tip-off to the social pressures at work. As for people who receive cards they were not expecting—that is, cards being sent upwards to them—and who then shamefacedly rush out on Christmas Eve to mail the forgotten sender one of theirs, they are simply insecure in their status position. Imagine the president of Chase Manhattan Bank receiving a Christmas card from the janitor and saying remorsefully, "Oh, my God, and I didn't send *him* one." Yet, thousands of people do roughly the same thing when they receive a card from someone who looks up to them. What should they do instead? The answer is nothing, except sit back and enjoy it. Of course, if the upward sender shows other indications of increased social status, it might be wise to send him a Christmas card next year, but that would depend on circumstances ranging far beyond the scope of this article.

In a recent film, "Diary of a Mad Housewife," the husband is shown counting the family's Christmas cards and remarking to his wife, "One hundred and fifty-three. That's fine. Three more weeks to go until Christmas, and we've already reached the half-way mark. . . . We sent out 300." He then goes on to instruct his wife to note carefully who has sent cards to them, since there's "no point" in sending cards the following year to people who have not sent them one this year. Here the authors of the film have missed a bet, however, since the husband is depicted as a social climber of the first water who would clearly insist on sending Christmas cards to certain "important" people—the same people whom he invites to his abysmal party and tries to cultivate in other ways.

In addition to scrutinizing the number of Christmas cards people send and receive for signs of social status and mobility aspirations, one can also tell a good deal about the personality of the sender by the kind of card he chooses. There may still be a few rare individuals who choose every Christmas card individually to suit the *recipient,* but for the most part those days went out with the advent of boxed cards. Somewhat more common is the tendency for people with two radically different constituencies—for example, businessmen who keep their business and private acquaintances well compartmentalized—to choose different sets of cards. However, in such cases it is not at all clear whether the two sets of cards are chosen to suit the different sets of recipients or to reflect the different personality that the businessman wishes to convey to each group—sober and elegant cards for his business acquaintances and mod, swingerish cards for his personal friends. In general, one may assume that cards reflect the sender rather than the receiver, and that a Madison Avenue executive would no more receive a museum card from his Aunt Emma in Vermont than he would send her a Hallmark Santa Claus with a rhymed poem inside.

How can one classify some of the cards that people consciously or subconsciously select to convey not only their Christmas wishes but also their personality? Among university types, whom I know best, there seem to be several distinct patterns. Well-established WASP professors tend to send museum cards or rather small studio cards of abstract design. Usually, the more powerful the professor, the smaller the card. (This appears to be a snobbish, willful inversion of the usual business pattern: the more important the executive, the bigger and more lavish the card. An academic friend argues that there are exceptions to this rule and cites Professor Henry Kissinger, from whom last year he received an absolutely gigantic Christmas card portraying both sides of the globe. I would maintain, however, that this Christmas card merely illustrates Professor Kissinger's defection from the academic ranks and his adoption of the big-business ethos of the Nixon Administration.) Jewish and youngish, slightly left-of-center professors tend to send UNICEF cards, often choosing a design that reflects their area of academic interest–India specialists send the Indian-designed card, Africa specialists send the African-designed card, and so forth. A similar tendency may be observed among government officials.

From professors who have (or think they have) artistic wives, we get hand-screened, hand-blocked, or otherwise handcrafted Christmas cards. From professors who have just had their first child we get (you guessed it) baby photographs; and from professors who are doing research abroad, we often get photos of their children in native dress. From professors abroad sans children, or from those who've been there before, we get interesting Chinese, Japanese, or Thai renderings of the nativity. (The most fascinating Thai card we ever received, from a high-ranking Thai army officer, was a photograph of the gentleman himself posed proudly beside his new Jaguar XKE. *Joyeux Noël* indeed!)

People with strong political convictions tend to remind us of these at Christmas time. Thus, we get our share of CORE and CND cards. From less political but equally morally outraged friends, we get a strange assortment of messages; cards that say on them "printed by spastics" or "designed by the deaf" and cards depicting felled redwood trees or oil-stained beaches. From our wealthier, nonacademic friends, we get cards supporting the Symphony Association and the Junior League.

In addition to all of these types of cards, we get, every year, a couple of photographs of houses. These are never from the academic world–although some professors I know live in very nice houses–because the houses displayed on Christmas cards have a special status significance. Most of the houses that I have seen on Christmas cards belonged to friends who had just retired to Florida or Hawaii, or they were the dream-come-true of people who had finally bought that acre in the country. Whatever the occasion, the house depicted is usually the visible sign of a major change in social status, and it is certainly no accident that the President's Christmas card almost always features the White House.

Finally, and perhaps hardest of all to pin down sociologically, there is the category of Christmas card known as the mimeographed Christmas letter. I would like to hold a contest sometime for the most fatuous Christmas letter, but I'm afraid I'd be deluged with entries. It is hard to attribute the Christmas letter to a particular type of person or a particular station in life, because almost everyone who has ever had an eventful year, taken an exciting trip, or accomplished a great deal has felt the urge to compose one. I have received them from internationally famous professors who were attempting to describe their world travels, from graduate students describing their Ph.D. research in the field, and from relatives recounting the latest family gossip. Perhaps mimeographed Christmas letters should be used as a vanity indicator, since they expose those among us who yielded to, rather than resisted, the pervasive temptation to blow one's own horn.

A MATTER OF TONE

The chief defect of the Christmas letter is its tone—that peculiar half-personal, half-distant note that makes most of them sound as if they were addressed to mentally defective thirteen-year-olds. This tone is the inevitable result of trying to address a single letter to a score or more of different friends. As any letter writer knows, one usually manipulates the tone of a letter to convey a certain personal image to a specific correspondent. If it is often difficult to send the same *card* to business as well as personal acquaintances because of the image to be conveyed to each group, how much more difficult to compose a letter that will ring true to a variety of recipients.

Not only is the tone of Christmas letters muddled by the lack of a clearly defined recipient, but it also often lacks the unifying voice of a single sender. Most Christmas cards can convey the status and life-style of a couple or a family as readily as they can those of an individual. But this is because cards deal in visual symbols, whereas letters traffic in words. It is always hard to believe that a mimeographed letter from "Betty and Bob" is really a joint verbal product, and so one looks for telltale "I's" and "he's" or "she's" to pin down the author. In a genuine Christmas letter, however, such slips never occur, and one is left to figure out for himself who is being the more sanctimonious from sentences that announce: "While Bob worked like a demon interviewing local politicians and village chiefs, Betty spent her time learning how to cook native dishes and teaching English to some of the wives and children." (For the full effect, one must try substituting "I" for each of the proper nouns in turn.)

There are doubtless still other sociological and psychological facets to the sending and receiving of Christmas cards. However, having said all of this, I would not want readers to conclude that I am trying to denigrate Christmas cards, or that I personally am above sending them. Far from it. Having already passed through my family-photograph, foreign, and UNICEF phases, I may even succumb to sending a Christmas letter one of these years. My card this year was a small, high-status museum number depicting a medieval knight being hoisted on his own petard. The motto on his banner reads: *Honi soit qui mal y pense*. I think it suits me rather well.

Is There a Culture of Poverty?

The Culture of Poverty*

Oscar Lewis

Because the research design of this study was concerned with testing the concept of a culture of poverty in different national contexts, and because this concept is helpful in understanding the Ríos family, I shall briefly summarize some of its dimensions here.

Although a great deal has been written about poverty and the poor, the concept of a culture of poverty is relatively new. I first suggested it in 1959 in my book *Five Families: Mexican Case Studies in the Culture of Poverty*. The phrase is a catchy one and has become widely used and misused. Michael Harrington used it extensively in his book *The Other America* (1961), which played an important role in sparking the national antipoverty program in the United States. However, he used it in a somewhat broader and less technical sense than I had intended. I shall try to define it more precisely as a conceptual model, with special emphasis upon the distinction between poverty and the culture of poverty. The absence of intensive anthropological studies of poor families from a wide variety of national and cultural contexts, and especially from the socialist countries, is a serious handicap in formulating valid cross-cultural regularities. The model presented here is therefore provisional and subject to modification as new studies become available.

Throughout recorded history, in literature, in proverbs, and in popular sayings, we find two opposite evaluations of the nature of the poor. Some characterize the poor as blessed, virtuous, upright, serene, independent, honest, kind, and happy. Others characterize them as evil, mean, violent, sordid, and criminal. These contradictory and confusing evaluations are also reflected in the infighting that is going on in the current war against poverty. Some stress the great potential of the poor for self-help, leadership, and community organization, while others point to the sometimes irreversible, destructive effect of poverty upon individual character and therefore emphasize the need for guidance and control to remain in the hands of the middle class, which presumably has better mental health.

* From *La Vida* (New York: Random House, 1966), pp. xlii-lii.

These opposing views reflect a political power struggle between competing groups. However, some of the confusion results from the failure to distinguish between poverty *per se* and the culture of poverty and the tendency to focus upon the individual personality rather than upon the group–that is, the family and the slum community.

As an anthropologist, I have tried to understand poverty and its associated traits as a culture or, more accurately, as a subculture[1] with its own structure and rationale, as a way of life that is passed down from generation to generation along family lines. This view directs attention to the fact that the culture of poverty in modern nations is not only a matter of economic deprivation, of disorganization, or of the absence of something. It is also something positive and provides some rewards without which the poor could hardly carry on.

Elsewhere, I have suggested that the culture of poverty transcends regional, rural-urban, and national differences and shows remarkable similarities in family structure, interpersonal relations, time orientation, value systems, and spending patterns. These cross-national similarities are examples of independent invention and convergence. They are common adaptations to common problems.

The culture of poverty can come into being in a variety of historical contexts. However, it tends to grow and flourish in societies with the following set of conditions: (1) a cash economy, wage labor, and production for profit; (2) a persistently high rate of unemployment and underemployment for unskilled labor; (3) low wages; (4) the failure to provide social, political, and economic organization, either on a voluntary basis or by government imposition, for the low-income population; (5) the existence of a bilateral kniship system rather than a unilateral one;[2] and, finally, (6) the

[1] While the term "subculture of poverty" is technically more accurate, I have used "culture of poverty" as a shorter form.

[2] In a unilineal kinship system, descent is reckoned either through males or through females. When traced exclusively through males, it is called patrilineal or agnatic descent; when reckoned exclusively through females, it is called matrilineal or uterine descent. In a bilateral or cognatic system, descent is traced through males and females without emphasis on either line.

In a unilineal system, the lineage consists of all the descendants of one ancestor. In a patrilineal system, the lineage is composed of all the descendants through males of one male ancestor. A matrilineage consists of all the descendants through females of one female ancestor. The lineage may thus contain a very large number of generations. If bilateral descent is reckoned, however, the number of generations that can be included in a social unit is limited, since the number of ancestors doubles every generation.

Unilineal descent groups ("lineages" or "clans") are corporate groups in the sense that the lineage or clan may act as a collectivity: It can take blood vengeance against another descent group, it can hold property, etc. However, the bilateral kin group (the "kindred") can rarely act as a collectivity, because it is not a "group" except from the point of view of a particular individual and, furthermore, has no continuity over time.

In a unilineal system, an individual is assigned to a group by virtue of his birth. In contrast, a person born into a bilateral system usually has a choice of relatives whom he chooses to recognize as "kin" and with whom he wants to associate. This generally leads to a greater diffuseness and fragmentation of ties with relatives over time.

existence of a set of values in the dominant class that stresses the accumulation of wealth and property, the possibility of upward mobility, and thrift, and explains low economic status as the result of personal inadequacy or inferiority.

The way of life that develops among some of the poor under these conditions is the culture of poverty. It can best be studied in urban or rural slums and can be described in terms of some seventy interrelated social, economic, and psychological traits. However, the number of traits and the relationships between them may vary from society to society and from family to family. For example, in a highly literate society, illiteracy may be more diagnostic of the culture of poverty than in a society where illiteracy is widespread and where even the well-to-do may be illiterate, as in some Mexican peasant villages before the revolution.

The culture of poverty is both an adaptation and a reaction of the poor to their marginal position in a class-stratified, highly individuated, capitalistic society. It represents an effort to cope with feelings of hopelessness and despair, which develop from the realization of the improbability of achieving success in terms of the values and goals of the larger society. Indeed, many of the traits of the culture of poverty can be viewed as attempts at local solutions for problems not met by existing institutions and agencies because the people are not eligible for them, cannot afford them, or are ignorant or suspicious of them. For example, unable to obtain credit from banks, they are thrown upon their own resources and organize informal credit devices without interest.

The culture of poverty, however, is not only an adaptation to a set of objective conditions of the larger society. Once it comes into existence, it tends to perpetuate itself from generation to generation because of its effect on the children. By the time slum children are age six or seven, they have usually absorbed the basic values and attitudes of their subculture and are not psychologically geared to take full advantage of changing conditions or increased opportunities that may occur in their lifetime.

Most frequently, the culture of poverty develops when a stratified social and economic system is breaking down or is being replaced by another, as in the case of the transition from feudalism to capitalism or during periods of rapid technological change. Often, it results from imperial conquest in which the native social and economic structure is smashed and the natives are maintained in a servile colonial status, sometimes for many generations. It can also occur in the process of detribalization, such as that now going on in Africa.

The most likely candidates for the culture of poverty are the people who come from the lower strata of a rapidly changing society and are already partially alienated from it. Thus, landless rural workers who migrate to the cities can be expected to develop a culture of poverty much more readily than migrants from stable peasant villages with a well-organized traditional culture. In this connection, there is a striking contrast between Latin America, where the rural population long ago made the transition from a tribal to a peasant society, and Africa, which is still close to its tribal heritage. The more corporate nature of many of the African tribal societies, in contrast to Latin American rural communities, and the persistence of village ties tend to inhibit or delay the formation of a full-blown culture of poverty in many of the African towns and cities. The special conditions of apartheid in South Africa, where the migrants are segregated into separate "locations" and do not enjoy freedom of movement, create special problems. Here, the institutionalization of repression and discrimination tend to develop a greater sense of identity and group consciousness.

The culture of poverty can be studied from various points of view: the relationship between the subculture and the larger society; the nature of the slum community; the nature of the family; and the attitudes, values, and character structure of the individual.

1. The lack of effective participation and integration of the poor in the major institutions of the larger society is one of the crucial characteristics of the culture of poverty. This is a complex matter and results from a variety of factors that may include lack of economic resources, segregation and discrimination, fear, suspicion or apathy, and the development of local solutions for problems. However, "participation" in some of the institutions of the larger society–for example, in the jails, the army, and the public relief system–does not *per se* eliminate the traits of the culture of poverty. In the case of a relief system that barely keeps people alive, both the basic poverty and the sense of hopelessness are perpetuated rather than eliminated.

Low wages, chronic unemployment, and underemployment lead to low income, lack of property ownership, absence of savings, absence of food reserves in the home, and a chronic shortage of cash. These conditions reduce the possibility of effective participation in the larger economic system. And, as a response to these conditions, we find in the culture of poverty a high incidence of pawning of personal goods, borrowing from local moneylenders at usurious rates of interest, spontaneous informal credit devices organized by neighbors, the use of secondhand clothing and furniture, and the pattern of frequent buying of small quantities of food many times a day as the need arises.

People with a culture of poverty produce very little wealth and receive very little in return. They have a low level of literacy and education, usually do not belong to labor unions, are not members of political parties, generally do not participate in the national welfare agencies, and make very little use of banks, hospitals, department stores, museums, or art galleries. They have a critical attitude toward some of the basic institutions of the dominant classes, hatred of the police, mistrust of government and those in high position, and a cynicism that extends even to the church. This gives the culture of poverty a high potential for protest and for being used in political movements aimed against the existing social order.

People with a culture of poverty are aware of middle-class values, talk about them, and even claim some of them as their own, but, on the whole, they do not live by them. Thus, it is important to distinguish between what they say and what they do. For example, many will tell you that marriage by law, by the church, or by both, is the ideal form of marriage, but few will marry. To men who have no steady jobs or other sources of income, who do not own property and have no wealth to pass on to their children, who are present-time oriented, and who want to avoid the expense and legal difficulties involved in formal marriage and divorce, free unions or consensual marriages makes a lot of sense. Women will often turn down offers of marriage, because they feel it ties them down to men who are immature, punishing, and generally unreliable. Women feel that consensual union gives them a better break; it gives them some of the freedom and flexibility that men have. By not giving the fathers of their children legal staus as husbands, the women have a stronger claim on their children if they decide to leave their men. It also gives women exclusive rights to a house or any other property they may own.

2. When we look at the culture of poverty on the local community level, we find poor housing conditions, crowding, gregariousness, but, above all, a minimum of organization beyond the level of the nuclear and extended family. Occasionally, there are informal, temporary groupings or voluntary associations with slums. The existence of neighborhood gangs that cut across slum settlements represents a considerable advance beyond the zero point of the continuum that I have in mind. Indeed, it is the low level of organization that gives the culture of poverty its marginal and anachronistic quality in our highly complex, specialized, organized society. Most primitive peoples have achieved a higher level of sociocultural organization than our modern urban slum dwellers.

In spite of the generally low level of organization, there may be a sense of community and *esprit de corps* in urban slums and in slum neighborhoods. This can vary within a single city, or from region to region or country to country. The major factors influencing this variation are the size of the slum, its location and physical characteristics, length of residence, incidence of home and landownership (versus squatter rights), rentals, ethnicity, kinship ties, and freedom or lack of freedom of movement. When slums are separated from the surrounding area by enclosing walls or other physical barriers, when rents are low and fixed and stability of residence is great (twenty or thirty years), when the population constitutes a distinct ethnic, racial, or language group [that] is bound by ties of kinship or *compadrazgo,* and when there are some internal voluntary associations, then the sense of local community approaches that of a village community. In many cases, this combination of favorable conditions does not exist. However, even where internal organization and *esprit de corps* is at a bare minimum and people move around a great deal, a sense of territoriality develops that sets off the slum neighborhoods from the rest of the city. In Mexico City and San Juan, this sense of territoriality results from the unavailability of low-income housing outside the slum areas. In South Africa, the sense of territoriality grows out of the segregation enforced by the government, which confines the rural migrants to specific locations.

3. On the family level, the major traits of the culture of poverty are the absence of childhood as a specially prolonged and protected stage in the life cycle; early initiation into sex; free unions or consensual marriages; a relatively high incidence of the abandonment of wives and children; a trend toward female- or mother-centered families and, consequently, a much greater knowledge of maternal relatives; a strong predisposition to authoritarianism; lack of privacy; verbal emphasis upon family solidarity, which is only rarely achieved because of sibling rivalry; and competition for limited goods and maternal affection.

4. On the level of the individual, the major characteristics are a strong feeling of marginality, of helplessness, of dependence, and of inferiority. I found this to be true of slum dwellers in Mexico City and San Juan among families who do not constitute a distinct ethnic or racial group and who do not suffer from racial discrimination. In the United States, of course, the culture of poverty of the Negroes has the additional disadvantage of racial discrimination; but, as I have already suggested, this additional disadvantage contains a great potential for revolutionary protest and organization that seems to be absent in the slums of Mexico City or among the poor whites of the South.

Other traits include a high incidence of maternal deprivation, of orality, of weak ego structure; confusion of sexual identification; a lack of impulse control; a strong present-time orientation, with relatively little ability to defer gratification and to plan for the future; a sense of resignation and fatalism; a widespread belief in male superiority; and a high tolerance for psychological pathology of all sorts.

People with a culture of poverty are provincial and locally oriented and have very little sense of history. They know only their own troubles, their own local conditions, their own neighborhood, their own way of life. Usually, they do not have the knowledge, the vision, or the ideology to see the similarities between their problems and those of their counterparts elsewhere in the world. They are not class-conscious, although they are very sensitive, indeed, to status distinctions.

When the poor become class-conscious or active members of trade-union organizations, or when they adopt an internationalist outlook on the world, they are no longer part of the culture of poverty, although, they may still be desperately poor. Any movement, be it religious, pacifist, or revolutionary, that organizes and gives hope to the poor, and effectively promotes solidarity and a sense of identification with larger groups, destroys the psychological and social core of the culture of poverty. In this connection, I suspect that the civil-rights movement among the Negroes in the United States has done more to improve their self-image and self-respect than have their economic advances, although, without doubt, the two are mutually reinforcing.

The distinction between poverty and the culture of poverty is basic to the model described here. There are degrees of poverty and many kinds of poor people. The culture of poverty refers to one way of life shared by poor people in given historical and social contexts. The economic traits that I have listed for the culture of poverty are necessary but not sufficient to define the phenomena I have in mind. There are a number of historical examples of very poor segments of the population that do not have a way of life that I would describe as a subculture of poverty. Here, I should like to give four examples:

1. Many of the primitive or preliterate peoples studied by anthropologists suffer from dire poverty, which is the result of poor technology and/or poor natural resources, or of both, but they do not have the traits of the subculture of poverty. Indeed, they do not constitute a subculture, because their societies are not highly stratified. In spite of their poverty, they have a relatively integrated, satisfying, and self-sufficient culture. Even the simplest food-gathering and hunting tribes have a considerable amount of organization, bands and band chiefs, tribal councils, and local self-government–traits that are not found in the culture of poverty.
2. In India, the lower castes (the Chamars, the leather workers, and the Bhangis, the sweepers) may be desperately poor, both in the villages and in the cities, but most of them are integrated into the larger society and have their own *panchayat*[3] organizations, which cut across village lines and give them a considerable amount of power.[4] In addition to the caste system, which gives individuals a sense of identity and belonging, there is still another factor, the clan system. Wherever there are unilateral kinship systems, or clans, one would not expect to find the culture of poverty, because a clan system gives people a sense of belonging to a corporate body with a history and a life of its own, thereby providing a sense of continuity, a sense of a past and of a future.
3. The Jews of Eastern Europe were very poor, but they did not have many of the traits of the culture of poverty because of their tradition of literacy, the great value placed upon learning, the organization of the community around the rabbi, the proliferation of local voluntary associations, and their religion, which taught that they were the chosen people.
4. My fourth example is speculative and relates to socialism. On the basis of my limited experience in one socialist country–Cuba–and on the basis of my reading, I am inclined to believe that the culture of poverty does not exist in the socialist countries. I first went to Cuba in 1947 as a visiting professor for the State Department. At that time, I began a study of a sugar plantation in Melena del Sur and of a slum in Havana. After the Castro Revolution, I made my second trip to

[3] A formal organization designed to provide caste leadership.

[4] It may be that in the slums of Calcutta and Bombay an incipient culture of poverty is developing. It would be highly desirable to do family studies there as a crucial test of the culture-of-poverty hypothesis.

> Cuba as a correspondent for a major magazine, and I revisited the same slum and some of the same families. The physical aspect of the slum had changed very little, except for a beautiful new nursery school. It was clear that the people were still desperately poor, but I found much less of the despair, apathy, and hopelessness that are so diagnostic of urban slums in the culture of poverty. They expressed great confidence in their leaders and hope for a better life in the future. The slum itself was now highly organized, with block committees, educational committees, party committees. The people had a new sense of power and importance. They were armed and were given a doctrine that glorified the lower class as the hope of humanity. (I was told by one Cuban official that they had practically eliminated delinquency by giving arms to the delinquents!)

It is my impression that the Castro regime—unlike Marx and Engels—did not write off the so-called lumpen proletariat as an inherently reactionary and antirevolutionary force but, rather, saw its revolutionary potential and tried to utilize it. In this connection, Frantz Fanon makes a similar evaluation of the role of the lumpen proletariat, based upon his experience in the Algerian struggle for independence. . . .

> It is within this mass of humanity, this people of the shanty towns, at the core of the lumpen proletariat, that the rebellion will find its urban spearhead. For the lumpen proletariat, that horde of starving men, uprooted from their tribe and from their clan, constitutes one of the most spontaneous and most radically revolutionary forces of a colonized people.

My own studies of the urban poor in the slums of San Juan do not support the generalizations of Fanon. I have found very little revolutionary spirit or radical ideology among low-income Puerto Ricans. On the contrary, most of the families I studied were quite conservative politically and about half of them were in favor of the Republican Statehood Party. It seems to me that the revolutionary potential of people with a culture of poverty will vary considerably according to the national context and the particular historical circumstances. In a country like Algeria, which was fighting for its independence, the lumpen proletariat was drawn into the struggle and became a vital force. However, in countries like Puerto Rico, in which the movement for independence has very little mass support, and in countries, like Mexico, that achieved their independence a long time ago and are now in their postrevolutionary period, the lumpen proletariat is not a leading source of rebellion or of revolutionary spirit.

In effect, we find that, in primitive societies and in caste societies, the culture of poverty does not develop. In socialist, fascist, and in highly developed capitalist societies with a welfare state, the culture of poverty tends to decline. I suspect that the culture of poverty flourishes in, and is generic to, the early free-enterprise stage of capitalism and that it is also endemic in colonialism.

It is important to distinguish between different profiles in the subculture of poverty, depending upon the national context in which these subcultures are found. If we think of the culture of poverty primarily in terms of the factor of integration in the larger society and a sense of identification with the great tradition of that society, or with a new emerging revolutionary tradition, then we will not be surprised that some slum dwellers with a lower per capita income may have moved further away from the core characteristics of the culture of poverty than others with a higher per capita income. For example, Puerto Rico has a much higher per capita income than Mexico, yet Mexicans have a deeper sense of identity.

I have listed fatalism and a low level of aspiration as one of the key traits for the subculture of poverty. Here, too, however, the national context makes a big difference. Certainly, the level of aspiration of even the poorest sector of the population in a country like the United States, with its traditional ideology of upward mobility and democracy, is much higher than in more backward countries like Ecuador and Peru, where both the ideology and the actual possibilities of upward mobility are extremely limited, and where authoritarian values still persist in both the urban and rural milieus.

Because of the advanced technology, high level of literacy, the development of mass media, and the relatively high aspiration level of all sectors of the population, especially when compared with underdeveloped nations, I believe that, although there is still a great deal of poverty in the United States (estimates range from thirty to fifty million people), there is relatively little of what I would call the culture of poverty. My rough guess would be that only about 20 per cent of the population below the poverty line (between six and ten million people) in the United States have characteristics that would justify classifying their way of life as that of a culture of poverty. Probably the largest sector within this group would consist of very low-income Negroes, Mexicans, Puerto Ricans, American Indians, and Southern poor whites. The relatively small number of people in the United States with a culture of poverty is a positive factor, because it is much more difficult to eliminate the culture of poverty than to eliminate poverty *per se*.

Middle-class people—and this would certainly include most social scientists—tend to concentrate on the negative aspects of the culture of poverty. They tend to associate negative valences to such traits as present-time orientation and concrete versus abstract orientation. I do not intend to idealize or romanticize the culture of poverty. As someone has said, "It is easier to praise poverty than to live in it"; yet, some of the positive aspects that may flow from these traits must not be overlooked. Living in the present may develop a capacity for spontaneity and adventure, for the enjoyment of the sensual, the indulgence of impulse, which is often blunted in the middle-class, future-oriented man. Perhaps it is this reality of the moment that the existentialist writers are so desperately trying to recapture, but which the culture of poverty experiences as natural, everyday phenomena. The frequent use of violence certainly provides a ready outlet for hostility, so that people in the culture of poverty suffer less from repression than does the middle class.

In the traditional view, anthropologists have said that culture provides human beings with a design for living, with a ready-made set of solutions for human problems, so that individuals don't have to begin all over again each generation. That is, the core of culture is its positive adaptive function. I, too, have called attention to some of the adaptive mechanisms in the culture of poverty—for example, the low aspiration level helps to reduce frustration, the legitimization of short-range hedonism makes possible spontaneity and enjoyment. However, on the whole, it seems to me that it is a relatively thin culture. There is a great deal of pathos, suffering, and emptiness among those who live in the culture of poverty. It does not provide much support or long-range satisfaction, and its encouragement of mistrust tends to magnify helplessness and isolation. Indeed, the poverty of culture is one of the crucial aspects of the culture of poverty.

The concept of the culture of poverty provides a high level of generalization that, hopefully, will unify and explain a number of phenomena viewed as distinctive characteristics of racial, national, or regional groups. For example, matrifocality, a high incidence of consensual unions, and a high percentage of households headed by women, which have been thought to be distinctive of Caribbean family organization or of Negro family life in the United States, turn out to be traits of the culture of poverty and are found among diverse peoples in many parts of the world and among peoples who have had no history of slavery.

The concept of a cross-societal subculture of poverty enables us to see that many of the problems we think of as distinctively our own or distinctively Negro problems (or that of any other special racial or ethnic group), also exist in countries where there are no distinct ethnic minority groups. This suggests that the elimination of physical poverty *per se* may not be enough to eliminate the culture of poverty, which is a whole way of life.

What is the future of the culture of poverty? In considering this question, one must distinguish between those countries in which it represents a relatively small segment of the population and those in which it constitutes a very large one. Obviously, the solutions will differ in these two situations. In the United States, the major solution proposed by planners and social workers in dealing with multiple-problem families and the so-called hard core of poverty has been to attempt slowly to raise their level of living and to incorporate them into the middle class. Wherever possible, there has been some reliance upon psychiatric treatment.

In the underdeveloped countries, however, where great masses of people live in the culture of poverty, a social-work solution does not seem feasible. Because of the magnitude of the problem, psychiatrists can hardly begin to cope with it. They have all they can do to care for their own growing middle class. In these countries, the people with a culture of poverty may seek a more revolutionary solution. By creating basic structural changes in society, by redistributing wealth, by organizing the poor and giving them a sense of belonging, of power, and of leadership, revolutions frequently succeed in abolishing some of the basic characteristics of the culture of poverty even when they do not succeed in abolishing poverty itself.

5. SUGGESTIONS FOR FURTHER READING

BALTZELL, E. DIGBY. *The Protestant Establishment* (New York: Random House, 1964).*

BENDIX, R., AND S. M. LIPSET (eds.). *Class, Status and Power* (New York: The Free Press, 1966).

BOTTOMORE, TOM. *Classes in Modern Society* (New York: Pantheon, 1966).*

DAHRENDORF, RALF. *Class and Class Conflict in Industrial Society* (Stanford, Calif.: Stanford University Press, 1959).*

DAVIS, ALLISON, B. GARDNER, AND M. GARDNER. *Deep South* (Chicago: University of Chicago Press, 1941).*

DJILAS, MILOVAN. *The New Class* (New York: Praeger, 1965).*

DOMHOFF, G. WILLIAM. *Who Rules America?* (Englewood Cliffs, N.J.: Prentice-Hall, 1967).*

GALBRAITH, JOHN K. *The New Industrial State* (Boston: Houghton Mifflin, 1967).*

HARRINGTON, MICHAEL. *The Other America* (New York: Macmillan, 1962).*

HELLER, CELIA (ed.). *Structured Social Inequality* (New York: Macmillan, 1969).

HODGES, HAROLD. *Social Stratification* (Cambridge, Mass.: Schenkman, 1969).

HOWE, LOUISE (ed.). *The White Majority* (New York: Vintage, 1970).*

HUNTER, FLOYD. *Community Power Structure* (Chapel Hill, N.C.: University of North Carolina Press, 1953).*

LEWIS, OSCAR. *La Vida* (New York: Random House, 1968).*

LIPSET, S. M., AND R. BENDIX. *Social Mobility in Industrial Society* (Berkeley: University of California Press, 1959).*

LYND, ROBERT, AND HELEN LYND. *Middletown* (New York: Harcourt, Brace, 1929).*

MAYER, KURT, AND W. BUCKLEY. *Class and Society,* 3rd ed. rev. (New York: Random House, 1969).*

MILLS, C. WRIGHT. *The Power Elite* (New York: Oxford University Press, 1957).*

———. *White Collar* (New York: Oxford University Press, 1951).*

SHOSTAK, A., AND W. GOMBERG (ed.). *Blue Collar World* (Englewood Cliffs, N.J.: Prentice-Hall, 1964).

VEBLEN, THORSTEIN. *The Theory of the Leisure Class* (New York: New American Library, 1953).*

* *Available in paperback.*

6. Minorities

INTRODUCTION

Every society is composed of a variety of groups differentiated from one another by race, national origin, religion, age, sex, kinship, economic status, political affiliation, and many other factors. Intergroup differences need not result in hostility and conflict; often, differences are more or less ignored or accepted as unimportant. However, when certain members of a given social order are singled out for distinctive treatment because of their group affiliations, intergroup animosity is likely to result.

The concept of minority, as used by sociologists, does not have any quantitative connotation. For example, the black people of the Union of South Africa vastly outnumber the white population but are decidedly a minority in the sociological sense. As we define minority, then, it is a category of people who (1) are subordinate in some way to the majority, (2) can be distinguished from the majority on the basis of physical or cultural characteristics, (3) are collectively regarded and treated as different and inferior on the basis of these characteristics, and (4) are excluded from full participation in the life of the society.[1]

Sociologists who study minorities generally distinguish between the concepts of prejudice and discrimination. Prejudice is a set of negative attitudes, feelings, and beliefs toward a particular group that has emotional weight behind it, is not readily amenable to alteration by reason or experience, and represents a predisposition to act in a particular way toward that group. Discrimination, by contrast, represents overt action involving differential treatment of individuals who belong to certain

[1] John Biesanz and Mavis Biesanz, *Introduction to Sociology* (Englewood Cliffs, N.J.: Prentice-Hall, 1969), p. 256.

groups. Generally, discrimination and prejudice go hand in hand. One who discriminates against given individuals usually harbors negative attitudes toward the groups to which they belong. Similarly, those who hold prejudicial sentiments are likely to engage in discriminatory actions. However, occasionally prejudice and discrimination are not in correspondence. Note, for example, the case of the "fair weather" white liberal who expresses his belief in equal opportunity for all people but, when a court order is issued requiring busing between his predominantly white community and an adjacent black district, keeps his own children home.

In light of the foregoing discussion, many sociologists would probably suggest that the last word in the title of Robert Hamblin's "Dynamics of Racial Discrimination" should be "prejudice." Few, indeed, would fault the study on any other ground, for it reports a most exacting and comprehensive research on the origins and functions of prejudice. Not only does the study examine the most important views of the causes of prejudice; it also suggests their relative significance in accounting for prejudice.

Probably the most critical of Hamblin's findings is the singularly important role of primary affiliations (i.e., family and friends) in the acquisition and maintenance of racial prejudice. Prejudice is learned and sustained by the supports received from close social intimates. If conditions can be created that expand the scope and heterogeneity of one's primary-group network, then perhaps a course can be set that may eventually mitigate prejudice.

The growing corpus of research on the reactionary, anti–civil-libertarian, authoritarian, and backlash views endorsed by the white lower-middle- and working-class segments of America seems to highlight the effects of fear of status competition in maintaining prejudice. Inasmuch as the lower-middle and working classes have thus far been among the vanguard in absorbing the effects of the continuing trend toward cybernation (they have experienced the greatest reductions of their work-weeks and more extensive unemployment), status insecurity may be at the root of their recent highly vocal manifestations of anti-minority feeling. This factor is a much more difficult matter to rectify than primary affiliation; what it requires is nothing less than wholesale changes in the American social structure. The society, and the economic institutions in particular, will require revamping before these fears can be successfully allayed.

But there are other courses to pursue as well. A great many researches, conducted over many years, show that equal-status interaction is the most effective means of reducing prejudice. The more opportunities people of different races, religions, nationalities, and cultures have to meet and associate with one another, the more they tend to like one another and the less they tend to have negative feelings toward one another. This has been demonstrated in military organizations, in business life, in educational institutions, and in housing, as well as in other areas. If we move significantly in the direction of expanding opportunities for equal-status interaction among all groups, a path will be opened for the reduction of intergroup hostility and prejudice.

Majority-minority relationships in any given society vary within a wide range of possibilities. The majority policy might prescribe cultural pluralism—that is, a willingness on the part of the dominant group to permit cultural differences. Amalgamation is another possibility, in which the best of majority and minority patterns are blended into a new synthesis, resulting in complete fusion. Still another alternative is assimilation, in which, under varying degrees of coercion, minorities absorb the dominant patterns of the majority. Still other possibilities include segregation, expulsion, and genocide.

The discriminatory behavior implicit in coerced majority-minority relationships is influenced by numerous factors, including heterogeneity in the population, rapid social change with attendant anomie, ignorance and barriers to communication, the size and relative density of the minority-group population, direct competition and realistic conflict, the exploitative advantages of discrimination, and customs and traditions that prescribe and sustain hostility.

Intergroup relations in America today are marked by a considerable amount of conflict, confusion, and dissent, which M. Yinger calls a pattern of "subcultural anomie." Ideologically, pluralism, amalgamation, and assimilation have been touted as the dominant majority policies. In practice, however, assimilation—with occasional flourishes of force—embodied in the "melting pot" theory, and segregation have been most pervasive.

Probably the most oppressed and excluded group on the national scene today is the first American, the American Indian. Of an estimated six million people who were here at the time of the conquest of the Americas, fewer than one million survive. The average American Indian has a life-span of 44 years, a yearly income of approximately $1,500 (for a family of four), and less than a sixth-grade education. Living on an Indian reservation, relegated to the most arid and barren land for agricultural and livestock production, he is totally excluded from everything that goes on in America. Everything that ever belonged to him and his forefathers has been successfully expropriated.

Our country's largest minority—51 per cent of the population—is the American female. Only recently, in the resurgence of the women's liberation movement, has the minority status of women begun to be appreciated. Jo Freeman, in "Growing Up Girlish," eloquently expounds on the subordinate position of the American female. Moreover, her essay highlights the concept of the self-fulfilling prophecy and how it applies to woman's status.

A self-fulfilling prophecy is a prediction of a social outcome that, because it is believed and acted upon as true, generates its own confirmation. The values and precepts of male-dominated America enjoin female ineptitude and incompetence. Consequently, in the socialization process women learn to develop negative conceptions of their own abilities and low achievement motivation. The most important lesson women learn is that, to be successful as women, they must fail in the socially significant areas of achievement. Thus, the full creative and productive capacity of women is stunted and circumscribed within the range of the traditionally subordinate female role.

Self-fulfilling prophecies are not limited to the case of the female minority; they are part of the experiences of all minorities. From Elliot Liebow's discussion of "Men and Jobs," we note that self-fulfilling prophecies play a most significant role in the subordination of the black American. White Americans, conceiving of the black man as "lazy, shiftless, irresponsible, immoral," and white employers especially, considering black men capable of handling only low-status, dead-end jobs, create conditions to make these prejudiced beliefs self-fulfilling. Liebow develops the position that, as the black American is subordinated in the workplace, his self-image suffers, his family life is disrupted, and his friendships become precarious. These effects, once observed, become justifications for more delimitation of opportunities.

Recently, many whites have become frightened and outspokenly hostile to the black man in the wake of newly emergent black militancy and ghetto riots. This militancy seems surprising to some whites, in light of the gains blacks have made in recent years in such areas as income and education. Yet, many of these gains are more apparent than real. Many are contradicted by setbacks in other important areas. In other cases, the old inequities remain. For example, the ratio of black incomes to white incomes has not changed substantially in the past twenty years. In every occupational category, black workers earn less than white workers doing the same jobs. Blacks are twice as likely to be subject to unemployment. Black college graduates can expect lower lifetime earnings than white high school graduates. There has been no slackening in housing segregation since 1900. Racial segregation in schools may actually have increased since 1954, when the Supreme Court ruled for school desegregation "with all deliberate speed."

Often, in a period of rising expectations, inequity develops a more disturbing character and tends to be more provocative. Otherwise, one's sights are set lower, or one is so overwhelmed by the quest for survival that protest of any kind becomes a luxury one cannot afford. This phenomenon is discussed at greater length by James Davies in Chapter 10, "Social Change." Rising expectations have no doubt played a part in the development of black militancy.

For many whites, the term "black power" has a menacing connotation; it suggests that blacks have the same racist and dominating aspirations that whites have shared and implemented in America for over

300 years. However, this is not how most black leaders and the black American population conceive of black power. From Charles Hamilton's explanation, we can readily see that the realization of black power will mean not only greater well-being for the black man but a better life for all people.

The Causes of Prejudice

The Dynamics of Racial Discrimination*

Robert L. Hamblin

This paper reports the results of a field survey designed to evaluate and interrelate nine hypotheses about the antecedents of racial discrimination. Three of the hypotheses were formulated at the beginning of the present investigation, but the others are familiar. Ultimately, the concern is a series of bivariate and multivariate tests designed to develop the empirical foundations for combining the hypotheses into an integrated theory of racial discrimination.

Our dependent variable is the *tendency to discriminate;* prejudice, or the tendency toward negative stereotyping, is treated as a separate variable, one of several possible antecedents of the tendency to discriminate. This procedure is followed for two reasons:

1. We found that, in answering pretest questions designed to get at prejudice, or negative stereotyping, respondents often hesitated in a way suggesting that they were prejudiced but did not want to "sound" prejudiced, whereas answers to the discrimination measure were quick, direct, and quite definite.

2. Discrimination is probably of more concern to racial minorities than prejudice, since discrimination is a direct form of aggression. An act is aggressive if (1) as a consequence of individual *S*'s act, *P,* another individual, suffers physical, psychological, or social injury, and (2) the injury is not accidental–that is, *S* proceeds with the act even though he is aware that it will injure *P*. An act is discriminatory if *S arbitrarily* excludes *P* from a status or position in society that is ordinarily valued by that society. Another way of putting it: *S* discriminates against *P* to the extent *S* does not allow *P* to compete for high statuses via differential achievement but by ascription relegates to him low statuses. Defined in this manner, discrimination does result in social and perhaps psychological injury. Furthermore,

* From *Social Problems,* 10, no. 2 (Fall, 1962), 103–12, 116–18.

those who discriminate are probably aware that their actions are injurious, even though at times they may try to fool themselves and others with denials. If those who discriminate were asked, "Would you want to be treated that way?" they would probably find it most difficult to say "Yes."

THE HYPOTHESES

Authoritarianism. The authoritarianism hypothesis, first proposed and tested by Adorno, Frenkel-Brunswik, Levinson, and Sanford,[1] is as follows:

> *The tendency to discriminate against members of a minority varies directly with authoritarianism,* or the degree to which the individual's personality is characterized by fascist tendencies, that is, rigidity, projection, and punitiveness. (1)

The authoritarian personality is supposed to develop in a family atmosphere of strict norms, where punishment for deviation is harsh and unreasoning. Through identification with his parents, a child internalizes their hostile, unreasoning attitude toward deviation. Consequently, in order to live with himself, he projects his faults onto others, whom he subsequently hates. Since minorities are usually deviant with respect to some of the majority's norms, and, perhaps more important, since members of the minority are often not allowed to retaliate against members of the majority, minorities become the focus of the authoritarian personality's projected hostility.

In the original tests of the authoritarianism hypothesis, correlations between measures of authoritarianism and prejudice ranged "from an average of about .6 to about .75 in later forms. . . ."[2] Subsequently, other tests conducted by a large number of other investigators, who have both attacked and supported the hypothesis, have produced inconclusive results. It is obvious from the evidence that authoritarianism probably has something to do with racial discrimination. The exact nature of this "something" has yet to be determined, however. This uncertainty is reflected in the range of correlations found thus far. They have been as high as .75 and as low as .18.[3]

Anomia. First proposed and tested by Srole,[4] the anomia hypothesis is:

[1] T. W. Adorno, Else Frenkel-Brunswik, Daniel J. Levinson, and R. Nevitt Sanford, *The Authoritarian Personality* (New York: Harper, 1950).

[2] Else Frenkel-Brunswik, Daniel J. Levinson, and R. Nevitt Sanford, "The Antidemocratic Personality," in Guy E. Swanson, Theodore M. Newcomb, and Eugene L. Hartley, eds., *Readings in Social Psychology* (New York: Henry Holt, 1952), p. 618.

[3] The .18 correlation was obtained in a study by Herbert Greenberg, Arthur L. Chase, and Thomas M. Cannon, Jr., "Attitudes of White and Negro High School Students in a W. Texas Town Toward School Integration," *Journal of Applied Psychology,* XLI, 1 (1957).

[4] Leo Srole, "Social Integration and Certain Corollaries: An Exploratory Study," *American Sociological Review,* 21 (December, 1956), pp. 709–16.

The tendency to discriminate against members of a minority varies directly with anomia, or the degree to which the individual perceives his milieu as being unpredictable or normless. (2)

Although the rationale has not been completely worked out, the theory behind this hypothesis seems to involve a certain amount of displaced aggression, resulting from severe frustration–the concomitant of anomia. Living in an unpredictable, normless social milieu is probably frustrating. Because it is difficult to fix the blame for this sort of frustration, the resulting instigation to aggression is easily displaced toward members of minorities, who are often ideal scapegoats, since retaliation is often prohibited by penalty of severe social sanctions.

Srole developed a measure of anomia that survived a latent structure analysis, as well as other tests indicating that the items composed a scale. He reports a correlation of .43 between this measure of anomia and a measure of discrimination against minorities in general. In a replication, Roberts and Rokeach report a correlation of .55 between scores from Srole's anomia scale and scores from a prejudice scale.[5]

Vertical mobility. Originating in the research of Bettelheim and Janowitz,[6] the vertical-mobility hypothesis is as follows:

The tendency to discriminate against members of a minority varies inversely with the amount of vertical mobility, or the degree to which the individual has experienced an increase (as opposed to a decrease) in occupational status. (3)

The relationship between vertical mobility and the tendency to discriminate is usually explained in terms of frustration and displaced aggression. Negative vertical mobility–a decrease in occupational status–results in frustration, which in turn results in instigation to aggression, which in turn is displaced against members of minority groups, who, as we have noted, are ideal scapegoats.

Data gathered by Bettelheim and Janowitz from depth interviews with veterans of World War II show an association between negative mobility and the tendency to discriminate against Negroes and Jews. The gammas we calculated from this data are —.37 for Negroes and —.35 for Jews.[7]

Perceived nonconformity. The perceived-nonconformity hypothesis is probably suggested most clearly in the works of Sumner:[8]

The tendency to discriminate against members of a minority varies directly with perceived nonconformity, or the degree to which the

[5] *Ibid.,* and Alan H. Roberts and Milton Rokeach, "Anomie, Authoritarianism, and Prejudice: A Replication," *American Journal of Sociology,* 61 (January, 1956), pp. 355–59.

[6] Bruno Bettelheim and Morris Janowitz, "Ethnic Tolerance: A Function of Social and Personal Control," in Swanson *et al., op. cit.,* pp. 593–602.

[7] *Ibid.*

[8] William G. Sumner, *Folkways: A Study of the Sociological Importance of Usages, Manners, Customs, Mores, and Morals* (Boston: Ginn, 1940).

members of the minority group are perceived by members of the majority as violating the norms of the majority. (4)

Sumner observed that those who violate the mores are punished, and those who abide by them are rewarded. He suggested, also, that the world is divided into in-groups and out-groups on the basis of differences in mores, and that humans are ordinarily ethnocentric—they judge others by their own mores. Consequently, members of in-groups exclude members of out-groups, who have different mores. In other theoretical contexts, Freud explained the tendency to punish deviants as a defense against temptation; Durkheim explained the same phenomenon as an attempt to maintain the solidarity of the in-group.[9] In any event, perceived nonconformity is threatening or frustrating. In turn, the threat or frustration instigates aggression in the form of discrimination. This hypothesis, then, makes discrimination against minorities analogous to punishment for crime. The crime committed by minorities is a violation of the mores of the majority. It is as though the majority said, "To be treated like a gentleman, one must act like a gentleman."

Jacobson and Rainwater[10] concluded that easy conformity (or lack of nonconformity) to middle-class norms was crucial in the Nisei's unprecedented acceptance in Chicago after World War II. Pettigrew recently reported a .62 correlation between scores from a "stereotyped-belief" scale and an "exclusion-discrimination" scale for a Northern sample, and a .72 correlation for a Southern sample.[11] These correlations, of course, are large but are expected by social scientists who have worked in intergroup relations. They have generally assumed that negative stereotypes—perceptions or accusations of inferiority and nonconformity—are simply a manifestation of the tendency to discriminate and, consequently, have usually combined items indicating negative stereotypes with items indicating a tendency to discriminate to form a prejudice scale. Actually, there is evidence that, in open conflict, accusations of inferiority and nonconformity often are fabricated to hurt others. This evidence suggests that hypothesis 4 is not complete, and that feedback probably should be postulated, so that perceived nonconformity in part varies with instigation to aggression.

Fully aware of these interpretative difficulties, we included the nonconformity hypothesis in the present investigation, feeling that previous tests were faulty and, thus, indeterminate. In studies like Pettigrew's, the nonconformity items have always been mixed with the discrimination items. This mixture instigates people to distort their perceptions of nonconformity in an effort to justify their aggressive, discriminatory responses. The per-

[9] Sigmund Freud, *Totem and Taboo,* reprinted in A. A. Brill, ed. and trans., *The Basic Writings of Sigmund Freud* (New York: The Modern Library, 1938), pp. 805–930; Émile Durkheim, *The Elementary Forms of Religious Life* (Glencoe, Ill.: The Free Press, 1947).

[10] Alan Jacobson and Lee Rainwater, "A Study of Management Representative Evaluations of Nisei Workers," *Social Forces,* 32 (October, 1953), pp. 35–41.

[11] Thomas F. Pettigrew, "Regional Differences in Anti-Negro Prejudice," *The Journal of Abnormal and Social Psychology,* 59 (July, 1959), pp. 28–36.

ceived-nonconformity questions should be separate from, and prior to, the discrimination questions. Furthermore, all past tests, including Pettigrew's, use Likert-type scales, which essentially ask people to agree or disagree with stereotyped, platitudinous statements. Thus, these past tests may be measuring perceived nonconformity and the tendency to discriminate, but they are also, in part, measuring a personality characteristic–acquiescence, a willingness to accept stereotyped, platitudinous statements. In a study such as Pettigrew's, then, the correlations may be spuriously high.

Equal-Status Contact. The equal-status contact hypothesis is as follows:

> *The tendency to discriminate against members of a minority varies inversely with equal-status contact,* or the degree to which the majority member has interacted with minority members who are his equals in occupational status. (5)

Although the origins of this hypothesis are obscure, a number of studies have been designed to test it.[12] In the best known of these, the Information and Education Division of the U.S. War Department carried out interviews of enlisted men who had contact with Negro troops during the Normandy invasion. The gamma between contact with, and hostility toward, Negroes, calculated from their published data, is —.50. Brophy interviewed merchant seamen who had shipped with Negroes. The gamma between contact with, and discrimination against, Negroes, calculated from his published data, is —.67. MacKenzie obtained data from university students who had worked with Negroes. The gamma between the status of the Negroes and the tendency to discriminate against Negroes calculated from the published data is —.52. All these coefficients support the equal-status contact hypothesis.

Competition. Although the competition hypothesis has had a long history in social science, Sherif recently reformulated it,[13] as follows:

> *The tendency to discriminate against members of a minority varies directly with competition,* or the degree to which the individual has experienced frustration in past competition with members of the minority group. (6)

The rationale is simple. People who actually lose in competition with members of the minority group–for such items as jobs, houses, schools, and recreation facilities–perceive the members as a potential or actual threat, as agents of frustration. Consequently, members of the majority are instigated to discriminate against the minority group as a defense.

Several experiments by Sherif show that, in the absence of institutional-

[12] Information and Education Division, U.S. War Department, "Opinions about Negro Infantry Platoons in White Companies of Seven Divisions," in Swanson *et al., op. cit.,* pp. 502–06; I. N. Brophy, "The Luxury of Anti-Negro Prejudice," *Public Opinion Quarterly,* 9 (1946), pp. 456–66; and Barbara K. MacKenzie, "The Importance of Contact in Determining Attitudes Toward Negroes," *Journal of Abnormal and Social Psychology,* 43 (October, 1948), pp. 417–41.

[13] Muzafer Sherif, "Experiments in Group Conflict," *Scientific American,* CXCV, 5 (1956), 54–58.

ized control, boys' groups normally develop very hostile, discriminatory relationships after a relatively short period of competition in sports and games. Although this is the only rigorous supportive evidence we could find, several writers of textbooks on intergroup relations emphasize competition as the most important cause of discrimination against minorities.

During our pretest, it occurred to us that people may not be so resentful about past competition with Negroes as they are fearful about possible future competition from Negroes given equal status and equal opportunity. Consequently, we formulated the following hypothesis:

> *The tendency to discriminate against members of a minority varies directly with the amount of fear of equal-status competition with members of the minority group.* (7)

As far as we could tell, this hypothesis had never been tested directly before.

Social pressures. Sumner suggested that the tendencies to discriminate against, and to be hostile toward, out-groups are in the mores,[14] which, he further suggested, cannot be changed. He thus became the hero of the Southern whites but the bane of modern sociologists, who like to think of the profession as being liberal, particularly about race relations. Even so, research like that conducted by Prothro and by Pettigrew[15] suggests that Sumner's hypothesis is true; that discrimination patterns are determined, in part, at least, by the mores. Whether or not the mores can be changed is another matter for investigation.

Sumner's mores hypothesis has not previously been investigated in an attempt to account for individual differences in the tendency to discriminate, because the mores are ordinarily assumed to be uniform for everyone.[16] Sutherland, however, has suggested that the mores are not uniform for everyone, that families and peer groups vary considerably in the mores they enforce.[17] From Sutherland's insight, and the assumption that the mores are experienced most directly as pressures from family and friends, it seemed likely that individuals might vary in their tendencies to discriminate against minorities because they experience differential pressures. Consequently, we formulated the following hypotheses:

> *The tendency to discriminate against members of a minority varies directly with the strength of family pressures to discriminate against members of that minority.* (8)

14 Sumner, *op. cit.*

15 E. T. Prothro, "Ethnocentrism and Anti-Negro Attitudes in the Deep South," *Journal of Abnormal and Social Psychology,* 47 (January, 1952), pp. 105–8; Pettigrew, *loc. cit.*: Thomas F. Pettigrew, "Personality and Sociocultural Factors in Intergroup Attitudes: A Cross-National Comparison," *Conflict Resolution,* 2 (March, 1958), pp. 29–42; and Thomas F. Pettigrew, "Social Distance Attitudes of South African Students," *Social Forces,* 38 (March, 1960), pp. 246–53.

16 Cf. Gordon W. Allport, *The Nature of Prejudice* (Cambridge, Mass.: Addison-Wesley, 1954), pp. 40–41.

17 E. H. Sutherland, *Principles of Criminology,* 4th ed. (Philadelphia: J. B. Lippincott, 1947).

The tendency to discriminate against members of a minority varies directly with the strength of friends' pressures to discriminate against members of that minority. (9)

The Horowitzes found that attitudes of school children on race were more firmly established, even among first-graders, than attitudes causing sex, age, and economic cleavages.[18] They also found that the primary source for learning race attitudes was the parents. Younger children were aware that their parents were teaching them about race, but older children had forgotten the source of their attitudes, or perhaps had internalized them, considering them as natural and reasonable. Since the Horowitzes' study, published in 1938, the hypothesis has been more or less neglected in empirical research. Even so, Allport recently guessed that perhaps half of all prejudiced-discriminatory attitudes "are based only on the need to conform to custom, to let well enough alone, to maintain the cultural pattern."[19]

The tests of the above hypotheses to be performed here will, in part, be bivariate tests, simply replicating much of the empirical work done to date in intergroup relations. In addition, a multivariate analysis will be used to establish the independent and the combined effects of the hypothesized antecedent variables. . . .

METHODS

Data for this investigation were obtained in interviews with two quota samples of 100 adults in the St. Louis metropolitan area. These quota samples were designed to be representative of the white adults in the St. Louis metropolitan area in occupation, education, and sex according to the 1950 census, and in religion according to the St. Louis Metropolitan Survey, conducted in 1956–57.[20] The first, or pretest, sample was used primarily for developing scales for measurement. The second, or final, sample was used for the actual tests.

* * *

In the pretest, many respondents seemed to be distorting their answers to some of the questions, evidently because they were involved in a serious moral conflict over racial "prejudice." Many felt that prejudice is wrong but, nevertheless, recognized it in themselves. Consequently, in verbal responses, some seemed at times to be defensive enough to distort or suppress answers to vital questions.

After trying several different methods of getting around these tendencies,

[18] Eugene L. Horowitz and Ruth E. Horowitz, "Development of Social Attitudes in Children," *Sociometry,* 1 (1938), pp. 301–38.

[19] Allport, *op. cit.,* p. 286.

[20] Sarah Lee Boggs, *The People of St. Louis, 1957: A Description and Comparison of the White and Non-White Populations in St. Louis and St. Louis County* (St. Louis: Health and Welfare Council of Metropolitan St. Louis and the Social Science Institute of Washington University, 1958).

we discovered people, in general, to be much more frank and accurate when answers do not have to be verbalized. In the final sample, therefore, the relatively educated respondents completed most of the schedule as a questionnaire, and the interviewers read the questions to the relatively uneducated respondents, who then wrote the answers themselves on a second interviewing schedule. These procedures worked for all but about eight respondents, who were relatively illiterate; for them, the entire interview was verbal. The moral conflict seemed to be absent for these illiterates, however, most being migrants from the rural South who had internalized definite mores and had been accustomed to telling outsiders exactly how they felt about Negroes.

RESULTS

This section will be divided into [two] parts: bivariate tests involving Pearsonian correlation coefficients between the discrimination index and the indexes of the nine possible antecedent variables; [and] a multivariate test involving a multiple regression-correlation analysis. . . .

The Bivariate Tests. In Table 1, there are two columns of correlations,

TABLE 1

Pearsonian Correlations Between the Discrimination Index (1) and Nine Possible Antecedent Variables (2)

Possible Antecedent Variables	Expected r_{12}	Obtained r_{12}
Authoritarianism	.75 to .18	.22
Anomia	.55 to .25	.37
Vertical mobility	−.37 to −.35	.06
Perceived nonconformity of Negroes	.72 to .40	.29
Negative-sympathetic stereotypes	———	.28
Equal-status contact	−.67 to −.23	−.17
Frustration from past competition	.40	.41
Fear of equal-status competition	———	.62
Family pressures to discriminate	.64	.75
Friends' pressures to discriminate	.60	.68

the "Expected" and the "Obtained." In the Expected column, coefficients of association from past research are given. Where more than one previous test has been conducted, the range in coefficients is used. These expected coefficients will include correlations from the pretest sample when available and appropriate. The Obtained column contains correlations calculated from the data obtained from the final sample.

Authoritarianism. For authoritarianism, the obtained correlation coefficient is .22, which is slightly larger than the .18 correlation at the bottom of the expected range. In recent years, the studies supplying the high correlations in the expected range[21] have been questioned, because both the authoritarianism and the prejudice items in the scales were formulated in a way that capitalized on an acquiescence-response set that critics claim inflated the correlations.[22] In the present study, this response set may have been avoided, since the format of the discrimination items differs in many ways from that of the authoritarianism items. Even so, the .22 correlation obtained in the final sample may be unusually low; the pretest sample correlation was .36.

Anomia. In Table 1, the expected correlation between anomia and prejudice or discrimination ranges from .55[23] to .25 (from the pretest sample). The obtained correlation is .37, which differs little from Srole's .43.

* * *

Vertical mobility. In Table 1, the gamma coefficients for the relationship between vertical mobility and prejudice range between —.37 and —.35.[24] The very different obtained .06 correlation between the vertical-mobility and the discrimination measures thus appears to be problematical, but in actuality it is not. Pettigrew found a negative relationship between mobility and discrimination in the North but a positive relationship in the South.[25] The St. Louis population being somewhat a mixture of the North and South, the near-zero correlation is consistent with Pettigrew's finding.

Perceived nonconformity. Measuring perceived nonconformity turned out to be difficult. Our attempt to minimize distortions from people who did not want to "sound prejudiced," by changing from verbal to written responses, evidently was somewhat successful, since the written responses resulted in a much greater frequency of perceived nonconformity.

At the end of the interview, the interviewer went over the perceived-nonconformity items with the respondent and asked why he answered the questions as he did. We received two classes of responses. One involved the typical negative stereotypes–"The Negro is inferior," "The Negro is amoral," and so on–and the other what we have called sympathetic stereotypes–the Negro is that way "because he cannot find a steady job," "because he is forced to live in poor neighborhoods," "because he has nothing else to do for recreation," and so on.

21 Frenkel-Brunswik *et al., loc. cit.,* pp. 612–22.

22 Loren J. Chapman and Donald T. Campbell, "Response Set in the F Scale," *Journal of Abnormal and Social Psychology,* 54 (January, 1957); Richard Christie, Joan Havel, and Bernard Seidenberg, "Is the F Scale Irreversible?" *Journal of Abnormal and Social Psychology,* 56 (March, 1958); N. L. Gage, George S. Leavitt, and George C. Stone, "The Psychological Meaning of Acquiescence Set for Authoritarianism," *Journal of Abnormal and Social Psychology,* 55 (July, 1957); Samuel Messick and Douglas N. Jackson, "Authoritarianism or Acquiescence in Bass's Data," *Journal of Abnormal and Social Psychology,* 54 (May, 1957); and Robert E. Mogar, "Three Versions of the F Scale and Performance on the Semantic Differential," *Journal of Abnormal and Social Psychology,* LX, 2 (1960).

23 Roberts and Rokeach, *loc. cit.*

24 Bettelheim and Janowitz, *loc. cit.*

25 Thomas F. Pettigrew, "Regional Differences in Anti-Negro Prejudice," *loc. cit.*

We utilized the data obtained in two ways. First, we factor analyzed the nonconformity items and thereby obtained an index of perceived nonconformity. Secondly, we developed a relatively simple, if somewhat arbitrary, measure: the number of negative stereotypes minus the number of sympathetic stereotypes expressed during the last part of the interview.

In Table 1, the expected correlations between perceived nonconformity and discrimination ranged from .72[26] to .40 (from the pretest sample). This range is, of course, quite large and may be attributed in part to the fact that, in the pretest sample, the formats of the nonconformity and the discrimination items differed markedly, to avoid the problem of an acquiescence-response set. Furthermore, the nonconformity items were not interspersed with the discrimination items but were given first, to avoid the aforementioned problem of justification. Note, however, that, when written responses were introduced, in the final sample, the obtained correlation is still smaller, .29. It is possible that respondents who perceived Negroes as a nonconforming group but had no desire to discriminate against them were able to express themselves more accurately in written answers than in verbal replies. Of the two correlations, then, the .29 in the final sample is probably more accurate. Also interesting is the .28 correlation between the maverick "negative-sympathetic stereotypes" index and the discrimination index.

The results of this investigation suggest that perceived nonconformity and stereotyping are not highly associated with the tendency to discriminate. The suggestion is that, when the methods are changed to minimize justification, the relationship between perceived nonconformity or stereotyping and the tendency to discriminate involves less than 10 per cent of the variance.

Equal-status contact. In Table 1, the expected coefficients ranged from —.67[27] to —.23 (from the pretest sample). The correlation obtained from the final sample is —.17. Just why the correlations in the pretest and final samples are so low is problematical. However, Sherif has presented data that suggest that the equal-status contact hypothesis does not obtain under conditions of strong intergroup competition and conflict.[28] Since the respondents in the pretest and final samples may have been threatened by the competition, the relationship between equal-status contact and discrimination may have been vitiated. We will see the results are consistent with the assumption that competition increases the tendency to discriminate.

Competition. In Table 1, the expected correlation coefficient, .40, between frustration experienced in past competition and discrimination came from the pretest sample. The measure involved is almost identical to that used in the final sample, where the obtained correlation is .41. These approximately equal correlation coefficients give some indication of the stability of the relationship, since they were calculated from data from two

[26] *Ibid.*
[27] Brophy, *loc. cit.*
[28] Sherif, *loc. cit.*

similar but independent samples, taken approximately a year apart. A much stronger correlation is found between the *fear* of equal-status competition with Negroes and the discrimination index, .62. These data suggest that the frustration and fear that sometimes accompany competition between the races could be major antecedents of the tendency to discriminate as postulated in hypotheses 6 and 7.

Social pressures. In Table 1, the expected correlations between the index of discrimination and the indexes of family and friends' pressures are .64 and .60, respectively, and come from the pretest sample. The correlation in the final sample are somewhat larger, .75 and .68, respectively. These pretest and final sample differences are probably due to a change in the measures used.

In the pretest sample, the respondent was asked to translate his family's and friends' feelings into what he thought they would actually do if he worked with a Negro, if he went to school with a Negro, if one of his children married a Negro, and so forth. Responses such as "They would praise me," "They would talk with me," "They would disown me" were then coded on the basis of direction–"favor" or "object"–and severity. In the final sample, the respondents were simply asked to indicate how their family and how their friends would feel. The change was made because we discovered that most people found it difficult to anticipate what their family and friends would actually do, but few were at a loss to know how their family and friends would feel. Possibly, then, since the correlations were higher, the feelings in the final sample indicate more accurately the importance of family and friends' pressures than the punitive or rewarding actions in the pretest sample. With either measure, however, the data suggests that family and friends' pressures may be important antecedents of the tendency to discriminate as postulated in hypotheses 8 and 9.

The multiple regression-correlation analysis. In the multiple regression-correlation analysis, we performed seven analyses on the computer, the first with all nine possible antecedent variables and the last with only three. These last three variables–fear of equal-status competition, family pressures to discriminate, and friends' pressures to discriminate–were the only ones that resulted in a substantial independent relationship with the discrimination index. This is shown, in part, by the fact that the multiple correlation of all nine possible antecedent variables with the index of discrimination is .82, but of only these three variables, .81. The three-variable analysis is presented in Table 2, where the data show that fear of equal-status competition independently explained 17 per cent of the variance; family pressures, 32 per cent; and friends' pressures, 16 per cent; the three variables together explaining 65 per cent of the variance. This multiple regression-correlation analysis indicates that there is considerable overlapping of effects among the independent variables, and, further, that we should not pay too much attention to zero-order correlation coefficients.

* * *

TABLE 2

Multiple Regression-Correlation Analysis Between Three Antecedent Variables and the Index of Discrimination

Antecedent Variables	Beta Weight	t*	Explained variance†
Fear of equal-status competition	.26	3.63	.17
Family pressures to discriminate	.43	4.62	.32
Friends' pressures to discriminate	.24	2.53	.16

* To be significant at the .05 level, *t* must be equal to, or greater than, 2.00 for a two-tailed test.

† R is .81. The total explained variance of the tendency to discriminate was partitioned among the three antecedent variables by means of the following formula:

$$R^2 = \beta_1 r_{01} + \beta_2 r_{02} + \beta_3 r_{03}$$

where the subscript *0* refers to the tendency to discriminate. The three terms on the right-hand side of the equation represent the unique contribution of each antecedent variable. However, this is not the only way to partition explained variance. Quinn McNemar, in *Psychological Statistics* (New York: Wiley, 1955), p. 177, has suggested that the independent contribution of each variable is equal to the square of its beta weight. Calculated this way, the sum of the unique effects can exceed 100 per cent. Furthermore, this approach necessitates additional terms, like $\beta_1\beta_2 r_{12}$, which represent the common contribution of each pair of antecedent variables. These terms can be negative and indicate thereby negative explained variance, a difficult concept to interpret. For both of these reasons, McNemar's approach was not used. A third approach is given by Philip H. Dubois, in *Multivariate Correlation Analysis* (New York: Harper, 1957). Since the variance calculated by the DuBois method for each variable is not unique–it varies according to the order in which the variables are eliminated–this approach was not used either.

DISCUSSION

It appears from the results that one major determinant of the tendency to discriminate is the actual and feared frustration arising out of competition with minority-group members. Of course, it has long been recognized that frustration instigates individuals to behave aggressively–to behave in ways they know will hurt others. Here, however, anticipated frustration seems to be more important than actual frustration as a possible antecedent of racial discrimination. . . . Thus, anticipated frustration may be an important concept to introduce into aggression theory, for the two types of frustration–anticipated and actual–may relate differentially to aggression.

The results also show that frustration, actual or anticipated, is not the most important antecedent of the tendency to discriminate. Together, family and friends' pressures may account for about 50 per cent of the variance. Actual frustration and family pressures do, of course, interact, but family pressures [are] by far the more important variable. These results suggest that, if we continue to assume that discrimination is a special case of aggression, aggression theory should be amended to include antecedents other than frustration, namely, social pressures.

Dollard and his associates suggested an important hypothesis involving one form of social pressure—anticipated punishment:[29]

The strength of inhibition of aggression varies directly with the strength of punishment anticipated as a consequence of aggression. (10)

Many respondents in the final sample—particularly those who had experienced considerable frustration in past competition with minority groups—did, in fact, experience family and peer pressures as anticipated punishment that did inhibit their tendency to discriminate. They apparently deviated from family pressures in a way that resulted in a net increase in the tendency to discriminate.

Many other respondents evidently had just the opposite experience, however. Family and friends may have exerted pressures that were experienced as instigations to discriminate. This is probably true of the respondents who expressed many sympathetic stereotypes. They, too, deviated from family pressures, but in a way that evidently resulted in a net decrease in the tendency to discriminate.

These results suggest a basic hypothesis that might be added to aggression theory:

The strength of instigation to aggression varies directly with the strength of punishment anticipated as a consequence of nonaggression. (11)

This hypothesis may be important in understanding aggressive exchanges in intergroup relations generally. It may apply not only to interracial rivalries but also to interfamily, intergang, intercommunity, even international rivalries. For example, how many people fight in wartime in order to escape governmental punishment anticipated as a consequence of refusing to fight?

It appears that individuals may be socialized either to discriminate or not to discriminate by family and friends just as they are socialized to favor one political party, a certain religion (or, perhaps, no religion), or a particular way of life over others. Just as families and friends, by exerting pressures, attempt to enforce norms about voting, religion, and a way of life, they also attempt to enforce norms about how the individual should relate to members of another race. Interestingly enough, the results indicate considerable variation, considerable conflict in the norms enforced by different families and friendship groups. If these norms are considered mores, evidently there are two conflicting sets of mores in operation in the Saint Louis area. Family and friends tend to enforce one or the other, but even the degree of enforcement varies.

* * *

Finally, the results suggest that the patterns of determinants of racial discrimination are not constant. The mores may vary from time to time

[29] John Dollard, Leonard W. Doob, Neal E. Miller, O. H. Mowrer, and Robert R. Sears, *Frustration and Aggression* (New Haven, Conn.: Yale University Press, 1939).

and from place to place, for instance. When they do, apparently the whole pattern of antecedents shifts, since most of the other factors exert influence on the individual tendency to discriminate only by modifying the individual's tendency to conform to normative, or social, pressures.

This is not exactly a new point. Lohman and Reitzes[30] presented case studies ten years ago that led them to similar but perhaps more spectacular conclusions. They found a case where most of the men in a working-class neighborhood worked in the same factory and belonged to the same union. At work, they accepted and even supported the union's position of equality of opportunity and desegregation, to the point of electing a Negro to the position of Vice President in the union. However, in the neighborhood, these same individuals accepted and even identified with the discriminatory objectives of the local neighborhood-improvement association to reject Negroes completely as potential neighbors. Thus, there were individuals caught in a work group and a community group where they experienced quite different mores and social pressures, but these individuals apparently accommodated themselves to both sets of mores. The results of our investigation suggest that some individuals in the Lohman-Reitzes case probably accommodated themselves more readily than others. Nevertheless, both sets of data suggest that the mores, the social pressures, are dominant in race relations–not only in determining behavior but perhaps attitudes themselves.

This suggests that, in order to understand the ideology of racial discrimination in a given locale, it is necessary to do a diagnostic study in that locale to determine the social pressures operating and the other factors that may modify the effects of these social pressures. Thus, in order to understand the ideology of racial discrimination in the United States, perhaps a national sample is required–from the North, the South, the East, the West; and this national sample stratified appropriately. . . .

The Minority Status of Women in Contemporary America

Growing Up Girlish*

Jo Freeman

The passivity that is the essential characteristic of the "feminine" woman is a trait that develops in her from the earliest years. But it is wrong to assert a bio-

[30] Joseph D. Lohman and Dietrich C. Reitzes, "Note on Race Relations in Mass Society," *American Journal of Sociology,* 58 (November, 1952), pp. 240–46.

* From *Trans-action,* vol. 8, nos. 1 and 2 (November–December, 1970), 36–43.

logical datum is concerned; it is, in fact, a destiny imposed upon her by her teachers and by society.

—Simone de Beauvoir

During the last thirty years, social science has paid scant attention to women, confining its explorations of humanity to the male. Research has generally reinforced the popular mythology that women are essentially nurturant, expressive, passive and men instrumental, active, aggressive. Social scientists have tended to justify these stereotypes rather than analyze their origins, their value, or their effect.

The result of this trend has been a social science that is more a mechanism of social control than of social inquiry. Rather than trying to analyze why, it has only described what. Rather than exploring how men and women came to be the way they are, it has taken their condition as irrevocably given and sought to explain this on the basis of "biological" differences.

Nonetheless, the assumption that psychology recapitulates physiology has begun to crack. William Masters and Virginia Johnson shattered the myth of woman's natural sexual passivity—on which her psychological passivity was claimed to rest. Research is just beginning in other areas, and, while evidence is being accumulated, new interpretations of the old data are being explored. What these new interpretations say is that women are the way they are because they've been trained to be that way—their motivations as well as their alternatives have been channeled by society.

This motivation is controlled through the socialization process. Women are raised to want to fill the social roles in which society needs them. They are trained to model themselves after the accepted image and to meet as individuals the expectations that are held for women as a group. Therefore, to understand how most women are socialized, we must first understand how they see themselves and are seen by others. Several studies have been done on this.

One thorough study asked men and women to choose, out of a long list of adjectives, those that most closely applied to themselves. The results showed that women strongly felt that they could accurately be described as uncertain, anxious, nervous, hasty, careless, fearful, dull, childish, helpless, sorry, timid, clumsy, stupid, silly, and domestic. On the more positive side, women felt they were understanding, tender, sympathetic, pure, generous, affectionate, loving, moral, kind, grateful, and patient. This is not a very favorable self-image, but it does correspond fairly well to the myths about what women are like. The image has some "nice" qualities, but they are not the ones normally required for the kinds of achievement to which society gives its highest rewards.

GROSS DISTORTIONS

Now, one can justifiably question both the idea of achievement and the qualities necessary for it, but this is not the place to do so. The fact remains that these standards are widely accepted, and that women have been told they do not meet them. My purpose here, then, is to look at the socialization process as a mechanism to keep them from doing so. All people are socialized to meet the social expectations held for them, and only when this process fails to work (as is currently happening on several fronts) is it at all questioned.

When we look at the *results* of female socialization, we find a strong similarity between what our society labels, even extols, as the typical "feminine" character structure and that of oppressed peoples in this country and elsewhere. In his classic study on *The Nature of Prejudice,* Gordon Allport devotes a chapter to "Traits Due to Victimization." Included are such personality characteristics as sensitivity, submission, fantasies of power, desire for protection, indirectness, ingratiation, petty revenge and sabotage, sympathy, extremes of both self and group hatred and self and group glorification, display of flashy status symbols, compassion for the underprivileged, identification with the dominant group's norms, and passivity. Allport was primarily concerned with Jews and Negroes, but his characterization is disturbingly congruent with the general profile of girls that Lewis Terman and Leona Tyler draw after a very thorough review of the literature on sex differences among young children. For girls, they listed such traits as sensitivity, conformity to social pressures, response to environment, ease of social control, ingratiation, sympathy, low levels of aspiration, compassion for the underprivileged, and anxiety. They found that girls, compared to boys, were more nervous, unstable, neurotic, socially dependent, [and] submissive; had less self-confidence, lower opinions of themselves and of girls in general; and were more timid, emotional, ministrative, fearful, and passive.

Girls' perceptions of themselves were also distorted. Although girls make consistently better school grades than boys until late high school, their opinion of themselves grows progressively worse with age, and their opinion of boys and boys' abilities grows better. Boys, however, have an increasingly better opinion of themselves and worse opinion of girls as they grow older.

These distortions become so gross that, according to Phillip Goldberg in an article in this magazine, by the time girls reach college they have become prejudiced against women. He gave college girls sets of booklets containing six identical professional articles in traditional male, female, and neutral fields. The articles were identical, but the names of the authors were not. For example, an article in one set would bear the name John T. McKay, and in another set the same article would be by-lined Joan T. McKay. Each booklet contained three articles by "women" and three by "men." Questions at the end of each article asked the students to rate the articles on value, persuasiveness and profundity and the authors for style and competence. The male authors fared better on every dimension, even such "feminine" areas as art history and dietetics. Goldberg concluded that "women are prejudiced against female professionals and, regardless of the actual accomplishments of these professionals, will firmly refuse to recognize them as the equals of their male colleagues."

This combination of group self-hate and a distortion of perceptions to justify that group self-hate is precisely typical of a minority-group character structure. It has been noted time and time again. Kenneth and Mamie Clark's finding of the same pattern in Negro children in segregated schools contributed to the 1954 Supreme Court decision that outlawed such schools. These traits, as well as the others typical of the "feminine" stereotype, have been found in the Indians under British rule, in the Algerians under the French, and in black Americans. It would seem, then, that being "feminine" is related to low social status.

This pattern repeats itself even within cultures. In giving Thematic Apperception Tests to women in Japanese villages, George De Vos discovered that those from fishing villages, where the status position of women was higher than in farming communities, were more assertive, not as guilt-ridden, and were more willing to ignore the traditional pattern of arranged marriages in favor of love marriages.

In Terman's famous fifty-year study of the gifted–a comparison of those men who conspicuously failed to fulfill their early promise with those who did–showed that the successful had more self-confidence, fewer background disabilities, and were less nervous and emotionally unstable. But, he concluded, "the disadvantages associated with lower social home status appeared to present the outstanding handicap."

SEXUAL CHARACTERISTICS

The fact that women do have lower social status than men in our society, and that both sexes tend to value men and male characteristics, values, and activities more highly than those of women, has been noted by many authorities. What has not been done is to make the connection between this status and its accompanying personality. The failure to analyze the effects and the causes of lower social status among women is surprising in light of the many efforts that have been made to uncover distinct psychological differences between men and women to account for the tremendous disparity in their social production and creativity. The Goldberg study implies that, even if women did achieve on a par with men, it would not be perceived or accepted as such, and that a woman's work must be of a much higher quality than that of a man to be given the same recognition. But these circumstances alone, or the fact that it is the male definition of achievement that is applied, are not sufficient to account for the relative failure of women to achieve. So, research has turned to male-female differences.

Most of this research, in the Freudian tradition, has focused on finding the psychological and developmental differences supposedly inherent in feminine nature and function. Despite all these efforts, the general findings of psychological testing indicate only that individual differences are greater than sex differences. In other words, sex is just one of the many characteristics that define a human being.

An examination of the work done on intellectual differences between the sexes discloses some interesting patterns, however. First of all, the statistics themselves show some regularity. Most conclusions of what is typical of one sex or the other are founded upon the performances of two-thirds of the subjects. For example, two-thirds of all boys do better on the math section of the College Board Exam than they do on the verbal section, and two-thirds of the girls do better on the verbal than the math. Robert Bales' studies show a similar distribution when he concludes that, in small groups, men are the task-oriented leaders and women are the social-emotional leaders. Not all tests show this two-thirds differential, but it is the mean about which most results of the ability tests cluster. Sex is an easily visible, differentiable, and testable criterion on which to draw conclusions; but it doesn't explain the one-third that do not fit. The only characteristic virtually all women seem to have in common, besides their anatomy, is their lower social status.

Secondly, girls get off to a very good start. They begin speaking, reading, and counting sooner. They articulate more clearly and put words into sentences earlier. They have fewer reading and stuttering problems. Girls are even better in math in the early school years. Consistent sex differences in favor of boys do not appear until high school age. Here, another pattern begins to develop.

During high school, girls' performance in school and on ability tests begins to drop, sometimes drastically. Although well over half of all high school graduates are girls, significantly [fewer] than half of all college students are girls. Presumably, this should mean that a higher percentage of the better female students go on to higher education, but their performance vis-à-vis boys' continues to decline.

ONLY MEN EXCEL

Girls start off better than boys and end up worse. This change in their performance occurs at a very significant point in time. It happens when their status changes, or, to be more precise, when girls become aware of what their adult status is supposed to be. It is during adolescence that peer group pressures to be "feminine" or "masculine" increase, and the conceptions of what is "feminine" and "masculine" become more narrow. It is also at this time that there is a personal drive for conformity. And one of the norms of our culture to which a girl learns to conform is that only men excel. This was evident in Beatrice Lipinski's study on *Sex-Role Conflict and Achievement Motivation in College Women,* which showed that thematic pictures depicting males as central characters elicited significantly more achievement imagery than those with females in them. One need only recall Asch's experiments to see how peer group pressures, armed only with our rigid ideas about "feminity" and "masculinity," could lead to a decline in girls' performance. Asch found that some 33 per cent of his subjects would go contrary to the evidence of their own senses about something as tangible as the comparative length of two lines when their judgments were at variance with those made by the other group members. All but a handful of the other 67 per cent experienced tremendous trauma in trying to stick to their correct perceptions.

When we move to something as intangible as sex role behavior, and to social sanctions far greater than the displeasure of a group of unknown experimental stooges, we can get an idea of how stifling social expectations can be. A corollary of the notion that only men can excel is the cultural norm that a girl should not appear too smart or surpass boys in anything. Again, the pressures to conform, so prevalent in adolescence, prompt girls to believe that the development of their minds will have only negative results. These pressures even affect the supposedly unchangeable I.Q. scores. Corresponding with the drive for social acceptance, girls' I.Q.'s drop below those of boys during high school, rise slightly if they go to college, and go into a steady and consistent decline when and if they become full-time housewives.

These are not the only consequences. Negative self-conceptions have negative effects. They stifle motivation and channel energies into areas more likely to get some positive social rewards. The clincher comes when the very people (women) who have been subjected to these pressures are condemned for not having striven for the highest rewards society has to offer.

A good example of this double bind is what psychologists call the "need for achievement." Achievement motivation in male college sophomores has been studied extensively. In women, it has barely been looked at. The reason for this is that women didn't fit the model social scientists set up to explain achievement in men. Nonetheless, some theories have been put forward that suggest that the real situation is not that women do not have achievement motivation but that this motivation is directed differently [from] that of men. In fact, the achievement orientation of both sexes goes precisely where it is socially directed–educational achievement for boys and marriage achievement for girls.

After considerable research on the question, James Pierce concluded that "girls see that to achieve in life as adult females they need to achieve in non-academic ways, that is, attaining the social graces, achieving beauty in person and dress, finding a desirable social status, marrying the right man. This is the successful adult woman. . . . Their achievement motivations are directed toward realizing personal goals through their relationship with men. . . . Girls who are following the normal course of development are most likely to seek adult status through marriage at an early age."

Achievement for women is adult status through marriage, not success in the usual use of the word. One might postulate that both kinds of success might be possible, particularly for the highly achievement-oriented woman.

But, in fact, the two are more often perceived as contradictory; success in one is seen to preclude success in the other.

Matina Horner recently completed a study at the University of Michigan from which she postulated a psychological barrier to achievement in women. She administered a test in which she asked undergraduates to complete the sentence "After first-term finals, Anne finds herself at the top of her medical school class" with a story of their own. A similar one for a male control group used a masculine name. The results were scored for imagery of fear of success, and Horner found that 65 per cent of the women and only 10 per cent of the men demonstrated a definite "motive to avoid success." She explained the results by hypothesizing that the prospect of success, or situations in which success or failure is a relevant dimension, are perceived as [having], and in fact do have, negative consequences for women.

While many of the choices and attitudes of women are determined by peer and cultural pressures, many other sex differences appear too early to be much affected by peer groups, and are not directly related to sex role attributes.

ANALYTIC CHILDREN

One such sex difference is spatial perception, or the ability to visualize objects out of their context. This is a test in which boys do better, although differences are usually not discernible before the early school years. Other tests, such as the Embedded Figures and the Rod and Frame Tests, likewise favor boys. They indicate that boys perceive more analytically, while girls are more contextual. Again, however, this ability to "break set" or be "field independent" also does not seem to appear until after the fourth or fifth year.

According to Eleanor Maccoby, this contextual mode of perception common to women is a distinct disadvantage for scientific production: "Girls on the average develop a somewhat different way of handling incoming information–their thinking is less analytic, more global, and more perservative [*sic*]–and this kind of thinking may serve very well for many kinds of functioning but it is not the kind of thinking most conducive to high-level intellectual productivity, especially in science."

Several social psychologists have postulated that the key developmental characteristic of analytic thinking is what is called early "independence and mastery training," or, as one group of researchers put it, "whether and how soon a child is encouraged to assume initiative, to take responsibility for himself, and to solve problems by himself, rather than rely on others for the direction of his activities." In other words, analytically inclined children are those who have not been subject to what Urie Bronfenbrenner calls "oversocialization," and there is a good deal of indirect evidence that such is the case. D. M. Levy has observed that "overprotected" boys tend to develop intellectually like girls. Bing found that those girls who were good at spatial tasks were those whose mothers left them alone to solve the problems by themselves, while the mothers of verbally inclined daughters insisted on helping them. H. A. Witkin similarly found that mothers of analytic children had encouraged their initiative, while mothers of nonanalytic children had encouraged dependence and discouraged self-assertion. One writer commented on these studies that "this is to be expected, for the independent child is less likely to accept superficial appearances of objects without exploring them for himself, while the dependent child will be afraid to reach out on his own, and will accept appearances without question. In other words, the independent child is likely to be more active, not only psychologically but physically, and the physically active child will naturally have more kinesthetic experience with spatial relationships in his environment."

The qualities associated with independence training also have an effect on I.Q. I. W. Sontag did a longitudinal study in which he compared children whose I.Q.'s had improved with those whose I.Q.'s had declined with age. He discovered that the child with increasing I.Q. was competitive, self-assertive, independent, and dominant in interaction with other children. Children with declining I.Q.'s were passive, shy, and dependent.

Maccoby commented on this study that "the characteristics associated with a rising I.Q. are not very feminine characteristics." When one of the people working on the Sontag study was asked about what kind of developmental history was necessary to make a girl into an intellectual person, he replied, "The simplest way to put it is that she must be a tomboy at some point in her childhood."

However, analytic abilities are not the only ones that are valued in our society. Being person-oriented and contextual in perception are very valuable attributes for many fields where, nevertheless, very few women are found. Such characteristics are also valuable in the arts and some of the social sciences. But, while women do succeed here more than in the sciences, their achievement is still not equivalent to that of men. One explanation of this, of course, is the study by Horner that established a "motive to avoid success" among women. But, when one looks further, it appears that there is an earlier cause here as well.

SONS AND DAUGHTERS

The very same early independence and mastery training that has such a beneficial effect on analytic thinking also determines the extent of one's achievement orientation. Although comparative studies of parental treatment of boys and girls are not extensive, those that have been made indicate that the traditional practices applied to girls are very different from those applied to boys. Girls receive more affection, more protectiveness, more control, and more restrictions. Boys are subjected to more achievement demands and higher expectations. In short, while girls are not always encouraged to be dependent *per se,* they are usually not encouraged to be independent and physically active. As Bronfenbrenner put it, "Such findings indicate that the differential treatment of the two sexes reflects in part a difference in goals. With sons, socialization seems to focus primarily on directing and constraining the boys' impact on the environment. With daughters, the aim is rather to protect the girl from the impact of environment. The boy is being prepared to mold his world, the girl to be molded by it."

Bronfenbrenner concludes that the crucial variable is the differential treatment by the father, and, "in fact, it is the father who is especially likely to treat children of the two sexes differently." His extremes of affection and of authority are both deleterious. Not only do his high degrees of nurturance and protectiveness toward girls result in oversocialization," but "the presence of strong paternal . . . power is particularly debilitating. In short, boys thrive in a patriarchal context, girls in a matriarchal one."

Bronfenbrenner's observations receive indirect support from Elizabeth Douvan, who noted that "part-time jobs of mothers have a beneficial effect on adolescent children, particularly daughters. This reflects the fact that adolescents may receive too much mothering."

ANXIETY

The importance of mothers, as well as mothering, was pointed out by Kagan and Moss. In looking at the kinds of role models that mothers provide for developing daughters, they discovered that it is those women who are looked upon as unfeminine whose daughters tend to achieve intellectually. These mothers are "aggressive and competitive women who were critical of their daughters and presented themselves to their daughters as intellectually competitive and aggressive role models. It is reasonable to assume that the girls identified with these intellectually aggressive women who valued mastery behavior."

To sum up, there seems to be some evidence that the sexes have been differentially socialized with different training practices, for different goals, and with different results. If David McClelland is right in all the relationships he finds between child-rearing practices, in particular independence and mastery training, achievement motivations scores of individuals tested, actual achievement of individuals, and, indeed, the economic growth of whole societies, there is no longer much question as to why the historical achievement of women has been so low. In fact, with the dependency training they receive so early in life, the wonder is that they have achieved so much.

But this is not the whole story. Maccoby, in her discussion of the relationship of independence training to analytic abilities, notes that the girl who does not succumb to overprotection and develop the appropriate personality and behavior for her sex has a major price to pay—a price in anxiety. Some anxiety is beneficial to creative thinking, but high or sustained levels of it are damaging. Anxiety is particularly manifest in college women, and, of course, they are the ones who experience the most conflict between their current–intellectual–activities and expectations about their future–unintellectual–careers.

Maccoby feels that "it is this anxiety which helps to account for the lack of productivity among those women who do make intellectual careers." The combination of social pressures, role expectations, and parental training together tells "something of a horror story. It would appear that even when a woman is suitably endowed intellectually and develops the right temperament and habits of thought to make use of her endowment, she must be fleet of foot indeed to scale the hurdles society has erected for her and to remain a whole and happy person while continuing to follow her intellectual bent."

The reasons for this horror story must by now be clearly evident. Traditionally, women have been defined as passive creatures, sexually, physically, and mentally. Their roles have been limited to the passive, dependent, auxiliary ones, and they have been trained from birth to fit these roles. However, those qualities by which one succeeds in this society are active ones. Achievement orientation, intellectuality, analytic ability, all require a certain amount of aggression.

As long as women were convinced that these qualities were beyond them, that they would be much happier if they stayed in their place, they remained quiescent under the paternalistic system of Western civilization. But paternalism was a preindustrial scheme of life, and its yoke was partially broken by the industrial revolution. With this loosening up of the social order, the talents of women began to appear.

In the eighteenth century, it was held that no woman had ever produced anything worthwhile in literature, with the possible exception of Sappho. But, in the first half of the nineteenth century, feminine writers of genius flooded the literary scene. It wasn't until the end of the nineteenth century that women scientists of note appeared, and still later that women philosophers were found.

LORDS AT HOME

In preindustrial societies, the family was the basic unit of social and economic organization, and women held a significant and functional role within it. This, coupled with the high birth and death rates of those times, gave women more than enough to do within the home. It was the center of production, and women could be both at home and in the world at the same time. But the industrial revolution, along with decreased infant mortality, increased life span, and changes in economic organization, has all but destroyed the family as the economic unit. Technological advances have taken men out of the home, and now those functions traditionally defined as female are being taken out also. For the first time in human history, women have had to devote themselves to being full-time mothers in order to have enough to do.

Conceptions of society have also changed. At one time, authoritarian hierarchies were the norm, and paternalism was reflective of a general social authoritarian attitude. While it is impossible to do retroactive studies on feudalistic society, we do know that authoritarianism as a personality trait does correlate strongly with a rigid conception of sex roles and with ethnocentrism. We also know from ethnological data that, as W. N. Stephens wrote, there is a "parallel between family relationships and the larger social hierarchy. Autocratic societies have autocratic families. As the king rules his subjects and the nobles subjugate and exploit the commoners, so does husband tend to lord it over wife, father rule over son."

According to Roy D'Andrade, "another variable that appears to affect the distribution of authority and deference between the sexes is the degree to which men rather than women control and mediate property." He presented evidence that showed a direct correlation between the extent to which inheritance, succession, and descent-group membership were patrilineal and the degree of subjection of women.

Even today, the equality of the sexes in the family is often reflective of the economic quality of the partners. In a Detroit sample, Robert Blood and D. M. Wolfe found that the relative power of the wife was low if she did not work and increased with her economic contribution to the family. "The employment of women affects the power structure of the family by equalizing the resources of husband and wife. A working wife's husband listens to her more, and she listens to herself more. She expresses herself and has more opinions. Instead of looking up into her husband's eyes and worshipping him, she levels with him, compromising on the issues at hand. Thus her power increases and, relatively speaking, the husband's falls."

William J. Goode also noted this pattern but said it varied inversely with class status. Toward the upper strata, wives are not only less likely to work, but, when they do, they contribute a smaller percentage of the total family income than is true in the lower classes. Reuben Hill went so far as to say, "Money is a source of power that supports male dominance in the family. . . . Money belongs to him who earns it, not to her who spends it, since he who earns it may withhold it." Phyllis Hallenbeck feels more than just economic resources are involved but does conclude that there is a balance of power in every family that affects "every other aspect of the marriage division of labor, amount of adaptation necessary for either spouse, methods used to resolve conflicts, and so forth." Blood feels the economic situation affects the whole family structure. "Daughters of working mothers are more independent, more self-reliant, more aggressive, more dominant, and more disobedient. Such girls are no longer meek, mild, submissive, and feminine [as] 'little ladies' ought to be. They are rough and tough, actively express their ideas, and refuse to take anything from anybody else. . . . Because their mothers have set an example, the daughters get up the courage and the desire to earn money as well. They take more part-time jobs after school and more jobs during summer vacation."

SEX AND WORK

Herbert Barry, M. K. Bacon, and Irvin Child did an ethnohistoriographic analysis that provides some further insights into the origins of male dominance. After examining the ethnographic reports of 110 cultures, they concluded that large sexual differentiation and male superiority occur concurrently and in "an economy that places a high premium on the superior strength and superior development of motor skills requiring strength, which characterize the male." It is those societies in which great physical strength and mobility are required for survival, in which hunting and herding, or warfare, play an important role, that the male, as the physically stronger and more mobile sex, tends to dominate.

Although there are a few tasks that virtually every society assigns only to men or women, there is a great deal of overlap for most jobs. Virtually every task, even in the most primitive societies, can be performed by either men or women. Equally important, what is defined as a man's task in one society may well be classified as a woman's job in another. Nonetheless, the sexual division of labor is much more narrow than dictated by physical limitations, and what any one culture defines as a woman's job will seldom be performed by a man, and vice versa. It seems that what originated as a division of labor based upon the necessities of survival has spilled over into many other areas and lasted long past the time of its social value. Where male strength and mobility have been crucial to social survival, male dominance and the aura of male superiority have been the strongest. The latter has been incorporated into the value structure and attained an existence of its own.

Thus, male superiority has not ceased with an end to the need for male strength. As Goode pointed out, there is one consistent element in the assignment of jobs to the sexes, even in modern societies: "Whatever the strictly male tasks are, they are defined as *more honorific* [emphasis his]. . . . Moreover, the tasks of control, management, decision, appeals to the gods–in short the higher level jobs that typically do not require strength, speed or traveling far from home–are male jobs."

He goes on to comment that "this element suggests that the sexual divisions of labor within family and society come perilously close to the racial or caste restrictions in some modern countries. That is, the low-ranking race, caste, or sex is defined as not being able to do certain types of prestigious work, but it is also considered a violation of propriety if they do. Obviously, if women really cannot do various kinds of male tasks, no moral or ethical prohibition would be necessary to keep them from it."

COMPANIONSHIP

These sex role differences may have served a natural function at one time, but it is doubtful that they still do so. The characteristics we observe in women and men today are a result of socialization practices developed for the survival of a primitive society. The value structure of male superiority is a reflection of the primitive orientations and values. But social and economic conditions have changed drastically since these values were developed. Technology has reduced to almost nothing the importance of muscular strength. In fact, the warlike attitude that goes along with an idealization of physical strength and dominance is coming to be seen as dreadfully dangerous. The value of large families has also come to be questioned. The result of all these changes is that the traditional sex roles and the traditional family structures have become dysfunctional.

To some extent, patterns of child rearing have also changed. Bronfenbrenner reports that at least middle-class parents are raising both boys and girls much the same. He noted that, over a fifty-year period, middle-class parents have been developing a "more acceptant, equalitarian relationship with their children." With an increase in the family's social position, the patterns of parental treatment of children begin to converge. He likewise noted that a similar phenomenon is beginning to develop in lower-class parents, and equality of treatment is slowly working its way down the social ladder.

The changes in patterns of child rearing correlate with changes in relationships within the family. Both are moving toward a less hierarchical and more egalitarian pattern of living. As Blood has pointed out, "today we may be on the verge of a new phase in American family history, when the companionship family is beginning to manifest itself. One distinguishing characteristic of this family is the dual employment of husband and wife. . . . Employment emancipates women from domination by their husbands and, secondarily, raises their daughters from inferiority to their brothers. . . . The classic differences between masculinity and femininity are disappearing as both sexes in the adult generation take on the same roles in the labor market. . . . The roles of men and women are converging for both adults and children. As a result the family will be far less segregated internally, far less stratified into different age generations and different sexes. The old asymmetry of male-dominated, female-serviced family life is being replaced by a new symmetry."

LEFTOVER DEFINITIONS

All these data indicate that several trends are converging at about the same time. Our value structure has changed from an authoritarian one to a more democratic one, although our social structure has not yet caught up. Social attitudes begin in the family; only a democratic family can raise children to be citizens in a democratic society. The social and economic organization of society that kept women in the home has likewise changed. The home is no longer the center of society. The primary male and female functions have left it, and there is no longer any major reason for maintaining the large sex role differentiations that the home supported. The value placed on physical strength, which reinforced the dominance of men, and the male superiority attitudes that this generated have also become dysfunctional. It is the mind, not the body, that society needs now, and woman's mind is the equal of man's. The pill has liberated women from the uncertainty of child-bearing and, with it, the necessity of being attached to a man for economic support. But our attitudes toward women, and toward the family, have not changed. There is a distinct "cultural lag." Definitions of the family, conceptions of women, and ideas about social function are left over from an era when they were necessary for social survival. They have persisted into an era in which they are no longer viable. The result can only be called severe role dysfunctionality for women.

The necessary relief for this dysfunctionality must come through changes in the social and economic organization of society and in social attitudes that will permit women to play a full and equal part in the social order. With this must come changes in the family, so that men and women are not only equal but can raise their children in a democratic atmosphere. These changes will not come easily, nor will they come through the simple evolution of social trends. Trends do not move all in the same direction or at the same rate. To the extent that changes are dysfunctional with each other, they create problems. These problems will be solved not by complacency but by conscious human direction. Only in this way can we have a real say in the shape of our future and the shape of our lives.

Discrimination Against Black Americans

Men and Jobs*

Elliot Liebow

A pickup truck drives slowly down the street. The truck stops as it comes abreast of a man sitting on a cast-iron porch, and the white driver calls out, asking if the man wants a day's work. The man shakes his head, and the truck moves on up the block, stopping again whenever idling men come within calling distance of the driver. At the Carry-out corner, five men debate the question briefly and shake their heads no to the truck. The truck turns the corner and repeats the same performance up the next street. In the distance, one can see one man, then another, climb into the back of the truck and sit down. In starts and stops, the truck finally disappears.

What is it we have witnessed here? A labor scavenger rebuffed by his would-be prey? Lazy, irresponsible men turning down an honest day's pay for an honest day's work? Or a more complex phenomenon, marking the

* From *Tally's Corner,* by Elliot Liebow, copyright © 1967 by Little, Brown and Co., Inc. Used by permission of Little, Brown and Co.

intersection of economic forces, social values, and individual states of mind and body?

Let us look again at the driver of the truck. He has been able to recruit only two or three men from each twenty or fifty he contacts. To him, it is clear that the others simply do not choose to work. Singly or in groups, belly-empty or belly-full, sullen or gregarious, drunk or sober, they confirm what he has read, heard, and knows from his own experience: These men wouldn't take a job if it were handed to them on a platter.[1]

Quite apart from the question of whether or not this is true of some of the men he sees on the street, it is clearly not true of all of them. If it were, he would not have come here in the first place; or, having come, he would have left with an empty truck. It is not even true of most of them, for most of the men he sees on the street this weekday morning do, in fact, have jobs. But since, at the moment, they are neither working nor sleeping, and since they hate the depressing room or apartment they live in, or because there is nothing to do there,[2] or because they want to get away from their wives or anyone else living there, they are out on the street, indistinguishable from those who do not have jobs or do not want them. Some, like Boley, a member of a trash-collection crew in a suburban housing development, work Saturdays and are off on this weekday. Some, like Sweets, work nights cleaning up middle-class trash, dirt, dishes, and garbage, and mopping the floors of the office buildings, hotels, restaurants, toilets, and other public places dirtied during the day. Some men work for retail businesses, such as liquor stores, that do not begin the day until ten o'clock. Some laborers, like Tally, have already come back from the job, because the ground was too wet for pick and shovel, or because the weather was too cold for pouring concrete. Other employed men stayed off the job today for personal reasons: Clarence to go to a funeral at eleven this morning, and Sea Cat to answer a subpoena as a witness in a criminal proceeding.

Also on the street, unwitting contributors to the impression taken away by the truck driver, are the halt and the lame. The man on the cast-iron steps strokes one gnarled arthritic hand with the other and says he doesn't know whether or not he'll live long enough to be eligible for Social Security. He pauses, then adds matter-of-factly, "Most times, I don't care whether I do or don't." Stoopy's left leg was polio-withered in childhood. Raymond, who looks as if he could tear out a fire hydrant, coughs up blood if he bends or moves suddenly. The quiet man who hangs out in front of the Saratoga apartments has a steel hook strapped onto his left elbow. And, had

[1] By different methods, perhaps, some social scientists have also located the problem in the men themselves, in their unwillingness or lack of desire to work: "To improve the underprivileged worker's performance, one must help him to learn *to want* . . . higher social goals for himself and his children. . . . The problem of changing the work habits and motivation of [lower class] people . . . is a problem of changing the goals, the ambitions, and the level of cultural and occupational aspiration of the underprivileged worker." Allison Davis, "The Motivation of the Underprivileged Worker," in W. F. Whyte, ed., *Industry and Society* (New York: McGraw-Hill, 1946), p. 90.

[2] The comparison of sitting at home alone with being in jail is commonplace.

the man in the truck been able to look into the wine-clouded eyes of the man in the green cap, he would have realized that the man did not even understand he was being offered a day's work.

Others, having had jobs and been laid off, are drawing unemployment compensation (up to $44 per week) and have nothing to gain by accepting work that pays little more than this and frequently less.

Still others, like Bumdoodle the numbers man, are working hard at illegal ways of making money—hustlers who are on the street to turn a dollar any way they can: buying and selling sex, liquor, narcotics, stolen goods, or anything else that turns up.

Only a handful remains unaccounted for. There is Tonk, who cannot bring himself to take a job away from the corner, because, according to the other men, he suspects his wife will be unfaithful if given the opportunity. There is Stanton, who has not reported to work for four days now, not since Bernice disappeared. He bought a brand-new knife against her return. She had done this twice before, he said, but not for so long and not without warning, and he had forgiven her. But this time, "I ain't got it in me to forgive her again." His rage and shame are there for all to see, as he paces the Carry-out and the corner, day and night, hoping to catch a glimpse of her.

And, finally, there are those like Arthur, able-bodied men who have no visible means of support, legal or illegal, who neither have jobs nor want them. The truck driver, among others, believes the Arthurs to be representative of all the men he sees idling on the street during his own working hours. They are not, but they cannot be dismissed simply because they are a small minority. It is not enough to explain them away as being lazy or irresponsible, or both, because an able-bodied man with responsibilities who refuses work is, by the truck driver's definition, lazy and irresponsible. Such an answer begs the question. It is descriptive of the facts; it does not explain them.

Moreover, despite their small numbers, the don't-work-and-don't-want-to-work minority [are] especially significant, because they represent the strongest and clearest expression of those values and attitudes associated with making a living that, to varying degrees, are found throughout the street-corner world. These men differ from the others in degree rather than in kind, the principal difference being that they are carrying out the implications of their values and experiences to their logical, inevitable conclusions. In this sense, the others have yet to come to terms with themselves and the world they live in.

Putting aside, for the moment, what the men say and feel, and looking at what they actually do and the choices they make, getting a job, keeping a job, and doing well at it is clearly of low priority. Arthur will not take a job at all. Leroy is supposed to be on his job at 4:00 P.M.; but it is already 4:10, and he still cannot bring himself to leave the free games he has accumulated on the pinball machine in the Carry-out. Tonk started a construction job on Wednesday, worked Thursday and Friday, then didn't go back again. On the same kind of job, Sea Cat quit in the second week. Sweets had been working three months as a busboy in a restaurant, then quit without notice, not sure himself why he did so. A real-estate agent, saying he was more interested in getting the job done than in the cost, asked Richard to give him an estimate on repairing and painting the inside of a house, but Richard, after looking over the job, somehow never got around to submitting an estimate. During one period, Tonk would not leave the corner to take a job because his wife might prove unfaithful; Stanton would not take a job because his woman had been unfaithful.

Thus, the man-job relationship is a tenuous one. At any given moment, a job may occupy a relatively low position on the street-corner scale of real values. Getting a job may be subordinated to relations with women or to other nonjob considerations; the commitment to a job one already has is frequently shallow and tentative.

The reasons are many. Some are objective and reside principally in the job; some are subjective and reside principally in the man. The line between them, however, is not a clear one. Behind the man's refusal to take a job or his decision to quit one is not a simple impulse or value choice but a complex combination of assessments of objective reality, on the one hand, and values, attitudes, and beliefs drawn from different levels of his experience, on the other.

Objective economic considerations are frequently a controlling factor in a man's refusal to take a job. How much the job pays is a crucial question but seldom asked. He knows how much it pays. Working as a stock clerk, a delivery boy, or even behind the counter of liquor stores, drug stores, and other retail businesses pays one dollar an hour. So, too, do most busboy, car-wash, janitorial, and other jobs available to him. Some jobs, such as dishwasher, may dip as low as eighty cents an hour, and others, such as elevator operator or work in a junk yard, may offer $1.15 or $1.25. Take-home pay for jobs such as these ranges from $35 to $50 a week, but a take-home pay of over $45 for a five-day week is the exception rather than the rule.

One of the principal advantages of these kinds of jobs is that they offer fairly regular work. Most of them involve essential services and are therefore somewhat less responsive to business conditions than are some higher-paying, less menial jobs. Most of them are also inside jobs not dependent on the weather, as are construction jobs and other higher-paying outside work.

Another seemingly important advantage of working in hotels, restaurants, office and apartment buildings, and retail establishments is that they frequently offer an opportunity for stealing on the job. But stealing can be a two-edged-sword. Apart from increasing the cost of the goods or services to the general public, a less obvious result is that the practice usually acts as a depressant on the employee's own wage level. Owners of small retail establishments and other employers frequently anticipate employee stealing and adjust the wage rate accordingly. Tonk's employer explained why he was paying Tonk $35 for a 55–60 hour workweek. These men will all steal, he said. Although he keeps close watch on Tonk, he estimates that Tonk steals from $35 to $40 a week.[3] What he steals, when added to his regular earnings, brings his take-home pay to $70 or $75 per week. The employer said he did not mind this, because Tonk is worth that much to the business. But, if he were to pay Tonk outright the full value of his labor, Tonk would still be stealing $35–$40 per week, and this, he said, the business simply would not support.

This wage arrangement, with stealing built-in, was satisfactory to both parties, with each one independently expressing his satisfaction. Such a wage-theft system, however, is not as balanced and equitable as it appears. Since the wage level rests on the premise that the employee will steal the unpaid value of his labor, the man who does not steal on the job is penalized. And, furthermore, even if he does not steal, no one would believe him; the employer and others believe he steals because the system presumes it.

Nor is the man who steals, as he is expected to, as well off as he believes himself to be. The employer may occasionally close his eyes to the worker's stealing but not often and not for long. He is, after all, a businessman and cannot always find it within himself to let a man steal from him, even if the man is stealing his own wages. Moreover, it is only by keeping close watch on the worker that the employer can control how much is stolen and thereby protect himself against the employee's stealing more than he is worth. From this viewpoint, then, the employer is not in wage-theft collusion with the employee. In the case of Tonk, for instance, the employer was not actively abetting the theft. His estimate of how much Tonk was stealing was based on what he thought Tonk was able to steal despite his own best efforts to prevent him from stealing anything at all. Were he to have caught Tonk in the act of stealing, he would, of course, have fired him from the job and perhaps called the police as well. Thus, in an actual, if not in a legal, sense, all the elements of entrapment are present. The employer knowingly provides the conditions that entice (force) the employee to steal the unpaid value of his labor, but, at the same time, he punishes him for theft if he catches him doing so.

Other consequences of the wage-theft system are even more damaging to the employee. Let us, for argument's sake, say that Tonk is in no danger of entrapment; that his employer is willing to wink at the stealing, and that Tonk, for his part, is perfectly willing to earn a little, steal a little. Let us say, too, that he is paid $35 a week and allowed to steal $35. His money income—as measured by the goods and services he can purchase with it—is, of course, $70. But not all of his income is available to him for all purposes. He cannot draw on what he steals to build his self-respect or to measure his self-worth. For this, he can draw only on his earnings—the

[3] Exactly the same estimate as the one made by Tonk himself. On the basis of personal knowledge of the stealing routine employed by Tonk, however, I suspect the actual amount is considerably smaller.

amount given him publicly and voluntarily in exchange for his labor. His "respect" and "self-worth" income remains at $35—only half [of] that of the man who also receives $70 but all of it in the form of wages. His earnings publicly measure the worth of his labor to his employer, and they are important to others and to himself in taking the measure of his worth as a man.[4]

With or without stealing, and quite apart from any interior processes going on in the man who refuses such a job or quits it casually and without apparent reason, the objective fact is that menial jobs in retailing or in the service trades simply do not pay enough to support a man and his family. This is not to say that the worker is underpaid; this may or may not be true. Whether he is or not, the plain fact is that, in such a job, he cannot make a living. Nor can he take much comfort in the fact that these jobs tend to offer more regular, steadier work. If he cannot live on the $45 or $50 he makes in one week, the longer he works, the longer he cannot live on what he makes.[5]

Construction work, even for unskilled laborers, usually pays better, with the hourly rate ranging from $1.50 to $2.60 an hour.[6] Importantly, too, good references, a good driving record, a tenth-grade (or any high school) education, previous experience, the ability to "bring police clearance with you" are not normally required of laborers as they frequently are for some of the jobs in retailing or in the service trades.

Construction work, however, has its own objective disadvantages. It is, first of all, seasonal work for the great bulk of the laborers, beginning early

[4] Some public credit may accrue to the clever thief but not respect.

[5] It might be profitable to compare, as Howard S. Becker suggests, gross aspects of income and housing costs in this particular area with those reported by Herbert Gans for the low-income working class in Boston's West End. In 1958, Gans reports, median income for the West Enders was just under $70 a week, a level considerably higher than that enjoyed by the people in the Carry-out neighborhood five years later. Gans himself rented a six-room apartment in the West End for $46 a month, about $10 more than the going rate for long-time residents. In the Carry-out neighborhood, rooms that could accommodate more than a cot and a miniature dresser—that is, rooms that qualified for family living—rented for $12–$22 a week. Ignoring differences that really can't be ignored—the privacy and self-contained efficiency of the multiroom apartment as against the fragmented, public living of the rooming-house "apartment," with a public toilet on a floor always different from the one your room is on (no matter, it probably doesn't work, anyway)—and assuming comparable states of disrepair, the West Enders were paying $6 or $7 a month for a room that cost the Carry-outers at least $50 a month, and frequently more. Looking at housing costs as a percentage of income—and again ignoring what cannot be ignored: that what goes by the name of "housing" in the two areas is not at all the same thing—the median-income West Ender could get a six-room apartment for about 12 per cent of his income, while his 1963 Carry-out counterpart, with a weekly income of $60 (to choose a figure from the upper end of the income range), often paid 20–33 per cent of his income for one room. See Herbert J. Gans, *The Urban Villagers,* pp. 10–13.

[6] The higher amount is 1962 union scale for building laborers. According to the Wage Agreement Contract for Heavy Construction Laborers (Washington, D.C., and vicinity) covering the period from May 1, 1963 to April 30, 1966, minimum hourly wage for heavy construction laborers was to go from $2.75 (May, 1963) by annual increments to $2.92, effective November 1, 1965.

in the spring and tapering off as winter weather sets in.[7] And, even during the season, the work is frequently irregular. Early or late in the season, snow or temperatures too low for concrete frequently sends the laborers back home, and, during late spring or summer, a heavy rain on Tuesday or Wednesday, leaving a lot of water and mud behind it, can mean a two- or three-day workweek for the pick-and-shovel men and other unskilled laborers.[8]

The elements are not the only hazard. As the project moves from one construction stage to another, laborers–usually without warning–are laid off, sometimes permanently or sometimes for weeks at a time. The more fortunate or the better workers are told periodically to "take a walk for two, three days."

Both getting the construction job and getting to it are also relatively more difficult than is the case for the menial jobs in retailing and the service trades. Job competition is always fierce. In the city, the large construction projects are unionized. One has to have ready cash to get into the union to become eligible to work on these projects, and, being eligible, one has to find an opening. Unless one "knows somebody"–say, a foreman or a laborer who knows the day before that they are going to take on new men in the morning–this can be a difficult and disheartening search.

Many of the nonunion jobs are in suburban Maryland or Virginia. The newspaper ads say "Report ready to work to the trailer at the intersection of Rte. 11 and Old Bridge Rd., Bunston, Virginia (or Maryland)," but this location may be ten, fifteen, or even twenty-five miles from the Carry-out. Public transportation would require two or more hours to get there, if it services the area at all. Without access to a car or to a car-pool arrangement, it is not worthwhile reading the ad. So the men do not. Jobs such as these are usually filled by word-of-mouth information, beginning with someone who knows someone or who is himself working there and looking for a paying rider. Furthermore, nonunion jobs in outlying areas tend to be smaller projects of relatively short duration and to pay somewhat less than scale.

[7] "Open-sky" work, such as building overpasses, highways, etc., in which the workers and materials are directly exposed to the elements, traditionally begins in March and ends around Thanksgiving. The same is true for much of the street repair work and the laying of sewer, electric, gas, and telephone lines by the city and public utilities, all important employers of laborers. Between Thanksgiving and March, they retain only skeleton crews selected from their best, most reliable men.

[8] In a recent year, the crime rate in Washington for the month of August jumped 18 per cent over the preceding month. A veteran police officer explained the increase to David L. Bazelon, Chief Judge, U.S. Court of Appeals for the District of Columbia. "It's quite simple. . . . You see, August was a very wet month. . . . These people wait on the street corner each morning around 6:00 or 6:30 for a truck to pick them up and take them to a construction site. If it's raining, that truck doesn't come, and the men are going to be idle that day. If the bad weather keeps up for three days . . . we know we are going to have trouble on our hands–and sure enough, there invariably follows a rash of purse-snatchings, house-breakings and the like. . . . These people have to eat like the rest of us, you know." David L. Bazelon, Address to the Federal Bar Association, p. 3.

Still another objective factor is the work itself. For some men, whether the job be digging, mixing mortar, pushing a wheelbarrow, unloading materials, carrying and placing steel rods for reinforcing concrete, or building or laying concrete forms, the work is simply too hard. Men such as Tally and Wee Tom can make such work look like child's play; some of the older work-hardened men, such as Budder and Stanton, can do it, too, though not without showing unmistakable signs of strain and weariness at the end of the workday. But those who lack the robustness of a Tally or the time-inured immunity of a Budder must either forego jobs such as these or pay a heavy toll to keep them. For Leroy, in his early twenties, almost six feet tall but weighing under 140 pounds, it would be as difficult to push a loaded wheelbarrow, or to unload and stack 96-pound bags of cement all day long, as it would be for Stoopy with his withered leg.

Heavy, backbreaking labor of the kind that used to be regularly associated with bull gangs or concrete gangs is no longer characteristic of laboring jobs, especially those with the larger, well-equipped construction companies. Brute strength is still required from time to time, as on smaller jobs, where it is not economical to bring in heavy equipment, or where the small, undercapitalized contractor has none to bring in. In many cases, however, the conveyor belt has replaced the wheelbarrow or the Georgia buggy, mechanized forklifts have eliminated heavy, manual lifting, and a variety of digging machines have replaced the pick and shovel. The result is fewer jobs for unskilled laborers and, in many cases, a work speed-up for those who do have jobs. Machines now set the pace formerly set by men. Formerly, a laborer pushed a wheelbarrow of wet cement to a particular spot, dumped it, and returned for another load. Another laborer, in hip boots, pushed the wet concrete around with a shovel or a hoe, geting it roughly level in preparation for the skilled finishers. He had relatively small loads to contend with and had only to keep up with the men pushing the wheelbarrows. Now, the job for the man pushing the wheelbarrow is gone, and the wet concrete comes rushing down a chute at the man in the hip boots, who must "spread it quick or drown."

Men who have been running an elevator, washing dishes, or "pulling trash" cannot easily move into laboring jobs. They lack the basic skills for "unskilled" construction labor, familiarity with tools and materials, and tricks of the trade without which hard jobs are made harder. Previously unused or untrained muscles rebel in pain against the new and insistent demands made upon them, seriously compromising the man's performance and testing his willingness to see the job through.

A healthy, sturdy, active man of good intelligence requires from two to four weeks to break in on a construction job.[9] Even if he is willing somehow to bull his way through the first few weeks, it frequently happens that

[9] Estimate of Mr. Francis Greenfield, President of the International Hod Carriers, Building and Common Laborers' District Council of Washington, D.C. and vicinity. I am indebted to Mr. Greenfield for several points in these paragraphs dealing with construction laborers.

his foreman or the craftsman he services with materials and general assistance is not willing to wait that long for him to get into condition or to learn at a glance the difference in size between a rough 2″ x 8″ and a finished 2″ x 10″. The foreman and the craftsman are themselves "under the gun" and cannot "carry" the man when other men, who are already used to the work and who know the tools and materials, are lined up to take the job.

Sea Cat was "healthy, sturdy, active, and of good intelligence." When a judge gave him six weeks in which to pay his wife $200 in back child-support payments, he left his grocery-store job in order to take a higher-paying job as a laborer, arranged for him by a foreman friend. During the first week, the weather was bad, and he worked only Wednesday and Friday, cursing the elements all the while for cheating him out of the money he could have made. The second week, the weather was fair, but he quit at the end of the fourth day, saying frankly that the work was too hard for him. He went back to his job at the grocery store and took a second job working nights as a dishwasher in a restaurant,[10] earning little, if any, more at the two jobs than he would have earned as a laborer and keeping at both of them until he had paid off his debts.

Tonk did not last as long as Sea Cat. No one made any predictions when he got a job in a parking lot; but, when the men on the corner learned he was to start on a road construction job, estimates of how long he would last ranged from one to three weeks. Wednesday was his first day. He spent that evening and night at home. He did the same on Thursday. He worked Friday and spent Friday evening and part of Saturday draped over the mailbox on the corner. Sunday afternoon, Tonk decided he was not going to report on the job the next morning. He explained that, after working three days, he knew enough about the job to know that it was too hard for him. He knew he wouldn't be able to keep up, and he'd just as soon quit now as get fired later.

Logan was a tall, two-hundred-pound man in his late twenties. His back used to hurt him only on the job, he said, but now he can't straighten up for increasingly longer periods of time. He said he had traced this to the awkward walk he was forced to adopt by the loaded wheelbarrows, which pull him down into a half-stoop. He's going to quit, he said, as soon as he can find another job. If he can't find one real soon, he guesses he'll quit anyway. It's not worth it, having to walk bent over and leaning to one side.

Sometimes, the strain and effort is greater than the man is willing to admit, even to himself. In the early summer of 1963, Richard was rooming at Nancy's place. His wife and children were "in the country" (his grandmother's home in Carolina), waiting for him to save up enough money so that he could bring them back to Washington and start over again after a disastrous attempt to "make it" in Philadelphia. Richard had gotten a job with a fence company in Virginia. It paid $1.60 an hour. The first few evenings, when he came home from work, he looked ill from exhaustion and the heat. Stanton said Richard would have to quit, "he's too small

[10] Not a sinecure, even by street-corner standards.

[thin] for that kind of work." Richard said he was doing O.K. and would stick with the job.

At Nancy's one night, when Richard had been working about two weeks, Nancy and three or four others were sitting around talking, drinking, and listening to music. Someone asked Nancy when was Richard going to bring his wife and children up from the country. Nancy said she didn't know, but it probably depended on how long it would take him to save up enough money. She said she didn't think he could stay with the fence job much longer. This morning, she said, the man Richard rode to work with knocked on the door, and Richard didn't answer. She looked in his room. Richard was still asleep. Nancy tried to shake him awake. "No more digging!" Richard cried out. "No more digging! I can't do no more God-damn digging!" When Nancy finally managed to wake him, he dressed quickly and went to work.

Richard stayed on the job two more weeks, then suddenly quit, ostensibly because his pay check was three dollars less than what he thought it should have been.

In summary of objective job considerations, then, the most important fact is that a man who is able and willing to work cannot earn enough money to support himself, his wife, and one or more children. A man's chances for working regularly are good only if he is willing to work for less than he can live on, and sometimes not even then. On some jobs, the wage rate is deceptively higher than on others; but the higher the wage rate, the more difficult it is to get the job, and the less the job security. Higher-paying construction work tends to be seasonal, and, during the season, the amount of work available is highly sensitive to business and weather conditions and to the changing requirements of individual projects.[11] Moreover, high-paying construction jobs are frequently beyond the physical capacity of some of the men, and some of the low-paying jobs are scaled down even lower in accordance with the self-fulfilling assumption that the man will steal part of his wages on the job.[12]

Bernard assesses the objective job situation dispassionately over a cup of coffee, sometimes poking at the coffee with his spoon, sometimes staring at it as if, like a crystal ball, it holds tomorrow's secrets. He is twenty-seven years old. He and the woman with whom he lives have a baby son, and she

[11] The over-all result is that, in the long run, a Negro laborer's earnings are not substantially greater—and may be less—than those of the busboy, janitor, or stock clerk. Herman P. Miller, for example, reports that, in 1960, 40 per cent of all jobs held by Negro men were as laborers or in the service trades. The average annual wage for nonwhite, nonfarm laborers was $2,400. The average earning of nonwhite service workers was $2,500 (*Rich Man, Poor Man,* p. 90). Francis Greenfield estimates that, in the Washington vicinity, the 1965 earnings of the union laborer who works whenever work is available will be about $3,200. Even this figure is high for the man on the street corner. Union men in heavy construction are the aristocrats of the laborers. Casual day labor and jobs with small firms in the building and construction trades, or with firms in other industries, pay considerably less.

[12] For an excellent discussion of the self-fulfilling assumption (or prophecy) as a social force, see "The Self-Fulfilling Prophecy," Chap. 11, in Robert K. Merton's *Social Theory and Social Structure*.

has another child by another man. Bernard does odd jobs—mostly painting—but here it is the end of January, and his last job was with the Post Office during the Christmas mail rush. He would like postal work as a steady job, he says. It pays well (about $2.00 an hour), but he has twice failed the Post Office examination (he graduated from a Washington high school) and has given up the idea as an impractical one. He is supposed to see a man tonight about a job as a parking attendant for a large apartment house. The man told him to bring his birth certificate and driver's license, but his license was suspended because of a backlog of unpaid traffic fines. A friend promised to lend him some money this evening. If he gets it, he will pay the fines tomorrow morning and have his license reinstated. He hopes the man with the job will wait till tomorrow night.

A "security job" is what he really wants, he said. He would like to save up money for a taxicab. (But, having twice failed the postal examination, and having a bad driving record as well, it is highly doubtful that he could meet the qualifications or pass the written test.) That would be "a good life." He can always get a job in a restaurant or as a clerk in a drugstore, but they don't pay enough, he said. He needs to take home at least $50–$55 a week. He thinks he can get that much driving a truck somewhere. . . . Sometimes, he wishes he had stayed in the army. . . . A security job, that's what he wants most of all, a real security job. . . .

Black Power

An Advocate of Black Power Defines It*

Charles V. Hamilton

Black power has many definitions and connotations in the rhetoric of race relations today. To some people, it is synonymous with premeditated acts of violence to destroy the political and economic institutions of this country. Others equate Black Power with plans to rid the civil-rights movement of whites who have been in it for years. The concept is understood by many to mean hatred of, and separation from, whites; it is associated with calling whites "honkies" and with shouts of "Burn, baby, burn!" Some understand it to be the use of pressure-group tactics in the accepted tradition of the American political process. And still others say that Black Power must be seen first of all as an attempt to instill a sense of identity and pride in black people.

* From the *New York Times Magazine,* April 14, 1968. Copyright 1968 by the New York Times Company. Reprinted by permission.

Ultimately, I suspect, we have to accept the fact that, in this highly charged atmosphere, it is virtually impossible to come up with a single definition satisfactory to all.

Even as some of us try to articulate our idea of Black Power and the way we relate to it and advocate it, we are categorized as "moderate" or "militant" or "reasonable" or "extremist." "I can accept your definition of Black Power," a listener will say to me. "But how does your position compare with what Stokely Carmichael said in Cuba, or with what H. Rap Brown said in Cambridge, Maryland?" Or, just as frequently, some young white New Left advocate will come up to me and proudly announce: "You're not radical enough. Watts, Newark, Detroit–that's what's happening, man! You're nothing but a reformist. We've got to blow up this society. Read Ché or Debray or Mao." All I can do is shrug and conclude that some people believe that making a revolution in this country involves rhetoric, Molotov cocktails, and being under thirty.

To have Black Power equated with calculated acts of violence would be very unfortunate. First, if black people have learned anything over the years, it is that he who shouts revolution the loudest is one of the first to run when the action starts. Second, open calls to violence are a sure way to have one's ranks immediately infiltrated. Third–and this is as important as any reason–violent revolution in this country would fail; it would be met with the kind of repression used in Sharpeville, South Africa, in 1960, when 67 Africans were killed and 186 wounded during a demonstration against apartheid. It is clear that America is not above this. There are many white bigots who would like nothing better than to embark on a program of black genocide, even though the imposition of such repressive measures would destroy civil liberties for whites as well as for blacks. Some whites are so panicky, irrational, and filled with racial hatred that they would welcome the opportunity to annihilate the black community. This was clearly shown in the senseless murder of Dr. Martin Luther King, Jr., which understandably–but nonetheless irrationally–prompted some black militants to advocate violent retaliation. Such cries for revenge intensify racial fear and animosity, when the need–now more than ever–is to establish solid, stable organizations and action programs.

Many whites will take comfort in these words of caution against violence. But they should not. The truth is that the black ghettos are going to continue to blow up out of sheer frustration and rage, and no amount of rhetoric from professors writing articles in magazines (which most black people in the ghettos do not read, anyway) will affect that. There comes a point beyond which people cannot be expected to endure prejudice, oppression, and deprivation, and they *will* explode.

Some of us can protect our positions by calling for "law and order" during a riot or by urging "peaceful" approaches, but we should not be confident that we are being listened to by black people legitimately fed up with intolerable conditions. If white America wants a solution to the violence in the ghettos by blacks, then let white America end the violence done to the ghettos by whites. We simply must come to understand that there can be no social order without social justice. "How long will the violence in the summers last?" another listener may ask. "How intransigent is white America?" is my answer. And the answer to that could be just more rhetoric, or it could be a sincere response to legitimate demands.

Black power must not be naïve about the intentions of white decision-makers to yield anything without a struggle and a confrontation by organized power. Black people will gain only as much as they can win through their ability to organize independent bases of economic and political power—through boycotts, electoral activity, rent strikes, work stoppages, pressure-group bargaining. And it must be clear that whites will have to bargain with blacks or continue to fight them in the streets of the Detroits and the Newarks. Rather than being a call to violence, this is a clear recognition that the ghetto rebellions, in addition to producing the possibility of apartheid-type repression, have been functional in moving *some* whites to see that viable solutions must be sought.

Black Power is concerned with organizing the rage of black people and with putting new, hard questions and demands to white America. As we do this, white America's responses will be crucial to the questions of violence and viability. Black Power must (1) deal with the obviously growing alienation of black people and their distrust of the institutions of this society, (2) work to create new values and to build a new sense of community and of belonging, and (3) to work to establish legitimate new institutions that make participants, not recipients, out of a people traditionally excluded from the fundamentally racist processes of this country. There is nothing glamorous about this; it involves persistence and hard, tedious, day-to-day work.

Black Power rejects the lessons of slavery and segregation that caused black people to look upon themselves with hatred and disdain. To be "integrated," it was necessary to deny one's heritage, one's own culture; to be ashamed of one's black skin, thick lips, and kinky hair. In their book, *Racial Crisis in America,* two Florida State University sociologists, Lewis M. Killian and Charles M. Grigg, wrote: "At the present time, integration as a solution to the race problem demands that the Negro forswear his identity as a Negro. But for a lasting solution, the meaning of 'American' must lose its implicit racial modifier, 'white.' " The black man must change his demeaning conception of himself; he must develop a sense of pride and self-respect. Then, if integration comes, it will deal with people who are psychologically and mentally healthy, with people who have a sense of their history and of themselves as whole human beings.

In the process of creating these new values, Black Power will, its advocates hope, build a new sense of community among black people. It will try to forge a bond in the black community between those who have "made it" and those "on the bottom." It will bring an end to the internal backbiting and suspicious bickering, the squabbling over tactics and personalities so characteristic of the black community. If Black Power can produce this unity, that in itself will be revolutionary—for the black community and for the country.

Black power recognizes that new forms of decision-making must be implemented in the black community. One purpose, clearly, is to overcome the alienation and distrust.

Let me deal with this specifically by looking at the situation in terms of "internal" and "external" ghetto problems and approaches. When I speak of internal problems, I refer to such things as exploitative merchants who invade the black communities, to absentee slumlords, to inferior schools and arbitrary law enforcement, to black people unable to develop their own independent economic and political bases. There are, of course, many problems facing black people that must be dealt with outside the ghettos—jobs, open occupancy, medical care, higher education.

The solution of the internal problems does not require the presence of massive numbers of whites marching arm in arm with blacks. Local all-black groups can organize boycotts of disreputable merchants and of those employers in the black communities who fail to hire and promote black people. Already, we see this approach spreading across the country with Operation Breadbasket, initiated by Dr. King's Southern Christian Leadership Conference. The national director of the program, the Reverend Jesse Jackson, who was with Dr. King when he was murdered in Memphis, has established several such projects from Los Angeles to Raleigh, North Carolina.

In Chicago alone, in fifteen months, approximately 2,000 jobs, worth more than $15 million in annual income, were obtained for black people. Negotiations are conducted on hiring and upgrading black people, marketing the products of black manufacturers and suppliers, and providing contracts to black companies. The operation relies heavily on the support of black businessmen, who are willing to work with Operation Breadbasket because it is mutually beneficial. They derive a profit and, in turn, contribute to the economic development of the black community.

This is Black Power in operation. But there is not nearly enough of this kind of work going on. In some instances, there is a lack of technical know-how coupled with a lack of adequate funds. These two defects constantly plague constructive pressure-group activity in the black communities.

CORE (Congress of Racial Equality) has developed a number of cooperatives around the country. In Opelousas, Louisiana, it has organized over 300 black farmers, growers of sweet potatoes, cabbages, and okra, in the Grand-Marie Co-op. They sell their produce, and some of the income goes back into the co-op as dues. Initially, 20 per cent of the cooperative's members were white farmers, but most of the whites dropped out as a result of social and economic pressures from the white community. An offshoot of the Grand-Marie group is the Southern Consumers' Cooperative in Lafayette, Louisiana, which makes and sells fruit cakes and candy. It has been in existence for more than a year, employs approximately 150 black people, and has led to the formation of several credit unions and buying clubs.

The major effort of Black Power–oriented CORE is in the direction of economic development. Antoine Perot, program director of CORE, says: "One big need in the black community is to develop capital-producing instruments which create jobs. Otherwise we are stuck with the one-crop commodity–labor–which does not produce wealth. Mere jobs are not enough. These will simply perpetuate black dependency."

Thus, small and medium-sized businesses are being developed in the black communities of Chicago, San Francisco, Detroit, Cleveland, New York, and several other urban centers. CORE hopes to call on some successful black businessmen around the country as consultants, and it is optimistic that they will respond favorably with their know-how and, in some instances, their money. The goal is to free as many black people as possible from economic dependency on the white man. It has been this dependency in many places that has hampered effective, independent political organizing.

In New York, Black Power, in the way we see it, operates through a group called NEGRO (National Economic Growth and Reconstruction Organization). Its acronym does not sit too well with some advocates of black consciousness who see in the use of the term "Negro" an indication of less than sufficient racial pride. Started in 1964, the group deals with economic self-help for the black community: a hospital in Queens, a chemical corporation, a textile company, and a construction company. NEGRO, with an annual payroll of $1 million and assets of $3 million, is headed by Dr. Thomas W. Matthew, a neurosurgeon who has been accused of failing to file federal income-tax returns for 1961, 1962, and 1963. He has asserted that he will pay all the Government says he owes, but not until "my patient is cured or one of us dies." His patient is the black community, and the emphasis of his group is on aiding blacks and reducing reliance on the white man. The organization creates a sense of identity and cohesiveness that is painfully lacking in much of the black community.

In helping oneself and one's race through hard work, NEGRO would appear to be following the Puritan ethic of work and achievement: If you work hard, you will succeed. One gets the impression that the organization is not necessarily idealistic about this. It believes that black people will never develop in this country as long as they must depend on handouts from the white man. This is realism, whatever ethic it is identified with. And this, too, is Black Power in operation.

More frequently than not, projects will not use the term "Black Power," but that is hardly necessary. There is, for instance, the Poor People's Corporation, formed by a former SNCC (Student Nonviolent Coordinating Committee) worker, Jessie Norris, in August, 1965. It has set up 15 cooperatives in Mississippi, employing about 200 black people. The employees, all shareholders, make handbags, hats, dresses, quilts, dolls, and other handcraft items that are marketed through Liberty House in Jackson, Mississippi. Always sensitive to the development of the black community, the Poor People's Corporation passed a rule that only registered voters could work in the co-ops.

These enterprises are small; they do not threaten the economic structure of this society, but their members look upon them as vital for the development of the black people. Their purpose is to establish a modicum of economic self-sufficiency without focusing too much attention on the impact they will have on the American economic system.

Absolutely crucial to the development of Black Power is the black middle class. These are people with sorely needed skills. There has been a lot of discussion about where the black middle class stands in relation to Black Power. Some people adopt the view that most members of the class opt out of the race (or at least try to do so); they get good jobs, a nice home, two cars, and forget about the masses of blacks who have not "made it." This has been largely true. Many middle-class blacks simply do not feel an obligation to help the less fortunate members of their race.

There is, however, a growing awareness among black middle-class people of their role in the black revolution. On January 20, [1968,] a small group of them (known, appropriately enough, as the Catalysts) called an all-day conference in a South Side Chicago church to discuss ways of linking black middle-class professionals with black people in the lower class. Present were about 370 people of all sorts—teachers, social workers, lawyers, accountants, three physicians, housewives, writers. They met in workshops to discuss ways of making their skills and positions relevant to the black society, and they held no press conferences. Although programs of action developed, the truth is that they remain the exception, not the rule, in the black middle class.

Another group has been formed by black teachers in Chicago, Detroit, and New York, and plans are being made to expand. In Chicago, the organization is called the Association of Afro-American Educators. These are people who have traditionally been the strongest supporters of the status quo. Education is intended to develop people who will support the existing values of the society, and "Negro" teachers have been helping this process over the years. But now some of them (more than 250 met on February 12 in Chicago) are organizing and beginning to redefine, first, their role as black educators vis-à-vis the black revolution and, second, the issues as they see them. Their motivation is outlined in the following statement:

> By tapping our vast resources of black intellectual expertise, we shall generate new ideas for *meaningful* educational programs, curricula and instructional materials that will contribute substantially toward raising the educational achievement of black children.
>
> Our purpose is to extricate ourselves momentarily from the dominant society in order to realign our priorities, to mobilize, and to "get ourselves together" to do what must be done by those best equipped to do it.

This is what they *say;* whether they can pull it off will depend initially on their ability to bring along their black colleagues, many of whom, admittedly, do not see the efficacy of such an attitude. Unless the link is made between the black middle-class professionals and the black masses, Black Power will probably die on the speaker's platform.

Another important phenomenon in the development of Black Power is the burgeoning of black students' groups on college campuses across the country. I have visited seventeen such campuses–from Harvard to Virginia to Wisconsin to UCLA–since October [, 1967]. The students are discussing problems of identity, of relevant curricula at their universities, of ways of helping their people when they graduate. Clearly, one sees in these hundreds (the figure could be in the thousands) of black students a little bit of Booker T. Washington (self-help and the dignity of common labor) and a lot of W. E. B. DuBois (vigorous insistence on equality and the liberal education of the most talented black men).

These are the people who are planning to implement social, political, and economic Black Power in their home towns. They will run for public office, aware that Richard Hatcher started from a political base in the black community. He would not be Mayor of Gary, Indiana, today if he had not first mobilized the black voters. Some people point out that he had to have white support. This is true; in many instances, such support is necessary, but internal unity is necessary first.

This brings us to a consideration of the external problems of the black community. It is clear that black people will need the help of whites at many places along the line. There simply are not sufficient economic resources –actual or potential–in the black community for a total, unilateral, bootstrap operation. Why should there be? Black people have been the target of deliberate denial for centuries, and racist America has done its job well. This is a serious problem that must be faced by Black Power advocates. On the one hand, they recognize the need to be independent of the "white power structure." And, on the other, they must frequently turn to that structure for help–technical and financial. Thus, the rhetoric and the reality often clash.

Resolution probably lies in the realization by white America that it is in her interest not to have a weak, dependent, alienated black community inhabiting the inner cities and blowing them up periodically. Society needs stability, and, as long as there is a sizable, powerless, restless group within it that considers the society illegitimate, stability is not possible. However it is calculated, the situation calls for a black-white rapprochement, which may well come only through additional confrontations and crises. More frequently than not, the self-interest of the dominant society is not clearly perceived until the brink is reached.

There are many ways whites can relate to this phenomenon. First, they must recognize that blacks are going to insist on an equitable distribution of *decision-making power.* Anything less will simply be perpetuating a welfare mentality among blacks. And, if the society thinks only in terms of *giving* more jobs, better schools, and more housing, the result will be the creation of more black recipients still dependent on whites.

The equitable distribution of power must result from a conviction that it is a matter of mutual self-interest, not from the feelings of guilt and altruism that were evident at the National Conference of New Politics convention in Chicago in August. An equitable distribution means that black men will have to occupy positions of political power in precincts, counties, Congressional districts, and cities where their numbers and organization warrant. It means the end of absentee white ward committeemen and precinct captains in Chicago's black precincts.

But this situation is much easier described than achieved. Black Americans generally are no more likely to vote independently than other Americans. In many Northern urban areas, especially, the job of wooing the black vote away from the Democratic party is gigantic. The established machine has the resources—patronage, tradition, apathy. In some instances, the change will take a catalytic event—a major racial incident, a dramatic black candidate, a serious boner by the white establishment (such as splitting the white vote). The mere call to "blackness" simply is not enough, even where the numbers are right.

In addition, many of the problems facing black people can be solved only to the extent that whites are willing to see such imperatives as an open-housing market and an expanding job market. White groups must continue to bring as much pressure as possible on local and national decision-makers to adopt sound policy in these fields. These enlightened whites *will* be able to work with Black Power groups.

There are many things that flow from this orientation to Black Power. It is not necessary that blacks create parallel agencies—political or economic —in all fields and places. In some areas, it is possible to work within, say, the two-party system. Richard Hatcher did so in Gary, but he first had to organize black voters to fight the Democratic machine in the primary. The same is true of Mayor Carl Stokes in Cleveland. At some point it may be wise to work with the existing agencies, but this must be done only from a base of independent, not subordinated, power.

On the other hand, dealing with a racist organization like George Wallace's Democratic party in Alabama would require forming an independent group. The same is true with some labor unions, especially in the South, that still practice discrimination, despite the condemnation of such a policy by their parent unions. Many union locals are willing to work with their black members on such matters as wages and working conditions but refuse to join the fight for open-housing laws.

The point is that black people must become much more pragmatic in their approach. Whether we try to work within or outside a particular agency should depend entirely on a hard-nosed, calculated examination of potential success in each situation—a careful analysis of cost and benefit. Thus, when we negotiate, the test will be: How will black people, not some political machine downtown or some labor union boss across town, benefit from this?

Black Power must insist that the institutions in the black community be led by, and, wherever possible, staffed by, blacks. This is advisable psychologically, and it is necessary as a challenge to the myth that black people are incapable of leadership. Admittedly, this violates the principle of egalitarianism ("We hire on the basis of merit alone, not color"). What black and white America must understand is that egalitarianism is just a *principle,* and [that] it implies a notion of "colorblindness" that is deceptive. It must be clear by now that any society that has been color-conscious all its life, to the detriment of a particular group, cannot simply become color-blind and expect that group to compete on equal terms.

Black Power clearly recognizes the need to perpetuate color consciousness, but in a positive way—to improve a group, not to subject it. When principles like egalitarianism have been so flagrantly violated for so long, it does not make sense to think that the victim of that violation can be equipped to benefit from opportunities simply upon their pronouncement. Obviously, some positive form of special treatment must be used to overcome centuries of negative special treatment.

This has been the argument of the Nation of Islam (the so-called Black Muslims) for years; it has also been the position of the National Urban League since its proposal for preferential treatment (the Domestic Marshall Plan, which urged a "special effort to overcome serious disabilities resulting from historic handicaps") was issued at its 1963 Denver convention. This is not racism. It is not intended to penalize or subordinate another group; its goal is the positive uplift of a deliberately repressed group. Thus, when some Black Power advocates call for the appointment of black people to head community-action poverty programs and to serve as school principals, they have in mind the deliberate projection of blacks into positions of leadership. This is important to give other black people a feeling of ability to achieve, if nothing else. And it is especially important for young black children.

An example of concentrated special treatment is the plan some of us are proposing for a new approach to education in some of the black ghettos. It goes beyond the decentralization plans in the Bundy Report; it goes beyond the community involvement at I.S. 201 in Harlem. It attempts to build on the idea proposed by Harlem CORE last year for an independent Board of Education for Harlem.

Harlem CORE and the New York Urban League saw the Bundy Report as a "step toward creating a structure which would bring meaningful education to the children of New York." CORE, led by Roy Innis, suggested an autonomous Harlem school system, chartered by the State Legislature and responsible to the state. "It will be run by an elected school board and an appointed administrator, as most school boards are," CORE said. "The elected members will be Harlem residents. It is important that much of the detailed planning and structure be the work of the Harlem community." Funds would come from city, state, and federal governments and from private sources. In describing the long-range goal of the proposal, CORE says: "Some have felt it is to create a permanently separate educational system. Others have felt it is a necessary step toward eventual integration. In any case, the ultimate outcome of this plan will be to make it possible for Harlem to choose."

Some of us propose that education in the black community should be family-oriented, not simply child-oriented. In many of the vast urban black ghettos (which will not be desegregated in the foreseeable future) the school should become the focal point of the community. This we call the Family-Community-School Comprehensive Plan. School would cease to be a 9-to-3, September-to-June, time-off-for-good-behavior institution. It would involve education and training for the entire family—all year round, day and evening. Black parents would be intimately involved as students, decision-makers, teachers. This is much more than a revised notion of adult education courses in the evening or the use of mothers as teachers' aides.

This plan would make the educational system the center of community life. We could have community health clinics and recreational programs built into the educational system. Above all, we could reorient the demeaning public welfare system, which sends caseworkers to "investigate" families. Why could we not funnel public assistance through the community educational program?

One major advantage would be the elimination of some of the bureaucratic chaos in which five to ten governmental agencies zero in on the black family on welfare, seldom if ever coordinating their programs. The welfare department, for one, while it would not need to be altered in other parts of the state, would have to work jointly with the educational system in the black community. This would obviously require administrative reorganization, which would not necessarily reduce bureaucracy but would consolidate and centralize it. In addition to being "investigators," for example, some caseworkers (with substantially reduced case loads) could become teachers of budgetary management, and family health consultants could report the economic needs of the family.

The teachers for such a system would be specially trained in a program similar to the National Teacher Corps, and recruits could include professionals as well as mothers who could teach classes in child rearing, home economics, art, music, or any number of skills they obviously possess. Unemployed fathers could learn new skills or teach the ones they know. The curriculum would be both academic and vocational, and it would contain courses in the culture and history of black people. The school would belong to the community. It would be a union of children, parents, teachers, social workers, psychologists, urban planners, doctors, community organizers. It would become a major vehicle for fashioning a sense of pride and group identity.

I see no reason why the local law-enforcement agency could not be integrated into this system. Perhaps this could take the form of training "community service officers," or junior policemen, as suggested in the report of the President's Commission on Civil Disorders. Or the local police precinct could be based in the school, working with the people on such things as crime prevention, first aid, and the training of police officers. In this way, mutual trust could be developed between the black community and the police.

Coordinating these programs would present problems to be worked out on the basis of the community involved, the agencies involved, and the size of the system. It seems quite obvious that, in innovations of this sort, there will be a tremendous amount of chaos and uncertainty, and there will be mistakes. This is understandable; it is the price to be paid for social change under circumstances of widespread alienation and deprivation. The recent furor about the Malcolm X memorial program at I.S. 201 in Harlem offers an example of the kind of problem to be anticipated. Rather than worrying about what one person said from a stage at a particular meeting, the authorities should be concerned about how the Board of Education will cooperate to transfer power to the community school board. When the transfer is made, confusion regarding lines of authority and program and curriculum content can be reduced.

The longer the delay in making the transfer, however, the greater the likelihood of disruption. One can expect misunderstanding, great differences of opinion, and a relatively low return on efforts at the beginning of such new programs. New standards of evaluation are being set, and the experimental concept developed at I.S. 201 should not be jeopardized by isolated incidents. It would be surprising if everything went smoothly from the outset.

Some programs *will* flounder, some will collapse out of sheer incompetence and faulty conception, but this presents an opportunity to build on mistakes. The precise details of the Comprehensive Plan would have to be worked out in conjunction with each community and agency involved. But the *idea* is seriously proposed. We must begin to think in entirely new terms of citizen involvement and decision-making.

Black power has been accused of emphasizing decentralization, of overlooking the obvious trend toward consolidation. This is not true with the kind of Black Power described here, which is ultimately not separatist or isolationist. Some Black Power advocates are aware that this country is simultaneously experiencing centralization and decentralization. As the federal government becomes more involved (and it must) in the lives of people, it is imperative that we broaden the base of citizen participation. It will be the new forms, new agencies and structures, developed by Black Power that will link these centralizing and decentralizing trends.

Black Power structures at the local level will activate people, instill faith (not alienation), and provide a habit of organization and a consciousness of ability. Alienation will be overcome and trust in society restored. It will be through these local agencies that the centralized forces will operate, not through insensitive, unresponsive city halls. Billions of dollars will be needed each year, and these funds must be provided through a more direct route from their sources to the people.

Black Power is a developmental process; it cannot be an end in itself. To the extent that black Americans can organize, and to the extent that white Americans can keep from panicking and begin to respond rationally to the demands of that organization—to that extent can we get on with the protracted business of creating not just law and order but a free and open society.

6. SUGGESTIONS FOR FURTHER READING

ADORNO, T. W., *et al. The Authoritarian Personality* (New York: Harper, 1950).*

ALLPORT, GORDON. *The Nature of Prejudice* (Garden City, N.Y.: Doubleday, 1958).*

CAHN, EDGAR (ed.). *Our Brothers' Keeper: The Indian in White America* (Washington, D.C.: New Community Press, 1969).*

CARMICHAEL, S., AND C. HAMILTON. *Black Power* (New York: Random House, 1967).*

CLEAVER, ELDRIDGE. *Soul on Ice* (New York: McGraw-Hill, 1968).*

DOLLARD, JOHN. *Class and Caste in a Southern Town* (New Haven, Conn.: Yale University Press, 1937).*

FANON, FRANTZ. *The Wretched of the Earth* (New York: Grove Press, 1963).*

GLAZER, N., AND D. P. MOYNIHAN. *Beyond the Melting Pot* (Cambridge, Mass.: MIT Press, 1963).*

GORDON, MILTON. *Assimilation in American Life* (New York: Oxford University Press, 1964).*

GRIER, W., AND P. COBB. *Black Rage* (New York: Basic Books, 1968).*

HANDLIN, OSCAR. *The Newcomers* (Garden City, N.Y.: Doubleday, 1962).*

HERBERG, WILL. *Protestant, Catholic, Jew* (Garden City, N.Y.: Doubleday, 1955.)*

KOZOL, JONATHAN. *Death at an Early Age* (Boston: Houghton Mifflin, 1967).*

LIEBOW, ELLIOT. *Tally's Corner* (Boston: Little Brown, 1967).*

LOPREATO, JOSEPH. *Italian Americans* (New York: Random House, 1970).*

MCWILLIAMS, CAREY. *Mexicans in America* (New York: Teachers College Press, 1968).*

MILLET, KATE. *Sexual Politics* (Garden City, N.Y.: Doubleday, 1970).*

MORGAN, ROBIN (ed.). *Sisterhood Is Powerful* (New York: Vintage, 1970).*

PARSONS, T., AND K. CLARK (eds.). *The Negro American* (Boston: Houghton Mifflin, 1965).*

ROSE, A., AND C. ROSE (eds.). *Minority Problems* (New York: Harper, 1965).*

SIMPSON, G., AND J. YINGER. *Racial and Cultural Minorities* (New York: Harper, 1965).

SKLARE, MARSHALL (ed.). *The Jews: Social Patterns of an American Group* (New York: The Free Press, 1958).

* *Available in paperback.*

7. The Family

INTRODUCTION

If we define the family as a structural unit composed of at least a man and a woman joined in a socially recognized union (marriage) with their children (i.e., biological or adopted offspring), every known society can be said to have a family. In actuality, in most of the world's societies, the family unit is composed of a greater number of individuals than are included in our definition. Other kin, possibly including grandparents, uncles, aunts, and cousins, among others, live together with parents and children in what sociologists call an extended family. Within any given society, there are also families composed of a mother (or father) with children but no spouse or of spouses without children. While these varying patterns are usually accepted in the societies where they may occur, in no society are they the norm, nor do they represent the cultural ideal. In all societies, the preferred family pattern conforms to our definition.

The family is a basic and universal institution. The survival of every society depends upon the continued existence and functioning of the family, not only to ensure the replacement of defunct members, but also to provide for the care, training, and role development of its infant population, enabling them to assume functioning positions in the social order. In every known society, the replacement function is performed in the context of the family. Although it is conceivably possible that sexual relations and child rearing could be deregulated or governed by norms that do not entail a family institution, everywhere in the world they are connected with the family. Except for a few communal societies, such as the Israeli kibbutz, socialization is performed primarily, if not exclusively, within the organization of the family.

In "The Attempt to Abolish the Family in Russia," Nicholas Timasheff describes a plan to correct inequities in the treatment of Soviet women and children. Although well intentioned, the plan proved unsuccessful. Why it failed, and why the Soviets found it necessary to resurrect the family institution almost as it was prior to the antifamily policies, may perhaps reflect the societal need to have these critical functions performed within the family.

In America, the family system is typically nuclear (spouses and their children), neolocal (the family lives apart from both spouses' kin groups), monogamous (the family consists of one husband and one wife), and patriarchal (power and authority are vested chiefly in the male). Compared with most of the world's societies, our family system is unusual.

In the overwhelming majority of societies, extended family life is most common. This is especially true among preindustrial societies, nearly universal among hunting and gathering societies, and very common among agricultural peoples. It appears that, as societies become more urban and industrial, family patterns move toward the nuclear structure.

Neolocal residence is also uncommon from a worldwide perspective. In most of the world's societies, patrilocal residence (living with or near the husband's kin group) is most popular. Where the family acts as the key economic unit—as is true in most of the preindustrial world—it is of fundamental importance to live near one's kin group.

Monogamy is not the most widely preferred marital form. The people of four-fifths of the world's societies, if they could chose, would prefer to live in polygynous society (in which one husband has several wives). However, in most polygynous societies, most members live in monogamy, mainly because they are financially unable to support more than one wife.

Polyandry (one wife with several husbands) and group marriage are the most uncommon patterns of all; fewer than 5 per cent of the world's societies live according to these modes.

Patriarchal society is most common throughout the world. Patriarchy still exists in American family life, especially among the working and upper classes. However, it appears that America is moving away from this pattern toward an equalitarian pattern, especially among the middle classes. As women participate to a growing extent in the labor force, the trend toward equalitarian family life will continue. The 1970 census found that nearly half of the married female population were holding jobs.

In the wake of the great urban industrial transformation, the modern American family has changed considerably since colonial days. Many functions once performed within the context of the family are now performed outside the home. The economic needs of the individual are no longer met within the family; it is now the corporation to which he looks for a livelihood. No longer is the home the place to learn specialized skills; the educational system now provides training. The state, organized religion, and professional caretakers (i.e., physicians, psychiatrists, social workers) also play a significant role in providing for the needs of people, furnishing many services that were once exclusively, or almost exclusively, provided within the family.

While the family has lost some important functions, it has become more specialized in function. Burgess and Locke argue that the family has changed from being an institution to a companionship. This transition implies that marriage is no longer a social "have to"; rather, it has become a "want to." One marries not simply for social propriety and social acceptance, but because marriage meets one's personal needs for friendship and companionship. In a world that has become ever more rationalized (codified in legal and official regulations), bureaucratized, and impersonal, the family is increasingly expected to provide for the emotional needs of the individual. The family is becoming the central, if not the only, place for the expression of intimacy and primary-group life. (Sociologists define primary groups as relatively small, durable, face-to-face, unspecialized groups within which relationships are highly personal and emotionally laden. In primary groups, free and extensive communication prevails, and individuals react to one another as whole personalities. Primary groups are believed to be the "cradle of personality development" and are vitally necessary for the maintenance of ego strength.)

In response to these factors, some trends have been noted. It appears that interest in family life has never been more widely shared; over the twentieth century, there have been continuous increases in the percentage of the population who marry. People are also marrying younger than they used to. And divorce and remarriage have reached new heights. All these changes could be related to the changing functions of the family and its increasing socio-emotional significance. Perhaps, too, the modern family has been emotionally overloaded by its members. It is also possible that we are moving toward what Bernard Farber calls the "permanent availability" model, where individuals are available to marry anyone at any time during their adulthood, thus reducing the durability of marital bonds and increasing voluntarism and fluidity in family life.

Intrafamily relationships are an important focus of the sociologist's interest in the family. In "The Split-Level American Family," reprinted here in Chapter 4, Urie Bronfenbrenner reviews the diminution in the role of the extended family with the advent of modern urban-industrial society. It is Bronfenbrenner's contention that suburbanization—which, among other effects, increases the father's commuting time to and from his workplace and hence decreases the time available to spend with his family—and the increase in the number of married women who hold jobs or pursue other interests outside the home have contributed toward fracturing normal family relationships, depriving children of necessary association with their parents and kin, relegating them to their peers, and leading to abnormally great exposure to television. It is Bronfenbrenner's view that these factors, together, are producing deleterious consequences for personality development and possibly contributing to the widening gap between the generations.

Another important aspect of the sociology of the family is the subject of courtship and mating. With the advent of industrial society, probably the most significant change in courtship patterns has been the diminution of arranged marriages, accompanied by a rise in marriage by individual choice and the development of romantic love as a basis for mate selection. James Carey's content analysis of the popular song suggests that postindustrial society may usher in still further changes in courtship; romantic love may lose its centrality to physical attractiveness, personal autonomy, and heightened recognition of how a mate contributes to one's psychic adjustment. When arranged marriage was the leading form of mate selection, considerable homogamy (marriage between individuals possessing similar characteristics) prevailed. In recent years, there has been increasing intermarriage, particularly across religious and ethnic lines. Class and racial intermarriage, while increasing somewhat, has shown the least change. Perhaps the new courtship patterns revealed in Carey's research will have the effect of producing more intermarriage in the future. There is no doubt that the patterns of marriage and the popularity of marriage itself will be affected by these changes.

Is the Family a Universal Societal Institution?

The Attempt to Abolish the Family in Russia*

Nicholas S. Timasheff

In their attempts to create a new culture, the revolutionists always meet resistance. This resistance is displayed by individuals, but they resist because they have been molded by mighty institutions through which social structure and culture are perpetuated. In modern society, these pillars of society are the family, the school, and the church. From the standpoint of the revolutionists, two of them, the family and the church, are hopeless, for it is

* From *The Great Retreat*, by Nicholas S. Timasheff. Copyright 1946 by E. P. Dutton & Co., Inc., and used with their permission.

their very nature to preserve tradition. But the school might, perhaps, be transformed into an instrument of cultural revolution.

Hence, for those who are eager to endow a nation with a new culture, a definite program of action follows: They must loosen the family ties; they must destroy, or at least weaken, the church; and they must transform the school into an accelerator of cultural revolution. This was the natural program of the Communists while they performed their Great Experiment.

With respect to the family, the destructive attitude is sometimes denied by pro-Communist writers outside of Russia.[1] The reason is obvious; the value of the family is beyond question, say, in this country, and a regime that is hostile to it cannot count on many sympathizers. But, in 1919, an authoritative representative of the regime said: "The family has ceased to be a necessity, both for its members and for the State." A few years later, another high dignitary declared that the Communists had to undermine the family, "this formidable stronghold of all the turpitudes of the old regime."[2] And acts were still more conclusive than words.

The family, which was to be destroyed, was of the patriarchal type. In old Russia, marriage was a religious institution. Only religious marriage and divorce were recognized, so that the rules of the corresponding religious communities were exclusively applied. The superiority of the husband over the wife was legally recognized, but there was no joint property of the consorts.[3] The wife received the husband's last name, but the Russians emphasized that, in contradistinction to the West, their women never were addressed as "Mrs. John Doe"; their first names had to be used. Parental authority was strong; up to the age of twenty-one, children needed parental consent for marriage and quite a few other significant acts. Naturally, the institution of inheritance existed. Thus, the strong family structure prevailed; this was especially the case among the peasants and the lower middle class, whereas, among the upper classes, the intellectuals, and the workers, there was a well-expressed tendency to weaken the family ties.

This stronghold of the old order, this instrument of culture tradition, was attacked by the Communists from the very start of their rule.[4] The general tendency was to destroy the stable character of marital relations and make marriage as easily soluble as possible. Naturally, marriage was liberated from all bonds with religion: After a certain date, church weddings ceased to be accorded any legal effect. Instead of going to church, the prospective consorts had to apply for "registration" of their marriage to local boards established for that purpose. Measures were taken to deprive

[1] See, for instance, Nathan Berman, "Juvenile Delinquency in the Soviet Union," *American Journal of Sociology,* March, 1937.

[2] A. Kollontay, "The Family and the Communist State" (Russian; 1919), p. 8; N. Bukharin, *Proceedings of the XIII Congress of the Communist Party* (Russian; 1924), p. 545.

[3] Cf. John Hazard in "Law and the Soviet Family," *Wisconsin Law Review,* 1939, p. 245.

[4] First by the decree of December 17 and 18, 1917, later on consolidated and expanded by the Family Code of October 22, 1918.

the registration of the character of an impressive ceremony. The boards were usually located in some dark and abject room of an office building, and no words about the significance of marriage were uttered by the officials.

The most drastic change concerned divorce: In contradistinction to the old law, which made it so difficult, the decrees of December 17 and 18, 1917, permitted every consort to declare that he wanted his marriage to be canceled. No reasons were to be given to the board. Receiving the application, it had to grant the cancellation immediately, if there was mutual consent; if this was not the case, divorce was to be granted by the court, but this was a meaningless formality, since the court had to do it at the request of each consort, even if the other one opposed it. If one of the consorts was absent, he or she was notified by a postcard.

In addition to this, incest, bigamy, and adultery were dropped from the list of criminal offenses. Abortion was explicitly permitted by the decree of November 20, 1920, provided that it was performed by an approved physician in a state hospital. Under these conditions, the physician had to accede to requests for abortion, even if no valid reasons could be established. Under war Communism, inheritance ceased to exist.

When marriage can be canceled by means of a postcard, when there is no distinction between legitimacy and illegitimacy, when inheritance is unknown, parental authority is naturally weakened, and this effect was one of the purposes of the measures described. In official propaganda, the idea was persistently emphasized that children had to obey their parents only insofar as the parents complied loyally with the directions of those in power. This signified, among other things, that, unless they wanted to risk placing themselves in a dangerous position, parents could not oppose the propaganda of the Marxist doctrine, including atheism, to which the children were exposed at school. There, they were taught to do their best to re-educate their parents in the Communist spirit and denounce them to the authorities if they displayed a marked counterrevolutionary attitude. Numerous family tragedies evolved on that basis, the state backing the children against the parents. Time and again the idea was publicly discussed as to whether family education ought not to be abolished and replaced by education in state institutions. Reluctantly, the idea was rejected as impractical, at least for the period of transition.

During the NEP[5] a partial restoration of the family could be expected, if the Marxist doctrine were correct and monogamy and the strong family were the counterpart of the individualistic manner of production. There was actually one almost unavoidable concession; this was the restoration of inheritance. But, in contrast with the Marxist scheme, the attack on the family was rather strengthened. A new Family Code was prepared in 1925, and the draft was submitted to an informal discussion. Voices from the countryside were unfavorable, but this did not stop the government, and the new code was enacted as of January 1, 1927. The main innovation

[5] New Economic Policy.

was the introduction of the institution of the "nonregistered marriage," legally equal to the registered one. This meant that courts and boards were obliged to consider every union of a man and woman as marriage, provided that at least one of the following conditions were present: (1) durable cohabitation, (2) common menage, (3) declaration of the relationship before third persons, or (4) mutual support and common education of the children. The unforeseen effect was the legalization of bigamy: Applying the new law, the Supreme Court prescribed the division of the estate of a deceased man between his registered and nonregistered wife.[6]

The period of the Second Socialist Offensive was characterized by additional efforts to uproot the traditional structure of the family. The labor law of the period made it obligatory to accept any job imposed on the individual, and often husband and wife were assigned work in different towns. To the complaint of a teacher that she was artificially separated from her husband, the Labor Board replied that divorce was easy, and that she probably could find another husband in the place of her occupation. In Stalingrad, it was decided to create "socialist suburbs" consisting of houses without apartments for family life, replaced by single rooms, refectories, and nurseries. The plan fell through, because nobody but bachelors agreed to live in such suburbs.

The antifamily policy was crowned by partial success: Around 1930, on the average, family ties were substantially weaker than they had been before the revolution. But this partial success was more than balanced by a number of detrimental effects unforeseen by the promoters of the Communist Experiment. About 1934, these detrimental effects were found to endanger the very stability of the new society and its capacity to stand the test of war. Let us review these effects:

1. The abuse of the freedom of divorce and abortion resulted in an ominous decrease of the birth rate. No natality figures have ever been published for the crucial years, but, in 1937, the population proved to be 13 million behind expectation, so that, around 1934, the deficit must already have been large. To what extent this was due to the freedoms just mentioned, cannot be established. But the following figures speak for themselves: In 1934, in the medical institutions of the city of Moscow, 57,000 children were born, but 154,000 abortions were performed; in 1935, already under changing conditions, the figures were 70,000 and 155,000. As to divorce, the frequency of which also pushes down the birth rate, the following figures were reported from Moscow: In 1934, in 100 marriages there were 37 divorces, and, in the first half of 1935, there were 38.3 divorces.[7]

2. The dissolution of family ties, especially of the parent-child relations, threatened to produce a wholesale dissolution of community ties, with rapidly increasing juvenile delinquency as the main symptom. In 1935, the

[6] Decision of the Supreme Court of the RSFSR, reported in *Sudebnaya Praktika,* 1929, No. 20.

[7] *Izvestia,* July 7, 1935.

Soviet papers were full of information and indignation about the rise of hooliganism–i.e., of crimes in which the sadistic joy of inflicting pain on somebody or destroying something of value was paramount. Everywhere, wrote the papers, gangs invaded workingmen's dwellings, ransacked them, and destroyed or spoiled what they did not take away; if somebody dared to resist, he was mercilessly killed. In trains, the hooligans sang obscene songs; to prolong the fun, they did not permit travelers to alight at their destinations if they had not finished singing. Sometimes, the schools were besieged by neglected children; other times, gangs beat the teachers and attacked women or regularly fought against one another.

3. Finally, the magnificent slogans of the liberation of sex and the emancipation of women proved to have worked in favor of the strong and reckless and against the weak and shy. Millions of girls saw their lives ruined by Don Juans in Communist garb, and millions of children had never known parental homes.

The disintegration of the family did not disturb the Communists, since this was precisely what they wanted to achieve; but they were disturbed by quite a few collateral effects of the disorganization. The unfavorable trend of the population figures threatened to undermine both the labor supply and the strength of the nation at arms–for wars to be waged by the next generation. In the specific circumstances of 1934, the waste of human energy in juvenile delinquency, the combat against it, and love affairs and the accumulation of unfavorable attitudes among the victims of the new family order–or perhaps disorder is the correct word–could no longer be tolerated: They undermined the strength of the nation for the war that was straight ahead. The unfavorable development had to be stopped, and, to achieve this, the government had no other choice than to re-enforce that pillar of society that is the family. These were the main lines of development:

1. Contrary to the teachings of the previous years, young people were instructed to consider marriage "as the most serious affair in life," since, in principle, it should be a union for life. Statements such as follow, which never could have appeared in the course of the Communist Experiment, now daily adorned the Soviet papers and magazines: "There are people who dare to assert that the Revolution destroys the family; this is entirely wrong: The family is an especially important phase of social relations in socialist society. . . . One of the basic rules of Communist morals is that of strengthening the family. . . . The right to divorce is not a right to sexual laxity. A poor husband and father cannot be a good citizen. People who abuse the freedom of divorce should be punished." And, actually, in 1935 the Soviet Government started to prosecute men for rape who "changed their wives as gloves," registering a marriage one day and divorce the next. *Pravda* told the following story:

Engineer P. seduced a girl by promising to marry her. When symptoms of pregnancy appeared, the girl reminded him of his promise. His reply was: "Look, dear, you are the seventh girl in my life to whom the same unpleasant thing has occurred. Here is a letter from another woman who is also bearing a child of mine. Could I marry her, too?" The girl insisted, but the engineer terminated the discussion by saying: "Forget about marriage. Do as you like. Here is money to pay for an abortion." Having told the story, the paper added: "This man should be tried, and his trial ought to be a 'demonstrative trial.' "[8]

In the official journal of the Commissariat of Justice these amazing statements may be found:

> The State cannot exist without the family. Marriage is a positive value for the Socialist Soviet State only if the partners see in it a lifelong union. So-called free love is a bourgeois invention and has nothing in common with the principles of conduct of a Soviet citizen. Moreover, marriage receives its full value for the State only if there is progeny, and the consorts experience the highest happiness of parenthood.[9]

To inculcate the rediscovered value of marriage into the minds of the younger generation, not only the negative method of deterrence by trials and producing indignation by well-chosen stories was used but also the positive method of glorifying marriage by well-staged ceremonies; perhaps one could speak of "demonstrative marriage." Here is a story from *Izvestia.* The people involved are a *kolhoz* brigadier, V., and the first parachutist among *kolhoz* girls, B. The scene is Northern Caucasus, one of Russia's granaries.

The romance lasted about two years. In the beginning, V. hated B. He did his best to organize a shock brigade,[10] but she preferred dancing and diverted the energy of youth toward that futility. When V. saw that he was unable to discourage that attraction, he joined the movement, even started helping young people organize dances and athletic performances, and in return was helped by them in work. Then, suddenly, when B. made her first jump, V. decided that life without her would be valueless and proposed to her. She accepted. The secretaries of the regional and local party organizations decided to sponsor the marriage. Stimulated by them, the collective farm took over all preparations and decorated the village beautifully for the great day. The people's commissar for agriculture was invited to come. He could not accept, but congratulated the young people by wire and offered them a magnificent gift—a phonograph and a set of records.

The story is continued in *Pravda.* Early in the morning, guests started arriving. Among them were leaders of the party, the Soviets, and the economic organizations, as well as the champion of the girl parachutists of the

[8] *Pravda,* June 4 and 26, 1935; *Molodaya Gvardiya,* 1935, No. 1.
[9] *Sotsialisticheskaya Zakonnost,* 1939, No. 2.
[10] A group of workers pledged to work substantially faster and better than required by regulations.

Union. About noon, a score of airplanes appeared in the sky. The betrothed were offered a ride, after which they were enthusiastically acclaimed by the crowd. About five o'clock, 800 guests were invited to dinner. Tables were overloaded with mutton, hams, ducks, chickens, pies, and other dishes. After a while, the regional party secretary rose and made a speech congratulating the V.'s on their marriage, the most serious step in their lives. He expressed the hope that they would live in perfect unity and procreate an abundant Bolshevik progeny. The 800 present rose and drank to the health of the newlyweds. The people danced and rejoiced far into the night.[11]

Was not this an invitation to millions of young people to reconsider those ideas about marriage that, until quite recently, they were taught as belonging to the very essence of the Doctrine? To re-enforce the new ideas, very simple, but probably very effective symbolic means were used. The registration offices ceased to be filthy places. Now, young people found them clean, comfortable, well furnished; the officers became polite, friendly, underlining the seriousness of the act. Marriage certificates started being issued on decent paper, no longer on wrapping paper, as was the case previously. For a small additional sum, the newlyweds could receive a marriage certificate designed by artists.[12] Then, in the fall of 1936, wedding rings started being sold in Soviet shops.[13] Since these rings are used in church weddings, this novelty could be interpreted as an invitation, on the part of the government, to have the civil marriage, or registration, re-enforced and made almost indissoluble by the Church.

2. The freedom of divorce was first curtailed and then almost abolished. The first phase appears in the law of June 27, 1936, which introduced a number of inhibitions. It calls for the summoning of both parties when a divorce is to be registered.

Moreover, according to the law of September 28, 1935, the fact of divorce must be marked in the passports and birth certificates of the consorts. Commenting on this regulation, *Izvestia* expressed the hope that, before marrying a "fluttering scoundrel," a girl would ask him to produce his papers and then perhaps renounce the honor of becoming his thirtieth bride.[14]

Finally, the fee for divorce, which previously had been rather nominal, was substantially raised; instead of three rubles, one had to pay 50 rubles for the first divorce, 150 for the second, and 300 for the third and each subsequent divorce.

The effect of the antidivorce drive may be measured by the following figures: In the course of the second half of the year 1936, the number of divorces in the Ukraine was 10,992, against 35,458 in the second half of 1935;[15] in other words, it decreased more than three times.

[11] *Izvestia,* September 9, 1935; *Pravda,* September 11, 1935.
[12] *Izvestia,* July 7, 1937; *Krasaya Gazeta,* November 4, 1934.
[13] *New York Times,* November 18, 1936.
[14] *Izvestia,* February 12, 1937.
[15] *New York Times,* July 11, 1944.

The second phase appears in the decree of July 8, 1944.

> Prospective applicants for a divorce will henceforth be obliged to state their reasons and satisfy the courts that these reasons are serious and valid. Both parties must appear personally before a lower court, which hears all the evidence and then seeks to determine if it cannot effect a reconciliation. If this is believed impossible, the petition can be carried to a higher court. Witnesses must be heard in both courts. The divorce fees have been raised to 2,000 rubles.

It is probable that the courts, obeying the government's directions, will demand very good reasons and irrefutable evidence to grant a divorce. In consequence, obtaining a divorce in Russia will probably become more difficult than in many states of this country.

Moreover, the decree of July 8, 1944, abolished the institution of "unregistered marriage" introduced in 1926. Now, only "registered marriage" is legally recognized; as a corollary, the "bourgeois" distinction between legitimate and illegitimate children has reappeared in Soviet law. In addition to this, "the research of paternity" has been explicitly forbidden, so that illegitimate children and their mothers will receive no alimony. Very definitely, this will prove a mighty deterrent to extramarital relations, insofar as girls are concerned.

3. The freedom to dispose of unborn children through abortion no longer exists. Early in 1935, a campaign against abortion was started. Articles began to appear in Soviet papers written by high medical authorities, explaining the harm that abortion, especially repeated abortion, inflicts on women.[16] Praising maternity, these authorities declared that the longing for children had suddenly reappeared among the women of the Soviet Union —a manner of saying that now Stalin wanted them to bear as many children as possible. Trials resulting in severe sentences finished the careers of persons operating clandestine "abortaria": Their very emergence disclosed that, without change in the law, Soviet hospitals no longer performed abortion at the simple request of the pregnant woman. Finally, a draft law prohibiting abortion was published and offered for public discussion. Numerous objections were raised, mainly based on intolerable dwelling conditions. Nevertheless, the law of June 27, 1936, abolished the freedom of abortion, which had been considered one of the highest achievements of Communism by many pro-Communists.

Repealing the notorious law of November 20, 1920, the new law prohibited abortion in all cases except where there was danger to life or health of the pregnant woman or danger of hereditary transmission of serious sickness. As in the former law, only medical men were permitted to perform the operation. Pressure exerted on a woman to induce her into abortion was declared a crime punishable by two years in prison. To make more childbearing possible, the law promised a large extension of the net-

[16] For instance, by Arkhangelski, member of the Academy of Sciences, *Izvestia,* June 5, 1935.

work of maternity hospitals, day nurseries, and kindergartens. Maternity grants were increased, and special allowances were promised to mothers of six or more children.[17]

4. The peculiar parent-child relationship that had obtained under the Communist Experiment, and which granted superiority to the children, was reversed to one that is considered normal in the world; once more, children have to recognize the authority of their parents. Obviously, the change could not be effected through legal enactment, and the method of persuasion through propaganda was used exactly in the same manner as it was used to stabilize marriage. Statements like these could be found almost daily on the pages of Soviet papers, beginning with the spring of 1935:

> Young people should respect their elders, especially their parents. . . . The respect and care of parents is an essential part of the Komsomol[18] morals. . . . One must respect and love his parents, even if they are old-fashioned and do not like the Komsomol.[19]

In 1939, the official journal of the Union Prosecutor declared:

> Sound moral ideas must be inculcated into the minds of young persons. They must know that lack of care for their parents is found only among savages, and that in every civilized society such conduct is considered dishonest and base.[20]

To corroborate these ideas, the journal cited the laws of Solon and Xenophon's works.

The method of positive demonstration was also used, and Stalin himself found it necessary to set the example. In October, 1935, he paid a visit to his old mother living in Tiflis,[21] and, in the detailed accounts of this visit, signs of love and respect to the old lady by the leader of the World Proletariat were emphasized. A high degree of intimacy in family relations was displayed through the reproduction of such questions as: How did Stalin's children like the jam made for them by their grandmother? Another day, Stalin appeared in one of Moscow's gardens with his children, something he had never done previously. Up to that time, the majority of Soviet citizens did not even know that Stalin had any children.

Gradually, the unlimited freedom granted to young people under the Communist Experiment was curbed. One of the most conspicuous items in the process has been the decree of July 15, 1943, excluding children below the age of sixteen from evening performances in theaters and movies.

To strengthen parental authority, an indirect method has been used in the new inheritance law of March 20, 1945. While previous laws limited

[17] The second antidivorce law (1944) substantially increased the advantages granted to mothers of numerous children. Honorary titles were granted to mothers of seven or more children.

[18] Young Communist League.

[19] *Komsomolskaya Pravda,* June 7 and September 29, 1935; *Pravda,* August 4, 1935.

[20] *Sovetskaya Yustitsia,* 1939, No. 4.

[21] *Izvestia,* December 23, 1935.

possible heirs to direct or adopted descendants, consorts, and needy dependents, the new law broadens this list to include parents, brothers, sisters, and public organizations. Although, according to the new law, the testator may not deprive his minor children or jobless heirs of their rightful portion, its impact on the family is clear: The greater the freedom to dispose of one's estate, the greater is the authority of the head of the family relating to presumptive heirs.

Courtship in Post-industrial Society

Changing Courtship Patterns in the Popular Song*

James T. Carey

Radio disc jockeys and rock and roll fans date the emergence of rock and roll as a distinct musical style with Bill Haley and the Comets' 1955 recording of "Rock Around the Clock." This musical style was a blend of blues and country Western and for the first time introduced mass white audiences to a Negro folk musical form. More recently, folk rock and psychedelic rock have appeared as variations within the same basic musical style. The emergence of rock and roll music has provided a vehicle for the development of a new perspective on boy-girl relationships. A look at . . . song content over the past eleven years reveals marked changes in orientation not only in the relationship between the sexes but also in the relationship of young people to the larger social order.

Any analysis of lyrics must take into account that only the verbal content, a secondary aspect of the music, lends itself to social examination. A superficial comparison of the mood of popular music in the 1950's [and] . . . 1960's suggests that the earlier music was languid, searching, "sweet"; the music of the late 1960's is more sensual, direct, sexual, and "gutsy."[1] Lyrics may reveal general values, but this is not necessarily the stated reason for listening to them. It seems to be the nature of the music itself, and not the vocal or lyrical aspects alone, that accounts for its popularity. The words are only part of the total sound and are responded to as such.

[1] See C. Keil, "Motion and Feeling Through Music," *Journal of Aesthetics and Art Criticism,* XXIV, no. 3 (Spring, 1966), 337–50, for a suggested classification of musical styles based on the combination of techniques used.

* From *American Journal of Sociology,* vol. 74 (May, 1969), 720–31. Reprinted by permission of the University of Chicago Press.

* * *

Content analyses of lyrics conducted by Peatman in 1944, by Horton in 1957, and the one discussed in this paper reveal that the overwhelming majority of songs are concerned with courtship and the boy-girl relationship. The courtship situation is viewed differently, however. This becomes clear by noting the difference in perspective between the lyrics analyzed by Horton and the present study.

We will rely on Horton's analysis of popular song lyrics for the verbal content of 1955 songs. His data were drawn from the June, 1955, issue of four magazines: *Hit Parader, Song Hits Magazine, Country Song Roundup,* and *Rhythm and Blues.* We have tried to repeat Horton's analysis by looking at the same magazines during a two-month period in the summer of 1966.[2] This was not completely possible, since *Rhythm and Blues* had discontinued publication several years earlier. In addition, we have used *Billboard* for the national top thirty listings in the same period[3] and the top thirty listings of one radio station in San Francisco for the Bay area. Both the national listing and the Bay area listing rate songs in terms of popularity. Our analysis should provide us with a comparison of courtship patterns at two different time periods based on a content analysis of song-magazine listings. Further, it should indicate, through the use of two more popularity listings in addition to the song magazines, the dramatic shift in value preferences of young people.[4] These value preferences relate

[2] The songs included in these magazines are drawn partly from a national popularity listing and partly from staff [opinion] of what songs are likely to gross well in retail sales. . . . In any given issue, at least 30 per cent [of the songs] are not drawn from any popularity chart.

[3] *Billboard* does include a separate rhythm and blues rating that lists songs popular among Negroes, based on radio-air play from Negro radio stations and retail sales in Negro neighborhoods. A preliminary check of the content of the songs, despite the distinctively different musical style, indicates that the themes do not differ substantially from [those in] the three song magazines, with one important qualification. There are few lyrics that suggest that women are on a pedestal or that sexual interests are anything less than normal. Horton, *op. cit.,* noted that there was nothing distinctive about the stages of the courtship relationship in his analysis of rhythm and blues lyrics. However, a more careful examination might reveal that the double standard characteristic of white popular music in the 1950's was absent in the rhythm and blues lyrics of the same period. In short, a case could probably be made that the "new" notions about boy-girl relationships in today's lyrics represent a general acceptance of Negro notions by a white audience.

[4] The inclusion of the national popularity ratings is an attempt to overcome the limitations of the song magazines as an indicator of youth preferences. The ratings are based on radio-air play and retail sales. The inclusion of the San Francisco ratings is an attempt to suggest that the new values being celebrated are related to particular groups, particular musical styles, and particular centers of popular culture. C. Hall, in "Detroit and L.A. Sales 'Happening Places,' " *Billboard,* LXXVIII (July 2, 1966), 1, reports that San Francisco had fifteen original record breakouts—i.e., records that first hit the top-thirty chart there—during the first six months of 1966, of which two went on to reach *Billboard*'s "Hot 100" chart. This was in contrast to New York with sixteen, of which six went on to reach the chart, and Los Angeles with sixteen, of which eight . . . reached the hit chart. Hall goes on to say: "In a similar survey last year [1965], New York took all the honors, not only having the most original breakouts —17—but having the most that reached the charts—19. San Francisco had been second, with 18 breakouts that reached the chart." *Billboard* classifies the country into twenty-two major markets, which include all the major cities in five regions—East, South, Midwest, Southwest, and West.

not only to idealized boy-girl relationships but also to a wider range of concerns.

A total of 227 different songs were analyzed, of which 52 per cent were classified as rock and roll.

* * *

Lyrics were classified in a general way in terms of whether they reflected "older" or "newer" values. Older values were found in lyrics that enjoined, implicitly or explicitly, the acceptance of conventional values—for example, romantic notions about boy-girl relationships or fatalistic acceptance of the demands placed on one by the larger community. Lyrics that expressed anxiety over social change were also classified as representing older values. Newer values were found in lyrics that seemed to advocate or imply a more autonomous relationship between the sexes . . . or criticized conventional society because of its misplaced preferences.[5] If we look at all the lyrics in our 1966 sample, we note that the new values are being communicated primarily through rock lyrics.

* * *

Our illustrations of the shift in perspective on boy-girl relationships will be primarily drawn from rock and roll lyrics, since it is here that the new outlook is most clearly stated.

Horton found that 83.4 per cent of the popular songs in 1955 were conversational songs about love.[6] The proportion of [such] songs . . . in three of the same magazines dropped in 1966 to 64.7 per cent, as shown in Table 1.

TABLE 1

Proportion of Love Songs in 1955 and 1966*

	1955	1966
Love songs in the conversational mode	83.4% (196)	64.7% (108)
Love songs not in the conversational mode	3.8% (9)	4.8% (8)
Themes other than love and courtship	12.8% (30)	30.5% (51)
TOTAL	100.0% (235)	100.0% (167)

* $\chi^2 = 20.02$, significant beyond .001 level.

The decline in conversational songs about love is more strikingly portrayed in . . . the national popularity rating reported by *Billboard* for the same period and [in] San Francisco's KYA listing.

Radio-air play, combined with retail sales, forms the basis for the *Bill-*

[5] Three judges sorted the lyrics into three categories—old values, new values, and other. Those classified as "other" included lyrics whose value content was neutral, . . . or songs that did not have enough verbal content to permit classification as old or new. . . . Disagreement among the judges occurred on those lyrics that were mixed, partly expressing old values, partly new. The final decision was made on the basis of which value was *most* represented in counting the lines.

[6] [This designation] . . . refers to songs written in the mode of direct address. The content can be an appeal, request, demand, complaint, or reproach, soliciting some kind of response, as though the songs were fragments of dialogue. Love songs not in the conversational mode are primarily narrative and descriptive ballads. . . .

board and KYA listings. Therefore, Table 2 highlights not only the declining interest in love lyrics from 1955 to 1966 but also the preferences of the youth audience. As we get closer to the center of popular culture, the proportion of love lyrics shows a marked decline to little more than half of the songs represented.[7]

Horton arranged his themes in terms of various stages of the love relationship. He called these stages the "drama of courtship." Basically, there were five:

1. The prologue to the courtship expresses the anticipations and longings of those who seek love affairs.
2. The initiation of courtship (Act I) describes the explosive beginning of the affair.
3. The honeymoon (Act II) portrays the euphoric phase of the courtship.
4. The downward course of love (Act III) depicts the appearance of forces hostile to love's happiness.
5. The all-alone stage (Act IV) laments . . . lost love and the ensuing loneliness.

How adequately can these phases characterize the 1966 songs? If we compare the two periods, we note that most of the lyrics about love can, with some difficulty, be classified using Horton's categories; that is, there are discernible stages in the relationship from the prologue through the lover's final isolation.[8] However, the characteristics of each stage or their content are different [for the two time periods]. The main difference is in terms of activity-passivity. The actors in the newer lyrics control their own destinies and are not fatalistic about the affair. To make a compari-

[7] J. Simmons and B. Winograd, in *It's Happening: A Portrait of the Youth Scene Today* (Santa Barbara, Calif.: Marc Laird Publications, 1966), p. 163, note the importance of San Francisco (and the West Coast generally) as an innovator in popular music: "A survey of the record buying public's tastes indicates that except for a few distinct styles . . . the music of today goes from West to East, no longer traveling from New York's Tin Pan Alley to the . . . hills of San Francisco."

[8] . . . To eliminate the possibility that the difference between the 1955 and 1966 data was simply a matter of reliability between two judges, a lengthy interview was conducted with one of Horton's judges. The author was instructed in the code originally used by Horton, and a sample of 1966 lyrics were sorted using the 1955 scheme. This constituted a reliability check of the author's assignment to specific categories. With the assistance of one of Horton's researchers, a further check was made in reclassifying the 1955 data into the new code. Almost 50 per cent of Horton's lyrics could not be classified. A count of the 1955 and 1966 lyrics revealed the following breakdown using the revised code:

	1955	1966
Active search	19.7% (38)	32.9% (57)
Happy stage	9.7% (19)	17.1% (29)
Breakup	8.6% (17)	33.5% (58)
Isolation	14.7% (29)	16.4% (28)
Other	47.4% (93)	
TOTAL	100.0% (196)	100.0% (172)

TABLE 2

Proportion of Love Songs by Popularity Rating in 1966

	*Billboard**	KYA*
Love songs in the conversational mode	62.9% (36)	52.0% (28)
Love songs not in the conversational mode		
Themes other than love and courtship	37.1% (21)	48.0% (26)
TOTAL	100.0% (57)	100.0% (54)

* *Billboard* and KYA were combined and compared with the 1955 data in computing $\chi^2 = 40.50$, significant beyond the .001 level.

son between 1955 and 1966 lyrics requires a slight reinterpretation of the earlier scheme to include a more active outlook on the love affair at each phase. Even with some modification, however, it was not possible to include 24 per cent of the lyrics drawn from the 1966 song magazines (see Table 3).

TABLE 3

Comparison of Courtship Stages in 1955 and 1966 Song Magazines

	1955	1966
Prologue*	5% (9)	1% (1)
Act I: courtship	39% (76)	25% (27)
Act II: honeymoon	9% (19)	14% (15)
Act III: downward course of love	17% (34)	19% (21)
Act IV: all alone	30% (58)	17% (18)
Other		24% (26)
TOTAL	100% (196)	100% (108)

* Prologue and Act I were combined in computing $\chi^2 = 58.52$, significant beyond .001 level.

If we look at the top thirty songs in the national listing included in *Billboard*'s popularity rating and San Francisco's KYA ranking, we note that an even larger proportion of lyrics do not fit into Horton's categories (see Table 4).

TABLE 4

Adequacy of Horton's Categories to 1966 Popularity Listings

	*Billboard**	KYA*
Songs that fit	67.7% (24)	66.6% (19)
Songs that do not fit	32.3% (12)	33.4% (9)
TOTAL	100.0% (36)	100.0% (28)

* *Billboard* and KYA were combined and compared with the 1955 data in computing $\chi^2 = 70.96$, significant beyond .001 level.

The shift in preoccupation is more dramatically noted in looking at San Francisco's KYA popularity rating for the same period. It is in the national popularity listings and rankings selected from key centers of popular culture that we would expect the new orientation toward boy-girl relationships to be most sharply drawn.

COURTSHIP IN 1966

The large proportion of song lyrics not included in Horton's categories suggests a reformulation of the phases of the love relationship to take into account a 1966 view of it.

Our sequence starts not with the longing for a relationship or the reveries associated with love but with looking for an affair. The lover is not wishing and dreaming for something to happen to him; he is actively seeking it. The sequence begins with Act I, the *active search,* which includes finding a partner.

Act II portrays the *happy stage* and seems somewhat related to Horton's honeymoon phase. It is different, in that there is no implication that the state is a permanent one, nor is it expected to be. The lover is less sentimental and romantic during this happy stage than previously. He is celebrating his enthusiasm over the physical relationship that has been established.

Act III describes the *breakup,* which occurs when something contaminates the relationship between two people. The breakup occurs because the relationship is not a healthy one and the lovers decide to end it.

Act IV depicts the *isolation* phase, which is viewed as an opportunity to discover one's real self.

Since most of the lyrics that could not be classified under Horton's stages were rock and roll lyrics, it is to these songs we must turn to describe in more detail the new orientation toward boy-girl relationships.

In Act I, people actively seek out lovers. They meet semicasually but with the intention of being lovers. The looking is preceded by a recognition that one needs some release, presumably through a physical relationship. The Mamas and the Papas describe this condition in "Somebody Groovy":

> I need somebody groovy,
> Someone who really can move me.
> Yeah, they gotta move me like they should
> And when I find somebody, yeah, I'm
> gonna treat 'em good.
> Oh, please, please believe me,
> I need someone to relieve me,
> Yeah, they gotta move me like they should
> And when I find somebody, yeah, I'm
> gonna treat 'em good.

When love is discussed in rock and roll poetry, it refers to a different phenomenon from romantic involvement. Love seems to be reduced simply to physical desire. This is not viewed as a bad thing–it is a reality that everyone must face. The description of love by the Supremes in "Love Is

Like an Itching in My Heart" finds one in the same kind of search as in the previous lyrics:

> Love is a nagging irritation
> Causing my heart complication
> Love is growing infection
> And I don't know the correction
> Got me rocking and a-reeling and I can't
> shake the feeling
> Love is like an itching in my heart
> Tearing it all apart
> Just an itching in my heart, baby,
> I can't scratch it
> Keeps me sighing, oh, oh,
> Keeps me yearning,
> Keeps me burning, keeps me tossing,
> Keeps me turning,
> Keeps me yearning.

The protagonist at first glance seems to be telling someone that she . . . is in love with him; but she is speaking only about her state of desire, which is not focused on anyone at this point.

The ideology of freedom is spelled out in the song "Go Where You Wanna Go," [which] enjoins one to seek out relationships with "whoever you wanna do it with." One enters a relationship with someone who moves him. The Troggs' "Wild Thing" suggests the character of the relationship:

> Wild thing, you make my heart sing,
> You make everything groovy
> Wild thing [*spoken*], Wild thing,
> I think you move me,
> [*sung*] But I wanna know for sure.
> [*spoken*] Come on and hold me tight.
> You move me . . .

The girl in these lyrics is viewed instrumentally. Love is depicted as basically physical. People are animals, but happy animals. Romantic involvement is not a necessary ingredient in the relationship. Indeed, it can actually be a hindrance to open, free enjoyment. Dusty Springfield expresses this sentiment in "You Don't Have to Say You Love Me":

> You don't have to say you love me,
> Just be close at hand.
> You don't have to stay forever,
> I will understand.

And, a little later in the song:

> But, believe me, I'll never tie you down.

Sam the Sham and the Pharaohs, in their "Lil' Red Riding Hood," also emphasize that physical attraction is the main reason for getting involved with someone. They describe her as very desirable, with big eyes and full lips, and they end by saying:

> Hey there, Lil' Red Riding Hood,
> You sure are looking good
> You're everything that a big bad
> wolf could want.

The next stage of the relationship, Act II, discusses what occurs after two people have found each other. The affair at this point is very happy. The lovers spend a great deal of time with each other, as Petula Clark states in "I Couldn't Live Without Your Love":

> I couldn't live without your love.
> Now I know you're really mine
> Gotta have you all the time.

The ecstatic happiness that characterizes the early stages of the new relationship is celebrated by the Shades of Blue in their "Oh, How Happy":

> Oh, how happy you have made me,
> Oh, how happy you have made me.
> I have kissed your lips a thousand times
> And more times than I can count I have
> called you mine.

The *happy stage* is soon followed by disturbing elements that enter the relationship. Alan Price, in "I Put a Spell on You," describes the lover's reaction to the beloved's behavior:

> I put a spell on you
> Because you're mine
> You better stop the things that you do
> I ain't lyin', no I ain't lyin'
> I just can't stand it, babe,
> The way you're always runnin' around
> I just can't stand it
> The way you always put me down
> I put a spell on you
> Because you're mine.

When unhappiness enters a relationship, then one must try to recover the original happiness. . . . In this case, the lover tries to recreate the earlier ecstasy by "putting a spell" on the girl. But the relationship continues to deteriorate, almost to the point of desperation. The Animals describe this stage in . . . "Don't Bring Me Down":

> When you complain and criticize
> I feel I'm nothing in your eyes.
> It makes me feel like giving up
> Because my best just ain't good enough.

Women are portrayed as unreasonable. This relationship, like all others, is seen as undesirable. The Animals go on to say:

Girl, I want to provide for you
And do all the things you want me to
Oh, but please,
Oh, darling, don't bring me down,
Oh, no, don't bring me down
I'm beggin' you, baby,
Please, don't bring me down.

The fundamental danger in this and other relationships is being "brought down." In love affairs, as in mental excursions with drugs, the idea of bringing down someone who is high is disparaged. In this case, the idea that the girl could bring the man down indicates that he is somehow "high" in terms of the relationship. The positive things he sees about the relationship are illusory. The necessity for the plea–"don't bring me down"–indicates that there is grave danger that the feared event will occur. The lyrics continue:

Girl, I know I can keep you satisfied
Just as long as you give me back my pride.
Baby, sacrifices I will make
I'm ready to give as well as take.
One thing I need is your respect.
One thing I can't take is your neglect.
More than anything I need your love
Then troubles are easy to rise above.

The lover needs the girl's response and is not getting it. In this vicious circle, he cannot come to terms with the present state of things, and she holds the power. He is unable to make the choice for detachment and independence. This is why there is danger of being brought down. The deteriorating relationship leads to the conclusion that certain kinds of involvements can be very bad. The Outsiders, in "Time Won't Let Me," philosophize on this point:

I can't wait forever
Even though you want me to
I can't wait forever
To know if you'll be true
Time won't let me, oh no
Time won't let me, oh no
Wait that long.

The key line is: "Even though you want me to." The implication is that a person has only one life, and that involvement with someone else complicates it. At this point in the relationship, the protagonist is urged to disengage. The girl in this song is insisting on continuing the relationship, even though the conditions are unfavorable to the man. The girl is informed that time won't let him wait that long.

The deterioration of the relationship is followed by the *breakup* in Act III. The breakup occurs because the protagonist comes to the realization that the relationship was bad in the first place. Since one cannot know this in advance, the injunction is to terminate the affair once this becomes known. The Syndicate of Sounds, in "Little Girl," describe this breakup:

> You can leave, little girl,
> I don't want you around no more.
> If you come knockin' you won't get past
> my door.
> You got nothin' to hide
> Everybody knows it's true
> Too bad, little girl, it's all over for you.

The decision to break up is difficult but must be made. The initiative seems to rest with the male to begin the relationship and terminate it. The Grass Roots, in "Where Were You When I Needed You?" describe some of the difficulties involved:

> Don't bother cryin', don't bother crawlin',
> It's all over now, no use in stallin'
> The love I once felt I don't feel any more
> for you.

What is revealed here is that it is undesirable to lose one's dignity. The boy is putting the girl down, but he doesn't want to see her cry or crawl, not for her sake but because he doesn't like watching such things.

When the affair is over, one realizes that the involvement was unhealthy. The Cyrkle, in "Red Rubber Ball," describe this realization:

> I should have known
> You did mean farewell.
> There's a lesson to be learned from this
> And I learned it very well.
> Now I know you're not the only starfish in
> the sea.
> If I never hear your name again it's all the
> same to me.
> [*chorus*] And I think it's gonna be all right.
> Yeah, the worst is over now,
> The morning sun is shining like a red rubber
> ball.

The lesson is: "Don't get involved." The choice for detachment ends the bad experience. The love affair was a big thing, but now it's a little thing. Happiness is equated with contentment and evenness—that is, keeping whole—rather than with risky involvements. If one is going to take chances, they should not be taken in interpersonal relationships.

The final stage in the sequence is Act IV, *isolation*. This is the inevitable result of the vicissitudes of human relationships. Isolation is an acceptable way out. In "Solitary Man," by Neil Diamond, a young man's bad experience with promiscuous women leads him to accept isolation as a way of life:

Don't know that I will but until I can
find me
A girl who'll stay and won't play games
behind me
I'll be what I am,
A solitary man.

He says: "Don't know that I will." Presumably, he is prepared to accept isolation for the rest of his life rather than be hurt in love again.

In Simon and Garfunkel's "I Am a Rock," the young man seems to be certain that total withdrawal is the answer to his problem. It is ironic. Throughout the song runs an undertone indicating that he knows his position to be impossible.

I have my books and my poetry to protect
me.
I am shielded in my armor.
Don't talk of love, I've heard the word
before.
It's sleeping in my memory.
I won't disturb the slumber of feelings that
have died.
If I'd never loved, I never would have cried.
I am a rock, I am an island.

He is describing the result of a bad experience. There is no cry that he wants his love back. There is no wish to see her. There is no specification of how he has been hurt. There is no relationship with anyone else at all. The isolation can be interpreted in a more general sense than that due to having been hurt. There is the process of deliberately cutting oneself off, which is experienced as a way of establishing one's own identity.

So ends the stylized love affair–from active searching through various stages of involvement to isolation.

The new perspective of the love affair that is depicted in the 1966 rock lyrics seems to support a new view of the courtship sequence. The change has not involved a shift in interest away from the boy-girl relationship but rather a shift in orientation toward the relationship. . . .

A NEW PATTERN

A comparison of the "drama of courtship" in 1955 and 1966 suggests a number of significant changes in the boy-girl relationship in the lyrics of songs over the last eleven years. One of the most conspicuous changes is in the conception of love.

The popular song lyrics of 1955 portrayed love as a deep, romantic involvement. The rock and roll lyrics of 1966 usually refer to a different phenomenon when they discuss love. Love often seems to have been reduced to physical attraction. Romantic love has been rejected as the exclusive requirement for engaging in a sexual relationship. While permissiveness with affection was acceptable eleven years ago, though entailing certain risks, today's songs legitimize permissiveness without affection. . . . The Mamas and Papas endorse this position in "Go Where You Wanna Go":

> You gotta go where you wanna go,
> Do what you wanna do
> With whoever you wanna do it with.

The new pattern, then, is that you can sleep with someone whether you have affection for him or not—*either* is acceptable.

One of the tragedies voiced in the 1955 lyrics was that everyone wants love but . . . the prerequisites make it difficult to find. The rock lyrics of today indicate that these prerequisites and preconditions to love have been reduced. Songs no longer dwell on approaches to courtship but focus more on an active search and involvement with a partner.

Similarly, on the downward course of love, rock and roll lyrics do not dwell for any length of time on the deteriorated relationship but rather value a quick break when the involvement is viewed as unhealthy and pervaded with guilt. This kind of involvement impedes one's freedom of action, and a choice for detachment and independence ends the bad experience. The [issues] posed in the lyrics no longer focus on "Are you still mine?" or "I'm afraid that you'll get careless, and someone will steal a kiss," but center closer to the theme the Grass Roots express in "Where Were You When I Needed You?":

> It's all over now, no use in stallin'
> The love I once felt I don't feel any more
> for you.

The new outlook on the love affair does not include the expectation of permanence. Freedom is celebrated for both partners. This highlights one of the dilemmas in the relationships portrayed in rock and roll lyrics. One is free not to become involved, but others have that freedom also. The relationship where each partner tries to maximize the other's freedom is a fragile arrangement that can be quickly terminated. Emphasis is on a rapid culmination of the affair as well as a quick ending when the involvement is an unhealthy one. The temporary quality of relationships is expressed in Dusty Springfield's "You Don't Have to Say You Love Me."

These sentiments seem far removed from those of 1955, when a relationship was expected to be permanent. It would be unusual to encounter lyrics today similar to those . . . in the 1955 song "As Long as I Live," in which the singer states that he will remember and love his partner forever.

The popular songs of the mid-1950's seem to have placed love in the hands of fate. Love is not something actively controlled by the lovers but something that happens to them. One "falls in love," and later the downward course of love is initiated by hostile forces external to one's control. . . . Because of the lack of control in the relationship, falling in love involves considerable risks; the outcome is not predictable. Since love in the

1955 song lyrics is experienced as externally controlled, it is often perceived as an object or a commodity rather than something the lovers mutually create. Love frequently appears in popular song lyrics as something to be "won" or something that is subject to theft.

The rock lyrics of 1966 reject this passive orientation toward the boy-girl relationship. Love is mutually created by the partners and is not perceived as external to their relationship. The affair is actively sought by the lovers rather than passively longed for.

Two other changes have occurred in the courtship patterns. The girls portrayed in the 1966 rock lyrics have been removed from their pedestal in boy-girl relations. "Wild Thing" by the Troggs reduces the girl to an object for sexual gratification. Furthermore, the boy is no longer at the mercy of the girl in the love affair. The 1955 lyrics often show the boy powerless and helpless in the face of the girl, who appears to hold the key to the relationship. The rock lyrics of today seem to have reversed this power situation. The initiative rests with the male to initiate the relationship and terminate it. The Syndicate of Sounds, in "Little Girl," capture this new pattern.

* * *

The major thrust of the 1966 rock and roll lyrics is toward an expansion of the boy-girl relationship to include a wider range of behavior and not just the limited "romantic love affair" that characterizes the 1955 lyrics. The possibility that the relationship between young people might be so quickly terminated today seems to suggest that different levels of involvement between two persons, in addition to the traditional romantic love affair, are now called for.

This whole development seems to reject the older double standard and opt for a more honest and open boy-girl relationship and has the effect of widening the range of choices for a satisfactory relationship. The net impact is to emphasize personal autonomy and eschew the kind of dependency revealed in earlier lyrics.

WIDER RANGE OF THEMES IN 1966

* * *

[We have noted that] the . . . rock and roll lyrics in 1966 deal with a wider range of themes than the popular songs of the preceding decade. Of the rock lyrics, 30 per cent are concerned with themes other than love and courtship, in contrast to almost 13 per cent of the 1955 lyrics.

The concerns expressed in the 1955 lyrics, apart from those of love and courtship, range widely and show no clear-cut focus. They include song dances, general narrative ballads on love themes, religious songs, comic songs, and others that could not be classified.

The 1966 lyrics reveal more specific concerns. The major preoccupation of rock and roll lyrics seems to be with *choice*. Choice permeates the themes, relating to many areas of interest besides those of boy-girl relationships. Choice is exercised in terms of freeing oneself from external constraints. The exercise of choice is enjoined in two crucial areas: (1) personal relations, and (2) the kind of society in which one will become involved. Choice in both relates to the individual's autonomy.

We have already seen how . . . the choice theme operates in the relationship between boy and girl. It functions to maximize the personal freedom of the persons in the relationship by widening the range of alternatives available to those involved.

The second crucial area in which choice operates is the individual's autonomy in relation to the conventional world. Will he become part of the conventional world, or will he choose to drop out and create his own scene? To do something about one's life, to think for oneself, no matter what the consequences, is generally enjoined.

SUMMARY

The major difference in orientation toward courtship in 1955 and 1966 is the active character of the boy-girl relationship [today]. The affair is created by the partners, and they can determine its outcome. If a position can be inferred from an analysis of the 1966 lyrics, it is that one makes his own choices. The value of existential choice is celebrated. It gives one the freedom to change, to become what he wants to be, to make of an affair what two people want it to be.

In the idealized sequence revealed by rock and roll lyrics today, one actively searches out and becomes involved with someone else rather than passively waiting for an affair. Relationships are initiated on the basis of mutual attraction, which includes both physical and "spiritual" elements. When these elements disappear, the expectation is that the relationship will be terminated. Relationships can also be ended if one or both of the parties diagnose it as "unhealthy." Usually, this means that it is tainted with dishonesty. Love is not placed in the hands of fate but is actively controlled by the lovers. Consequently, rock and roll lyrics are not likely to talk about "falling in love," since that phrase refers to a romantic conception of boy-girl relationships that is rejected.

Another striking difference between the 1955 and 1966 lyrics is in the attitude toward being alone—the isolation at the end of the affair. It is viewed negatively in 1955, more positively in 1966. There is pain and suffering associated with the dissolution of an affair in 1966, but it can also be the first step in exploring those facets of the self that can only be explored when one is alone. The description of the isolation phase of the courtship cycle suggests the Zen influence operative among the more recent songwriters.

The fact that there is a distinctive set of beliefs associated with a large proportion of 1966 lyrics may reflect the growing disaffection among younger people who constitute the audience for the new lyrics, or it may simply reflect a change in those who write them.

The significance of the changing orientation depicted here can be established more clearly by a further inquiry into two related areas: the emergence of more democratic controls over songs written since 1955, and the extent to which the new belief system is incorporated ideologically into the social movements of young people today.

7. SUGGESTIONS FOR FURTHER READING

BARTELL, GILBERT. *Group Sex* (New York: Peter H. Wyden, 1971).*

BELL, N. W., AND E. VOGEL (eds.). *A Modern Introduction to the Family* (New York: The Free Press, 1960).

BELL, ROBERT. *Premarital Sex in a Changing Society* (Englewood Cliffs, N.J.: Prentice-Hall, 1966).*

BILLINGSLEY, ANDREW. *Black Families in White America* (Englewood Cliffs, N.J.: Prentice-Hall, 1968).*

CHRISTENSEN, HAROLD (ed.). *Handbook of Marriage and the Family* (Chicago: Rand McNally, 1964).

FORD, C. S., AND F. A. BEACH. *Patterns of Sexual Behavior* (New York: Ace Books, 1951).*

FRIEDAN, BETTY. *The Feminine Mystique* (New York: Norton, 1963).*

GEIGER, KENT. *The Family in Soviet Russia* (Cambridge, Mass.: Harvard University Press, 1968).

GOODE, WILLIAM J. *Women in Divorce* (New York: The Free Press, 1956).*

———. *World Revolution and Family Patterns* (New York: The Free Press, 1968).*

HUNT, MORTON. *The World of the Formerly Married* (New York: McGraw-Hill, 1966).*

KOMAROVSKY, MIRRA. *Blue Collar Marriage* (New York: Random House, 1962).*

LEWIS, OSCAR. *Five Families* (New York: John Wiley & Sons, 1962).*

NYE, I., AND L. HOFFMAN. *The Employed Mother in America* (Chicago: Rand McNally, 1963).

RAINWATER, LEE. *And the Poor Get Children* (Chicago: Quadrangle Books, 1960).*

SKOLNICK, A., AND J. SKOLNICK (eds.). *Family in Transition* (Boston: Little Brown, 1971).*

SPIRO, MELFORD. *Kibbutz: Venture in Utopia* (Cambridge, Mass.: Harvard University Press, 1956).*

STEPHENS, WILLIAM. *The Family in Cross Cultural Perspective* (New York: Holt, Rinehart & Winston, 1963).*

WESTOFF, L., AND C. WESTOFF. *From Now to Zero* (Boston: Little Brown, 1968).*

WINCH, ROBERT. *The Modern Family,* 3rd ed. (New York: Holt, Rinehart & Winston, 1971).

YOUNG, M., AND P. WILLMOTT. *Family and Kinship in East London* (Baltimore: Penguin, 1957).*

* *Available in paperback.*

8. Deviance

INTRODUCTION

Deviance may be defined as behavior that departs from societal expectations. It is viewed by the members of the social body with varying degrees of moral disapproval, depending on the nature of the act, the characteristics of the actor, and the values of the particular society. For example, our own society deviance embraces a broad range of phenomena, including mental illness, minority-group membership, political nonconformity, physical handicaps, criminal behavior, sexual aberrations, and drug use.

What is considered deviant in one society may be perfectly acceptable, if not socially desired, in another. For example, in our own society mate swapping, or "swinging," as it most recently has been called, is generally regarded as morally offensive or "perverse." However, among numerous Eskimo peoples, wife sharing does not signify deviance; it is an expression of hospitality and friendship. Deviance is a matter of social definition. Its content tends to reflect the values that are endorsed in a given society.

Because every society has a number of ideal values that are not generally achieved and prescriptions governing conduct that are logically contradictory, deviance is inevitable and universal. The renowned French sociologist Émile Durkheim argued that even a society of saints would detect deviance among its members; those whose behavior was somewhat divergent from the rest would be viewed with moral disapproval.

Durkheim argued that a certain amount of deviant behavior was not only inevitable but socially functional and indicative of a healthy society. He was one of the first to recognize that deviance may introduce needed social change; the deviant pattern may eventually become the socially accepted pattern, and the deviant may thus be transformed into an innovator or cultural hero. Deviance also helps to clarify and define the social rules shared within a group. Until a rule is broken, many members may be unaware of its existence or its importance to group life. Deviance may unify a group by bringing the members together in disapproval of the deviant. Punishment of the deviant may encourage other members of the society to abide by the social rules. However, when deviance increases dramatically, or is widely pervasive, the most likely result is social disorganization.

The origins of deviance are many and varied. As an introduction to this important question, we shall examine three leading sociological viewpoints. According to Robert Merton, every society has a set of culturally prescribed goals to which its members aspire as well as a set of socially approved means of obtaining or achieving these goals. When the goals and the means of realizing them are in correspondence, normal conforming behavior is encouraged. When the goals are emphasized far more than the means, then the regulatory agencies lose their credibility and authority, a moral breakdown (anomie) results, and deviance is engendered. This experience usually does not affect the whole social body; it may prevail for a sizable social segment, such as a social class or a minority group.

As an example of this imbalance in America, Merton observes that the gospel of financial success is emphasized to a great degree; yet, for many Americans, and for a great number of the American underclasses in particular, the means of obtaining success—getting an education, finding a good job, and advancing through a series of positions—are considerably few. This tends to produce anomie and deviance, particularly among those social segments that are most deprived.

One adaptation to the imbalance of socially approved goals and means is *innovation*—accepting the goals of society and rejecting the approved means of achieving them; for example, a bank teller may embezzle funds to buy a house in the suburbs. Another response may be *ritualism*—following the rules but losing sight of the goals; as exemplified by the overzealous clerk at the motor-vehicle bureau who sends an applicant back to the end of the queue—creating office chaos—because he failed to indicate his middle initial on one of the forms. Another response is *retreatism*—rejecting both goals and means; the skid-row alcoholic typifies this adaptation. A fourth possibility is *rebellion*—rejecting both ends and means and substituting new ones in their place; this is typified in the behavior of the revolutionary.

Edwin Sutherland's differential-association theory represents another perspective on deviant behavior. Sutherland argued that people are exposed to a variety of social influences, differing in values and attitudes and in the socializing techniques used. The groups in society with which one has the most extensive association have the greatest effect on one's personality and behavior patterns. According to this theory, an individual becomes deviant by being exposed to deviant patterns and having relatively little exposure to nondeviant patterns. Moreover, the individual with a preponderance of deviant or criminal role models is likely to internalize ideas favorable to deviance and to act in a deviant way. Essentially, deviance is learned in the same way conventional behavior patterns are acquired.

Many conceptions of deviance place the primary causative emphasis at least indirectly on the deviant person. By contrast, in labeling theory the social-sanctioning process is seen as the most important contributor to deviance. For Howard Becker, a leading proponent of labeling theory, a deviant act—or even a series of deviant acts—does not make a person deviant; to acquire that status, one's behavior must be perceived, defined, and labeled as deviant by society. Being publicly labeled a deviant (being arrested, reputed to be a "queer," etc.) is probably the most significant step in developing what Becker calls a "deviant career"—that is, adopting deviance as a way of life. A person who commits an improper act and is caught at it is placed in a new status and treated accordingly. The deviant is stigmatized; his freedom is curtailed; and opportunities available to the average citizen are now denied him. He must, therefore, develop illegitimate practices, thus moving toward increasing deviance. For example, lacking conventional employment prospects, the ex-convict returns to theft. Or the drug experimenter, once labeled an addict and rejected by his family and friends, is led to seek acceptance among the drug subculture. The final step in the development of a deviant career is movement into an organized deviant group. This has a powerful impact on the deviant's self-conception. As the members of a deviant group share an *esprit de corps,* they justify and rationalize their position with respect to the larger, nondeviant culture. The group ideology serves to insulate and protect them and makes the rewards of their deviant activities personally meaningful and gratifying. Membership in the deviant group also mobilizes the experiences and skills of the members, so that the deviant activity may be carried on with a minimum of trouble.

The notion of a deviant subculture is illustrated in Weinberg's essay on the nudist camp, in Chapter 2, "Culture." In such subculture, the deviant act is socially accepted and regarded as desirable; hence, in this context, it is no longer deviant. Weinberg's finding that single males tend to be rejected by nudist groups suggests, further, that the basis of social acceptance and ranking in the deviant subculture parallels in an inverted order the system found in the conventional world.

Another aspect of Becker's theory concerns the initiation of the labeling or social-sanctioning process. Enforcement of social rules is an enterprising act. Labeling requires "moral entrepreneurs," people who "blow the whistle" or call attention to the deviation. They may be "rule creators" (i.e., crusading reformers) or "rule enforcers" (i.e., the police and regulatory agencies). According to Becker, people may blow the whistle, making enforcement necessary, when they see some personal advantage in doing so. Within the moral community, there may be several competing groups, some of which want enforcement and others that do not. Enforcement is likely to be affected by the relative power of the groups opting for and against it, by their abilities to mobilize coordinate groups in their support, and by their access to the means of communication to facilitate a favorable climate of opinion.

General theories are especially valuable for identifying common causal features in the multifarious types of deviant behavior. However, our knowledge can be greatly extended by focusing in depth on particular deviant patterns. With this proviso in mind, let us briefly explore two deviant activities, homosexuality and suicide.

In all modern industrial societies, homosexual behavior (relations with members of one's own sex) is viewed as morally disreputable, and in many places it is treated as a crime. Because of the highly privatized conception of sexual behavior in Western society, systematic sociological research has been most difficult. Consequently, to date, estimates of the incidence, prevalence, and increase of homosexuality are based, for the most part, on inadequate and unrepresentative data. Nevertheless, the best studies available[1] have found that about 5 per cent of American and British males are career homosexuals, and about a third have at least one homosexual experience some time between adolescence and old age. For women, the incidence of homosexuality is approximately half that for males. These differences between the sexes may be partly due to the widely shared belief in the West that males possess substantially greater interest in sex.

"Cruising" probably represents the major locus of male homosexual activity in urban areas. Homosexual contacts are frequently made around the shadowy places of public parks, public toilets, "gay bars," and the downtown city streets. The limited, yet steadily growing, body of research on the subject suggests that most male homosexual relationships are short-lived, and that there is considerable commercialism associated with homosexuality (homosexual prostitution).

Criminologist Laud Humphreys, in a recent article on "New Styles of Homosexual Manliness,"[2] suggests that there appears to be a trend away from the traditional cruising for pickups as the major activity in the homosexual market. Humphreys sees a polarization taking place between virilization of homosexuality, on the one hand, and impersonal homosexuality, on the other. He claims these changes may be caused by increasing crime in the streets, leaving the homosexual more vulnerable to assault and robbery; by the growing scarcity of leisure

[1] A. Kinsey *et al., Sexual Behavior in the Human Male* (Philadelphia: W. B. Saunders, 1948); A. Kinsey *et al., Sexual Behavior in the Human Female* (Philadelphia: W. B. Saunders, 1953); and Bryan Magee, *One in Twenty* (New York: Stein and Day, 1966).

[2] *Trans-action,* vol. 8, nos. 5 and 6 (March–April, 1971), 38–46.

time; and by the development of a new morality among the youth counterculture.

Virilization refers to the increasingly masculine image of the "gay" scene. More male homosexuals evince traditional male characteristics in their dress, appearance, and manner. Homosexuality appears to be pursued increasingly along with heterosexual activities, accompanied by the advent of the "swinger" set and the orgy set. There is now more frank and open involvement in the cause of civil rights for homosexuals, as embodied in the growing and increasingly organized homophile movement.

At the same time, Humphreys feels that impersonal sex in public places is on the increase, furnishing an anonymous, short-term, immediate mode of homosexual gratification. Through a combination of ingenious and resourceful research methods, Humphreys was able to illuminate this behavior, providing us with a detailed, systematic understanding of its characteristics and its social bases. His work breaks new ground in delineating some of the identity problems faced by the career homosexual and those who are involved in homosexual activity but maintain a heterosexual style of life.

Ever since the publication of Émile Durkheim's *Suicide* in 1897, which illuminated for the first time the sociological factors involved in suicide, sociologists have exhibited continuing interest in this deviant behavior. In his research, which compared fluctuations in the rates of suicide throughout the provinces of France, Durkheim identified three types of suicide—altruistic, egoistic, and anomic suicide.

Altruistic suicide represents a willful act performed in behalf of others. Examples are the deliberate crashes of the Japanese Kamikaze pilots during World War II and the self-immolations of the Vietnamese Buddhist priests protesting the war. Altruistic suicide is the predominant type in folk societies. Among some Eskimo groups, old people who can no longer hunt or work kill themselves to help the group survive. In some folk societies, the death of a spouse customarily prompts an individual to commit suicide as part of religious observance. In modern industrial societies, some of the elderly and incurably ill may end their lives so as not to be a burden to others.

Egoistic suicide represents the polar opposite of the altruistic type; it is a form of suicide that results from a diminished attachment to others and is most pervasive in modern industrial societies. Durkheim identified three dimensions of estrangement from society—family, religious, and political. He noted the relatively high likelihood of suicide among single people and those belonging to small families. Protestants have higher rates of suicide than Catholics or Jews. Suicide is higher in peacetime than during periods of war, when people are united against a common enemy and need to solve common problems.

Anomic suicide results from a disruption in the group-affiliational networks of the individual, which presents him with conflicting and competing norms, thrusting him into a mood of profound moral ambiguity and confusion. Durkheim notes that anomic suicide is exemplified in rapid and abrupt social change, such as during periods of economic catastrophe or marked spurts of prosperity, and is more likely among the divorced than the married.

Most of the Durkheim's hypotheses have been supported by contemporary suicide research. Ronald Maris, in "The Sociology of Suicide Prevention," presents a comprehensive and up-to-date view of the social correlates of suicide. Moreover, his research uncovers a very problematic disparity between those who actually commit suicide and those who receive care from suicide-prevention agencies; those who succeed in killing themselves have not generally received prior treatment from prevention services.

This disparity may be caused in part by the different motives and methods of "successful" suicides and those "attempting" suicide. It may also reflect discrimination against the aged, who, Maris finds, are overrepresented among successful suicides and who receive relatively few educational, rehabilitative, or economic benefits from social service agencies.[3] Possibly, also, the precarious economic status and prestige of many social-service agencies promote a preoccupation with organizational maintenance, diverting them from pursuing their stated objectives. Accurate social-science knowledge and adequate public support are essential for effective remedial social action in suicide prevention and other deviant-treatment programs or social-problem reform.

Homosexuality

Tearoom Trade: Impersonal Sex in Public Places*

Laud Humphreys

At shortly after five o'clock on a weekday evening, four men enter a public restroom in the city park. One wears a well-tailored business suit; another wears tennis shoes, shorts, and teeshirt; the third man is still clad in the

[3] Robert Scott, "Selecting Clients for Welfare Agencies," *Social Problems,* XIV, no. 3 (Winter, 1967), 248–57.

* From Laud Humphries, *Tearoom Trade* (Chicago: Aldine Publishing Company, 1970); copyright © 1970 by R. A. Laud Humphreys. Reprinted by permission of Aldine-Atherton, Inc.

khaki uniform of his filling station; the last, a salesman, has loosened his tie and left his sports coat in the car. What has caused these men to leave the company of other homeward-bound commuters on the freeway? What common interest brings these men, with their divergent background, to this public facility?

They have come here not for the obvious reason but in a search for "instant sex." Many men–married and unmarried, those with heterosexual identities and those whose self-image is a homosexual one–seek such impersonal sex, shunning involvement, desiring kicks without commitment. Whatever reasons–social, physiological, or psychological–might be postulated for this search, the phenomenon of impersonal sex persists as a widespread but rarely studied form of human interaction.

There are several settings for this type of deviant activity–the balconies of movie theaters, automobiles, behind bushes–but few offer the advantages for these men that public restrooms provide. "Tearooms," as these facilities are called in the language of the homosexual subculture, have several characteristics that make them attractive as locales for sexual encounters without involvement.

Like most other words in the homosexual vocabulary, the origin of *tearoom* is unknown. British slang has used "tea" to denote "urine." Another British usage is as a verb, meaning "to engage with, encounter, go in against." According to its most precise meaning in the argot, the only "true" tearoom is one that gains a reputation as a place where homosexual encounters occur. Presumably, any restroom could qualify for this distinction, but comparatively few are singled out at any one time. For instance, I have researched a metropolitan area with more than 90 public toilets in its parks, only 20 of which are in regular use as locales for sexual games. Restrooms thus designated join the company of automobiles and bathhouses as places for deviant sexual activity, second only to private bedrooms in popularity. During certain seasons of the year–roughly, that period from April through October that Midwestern homosexuals call "the hunting season"–tearooms may surpass any other locale of homoerotic enterprise in volume of activity.

Public restrooms are chosen by those who want homoerotic activity without commitment for a number of reasons. They are accessible, easily recognized by the initiate, and provide little public visibility. Tearooms thus offer the advantages of both public and private settings. They are available and recognizable enough to attract a large volume of potential sexual partners, providing an opportunity for rapid action with a variety of men. When added to the relative privacy of these settings, such features enhance the impersonality of the sheltered interaction.

In the first place, tearooms are easily accessible to the male population. They may be located in any sort of public gathering place–department stores, bus stations, libraries, hotels, YMCA's, or courthouses. In keeping with the drive-in craze of American society, however, the more popular facilities are those readily accessible to the roadways. The restrooms of public parks and beaches—and, more recently, the rest stops set at programmed intervals along superhighways—are now attracting the clientele that, in a more pedestrian age, frequented great buildings of the inner cities. My research is focused on the activity that takes place in the restrooms of public parks, not only because (with some seasonal variation) they provide the most action but also because of other factors that make them suitable for sociological study.

There is a great deal of difference in the volumes of homosexual activity that these accommodations shelter. In some, one might wait for months before observing a deviant act (unless solitary masturbation is considered deviant). In others, the volume approaches orgiastic dimensions. One summer afternoon, for instance, I witnessed twenty acts of fellatio in the course of an hour while waiting out a thunderstorm in a tearoom. For one who wishes to participate in (or study) such activity, the primary consideration is finding where the action is.

Occasionally, tips about the more active places may be gained from unexpected sources. Early in my research, I was approached by a man (whom I later surmised to be a park patrolman in plain clothes) while waiting at the window of a tearoom for some patrons to arrive. After finishing his business at the urinal and exchanging some remarks about the weather (it had been raining), the man came abruptly to the point: "Look, fellow, if you're looking for sex, this isn't the place. We're clamping down on this park because of trouble with the niggers. Try the john at the northeast corner of [Reagan] Park. You'll find plenty of action there." He was right. Some of my best observations were made at the spot he recommended. In most cases, however, I could only enter, wait, and watch—a method that was costly in both time and gasoline. After surveying a couple of dozen such rooms in this way, however, I became able to identify the more popular tearooms by observing certain physical evidence, the most obvious of which is the location of the facility. During the warm seasons, those restrooms that are isolated from other park facilities, such as administration buildings, shops, tennis courts, playgrounds and picnic areas, are the more popular for deviant activity. The most active tearooms studied were all isolated from recreational areas, cut off by drives or lakes from baseball diamonds and picnic tables.

I have chosen the term "purlieu" (with its ancient meaning of land severed from a royal forest by perambulation) to describe the immediate environs best suited to the tearoom trade. Drives and walks that separate a public toilet from the rest of the park are almost certain guides to deviant sex. The ideal setting for homosexual activity is a tearoom situated on an island of grass, with roads close by on every side. The getaway car is just a few steps away; children are not apt to wander over from the playground; no one can surprise the participants by walking in from the woods or from over a hill; it is not likely that straight people will stop there. According to my observations, the women's side of these buildings is seldom used at all.

WHAT THEY WANT, WHEN THEY WANT IT

The availability of facilities they can recognize attracts a great number of men who wish, for whatever reason, to engage in impersonal homoerotic activity. Simple observation is enough to guide these participants, the researcher, and, perhaps, the police to active tearooms. It is much more difficult to make an accurate appraisal of the proportion of the male population who engage in such activity over a representative length of time. Even with good sampling procedures, a large staff of assistants would be needed to make the observations necessary for an adequate census of this mobile population. All that may be said with some degree of certainty is that the percentage of the male population who participate in tearoom sex in the United States is somewhat less than the 16 per cent of the adult white male population Kinsey found to have "at least as much of the homosexual as the heterosexual in their histories."

Participants assure me that it is not uncommon in tearooms for one man to fellate as many as ten others in a day. I have personally watched a fellator take on three men in succession in a half hour of observation. One respondent, who has cooperated with the researcher in a number of taped interviews, claims to average three men each day during the busy season.

I have seen some waiting turn for this type of service. Leaving one such scene on a warm September Saturday, I remarked to a man who left close behind me: "Kind of crowded in there, isn't it?" "Hell, yes," he answered. "It's getting so you have to take a number and wait in line in these places!"

There are many who frequent the same facility repeatedly. Men will come to be known as regular, even daily, participants, stopping off at the same tearoom on the way to or from work. One physician in his late fifties was so punctual in his appearance at a particular restroom that I began to look forward to our daily chats. This robust, affable respondent said he had stopped at this tearoom every evening of the week (except Wednesday, his day off) for years "for a blow job." Another respondent, a salesman whose schedule is flexible, may "make the scene" more than once a day–usually at his favorite men's room. At the time of our interview, this man claimed to have had four orgasms in the past twenty-four hours.

According to the participants I have interviewed, those who are looking for impersonal sex in tearooms are relatively certain of finding the sort of partner they want–

> You go into the tearoom. You can pick up some really nice things in there. Again, it is a matter of sex real quick; and, if you like this kind, fine–you've got it. You get one and he is done; and, before long, you've got another one.

–and when they want it:

> Well, I go there; and you can always find someone to suck your cock, morning, noon, or night. I know lots of guys who stop by there on their way to work–and all during the day.

It is this sort of volume and variety that keeps the tearooms viable as market places of the one-night-stand variety.

Of the bar crowd in gay (homosexual) society, only a small percentage would be found in park restrooms. But this more overt, gay bar clientele constitutes a minor part of those in any American city who follow a predominantly homosexual pattern. The so-called closet queens and other types of covert deviants make up the vast majority of those who engage in homosexual acts—and these are the persons most attracted to tearoom encounters.

Tearooms are popular, not because they serve as gathering places for homosexuals, but because they attract a variety of men, a *minority* of whom are active in the homosexual subculture and a large group of whom have no homosexual self-identity. For various reasons, they do not want to be seen with those who might be identified as such or to become involved with them on a "social" basis.

SHELTERING SILENCE

There is another aspect of the tearoom encounter that is crucial. I refer to the silence of the interaction.

Throughout most homosexual encounters in public restrooms, nothing is spoken. One may spend many hours in these buildings and witness dozens of sexual acts without hearing a word. Of 50 encounters on which I made extensive notes, only in 15 was any word spoken. Two were encounters in which I sought to ease the strain of legitimizing myself as lookout by saying, "You go ahead—I'll watch." Four were whispered remarks between sexual partners, such as "Not so hard!" or "Thanks." One was an exchange of greetings between friends.

The other eight verbal exchanges were in full voice and more extensive, but they reflected an attendant circumstance that was exceptional. When a group of us were locked in a restroom and attacked by several youths, we spoke for defense and out of fear. This event ruptured the reserve among us and resulted in a series of conversations among those who shared this adventure for several days afterward. Gradually, this sudden unity subsided, and the encounters drifted back into silence.

Barring such unusual events, an occasionally whispered "thanks" at the conclusion of the act constitutes the bulk of even whispered communication. At first, I presumed that speech was avoided for fear of incrimination. The excuse that intentions have been misunderstood is much weaker when those proposals are expressed in words rather than signaled by body movements. As research progressed, however, it became evident that the privacy of silent interaction accomplishes much more than mere defense against exposure to a hostile world. Even when a careful lookout is maintaining the boundaries of an encounter against intrusion, the sexual participants tend to be silent. The mechanism of silence goes beyond satisfying the demand for privacy.

Like all other characteristics of the tearoom setting, it serves to guarantee anonymity, to assure the impersonality of the sexual liaison.

Tearoom sex is distinctly less personal than any other form of sexual activity, with the single exception of solitary masturbation. What I mean by "less personal" is simply that there is less emotional and physical involvement in restroom fellatio—less, even, than in the furtive action that takes place in autos and behind bushes. In those instances, at least, there is generally some verbal involvement. Often, in tearoom stalls, the only portions of the players' bodies that touch are the mouth of the insertee and the penis of the insertor; and the mouths of these partners seldom open for speech.

Only a public place, such as a park restroom, could provide the lack of personal involvement in sex that certain men desire. The setting fosters the necessary turnover in participants by its accessibility and visibility to the "right" men. In these public settings, too, there exists a sort of democracy that is endemic to impersonal sex. Men of all racial, social, educational, and physical characteristics meet in these places for sexual union. With the lack of involvement, personal preferences tend to be minimized.

If a person is going to entangle his body with another's in bed—or allow his mind to become involved with another mind—he will have certain standards of appearance, cleanliness, personality, or age that the prospective partner must meet. Age, looks, and other external variables are germane to the sexual action. As the amount of anticipated contact of body and mind in the sex act decreases, so do the standards expected of the partner. As one respondent told me:

> I go to bed with gay people, too. But if I am going to bed with a gay person, I have certain standards that I prefer them to meet. And in the tearooms you don't have to worry about these things—because it is just a purely one-sided affair.

Participants may develop strong attachments to the settings of their adventures in impersonal sex. I have noted more than once that these men seem to acquire stronger sentimental attachments to the buildings in which they meet for sex than to the persons with whom they engage in it. One respondent tells the following story: We had been discussing the relative merits of various facilities, when I asked him: "Do you remember that old tearoom across from the park garage—the one they tore down last winter?"

> Do I ever! That was the greatest place in the park. Do you know what my roommate did last Christmas, after they tore the place down? He took a wreath, sprayed it with black paint, and laid it on top of the snow—right where that corner stall had stood. . . . He was really broken up!

The walls and fixtures of these public facilities are provided by society at large, but much remains for the participants to provide for themselves. Silence in these settings is the product of years of interaction. It is a normative response to the demand for privacy without involvement, a rule that has been developed and taught. Except for solitary masturbation, sex necessitates joint action; but impersonal sex requires that this interaction be as unrevealing as possible.

PEOPLE NEXT DOOR

Tearoom activity attracts a large number of participants–enough to produce the majority of arrests for homosexual offenses in the United States. Now, employing data gained from both formal and informal interviews, we shall consider what these men are like away from the scenes of impersonal sex. "For some people," says Evelyn Hooker, an authority on male homosexuality, "the seeking of sexual contacts with other males is an activity isolated from all other aspects of their lives." Such segregation is apparent with most men who engage in the homosexual activity of public restrooms; but the degree and manner in which "deviant" is isolated from "normal" behavior in their lives will be seen to vary along social dimensions.

For the man who lives next door, the tearoom participant is just another neighbor–and probably a very good one at that. He may make a little more money than the next man and work a little harder for it. It is likely that he will drive a nicer car and maintain a neater yard than do other neighbors in the block. Maybe, like some tearoom regulars, he will work with Boy Scouts in the evenings and spend much of his weekend at the church. It may be more surprising for the outsider to discover that most of these men are married.

Indeed, 54 per cent of my research subjects are married and living with their wives. From the data at hand, there is no evidence that these unions are particularly unstable; nor does it appear that any of the wives are aware of their husbands' secret sexual activity. Indeed, the husbands choose public restrooms as sexual settings partly to avoid just such exposure. I see no reason to dispute the claim of a number of tearoom respondents that their preference for a form of concerted action that is fast and impersonal is largely predicated on a desire to protect their family relationships.

Superficial analysis of the data indicates that the maintenance of exemplary marriages–at least in appearance–is very important to the subjects of this study. In answering questions such as "When it comes to making decisions in your household, who generally makes them?" the participants indicate they are more apt to defer to their mates than are those in the control sample. They also indicate that they find it more important to "get along well" with their wives. In the open-ended questions regarding marital relationships, they tend to speak of them in more glowing terms.

TOM AND MYRA

This handsome couple live in ranch-style suburbia with their two young children. Tom is in his early thirties–an aggressive, muscular, and virile-looking male. He works "about 75 hours a week" at his new job as a chemist.

"I am *wild* about my job," he says. "I really love it!" Both of Tom's "really close" friends he met at work.

He is a Methodist, and Myra a Roman Catholic, but each goes to his or her own church. Although he claims to have broad interests in life, they boil down to "games–sports like touch football or baseball."

When I asked him to tell me something about his family, Tom replied only in terms of their "good fortune" that things are not worse:

> We've been fortunate that a religious problem has not occurred. We're fortunate in having two healthy children. We're fortunate that we decided to leave my last job. Being married has made me more stable.

They have been married for eleven years, and Myra is the older of the two. When asked who makes what kinds of decisions in his family, he said: "She makes most decisions about the family. She keeps the books. But I make the *major* decisions."

Myra does the household work and takes care of the children. Perceiving his main duties as those of "keeping the yard up" and "bringing home the bacon," Tom sees as his wife's only shortcoming "her lack of discipline in organization." He remarked: "She's very attractive . . . has a fair amount of poise. The best thing is that she gets along well and is able to establish close relationships with other women."

Finally, when asked how he thinks his wife feels about him and his behavior in the family, Tom replied: "She'd like to have me around more–would like for me to have a closer relationship with her and the kids." He believes it is "very important" to have the kind of sex life he needs. Reporting that he and Myra have intercourse about twice a month, he feels that his sexual needs are "adequately met" in his relationships with his wife. I also know that, from time to time, Tom has sex in the restrooms of a public park.

As an upwardly mobile man, Tom was added to the sample at a point of transition in his career as a tearoom participant. If Tom is like others who share working-class origins, he may have learned of the tearoom as an economical means of achieving orgasm during his navy years. Of late, he has returned to the restrooms for occasional sexual "relief," since his wife, objecting to the use of birth control devices, has limited his conjugal outlets.

Tom still perceives his sexual needs in the symbolic terms of the class in which he was socialized: "About twice a month" is the frequency of intercourse generally reported by working-class men; and, although they are reticent in reporting it, they do not perceive this frequency as adequate to meet their sexual needs, which they estimate are about the same as those felt by others of their age. My interviews indicate that such perceptions of sexual drive and satisfaction prevail among respondents of the lower-middle to upper-lower classes, whereas they are uncommon for those of the upper-middle and upper classes. Among the latter, the reported perception is of a much higher frequency of intercourse, and they estimate their needs to be greater than those of "most other men."

AGING CRISIS

Not only is Tom moving into a social position that may cause him to reinterpret his sexual drive, he is also approaching a point of major crisis in his career as a tearoom participant. At the time when I observed him in an act of fellatio, he played the insertor role. Still relatively young and handsome, Tom finds himself sought out as "trade"—that is, those men who make themselves available for acts of fellatio, but who, regarding themselves as "straight," refuse to reciprocate in the sexual act. Not only is that the role he expects to play in the tearoom encounters, it is the role others expect of him.

"I'm not toned up anymore," Tom complains. He is gaining weight around the middle and losing hair. As he moves past 35, Tom will face the aging crisis of the tearooms. Less and less frequently will he find himself the one sought out in these meetings. Presuming that he has been sufficiently reinforced to continue this form of sexual operation, he will be forced to seek other men. As trade, he was not expected to reciprocate, but he will soon be increasingly expected to serve as insertee for those who have first taken that role for him.

In most cases, fellatio is a service performed by an older man upon a younger. In one encounter, for example, a man appearing to be around forty was observed as insertee with a man in his twenties as insertor. A few minutes later, the man of forty was being sucked by one in his fifties. Analyzing the estimated ages of the principal partners in 53 observed acts of fellatio, I arrived at these conclusions: The insertee was judged to be older than the insertor in 40 cases; they were approximately the same age in 3; and the insertor was the older in 10 instances. The age differences ranged from an insertee estimated to be twenty-five years older than his partner to an insertee thought to be ten years younger than his insertor.

Strong references to this crisis of aging are found in my interviews with cooperating respondents, one of whom had this to say:

> Well, I started off as the straight young thing. Everyone wanted to suck my cock. I wouldn't have been caught dead with one of the things in my mouth! . . . So, here I am at forty—with grown kids—and the biggest cocksucker in [the city]!

Similar experiences were expressed, in more reserved language, by another man, some 15 years his senior:

> I suppose I was around thirty-five—or thirty-six—when I started giving out blow jobs. It just got so I couldn't operate any other way in the park johns. I'd still rather have a good blow job any day, but I've gotten so I like it the way it is now.

Perhaps by now there is enough real knowledge abroad to have dispelled the idea that men who engage in homosexual acts may be typed by any consistency of performance in one or another sexual role. Undoubtedly, there are preferences: Few persons are so adaptable, their conditioning so undifferentiated, that they fail to exercise choice between various sexual roles and positions. Such preferences, however, are learned, and sexual repertories tend to expand with time and experience. This study of restroom sex indicates that sexual roles within these encounters are far from stable. They are apt to change within an encounter, from one encounter to another, with age, and with the amount of exposure to influences from a sexually deviant subculture.

It is to this last factor that I should like to direct the reader's attention. The degree of contact with a network of friends who share the actor's sexual interests takes a central position in mediating not only his preferences for sex roles but his style of adaptation to–and rationalization of–the deviant activity in which he participates. There are, however, two reasons why I have not classified research subjects in terms of their participation in the homosexual subculture. It is difficult to measure accurately the degree of such involvement; and such subcultural interaction depends upon other social variables, two of which are easily measured.

Family status has a definitive effect on the deviant careers of those whose concern is with controlling information about their sexual behavior. The married man who engages in homosexual activity must be much more cautious about his involvement in the subculture than his single counterpart. As a determinant of life-style and sexual activity, marital status is also a determinant of the patterns of deviant adaptation and rationalization. Only those in my sample who were divorced or separated from their wives were difficult to categorize as either married or single. Those who had been married, however, showed a tendency to remain in friendship networks with married men. Three of the four were still limited in freedom by responsibilities for their children. For these reasons, I have included all men who were once married in the "married" categories.

The second determining variable is the relative autonomy of the respondent's occupation. A man is "independently" employed when his job allows him freedom of movement and security from being fired; the most obvious example is self-employment. Occupational "dependence" leaves a man little freedom for engaging in disreputable activity. The sales manager or other executive of a business firm has greater freedom than the salesman or attorney who is employed in the lower echelons of a large industry or by the federal government. The sales representative whose territory is far removed from the home office has greater independence, in terms of information control, than the minister of a local congregation. The majority of those placed in both the married and unmarried categories with *dependent* occupations were employed by large industries or the government.

Median education levels and annual family incomes indicate that those with dependent occupations rank lower on the socio-economic scale. Only in the case of married men, however, is this correlation between social class and occupational autonomy strongly supported by the ratings of these respondents on Warner's Index of Status Characteristics. Nearly all the married men with dependent occupations are of the upper-lower or lower-middle classes, whereas those with independent occupations are of the upper-middle or upper classes. For single men, the social-class variable is neither so easily identifiable nor so clearly divided. Nearly all single men in the sample can be classified only as "vaguely middle class."

As occupational autonomy and marital status remain the most important dimensions along which participants may be ranked, we shall consider four general types of tearoom customers: (1) married men with dependent occupations, (2) married men with independent occupations, (3) unmarried men with independent occupations, and (4) unmarried men with dependent occupations. As will become evident with the discussion of each type, I have employed labels from the homosexual argot, along with pseudonyms, to designate each class of participants. This is done not only to facilitate reading but to emphasize that we are describing persons rather than merely "typical" constructs.

TYPE I: TRADE

The first classification, which includes 19 of the participants (38 per cent), may be called "trade," since most would earn that appellation from the gay subculture. All of these men are, or have been, married–one was separated from his wife at the time of interviewing and another was divorced.

Most work as truck drivers, machine operators, or clerical workers. There is a member of the armed forces, a carpenter, and the minister of a pentecostal church. Most of their wives work, at least part time, to help raise their median annual family income to $8,000. One in six of these men is black. All are normally masculine in appearance and mannerism. Although 14 have completed high school, there are only 3 college graduates among them, and 5 have had less than twelve years of schooling.

George is representative of this largest group of respondents.

* * *

At the age of twenty, he married a Roman Catholic girl and has since joined her church, although he classifies himself as "lapsed." In the fourteen years of their marriage, they have had seven children, one of whom is less than a year old. George doesn't think they should have more children, but his wife objects to using any type of birth control other than the rhythm method. With his wife working part time as a waitress, they have an income of about $5,000.

"How often do you have intercourse with your wife?" I asked. "Not very much the last few years," he replied. "It's up to when she feels like giving it to me–which ain't very often. I never suggest it."

* * *

While more open than most in his acknowledgment of marital tension, George's appraisal of sexual relations in the marriage is typical of those respondents classified as trade. In 63 per cent of these marriages, the wife, husband, or both are Roman Catholic. When answering questions about their sexual lives, a story much like George's emerged: At least since the birth of the last child, conjugal relations have been very rare.

These data suggest that, along with providing an excuse for diminishing intercourse with their wives, the religious teachings to which most of these families adhere may cause the husbands to search for sex in the tearooms. Whatever the causes that turn them unsatisfied from the marriage bed, however, the alternate outlet must be quick, inexpensive, and impersonal. Any personal, ongoing affair—any outlet requiring money or hours away from home—would threaten a marriage that is already shaky and jeopardize the most important thing these men possess, their standing as father of their children.

Around the turn of the century, before the vice squads moved in (in their never-ending process of narrowing the behavioral options of those in the lower classes), the Georges of this study would probably have made regular visits to the two-bit bordellos. With a madam watching a clock to limit the time, these cheap whorehouses provided the same sort of fast, impersonal service as today's public restrooms. I find no indication that these men seek homosexual contact as such; rather, they want a form of orgasm-producing action that is less lonely than masturbation and less involving than a love relationship. As the forces of social control deprive them of one outlet, they provide another. The newer form, it should be noted, is more stigmatizing than the previous one—thus giving "proof" to the adage that "the sinful are drawn ever deeper into perversity."

* * *

For George, no doubt, the aging crisis is also an identity crisis. Only with reluctance—and perhaps never—will he turn to the insertee role. The threat of such a role to his masculine self-image is too great. Like others of his class with whom I have had more extensive interviews, George may have learned that sexual game as a teen-age hustler, or else when serving in the army during the Korean war. In either case, his socialization into homosexual experience took place in a masculine world where it is permissible to accept money from a "queer" in return for carefully limited sexual favors. But to use one's own mouth as a substitute for the female organ, or even to express enjoyment of the action, is taboo in the trade code.

Moreover, for men of George's occupational and marital status, there is no network of friends engaged in tearoom activity to help them adapt to the changes aging will bring. I found no evidence of friendship networks among respondents of this type, who enter and leave the restrooms alone, avoiding conversation while within. Marginal to both the heterosexual and homosexual worlds, these men shun involvement in any form of gay subculture. Type I participants report fewer friends of any sort than do those of other classes. When asked how many close friends he has, George answered: "None. I haven't got time for that."

TYPE II: AMBISEXUALS

* * *

Three-fourths of the married participants with independent occupations were observed, at one time or another, participating as insertees in fellatio, compared to only one-third of the trade. Not only do the Type II participants tend to switch roles with greater facility, they seem inclined to search beyond the tearooms for more exotic forms of sexual experience. Dwight, along with others in his class, expresses a liking for anal intercourse (both as insertee and insertor), for group activity, and even for mild forms of sadomasochistic sex. . . . Two-thirds of the married participants with occupational independence are college graduates.

. . . Although the upper-class deviants may have more to lose from exposure (in the sense that the mighty have farther to fall), they also have more means at their disposal with which to protect their moral histories. Some need only tap their spending money to pay off a member of the vice squad. In other instances, social contacts with police commissioners or newspaper publishers make it possible to squelch either record or publicity of an arrest. One respondent has made substantial contributions to a police charity fund, while another hired private detectives to track down a blackmailer. Not least in their capacity to cover for errors in judgment is the fact that their word has the backing of economic and social influence. Evidence must be strong to prosecute a man who can hire the best attorneys. Lower-class men are rightfully more suspicious, for they have fewer resources with which to defend themselves if exposed.

This does not mean that Type II participants are immune to the risks of the game, but simply that they are bidding from strength. To them, the risks of arrest, exposure, blackmail, or physical assault contribute to the excitement quotient. It is not unusual for them to speak of cruising as an adventure, in contrast with the trade, who engage in a furtive search for sexual relief. On the whole, then, the action of Type II respondents is apt to be somewhat bolder and their search for "kicks" less inhibited than that of most other types of participants.

Dwight is not fleeing from an unhappy home life or sexless marriage to the encounters in the parks. He expresses great devotion to his wife and children: "They're my whole life," he exclaims. All evidence indicates that, as father, citizen, businessman and, church member, Dwight's behavior patterns—as viewed by his peers—are exemplary.

Five of the twelve participants in Dwight's class are members of the Episcopal church. Dwight is one of two who were raised in that church, although he is not as active a churchman as some who became Episcopalians later in life. In spite of his infrequent attendance to worship, he feels his church is "just right" for him and needs no changing. Its tradition and ceremony are intellectually and esthetically pleasing to him. Its liberal outlook on questions of morality round out a religious orientation that he finds generally supportive.

* * *

Unlike the trade, Type II participants recognize their homosexual activity as indicative of their own psychosexual orientations. They think of themselves as bisexual, or ambisexual, and have intellectualized their deviant tendencies in terms of the pseudopsychology of the popular press. They speak often of the great men of history, as well as of certain movie stars and others of contemporary fame, who are also "AC/DC." Erving Goffman has remarked that stigmatized Americans "tend to live in a literarily defined world." This is nowhere truer than of the subculturally oriented participants of this study. Not only do they read a great deal about homosexuality, they discuss it within their network of friends. For the Dwights, there is subcultural support that enables them to integrate their deviance with the remainder of their lives, while maintaining control over the information that could discredit their whole being. For these reasons, they look upon the gaming encounters in the parks as enjoyable experiences.

TYPE III: GAY GUYS

Like the ambisexuals, unmarried respondents with independent occupations are locked into a strong subculture, a community that provides them with knowledge about the tearooms and reinforcement in their particular brand of deviant activity. This open participation in the gay community distinguishes these single men from the larger group of unmarrieds with dependent occupations. These men take the homosexual role of our society and are thus the most truly "gay" of all participant types. Except for Tim, who was recruited as a decoy in the tearooms by the vice squad of a police department, Type III participants learned the strategies of the tearooms through friends already experienced in this branch of the sexual market.

Typical of this group is Ricky, a twenty-four-year-old university student whose older male lover supports him. Ricky stands at the median age of his type, who range from nineteen to fifty years. Half of them are college graduates, and all but one other are at least part-time students, a characteristic that explains their low median income of $3,000. Because Ricky's lover is a good provider, he is comfortably situated in a midtown apartment, a more pleasant residence than most of his friends enjoy.

* * *

Having met his lover in a park, Ricky returns there only when his mate is on a business trip or their relationship is strained. Then Ricky becomes, as he puts it, "horny," and he goes to the park to study, cruise, and engage in tearoom sex:

> The bars are O.K.—but a little too public for a "married" man like me. . . . Tearooms are just another kind of action, and they do quite well when nothing better is available.

Like other Type III respondents, he shows little preference in sexual roles. "It depends on the other guy," Ricky says, "and whether I like his looks or not. Some men I'd crawl across the street on my knees for—others I wouldn't piss on!" His aging crisis will be shared with all others in the gay world. It will take the nightmarish form of waning attractiveness and the search for a permanent lover to fill his later years, but it will have no direct relationship with the tearoom roles. Because of his socialization in the homosexual society, taking the insertee role is neither traumatic for him nor related to aging.

Ricky's life revolves around his sexual deviance in a way that is not true of George or even of Dwight. Most of his friends and social contacts are connected with the homosexual subculture. His attitudes toward, and rationalization of, his sexual behavior are largely gained from this wide circle of friends. The gay men claim to have more close friends than do any other type of control or participant respondents. As frequency of orgasm is reported, this class also has more sex than any other group sampled, averaging 2.5 acts per week. They seem relatively satisfied with this aspect of their lives and regard their sexual drive as normal—although Ricky perceives his sexual needs as less than most.

* * *

All three of the Unitarians in the sample are Type III men, although none was raised in that faith; and their jobs are uniformly of the sort to which their sexual activity, if exposed, would present little threat.

Although these men correspond most closely to society's homosexual stereotype, they are least representative of the tearoom population, constituting only 14 per cent of the participant sample. More than any other type, the Rickys seem at ease with their behavior in the sexual market, and their scarcity in the tearooms is indicative of this. They want personal sex—more permanent relationships—and the public restrooms are not where this is to be found.

That any of them patronize the tearooms at all is the result of incidental factors: They fear that open cruising in the more common homosexual market places of the baths and bars might disrupt a current love affair; or they drop in at a tearoom while waiting for a friend at one of the "watering places" where homosexuals congregate in the parks. They find the anonymity of the tearooms suitable for their purposes, but not inviting enough to provide the primary setting for sexual activity.

TYPE IV: CLOSET QUEENS

Another dozen of the 50 participants interviewed may be classified as single deviants with dependent occupations—"closet queens," in homosexual slang. Again, the label may be applied to others who keep their deviance hidden, whether married or single, but the covert, unmarried men are most apt to earn this appellation. With them, we have moved full circle in our classifications, for they parallel the trade in a number of ways.

1. They have few friends, only a minority of whom are involved in tearoom activity.
2. They tend to play the insertor role, at least until they confront the crisis of aging.
3. Half of them are Roman Catholic in religion.
4. Their median annual income is $6,000; and they work as teachers, postmen, salesmen, clerks–usually for large corporations or agencies.
5. Most of them have completed only high school, although there are a few exceptionally well-educated men in this group.
6. One in six is black.
7. Not only are they afraid of becoming involved in other forms of the sexual market, they share with the trade a relatively furtive involvement in the tearoom encounters.

. . . They report poorer childhood relationships with their fathers than do those of any other group. As is the case with Arnold's roommate, many closet queens seem to prefer teen-age boys as sexual objects. This is one of the features that distinguishes them from all other participant types. Although scarce in tearooms, teen-agers make themselves available for sexual activity in other places frequented by closet queens. A number of these men regularly cruise the streets where boys thumb rides each afternoon when school is over. One closet queen from my sample has been arrested for luring boys in their early teens to his home.

Interactions between these men and the youths they seek frequently results in the sort of scandal feared by the gay community. Newspaper reports of molestations usually contain clues of the closet-queen style of adaptation on the part of such offenders. Those respondents whose lives had been threatened by teen-age toughs were generally of this type. One of the standard rules governing one-night-stand operations cautions against becoming involved with such "chicken." The frequent violation of this rule by closet queens may contribute to their general disrepute among the bar set of the homosexual subculture, where "closet queen" is a pejorative term.

* * *

STYLES OF DEVIANT ADAPTATION

Social isolation is characteristic of Type IV participants. Generally, it is more severe even than that encountered among the trade, most of whom enjoy at least a vestigial family life. Although painfully aware of their homosexual orientations, these men find little solace in association with others who share their deviant interests. Fearing exposure, arrest, the stigmatization that might result from a participation in the homosexual subculture, they are driven to a desperate, lone-wolf sort of activity that may prove most dangerous to themselves and the rest of society. Although it is tempting to look for psychological explanations of their apparent preference for chicken, the sociological ones are evident. They resort to the more dangerous game because of a lack of both the normative restraints and adult markets that prevail in the more overt subculture. To them, the costs (financial and otherwise) of operating among street-corner youths are more acceptable than those of active participation in the gay subculture. Only the tearooms provide a less expensive alternative for the closet queens.

* * *

In delineating styles of adaptation, I do not intend to imply that these men are faced with an array of styles from which they may pick one or even a combination. No man's freedom is that great. They have been able to choose only among the limited options offered them by society. These sets of alternatives, which determine the modes of adaptation to deviant pressures, are defined and allocated in accordance with major sociological variables: occupation, marital status, age, race, amount of education. That is one meaning of social probability.

THE SOCIOLOGIST AS VOYEUR

The methods employed in this study of men who engage in restroom sex are the outgrowth of three ethical assumptions: First, I do not believe the social scientist should ever ignore or avoid an area of research simply because it is difficult or socially sensitive. Second, he should approach any aspect of human behavior with those means that least distort the observed phenomena. Third, he must protect respondents from harm–regardless of what such protection may cost the researcher.

Because the majority of arrests on homosexual charges in the United States result from encounters in public restrooms, I felt this form of sexual behavior to provide a legitimate, even essential, topic for sociological investigation. In our society, the social control forces, not the criminologist, determine what the latter shall study.

Following this decision, the question is one of choosing research methods that permit the investigator to achieve maximum fidelity to the world he is studying. I believe ethnographic methods are the only truly empirical ones for the social scientist. When human behavior is being examined, systematic observation is essential; so, I had to become a participant-observer of furtive, felonious acts.

Fortunately, the very fear and suspicion of tearoom participants produces a mechanism that makes such observation possible: A third man (generally one who obtains voyeuristic pleasure from his duties) serves as a lookout, moving back and forth from door to windows. Such a "watchqueen," as he is labeled in the homosexual argot, coughs when a police car stops nearby or when a stranger approaches. He nods affirmatively when he recognizes a man entering as being a "regular." Having been taught the watchqueen role by a cooperating respondent, I played that part faithfully while observing hundreds of acts of fellatio. After developing a systematic observation sheet, I recorded 50 of these encounters (involving 53 sexual acts) in great detail. These records were compared with another 30 made by a cooperating respondent who was himself a sexual participant. The bulk of information presented in "Tearoom Trade" results from these observations.

Although primarily interested in the stigmatized behavior, I also wanted to know about the men who take such risks for a few moments of impersonal sex. I was able to engage a number of participants in conversation outside the restrooms; and, eventually, by revealing the purpose of my study to them, I gained a dozen respondents who contributed hundreds of hours of interview time. This sample I knew to be biased in favor of the more outgoing and better educated of the tearoom population.

To overcome this bias, I cut short a number of my observations of encounters and hurried to my automobile. There, with the help of a tape recorder, I noted a brief description of each participant, his sexual role in the encounter just observed, his license number, and a brief description of his car. I varied such records from park to park . . . to correspond with previously observed changes in volume at various times of the day. This provided me with a time-and-place-representative sample of 134 participants. With attrition, chiefly of those who had changed address or who drove rented cars, and the addition of two persons who walked to the tearooms, I ended up with a sample of 100 men, each of whom I had actually observed engaging in fellatio.

At this stage, my third ethical concern impinged. I already knew that many of my respondents were married, and that all were in a highly discreditable position and fearful of discovery. How could I approach these covert deviants for interviews? By passing as deviant, I had observed their sexual behavior without disturbing it. Now, I was faced with interviewing these men (often in the presence of their wives) without destroying them. Fortunately, I held another research job that placed me in the position of preparing the interview schedule for a social-health survey of a random selection of male subjects throughout the community. With permission from the survey's directors, I could add my sample to the larger group (thus enhancing their anonymity) and interview them as part of the social-health survey.

To overcome the danger of having a subject recognize me as a watchqueen, I changed my hair style, attire, and automobile. At the risk of losing more transient respondents, I waited a year between the sample gathering and the interviews, during which time I took notes on their homes and neighborhoods and acquired data on them from the city and county directories.

Having randomized the sample, I completed 50 interviews with tearoom participants and added another 50 interviews from the social-health survey sample. The latter control group was matched with the participants on the bases of marital status, race, job classification, and area of residence.

This study, then, results from a confluence of strategies: systematic, firsthand observation, in-depth interviews with available respondents, the use of archival data, and structured interviews of a representative sample and a matched control group. At each level of research, I applied those measures that provided maximum protection for research subjects and the truest measurement of persons and behavior observed.

Suicide

The Sociology of Suicide Prevention*

Ronald W. Maris

It is remarkable how stable the suicide rate has been in twentieth-century America.[1] Except for slight peaks during depression years and troughs during the two world wars, the rate of suicide has been constant for the last sixty-eight years. This constancy is all the more striking when contrasted with the variability of other causes of death. . . . Deaths by diseases of childhood (scarlet fever, diphtheria, measles, etc.) have been virtually eliminated. Deaths by pneumonia are one fifth what they were at the turn of the century. Tuberculosis deaths are 2 per cent of their 1900–1904 rate; chronic nephritis deaths, 6 per cent. Generally, the crude death rate has decreased from 17.2 per 1,000 population to 9.4 from 1900 to 1967. Durkheim (1951:305) noted a similar stability of suicide rates in nineteenth-century France, arguing that suicide rates reflected the temperament or collective conscience of a group or nation that itself was resistant to change:

> From this point of view, there is no longer anything mysterious about the stability of the suicide rate, any more than about its individual manifestations. For, since each society has its own temperament, unchangeable within brief periods, and since this inclination to suicide has its source in the moral constitution of groups, it must differ from group to group and in each of them remain for long periods practically the same. It is one of the essential elements of social coenaesthesia. Now this coenaesthetic state among collective existences, as well as among individuals, is their most personal and unchangeable quality, because nothing is more fundamental. But then the effects springing from it must have both the same personality and the same stability. It is even natural for them to possess a higher stability than that of the general mortality. For . . . the various conditions on which public health depends change much more readily from year to year than the temperament of peoples.

[1] This is not to deny that different countries, communities, occupational groups, and social role categories evidence considerable variation in the suicide rate (cf. Labovitz, 1968: 57–73).

* From *Social Problems,* vol. 17, no. 1 (Summer, 1969), 132–49. Reprinted by permission of The Society for the Study of Social Problems.

Regardless of how one explains the relative stability of the suicide rate, two implications stand out: First, suicide is becoming an increasingly important factor in the death rate; and, second, suicide is not being prevented.

Of course, suicide is still not among the leading causes of death, except for young adults (and even here the rate of suicide is very low). In other words, even though the suicide rate has not declined, neither has it increased appreciably. For example, during this century, the death rates of cancer, heart disease, and motor-vehicle accidents have doubled–in some instances, multiplying rates that were staggering to begin with. Yet, paradoxically, this very variability of the leading causes of death enhances their control potential. That is, there is always the possibility of determining what has varied with cancer or heart disease. One would predict a drastic decline in cancer deaths, if cigarette smoking could be controlled for a sufficient time. Suicide rates, however, seem relatively impervious to changes in the physical and social-psychological constitution of the American people. Thus, it is more difficult to conceive of effective suicide-prevention programs.

There are many other possible explanations for the failure to prevent suicide: The general determinants of suicide are not known; suicide is not solely the product of physiochemical forces; the taboo aura surrounding suicide (cf. Schneidman, 1966:33–43) has hindered basic research; official statistics (cf. Douglas, 1967) has often proved unreliable for hypothesis testing. The list could be extended. In this paper, it is hypothesized that suicide-prevention efforts have failed, in large part, because suicide prevention agencies, physicians, and public health workers in general do not contact highly suicidal persons and, thus, have formulated prevention policies based on experience with an essentially nonsuicidal or low-lethality population. As a case in point, . . . compare suicide-prevention-center patients with completed suicides in Cook County, Illinois. . . . There is a moderate negative association (–.30) between suicidal patients and completed suicides in Cook County; the two populations tend to be opposite types. Suicide rates are highest among old, white males; patient rates are highest for young black females. The Chicago area data are supported by similar research in suicide-prevention centers in St. Louis (Wetzel, 1968) and Los Angeles (Wold, 1968). For example, the St. Louis suicide-prevention center found that fewer than 2 per cent of the completed suicides in St. Louis had never contacted the center.

It follows that, if the suicide rate is to be lowered, more information is needed on the life-style of the completed suicide vis-à-vis the suicidal patient. Thus, the major objective of this paper is to describe and sketch plausible explanations of some statistically significant differences between patients at a suicide-prevention center and completed suicides to the end of suggesting policy changes that would enhance the control of completed suicides.

DATA, ASSUMPTIONS, AND METHODOLOGY

In an effort to test the major hypothesis that suicide-prevention-center patients and completed suicides are different populations, a 67-item schedule was constructed and administered to 150 subjects in New Hampshire.[2] Since the major suicide-prevention agency in New Hampshire is the state hospital, 75 consecutive admissions for suicide attempts, or problems, were interviewed. Each interview lasted about an hour. Note that those interviewed were patients in a state hospital. It follows that the subjects were probably more seriously suicidal than the average suicide-prevention-center client.[3] This has the effect of making it more difficult to reject the null hypothesis of no differences between suicidal patients and completed suicides. It should also be pointed out that the present comparison is not simply between attempted suicides and completed suicides but rather between subjects who came to the attention of a suicide-prevention agency and completed suicides.[4]

The same schedule was given to the coroner's informant on 75 suicides completed in New Hampshire in 1964 or 1965. Because many of the informants had moved out of the state or were widely scattered throughout the state, it was necessary to utilize a mailed questionnaire for the completed suicides. Of the 153 questionnaires mailed, 95 were returned–a response rate of 62 per cent. Of these 95, 20 were judged unusable, leaving 75 responses or a response rate of about 50 per cent. Given the difficulty of obtaining any data on such a taboo topic, especially after the lapse of three or four years, the response rate was considered adequate. When the informant requested it, a personal interview was conducted. Generally, the information from the mailed questionnaires was more complete than that obtained from the patients.

All data were dichotomized and analyzed in 2×2 tables in order to keep the marginal and cell frequencies at a statistically meaningful size. X^2 was used to test for significant differences and Q to indicate the strength of associations. The level of measurement was two nominal scales, and the two samples were assumed independent and random. As in most cases of

[2] As the reader will see, 18 of the 67 items differentiated suicide-prevention-center patients from completed suicides. Some of the items on which no significant differences were found include education, occupation, number of children, having a telephone, church attendance, order of birth, kind of discipline (family of orientation), alcohol intake, guilt feelings, and number of misfortunes.

[3] At present New Hampshire has a fledgling suicide-prevention center, not a mature center like the Los Angeles Center. The state hospital has had a two-year grant from the National Institute of Mental Health to prepare for a suicide-prevention center. Suicide problems are currently managed mainly through the community mental-health centers. The state hospital has a consultant in each of these centers who reports on completed suicides and refers clients to the state hospital. Thus, the state hospital is the major suicide-prevention agency in New Hampshire, although still in a relatively embryonic phase.

[4] Comparisons between attempted suicides and completed suicides have been made previously, but the implications of the differences for suicide prevention have not been seriously considered (cf. Stengel, 1964).

statistical testing, the assumptions were not strictly met. For example, over 10 per cent of the completed suicides had also been patients at the state hospital.

* * *

DIFFERENCES WITH CONTROLS

Before proceeding to the differences between suicidal patients and completed suicides, some mention should be made of differences between the total sample of suicidal actors and nonsuicidal controls. These differences should not be overlooked, for the difference between patients and suicides on an item may be less than the difference between suicidal actors as a whole and the nonsuicidal population. Or, while an item may not differentiate suicidal patients and completed suicides, it still might set the suicidal actors apart from the nonsuicidal population. For example, there were no significant differences between patients and suicides on population per household. Yet, the suicidal actors as a group have fewer people living with them. The average household size in the United States in 1960 was 3.38. Seventy-five per cent of the patients and suicides had households of less than 3.38. It would appear that suicidal acts of all types are encouraged by relative social isolation. Another item lends additional support to this finding. The lowest standard score of Chapin's Social Participation Scale for a nonsuicidal occupational category was four for unskilled workers. Yet, 83 per cent of the patients and suicides scored three or less; 71 per cent scored zero. While the evidence is far from conclusive, it is likely that this pattern of social isolation is coupled with a heavy use of alcohol by suicidal actors. Twenty-eight per cent of the total sample consumed on the average of three or more drinks each day.[5]

Data on social class and social mobility are more conclusive. Previous research (Maris, 1967:246–56) has documented the greater proportion of those in lower social classes among suicides. For example, Breed (1963: 179–88) found that 49 per cent of his New Orleans sample of suicides were either operatives, service workers, or laborers, compared with 24 per cent of the nonsuicidal controls. Fifty per cent of the suicidal actors in the present New Hampshire sample were in one of these three occupational categories. Not only were the suicidal actors disproportionately lower class, they were also more downwardly mobile. . . . As might be expected, since the New Hampshire sample includes suicidal patients as well as completed suicides, it stands between suicides and nonsuicides in income for the last two years before the suicidal event or interview. Generally, the more suicidal the group, the greater the loss of income in the preceding two years. When job mobility is compared, it is clear that the skidding pattern Breed found among New Orleans suicides also holds for the New Hampshire sample.

[5] Thirty-three per cent of the New Hampshire sample claimed not to consume alcohol at all. This is about the norm for the United States adult population as a whole (cf. Straus, 1966:250).

In some cases, items that differentiated suicidal patients and suicides do not differentiate suicidal actors as a whole from nonsuicidal controls. For example, when the physical health of the New Hampshire sample is compared with a nonsuicidal neuropsychiatric-patient group, no significant differences are found in physical health.

* * *

RESULTS

. . . Only 43 per cent of the patients were male, while 76 per cent of the suicides were male. This is an especially important finding, since sex and lethality of method of suicide attempt are related +.71. Eighty-one per cent of the serious suicide attempts were by males but only 42 per cent of the nonserious suicide attempts. As would be expected, the lethality of the method of attempting suicide is related +.81 with suicide; the more lethal the attempt, the greater the probability of accomplishing suicide. . . . These data suggest a possible causal sequence for future research; viz., that the method of attempting suicide contributes to the relationship between sex and suicide. The more males in a population, the more lethal the method of suicide attempt and the greater [the] probability of completing suicide. The partial Q between sex and suicide, controlling for method of attempt, is +.47. Since the zero-order association between sex and suicide is substantially reduced, it is reasonable to assume that method of attempt helps to interpret the correlation between sex and suicide.

Sex is also associated highly with the number of years on one's last job, mental health, and mental hospitalization. The job data are biased by the large number of females who never worked and the hospitalization data by the patients' confusion of their present institutionalization with hospitalization prior to the suicide event. This leaves only mental health, which is related +.51 with sex. Forty per cent of the males were classified as mentally healthy, contrasted with 18 per cent of the females who were judged mentally healthy. Mental health and suicide were related +.65 per cent. Paradoxically, the better one's mental health, the greater the chances of completing suicide; the poorer one's mental health, the greater one's chance of being a suicidal patient. Forty-eight per cent of the suicides were mentally healthy; 17 per cent of the patients were mentally healthy. Nevertheless, mental health in itself does not interpret the relationship between sex and suicide. The partial Q controlling for mental health only reduces the zero-order association from +.57 to +.53. But notice that the correlation between mental and suicide attempts is —.84; that between suicide attempts and suicide is —.51. Thus, in the New Hampshire data, the more females, the poorer the mental health; the poorer the mental health, the greater the number of suicide attempts; and, somewhat paradoxically, the more suicide attempts, the less suicide. This paradox is resolved, in part, by noting that a greater number of suicide attempts is associated with the use of less lethal methods (Q = —.22). One interpretation (Stengel, 1964:97–99, 108–10) is that frequent suicide attempters do not want to die as much as they want to "appeal" to significant others. Another interpretation (Menninger, 1938: 16–70) is that the wish to kill is greater than the wish to die. In any event, one plausible causal chain from sex to suicide would be:

The partial between sex and suicide attempts, controlling for mental health, is —.29, compared with an original zero-order correlation of —.39; and the partial between mental health and suicide, controlling for suicide attempts, is +.57, compared with +.65. While these differences are not large, they are in the direction predicted.

But what accounts for the patients' poorer mental health? It would appear that home life might be a factor; the association between home life and mental health is +.59. Fifty-seven per cent of the suicides came from normal homes; 33 per cent of the patients came from normal homes. It is hypothesized that the more broken homes, the greater dependency needs in later life; the greater the dependency needs, the poorer the mental health. The zero-order associations between home life, dependency, and mental health offer no evidence to doubt this suggested causal sequence. The partial between home life and mental health (+.54), controlling for dependency, is less than the zero-order association. It seems that home life and dependency make a slight contribution to the poorer mental health of the patients.

In passing, attention is called to the poorer communication of the suicides vis-à-vis the patients.[6] For example, 77 per cent of the suicides were visited by friends fewer than four times in a month immediately prior to the suicide; whereas 61 per cent of the patients had friends over fewer than four times. Seventy-five per cent of the suicides had read no books in the year before their suicide (this may be, in part, a function of age); 50 per cent of the patients had read no books in the year before their suicidal event. At this point, it is tempting to conclude that, since patients were more likely to have parents living, their relationship with their parents restrained them from suicide. While there is probably some truth in this speculation, the age of the suicidal actor is probably more crucial in determining suicide. Certainly, age explains a large part of the correlation between the variables "parents alive" and suicide. Furthermore, age is highly interrelated with several other variables associated with suicide.

One of the most striking associations with age is that of marital status (—1.0). All persons 45 or older were married; even though 64 per cent of the suicides and 24 per cent of the patients were 45 or older. Somewhat surprisingly, marital status is negatively related to suicide (—.69). The more married persons, the greater the number of suicides. Ninety-one per cent of the suicides were married, compared with 64 per cent of the patients. Given the previously documented prophylactic effect of marriage on suicide, it is likely that age explains the association between marital status and suicide (cf. Durkheim, 1951:171–216). That is, it is the age of those

[6] Remember that suicidal actors *as a whole* are more socially isolated than nonsuicidal controls.

not married that explains their suicidal behavior. The partial Q between marital status and suicide, controlling for age, is —.36, which supports the proposed causal model. Age is one of the variables contributing to the explanation of the relationship between marital status and suicide.[7]

Age, also, has a very strong negative association (—.71) with physical health. Seventy-six per cent of those less than 45 years old were in good to excellent physical health; whereas 35 per cent of those 45 or older were in good to excellent physical health. Physical health, on the other hand, has a substantial negative association with suicide (—.55). Sixty-two per cent of the suicides had fair to bad physical health. Only 32 per cent of the patients had fair to bad physical health. Thus, the older one is, the poorer one's physical health; and the poorer one's physical health, the greater the incidence of suicide.

It is hypothesized that age determines physical health, which in turn determines suicide. It follows that the partial Q for physical health and suicide, controlling for age, should be less than —.55. In fact, it is considerably less, —.34. Thus, the proposed causal model is supported.

Physical health and age are both related to the lethality of the method of suicide attempt (—.42 and +.54, respectively). Sixty per cent of those 45 or older used lethal methods, but only 31 per cent of those under age 45 used lethal methods. As one might expect, method of attempt and suicide are related +.81. Therefore, the older one is, the more lethal the method used; the more lethal the method used, the greater the incidence of suicide. . . . When the relationship between the method and suicide is controlled for age, the partial is +.76. Thus, while age does not explain the relationship between method of attempt and suicide, it does contribute to the explanation.

Finally, observe that the patients failed at their work more than the suicides. Sixty-eight per cent of the suicides had been on their last job one or more years; whereas only 27 per cent of the patients had been on their last job for one or more years. Seventy-six per cent of the suicides had not been fired from or quit their job two years before the suicide, compared with 41 per cent of the patients who had not been fired or quit two years before their suicide event. Seventy per cent of the suicides were considered successful by their friends; 41 per cent of the patients were considered successful. Forty per cent of the suicides had achieved their life goals, but only 14 per cent of the patients had achieved their life goals. These four variables indicate that work failure is associated primarily with being a suicidal patient and work success with completing suicide. In all four work-situation variables, age and marital status contribute to the explanation of the associations with suicide. That is, the zero-order associations are all reduced when marital status and age are controlled for. Sex is a contributing factor

[7] More of the patients had marital problems ($X^2 = 2.9$; $p = <.10$), which probably contributed to their not being married. Furthermore, home life was significantly associated with marital status ($Q = -.38$; $p = .05$). Thus, broken homes also seem to discourage marriage among patients.

only in the case of time spent on last job. Females were more likely to spend less time on their last job.

To recapitulate, clearly not all the differences between suicidal patients and completed suicides have been considered. Hopefully, the more salient ones have been. The major conclusion of this section is that the null hypothesis of no differences must be rejected. More specifically, patients tended to be young, female, and not married. Often, they were divorced or separated. They had problems with work–jobs were changed frequently; they were not very successful; they accomplished fewer life-goals than the suicides. It was hypothesized that broken homes in the patients' family of orientation were a factor in the etiology of their failure pattern. Broken homes were associated with increased dependency, which in turn was related to being not married, or unhappily married, and to poor mental health. Poor mental health, work, and marital failure all seemed to encourage many suicide attempts, which were relatively nonlethal. The social involvement, youth, and sex of the patients mitigated the lethality of their suicide attempts. The attempts appeared to constitute more of an appeal for help with a troubled life and introverted aggression intended primarily for the patients' spouses and parents rather than a genuine wish to die.

As contrasted with the patients, suicides tended to be male, old, and married. Their work history was comparatively positive. They had held jobs longer, accomplished more of their life-goals, and were regarded by others as more successful. Their childhood home life was relatively normal. Instead of becoming dependent, they became more independent than the patients. This independence, coupled with poor physical health, social isolation, and old age, proved to be fatal for them. A few, highly lethal attempts accomplished their suicides. Thus, the suicides were sick, old men who had been relatively happily married [and] fairly successful in accomplishing their life aspirations, and who were simply tired of living. Being independent, having little left to live for, actually wanting to die, they completed suicide more readily than the patients.[8]

CONCLUSIONS

What would a more effective suicide-prevention program based on the present research include? What modifications of prevention policy are called for? First and foremost, prevention programs must be reoriented to accommodate the life-style of the completed suicide. This necessitates putting more effort and money into basic research on a group that previously

[8] The author is aware that assessing the attitudes (e.g., feelings of success, weariness with life, etc.) in a retrospective study through second-party informants is problematic. Interpretations of these data are more impressionistic than those of behavioral data. However, there is some truth to the statement "My wife knows me better than I know myself." Furthermore, suicide notes were reviewed to assess attitudes, several informants' descriptions of the deceased were compared for consistency, therapy records were studied, and miraculous survivors making highly lethal attempts were interviewed. As a result, the attitude data are more reliable and valid than they might appear.

has been relatively inaccessible. Given that as many as 98 per cent of the completed suicides never set foot in a prevention agency, and that death-certificate data are skimpy and unreliable, the fact of the matter is that, at this moment, prevention agencies simply do not know much about the behavior and attitudes of the very group they are seeking to control.

But that knowledge of the dynamics of suicidal careers is slowly beginning to accumulate. Evidence has been presented that suicides are disproportionately recruited from lower social classes, and that they have suffered from occupational and financial "skidding." While these social characteristics may be more symptoms than causes of suicides, programs could at least help to eradicate these symptoms. Since the publication of Durkheim's (1951) classic work on suicide, prevention agencies have labored under the misconception that suicide [is] particularly a characteristic of the upper social classes, of the better educated, and that poverty acts as a restraint on suicide (cf. Henry and Short, 1954:27, 55, and 70). It is becoming increasingly difficult to accept Durkheim's argument. The time has come to think more seriously of action programs tailored to counteract the deprivations of belonging to a lower social class. More, and more equal, job opportunities; greater social-security benefits for the aged; better medical and psychiatric facilities for the poor; greater attention to the problem of developing a sense of pride in work among operatives, service workers, and laborers; coming to grips with retirement problems—all these would be a general step in the right direction.

Suicides were low in social participation; they had friends over fewer times than the patients; they read less; they were more self-sufficient. It follows that, if the suicide rate is to be lowered, older males must have more social involvement with significant others and more communication channels open for them. This raises the intriguing possibility of the decentralization and invasion of suicide-prevention services to predetermined ecological areas of cities (viz., those areas with the highest suicide rates) and hints that the very notion of a *center* for suicide prevention may be at cross-purposes with the stated goals of the institution. Having failed to establish social contacts, being generally uninformed, hopeless, and self-sufficient, the would-be suicide needs to be more aggressively sought out. Most emphatically, he must not be expected to know about, and come running to a highly formalized center for, suicide prevention and initiate a social relationship with an upper middle-class professional, who is a perfect stranger.

Surely, given the present data, it is naïve to think very many near-suicides will dial a telephone number and ask for help. If any communication medium were to be used, it should probably be television. Suicidal types watch television as much as, or more than, nonsuicidal types. Since most suicides are married (even though the rates are higher for the unmarried), a program could be developed to inform spouses of the presuicidal clues (even though not a single sufficient condition for suicide is known at this time). They, in turn, could make contact with prevention professionals; more indirection is required to reach potential suicides. Finally, someone could explore the suicide rates in communities solely for the elderly. A beginning could be made by investigating the suicide rates of retirement communities like Sun City, Arizona.[9]

Poor physical health was another salient attribute of suicides. Since three out of four suicides have been seen by a physician within four months of their death, it follows that M.D.'s have an opportunity to prevent as many as 75 per cent of all suicides (cf. Schneidman and Mandelkorn: 1967). The reasons for their failure [to do so] ought to be more thoroughly explored. At the very least, physicians should be informed of presuicidal syndromes. At the same time, physicians need to be given a more sophisticated instrument to sift out potential suicides. As a research task, someone could compare the characteristics of males with terminal illness who [commit] suicide with those who die a natural death. After all, most sick, old men do not [commit] suicide.

Finally, suicides make a small number of lethal attempts. Here is another instance where stricter control of firearms would be beneficial. It is well documented that most American male suicides shoot themselves. Females make more attempts than males, but their completion rate is one-third as high (cf. Dublin, 1963:22 ff.). This is largely the result of females using less lethal methods. Note, also, that four out of five completed suicides have made at least one prior nonfatal attempt.[10] Since many of these nonfatal attempts come to the attention of a professional, this is a unique opportunity to intervene. In other words, 80 per cent of completed suicides give concrete, highly visible statements of their intention to [commit] suicide.

These, then, are a few examples of the kinds of recommendations that can be made. More specific proposals must wait on future basic research. However, one fact is clear—success in suicide prevention is contingent upon reorienting current programs to accommodate the life-style of the completed suicide. Without such changes, there is little hope for lowering the suicide rate.

REFERENCES

BREED, WARREN. "Occupational Mobility and Suicide Among White Males," *American Sociological Review,* XXVIII (April, 1963), 179–88.

DOUGLAS, JACK D. "The Nature and Use of Official Statistics on Suicide," *The Social Meanings of Suicide* (Princeton, N.J.: Princeton University Press, 1967).

DUBLIN, LOUIS I. *Suicide* (New York: Ronald Press, 1963).

DURKHEIM, ÉMILE. *Suicide* (Glencoe, Ill.: The Free Press, 1951).

FARBEROW, NORMAN L., *et al.* "Case Histories and Hospitalization Factors in Suicides of Neuropsychiatric Hospital Patients," *Journal of Nervous and Mental Diseases* CXLII (January, 1966), 32–44.

[9] Of course, one must be careful to control for selection biases in recruiting for such communities.

[10] However, only about 10 per cent of attempters ever complete suicide. Still, this gives known attempters a suicide rate of 10,000 per 100,000 population—a high-risk group, to say the least.

HENRY, ANDREW F., AND SHORT, JAMES F., JR. *Suicide and Homicide* (New York: The Free Press, 1954).

KENDALL, PATRICIA L., AND LAZARSFELD, PAUL F. "Problems in Survey Analysis," Robert K. Merton and Paul F. Lazarsfeld (eds.), *Continuities in Social Research* (Glencoe, Ill.: The Free Press, 1950).

LABOVITZ, SANFORD. "Variation in Suicide Rates," in Jack P. Gibbs (ed.), *Suicide* (New York: Harper & Row, 1968), pp. 57–73).

MARIS, RONALD W. *Social Forces in Urban Suicide* (Homewood, Ill.: Dorsey Press, 1969).

———. "Suicide, Status, and Mobility in Chicago," *Social Forces,* XLVI (December, 1967), 246–56.

MENNINGER, KARL. *Man Against Himself* (New York: Harcourt, Brace & World, 1938).

PARKS, FRANCIS M., AND DARLENE WOLF. "A Suicide Prevention Center in Chicago." Unpublished manuscript.

SCHNEIDMAN, EDWIN S. "Suicide," in Norman L. Farberow (ed.), *Taboo Topics* (New York: Atherton Press, 1969), pp. 33–43.

——— AND PHILIP MANDELKORN. "How to Prevent Suicide," *Public Affairs Pamphlet No. 406* (1967).

STENGEL, ERWIN. *Suicide and Attempted Suicide* (Great Britain: C. Nicholls, 1964).

STRAUS, ROBERT. "Alcohol," in Robert K. Merton and Robert A. Nisbet (eds.), *Contemporary Social Problems* (New York: Harcourt, Brace & World, 1966), pp. 236–80.

WETZEL, RICHARD D. "Suicide Prevention, Inc. of St. Louis." Paper presented at the First Annual National Conference on Suicidology, March 20, 1968, Chicago.

WILKINS, JAMES. Unpublished manuscript (1969).

WOLD, CARL I. "Who Calls the Suicide Prevention Center in Los Angeles?" Paper presented at the First Annual National Conference on Suicidology, March 20, 1968, Chicago.

8. SUGGESTIONS FOR FURTHER READING

BECKER, HOWARD (ed.). *The Other Side* (New York: The Free Press, 1964).*

———. *Outsiders: Studies in the Sociology of Deviance* (New York: The Free Press, 1963).*

CLINARD, MARSHALL. *Sociology of Deviant Behavior,* 3rd ed. (New York: Holt, Rinehart & Winston, 1968).

COHEN, ALBERT. *Deviance and Control* (Englewood Cliffs, N.J.: Prentice-Hall, 1966).*

DOUGLAS, JACK (ed.). *Observations of Deviance* (New York: Random House, 1970).*

DURKHEIM, ÉMILE. *Suicide* (New York: The Free Press, 1951).*

ERIKSON, KAI. *Wayward Puritans* (New York: John Wiley & Sons, 1966).*

GOFFMAN, ERVING. *Stigma: Notes on the Management of Spoiled Identity* (Englewood Cliffs, N.J.: Prentice-Hall, 1963).*

HENRY, ANDREW, AND JAMES SHORT. *Suicide and Homicide* (New York: The Free Press, 1954).*

HUMPHREYS, LAUD. *Tearoom Trade: Impersonal Sex in Public Places* (Chicago: Aldine-Atherton, 1969).

JACKSON, GEORGE. *Soledad Brothers: The Prison Letters of George Jackson* (New York: Coward, McCann & Geoghegan, 1970).*

MATZA, DAVID. *Delinquency and Drift* (New York: John Wiley & Sons, 1964).*

MURTON, TOM, AND JOE HYAMS. *Accomplices to the Crime* (New York: Grove Press, 1969).*
SCHUR, EDWIN. *Crimes Without Victims* (Englewood Cliffs, N.J.: Prentice-Hall, 1965).*
———, *Our Criminal Society* (Englewood Cliffs, N.J.: Prentice-Hall, 1969).*
SKOLNICK, JEROME. *Justice Without Trial* (New York: John Wiley & Sons, 1966).*
STENGEL, ERWIN. *Suicide and Attempted Suicide* (Baltimore: Penguin, 1969).*
SUTHERLAND, EDWIN. *The Professional Thief* (Chicago: University of Chicago Press, 1937).*
———. *White Collar Crime* (New York: Holt, Rinehart & Winston, reissue 1960).*
SYKES, GRESHAM. *The Society of Captives* (Princeton, N.J.: Princeton University Press, 1958).*
THRASHER, FREDERIC. *The Gang* (Chicago: University of Chicago Press, 1927).*

* *Available in paperback.*

9. Political Sociology

INTRODUCTION

To understand the field of interest of the political sociologist, one must be familiar with several basic terms. *Power* refers to a relationship in which one person is able to exercise his will in determining the behavior of another. Power may be exerted by force, domination, manipulation, or any combination of these—for example, by the gunman who insists that the storekeeper open his cash drawer, the parent who demands that the child go to bed at a certain hour, the advertiser who convinces the public of the worth of his product.

Authority refers to legitimate power—that is, influence exercised by persons entitled to give commands to others obliged to obey them. When we say that power is legitimate, we mean that it is recognized as socially right and proper. For example, the policeman has the authority to stop traffic; the judge has the authority to order that a convicted offender pay a fine or spend a certain period of time in confinement.

We may define *government* as a social institution consisting of an enduring complex of norms and statuses through which the functions of maintaining order and enforcing norms are performed. Thus, the American Government includes the Constitution and the laws; the structure of the legislative, executive, and judiciary branches; the statuses of senator, congressman, President, Supreme Court justice, cabinet member, Federal Bureau of Investigation personnel, member of the U.S. Army, and the many other elected and appointed officials. The *state,* the agency that performs governmental functions, may be defined as having a "monopoly of the legitimate use of physical force within a given territory."[1] Thus, the state possesses the supreme power within a society.

The transition from one ruling group or system to another within a given society may take place over so extended a period of time and be so unceremonious that the members of the society find it difficult to discern when it has taken place. On the other hand, the transfer of power may be very abrupt and may involve considerable violence, in which case it is termed a revolution. In Chapter 10, "Social Change," James Davies examines a number of leading causal explanations of revolutionary political change, in addition to offering his own theory.

The political sociologist is especially interested in the underlying social conditions that affect government and power. According to Broom and Selznick,[2] three main areas within political sociology may be distinguished: (1) the social foundations of political institutions, especially the way in which political structures depend upon social organization and cultural values; (2) the social bases of political behavior—that is, why and how individuals vote, hold political opinions, support political associations and movements; and (3) the social aspect of political process, involving the identification of types of organized groups in politics and their patterns of association, in order to evaluate how interest groups, parties, and political movements affect political life.

In order for any society to remain in existence, there must be provisions for the accommodation of conflicts, the protection of the members, and the maintenance of order. Since every society must deal with these basic sociopolitical problems, political institutions, in some form, are universal phenomena. Differentiated political institutions are not often found in preindustrial societies, where political structures are likely to be inseparable from the system of kinship. In these simpler societies, social control is most often maintained informally, through the mores and the folkways, rather than regulated through judicial and police systems. The relative paucity of specialized political and legal institutions in simpler societies is examined more closely in Robert Redfield's discussion of "The Folk Society," presented in Chapter 3, "Social Organization." By contrast, in modern industrial societies one finds the nation-state, a formally organized, specialized, and highly differentiated political institution. In such complex and heterogeneous societies, social control is most often exercised by law.

Claude Lévi-Strauss asserts that, in studying simple societies, one can identify generic patterns of behavior that are invaluable for understanding more complex social worlds. Using this approach and the method he calls structuralism, he examines political institutions among the Nambikuara of Brazil in an effort to shed light on our own political arrangements. His research uncovers a basic feature of political rela-

[1] H. H. Gerth and C. Wright Mills, eds., *From Max Weber: Essays in Sociology* (New York: Oxford University Press, 1958), p. 78.

[2] L. Broom and P. Selznick, *Sociology* (New York: Harper & Row, 1963), p. 670.

tions everywhere: the reciprocity between the leaders of society and the led. The Nambikuara tribesmen receive numerous benefits from the chief in exchange for their deferential behavior. The chief, while receiving the benefits of polygyny and other rewards, is obliged to demonstrate unremitting generosity and especial hunting proficiency. These pressures have made this role a somewhat unattractive social position to the Nambikuara. Lévi-Strauss's findings appear to support the views of a number of political theorists of the Enlightenment, including Rousseau and Locke, who advanced the idea of a "social contract" between rulers and ruled as essential for stable political relations. No society, no matter how effective its coercive powers, can maintain its existence for very long without some modicum of consent on the part of those governed.

The stabilization of power relationships in society revolves around the nature of authority. The legitimation of power comes from many sources. The late German sociologist Max Weber classified authority into three main types, suggesting the most common and important sources of each:

Charismatic authority is based on the extraordinary personal characteristics of the leader. For example, the authority of Mao Tse-tung, Mahatma Gandhi, or the Nambikuara chief more or less typifies the charismatic type.

Traditional authority, by contrast, bases its legitimacy on custom and accepted practice. The ascribed power of the king in a monarchy or of the tribal chief who inherits his status are examples of legitimacy based on tradition.

In the third type, *rational-legal* authority, a body of generalized rules that apply impersonally to both the ruler and the ruled is the basis of legitimacy. Authority accompanies a particular office or status and is distinct from the person who occupies it at a given time. For instance, the Presidency of the United States or the executives of any corporation exemplify rational-legal authority.

In most societies, all three types of authority are represented, although one type usually is the most pervasive, as rational-legal authority is in the United States. But no recent American president has relied exclusively on rational-legal authority: Most have attempted to achieve some degree of charismatic authority by presenting themselves to the public in an attractive personal manner; most have followed their predecessors' policies, to varying degrees, in an effort to maintain a semblance of traditional continuity.

It was Weber's belief that the long-run trend will be marked by the increasing development of rational-legal authority. This form of authority corresponds most closely with bureaucratization. While there will be occasional eruptions of the charismatic, associated with revolutionary social movements, this basis of authority will eventually decline because of its inherent instability. Like charismatic authority, traditional authority, embodied as it is in the person of the monarch or the patriarch, presents problems of succession and expansion that will ultimately lead to its transformation into rational-legal authority.

Political sociologists have pursued other lines of inquiry, including, as we have noted, the social bases of individual political behavior. In this venture, probably the greatest effort has been expended in the area of voting behavior. The article by S. M. Lipset and Earl Raab on "Wallace Whitelash" is an excellent prototype of a sociological voting study, offering an exhaustive and penetrating examination of the social bases of support behind a Presidential campaign. This research suggests that the Wallace movement, though unlikely to pose a serious bid for leadership, is by no means doomed to extinction. Its many youthful supporters, unexpectedly revealed by the study, suggest that the movement will have adherents in the future. Lipset and Raab see the George Wallace phenomenon as a right-wing extremist political movement; in another research,[3] they have traced this trend back to America's early colonial days. That Wallace's following appears to have increased somewhat in the 1972 campaign may suggest that American political life is becoming increasingly polarized.

The extensive research on voting patterns in the United States has produced a great fund of knowledge on Americans' voting behavior.[4] In presidential elections, voter participation is approximately 60 per cent of the eligible electorate; in regional and local elections, participation is usually lower. The social factors associated with voting include high income, high educational attainment, white-collar occupation, government employment, long-term residence in the community, and membership in voluntary associations. Men vote more frequently than women; whites, more frequently than blacks; middle-aged citizens, more frequently than the young or old. Married people vote more regularly than nonmarried. Jews vote more often than Catholics, with Protestants occupying an intermediate position. Voting is more frequent among those whose personal interests are strongly affected by government policies. For example, during periods of national crisis, the electorate as a whole takes a greater interest in politics.

Political sociologists have noted a number of social correlates associated with political-party membership. In general, the higher one's occupational status, income, and educational attainment, the greater one's support for conservative political parties. Males somewhat more than females, blacks more than whites, Jews and Catholics, and labor-union members—all are more inclined to endorse the parties of the

[3] S. M. Lipset and Earl Raab, *The Politics of Unreason: Right-Wing Extremism in the United States, 1790–1970* (New York: Harper & Row, 1970).

[4] For excellent summaries of these findings, upon which the following discussion relies heavily, see Angus Campbell *et al., The American Voter* (New York: John Wiley & Sons, 1960); and S. M. Lipset, *Political Man* (Garden City, N.Y.: Doubleday, 1960).

left. While there are shifts from time to time, those whose views would be classified as "conservative" generally are more likely to support the Republican Party; those with more "liberal" views tend to be aligned with the Democratic Party.

As people move up the social ladder, they tend to adopt more conservative political positions. This tendency appears to be more pronounced in the United States than in many European countries. Lipset and Bendix suggest that European men who move up in the economic hierarchy find it difficult to adjust their life-style to a higher level, while American men do so more readily.[5] Perhaps European men identify more closely with the political ideology of their original class affiliation than is true of the less class-conscious American.

Those who are mobile in social status as well as those who are torn by conflicting sociopolitical memberships—e.g., being both a Catholic (Democratic influence) and a bank president (Republican influence)—are more likely to consider themselves political independents, to shift their vote from one election to the next, and to abstain from electoral participation.

Political life and political decision-making consist of more than the sum of individual political actions or electoral results. The activities of a vast array of groups, organized for the pursuit of political goals, have considerable importance in determining political affairs. The political sociologist has a deep interest in the variety of group life and how it affects political action.

In characterizing American political life, there appear to be two widely shared, competing views of the political process. Some students of American politics have advanced a "pluralist" theory of national power, in which political action is seen as a result of the diversified and balanced plurality of interest groups, each of which is chiefly concerned with protecting its own interests and blocking the threatening actions of others. On some issues, coalitions of various groups are formed to pursue specific aims or goals, which may be opposed by other coalitions. In this perspective, as the issues change, accompanying changes take place in the structure of coalition forces. There is no stable structure of power; power is ever shifting, changing with the issues involved and affected by the varying success of groups in mobilizing their resources against others.

In contrast to this view is the "power-elite" thesis advocated by the late C. Wright Mills and G. William Domhoff, among others. In this conception, political affairs are determined by a very small number of individuals and groups. Decisions are frequently made outside the formal structures of government. According to Mills, the real rulers of America come from among three groups: leading corporate executives, military leaders, and high-ranking politicians. These individuals have

[5] S. M. Lipset and R. Bendix, *Social Mobility in Industrial Society* (Berkeley: University of California Press, 1959), p. 68.

similar socialization experiences (they attend the same private schools, academies, and ivy-league colleges) and travel in the same social circles. They share similar outlooks and form an interlocking directorate of power. These individuals comprise a stable and enduring power base whose power is not diminished by electoral process; they are subject to little control by others, least of all by the average citizen.

There are still other views of the American political scene, such as the argument advanced by Theodore Roszak in his popular *The Making of a Counter-Culture* (Doubleday, 1969). Roszak argues that a new kind of political cleavage is beginning to appear in America and other advanced industrial societies—adult-youth conflict. Further technological development, he claims, has rendered some of the previous political cleavage points—conservative versus liberal, right-wing versus left-wing, capitalist versus socialist—less meaningful. The new conflict groups are beginning to consist of a "militant minority of dissenting youth" versus "the sluggish, consensus-and-coalition politics of their middle-aged elders."

In *The Making of a Counter-Culture,* Roszak asserts that the newly emerging conflict between youth and adults is not simply political but represents an almost total opposition, in which most of the components of culture—fundamental values, moral prescriptions, and institutional matrix—are matters of contention. The youthful counterculture includes opposition to rationality, bureaucracy, authority, and technology, combined with an emphasis on spontaneity, immediacy, self-expression, and self-actualization. The outlook highlights authenticity, commitment, and a quest for community. Whether these values will become more widely shared and will come to represent a major axis of political cleavage, only the future will reveal.

The Basis of Social Power

The Social and Psychological Aspects of Chieftainship in a Primitive Tribe*

Claude Lévi-Strauss

. . . **I do not** believe that the data I am going to present, if considered only as data on chieftainship among a hitherto little known group, would honestly deserve one hour of attention. Similar facts have been recorded many times,

* From *Transactions of the New York Academy of Sciences,* Section of Anthropology, vol. 7 (October 23, 1944), pp. 16–32. Reprinted by permission of the author and The New York Academy of Sciences.

either joined or separately. The particular interest offered by the Nambikuara is that they confront us with one of the simplest conceivable forms of social and political organization. Chiefs and chieftainship exist, among all human groups, under very different forms, but it would be vain to assign a special functional value to each of the modalities down to their smallest details. There is, undoubtedly, a function in chieftainship. This can, however, be reached only through analysis as the underlying principle of the institution. In other words, the differing structure of the digestive organs in man, ox, fish, and clam do not point toward different functions of the digestive system. The function is always and everywhere the same and can be better studied, and more fully understood, where it exists under a simple form–for instance, in a mollusc. Similarly, and as Professor Lowie once wrote, if anthropology is to be considered as a scientific study, its subject matter cannot be individual cultures but culture taken as a whole; the role of individual cultures being to offer, according to their own characteristics, special angles from which the basic functions of culture, although universal in application, can be more easily reached.

This will, perhaps, help us to eliminate preliminary questions that otherwise could have proved very difficult. Anthropologists in South America and elsewhere have been eagerly debating the question of whether these South American tribes–nomadic, relying mostly on collecting and gathering, with little or no agriculture, little or no pottery, and, in some cases, with no dwelling other than crude shelters–should be considered as truly primitive and as having preserved their exceptionally low cultural level through tarriance, or whether they did not previously possess a higher type of social and material organization and have regressed to a pseudoarchaism under unfavorable circumstances. The Nambikuara are one of those tribes that, together with the Siriono, on the other side of the Guaporé valley, the Cayapo, Bororo, Karaja of central Brazil, the so-called *Gé* of Central and Eastern Brazil, and some others, form a kernel of primitiveness surrounded, in the West, by the higher tribes of the upper Amazon, the Bolivian plain and the Chaco, and from the Orinoco's to the La Plata's estuaries, by a coastal strip inhabited mostly by the Arawak, Carib, and Tupi-Guarani linguistic families. An independent linguistic stock divided into several dialects, the Nambikuara seem to display one of the more backward cultures in South America. At least, some of their bands do not build huts and are wholly ignorant of pottery–and, even among the others, these two arts are exceedingly poor. There is no weaving, except for the narrow arm and leg bands that are made of cotton; no dress whatsoever, either for the men or for the women; no sleeping contrivances, such as hammocks or platforms, the natives being used to sleeping on the bare ground without the protection of blankets, mats, or hides. Gardening exists only during the rainy season and does not free the Nambikuara from wandering during the seven months of the dry season, looking for wild roots, fruits, and seeds, small animals such as lizards, snakes, bats, spiders, and grasshoppers, and, generally speaking, anything that may prevent them from starving. As a matter of fact, their geographical surroundings, which are located in the northwestern part of the state of Mato Grosso and include the headwaters of the Tapajoz, Rio Roosevelt, and Rio Gi-Parana, consist of a desolated savanna with few vegetal resources and still less game.

Had I approached my subject from a point of view other than the one outlined above, I could not have avoided a long discussion in South American cultural history, aimed at clearing up this apparent primitiveness, on the question as to whether the survival of early conditions of life in South America is genuine, or whether we should consider it as a more recent—though undoubtedly pre-Columbian—result of culture clashes and processes of acculturation. Whatever the answer may be, it cannot substantially change our problem: Whether tarriant or recessive, the Nambikuara society functions, in the present, as one of the simplest forms of human society to be conceived. We shall not seek information from the particular history that kept them in their exceptionally crude organization or brought them back to it. We shall only look at the experiment in social anthropology that they now enact under our very eyes.

This holds especially true in respect to their social and political life. For, if we do not know what was the material culture of the Nambikuara forty years ago (they were discovered only in 1907), we do know that their numbers became tremendously reduced after their contact with white civilization. General (then Colonel) Candido Mariano da Silva Rondon, who discovered and studied them, first stated that their number was about 20,000. This was around 1915. I take this figure as greatly exaggerated; but, even if reduced by one-half, it considerably exceeds the present number, which is hardly more than 2,000. Epidemics have taken care of difference. What does this mean, from the point of view of our study? During the dry season, the Nambikuara live in nomadic bands, each one under the leadership of a chief, who, during the sedentary life of the rainy months, may be either a village chief or a person of position. General Rondon wrote that, at the time he was exploring the country, it was not rare to see bands averaging two or three hundred individuals. Now, sixty or seventy people are seldom met together, the average size of the bands being twenty individuals, women and children included. This demographic collapse cannot possibly have taken place without affecting the structure of the band. But here, too, we do not need to concern ourselves with such questions as the type of political organization in earlier times. It is probably more difficult to understand Nambikuara sociology now than it was thirty years ago. Perhaps, on the contrary, the much reduced Nambikuara band offers, better than in the past, a privileged field for a study in social anthropology. My contention is that, precisely on account of its extreme impoverishment, Nambikuara political structure lays bare some basic functions that may remain hidden in more complex and elaborate systems of government.

Each year, at the end of the rainy season—that is, in April or in early May—the semipermanent dwellings laid in the vicinity of the gallery-forest where the gardens are cleared and tilled are abandoned, and the population splits into several bands formed on a free-choice basis. Each band includes from two to about ten families usually tied by kinship. This may be misleading when a band is met, for one easily gets the impression that it is formed as an extensive family. It does not take long to discover, however, that the kinship tie between two families belonging to separate bands may be as close [as], and eventually closer than, between two families inside the same band. The Nambikuara have a simple kinship system based on cross-cousin marriage and the subsequent dichotomy between "cross" and "parallel" in every generation. Therefore, all the men in one generation are either "brothers" or "brothers-in-law," and men and women are to one another either siblings (true or classificatory) or spouses (true or classificatory). Similarly, children are, in relation to the adults, either sons and daughters (true or classificatory) or nephews and nieces, which is the same as actual or potential children-in-law.[1] As a result, there is no great choice of terms to express kinship, and this explains why kinship inside the band may appear closer than it actually is, and kinship between people belonging to different bands more remote than shown by genealogies. Furthermore, a bilateral, cross-cousin marriage system functioning in a relatively small tribe must produce a progressive narrowing, and even a multiplication, of the kinship ties between any two individuals. This is a supplementary reason preventing family relationship from becoming really operative in the constitution of the band. It can be said that, inside the band as well as between the different bands that are the offspring of the same temporary village, everybody is everybody's kin, in pretty much the same fashion.

Why, then, the splitting-up process? Two different considerations must be brought forth to answer this question. From an economic point of view, the scarcity of wild-food resources and the subsequent high square-mileage needed to feed one individual during the nomadic period make the division into small bands almost compulsory. The real question is not why there is a division but, rather, on what basis it takes place. I have said that this is done by free choice, but this freedom is not arbitrary. There are, in the initial group, several men acknowledged as leaders (who likely acquired this reputation from their behavior during the nomadic life), and who make the relatively stable nuclei around which the different aggregates center. The importance, as well as the permanence of the aggregate through successive years, depends largely upon the ability of each of these leaders to keep his rank and eventually to improve it. Thus, it may be said that leadership does not exist as a result of the band's needs, but, instead, that the band receives its shape, its size, and even its origin from the potential leader who antedates it.

There is, however, a continuous function of leadership, although not permanently assumed by the same individual. Among the Nambikuara, chieftainship is not hereditary. When a chief grows old or is taken ill, and when he does not feel able to fulfill his heavy duty any more, he himself

[1] Claude Lévi-Strauss, "The Social Use of Kinship Terms Among Brazilian Indians." *American Anthropologist,* XLV, no. 3 (1943).

designates his successor. "This one–this one will be the chief . . ." he says. It seems likely that this autocratic power to insure one's own succession is more apparent than real. We shall emphasize later . . . the small amount of authority enjoyed by the chief; and, in this case as in many others, the final decision is probably preceded by a careful survey of public opinion, the designated heir being, at the same time, the one with the greate[st] support from the members of the band. The appointment of the new chief is not only limited by the wishes or disapproval of the band; it needs also to correspond to the plans of the individual to be chosen. Not seldom does the offer of leadership meet with a vehement refusal: "I don't want to be the chief." Then, a new choice must be made. As a matter of fact, chieftainship does not seem to be coveted by many people, and the general attitude of the different chiefs I happened to know was less to brag about their importance and authority than to complain of their many duties and heavy responsibilities. What, then, are the privileges of the chief, and what are his obligations?

When, about 1560, the great French moralist of the sixteenth century, Montaigne, met in Rouen with three Brazilian Indians brought there by some navigator, he asked one of them what were the privileges of the chief (Montaigne said the "King") in his country; and the native, himself a chief, answered: "To walk ahead on the warpath." Montaigne related this story in a famous chapter of the *Essays* where he wondered a great deal about this proud definition;[2] but it was a greater wonder to me when, almost four centuries later, putting the same question to my informants, I was given the same answer. Civilized countries are certainly not accustomed to such constancy in the field of political philosophy! Striking as it may be, this answer is less significant than the name by which the chief is designated in the Nambikuara language. *Uilikande,* the native word for chief, seems to mean "the one who unites" or "the one who joins together." This etymology suggests that the native mind is fully conscious of this extremely important phenomenon that I have pointed out from the beginning; namely, that the leader appears as the cause of the group's willingness to aggregate rather than as the result of the need for a central authority felt by a group already constituted.

Personal prestige and the ability to inspire confidence are thus the foundations of leadership in Nambikuara society. As a matter of fact, both are necessary in the man who will become the guide of this adventurous experiment–the nomadic life of the dry season. For six or seven months, the chief will be entirely responsible for the management of his band. It is he who orders the start of the wandering period, selects the routes, chooses the stopping points and the duration of the stay at each of them, whether a few days or several weeks. He also orders and organizes the hunting, fishing, collecting and gathering expeditions and determines the conduct of the band in relation to neighboring groups. When the band's chief is, at the same

[2] Michel de Montaigne. "Des Cannibales." *Essais,* Livre I, XXXI (end of the chapter).

time, a village chief (taking the word village with the restricted meaning of semipermanent dwelling for the rainy season), his duties do not stop there. He will determine the moment when, and the place where, the group will settle; he will also direct the gardening and decide what plants are to be cultivated; and, generally speaking, he will organize the occupations according to the season's needs and possibilities.

These rather versatile duties, it should be pointed out from the start, are not facilitated by any fixed power or recognized authority. Consent is at the origin of leadership, and consent, too, furnishes the only measure of its legitimacy. Disorderly conduct (according to the native standards) and unwillingness to work on the part of one or two discontented individuals may seriously jeopardize the chief's program and the welfare of his small group. In this eventuality, however, the chief has no coercive power at his disposal. The eviction of the bad people can take place only insofar as the chief is able to make public feeling coincide with his own opinion. Thus, he must continuously display a skill belonging more to the politician trying to keep hold of his fluctuating majority than to an overpowering ruler. Furthermore, he does not only need to keep his group together. Although the band lives practically alone and by itself during the nomadic period, the existence of the other bands is not forgotten. It is not enough to do well; the chief must try–and his people count on him for that–to do better than the others.

No social structure is weaker and more fragile than the Nambikuara band. If the chief's authority appears too exacting, if he keeps too many women for himself (I shall later analyze the special features of the chief's polygamy), or if he does not satisfactorily solve the food problem in times of scarcity, discontent will very likely appear. Then, individuals, or families, will separate from the group and join another band believed to be better managed. For instance, this band may get better fare from the discovery of new hunting or gathering emplacements; or it may have become richer in ornaments or implements, through trade with neighboring groups, or more powerful as a result of a successful war expedition. The day will come when the chief finds himself heading a group too small to face the problems of daily life and to protect his women from the covetousness of other bands. In such cases, he will have no alternative but to give up his command and to rally, together with his last followers, a happier faction. Therefore, Nambikuara social structure appears continuously on the move. The bands take shape, then disorganize; they increase, and they vanish. Within a few months, sometimes, their composition, number, and distribution cannot be recognized. Political intrigues within the same band and conflicts between bands impose their rhythm upon these fluctuations, and the ascent [and] decline of individuals and groups follow each other in a rather surprising manner.

How will the chief be able to overcome these difficulties? The first instrumental force of his power lies in his generosity. Generosity–an all-important feature of chieftainship among most primitive peoples, especially in America—plays an outstanding part even on those crude cultural levels where worldly goods are limited to the most primitive weapons and tools, coarse ornaments made of feathers, shells and bones, and raw materials, such as lumps of rosin and wax, hanks of fiber and splinters of bamboo for arrow-making. There cannot be great economic distinctions between families, each of which can pack all of its belongings in the baskets carried along by the women during the long travels of the dry season. But, although the chief does not seem to fare better, in this respect, than the others, he must always have at hand surpluses of food, tools, weapons, ornaments that, while being small indeed, acquire great value because of the scarcity that is the prevalent condition. When an individual, a family, or the band itself needs or covets something, the chief is called upon to secure the desired article. Generosity is the quality, much speculated on, that is expected of a new chief. Generosity is the string constantly struck that makes the general consent to one's leadership sound clear or out of tune. There is little doubt that, in this respect, the chief's ability to give is exploited to the utmost. Band chiefs used to be my best informants, and, well aware of their difficult position, I liked to reward them liberally; but I seldom saw one of my many gifts remain in their hands for more than a few days. Each time I took leave of a band, after a few weeks or a few months, its members had time to become the happy hoarders of axes, knives, beads, and so on. As a rule, however, the chief was exactly as poor as at my first arrival. Everything he had received from me (and this was considerably more than the average) had already been squeezed out of him. This collective greediness not seldom drives the chief to an almost desperate position; then the refusal to give plays about the same part, in this primitive democracy, as the threat to resign followed by a vote of confidence in a modern parliament. When a chief reaches the point where he must say, "To give away is over! To be generous is over! Let another be generous in my place!" he must, indeed, be sure of his power and prestige, for his rule is undergoing its severest crisis.

Ingenuity is but the intellectual form of generosity. A great deal of skill and initiative are the prerequisites of a good leader. It is he who makes the arrow-poison, although the preparation of *curare* among the Nambikuara is a purely profane activity surrounded by no ceremonial taboos or magic prescriptions. It is he, also, who makes the rubber ball used in the head-ball games that are played occasionally. The chief must be a good singer and dancer, a merrymaker always ready to cheer up the band and to brighten the dullness of daily life. This could easily lead to shamanism; and, in some cases, I have met with chiefs who were at the same time healers and trance addicts. Mystical life, however, is kept in the background among the Nambikuara, and, wherever they exist, magical functions are only secondary attributes of the leader. More often, chieftainship and sorcery are divided between two different individuals. In this respect, there is a strong difference between the Nambikuara and their northwestern neighbors, the Tupi-Kawahib, among whom the chief is, first of all, a shaman, usually a psychotic addicted to dreams, visions, trances, and impersonations.

But, although they are oriented in a more positive direction, the Nambikuara chief's skill and ingenuity are nonetheless amazing. He must have a perfect knowledge of the territories haunted by his and other groups; be familiar with the hunting grounds, the location of fruit-bearing trees, and the time of their ripening; have some idea of the itineraries followed by other bands, whether hostile or friendly. Therefore, he must travel more, and more quickly, than his people, have a good memory, and sometimes gamble his prestige on hazardous contacts with foreign and dangerous people. He is constantly engaged in some task of reconnoitering and exploring and seems to flutter around his band rather than lead it.

Except for one or two men without actual power, but eager to cooperate and to receive occasional rewards, the passivity of the band makes a strong contrast with its dynamic leader. It seems as if the band, having relinquished certain advantages to the chief, were in exchange relying entirely upon him for its interests and safety. I received a particularly striking demonstration of this under rather strange circumstances. After several weeks' discussion, I had obtained from a chief the favor of taking me, together with a few companions and some animals loaded with presents, to the semipermanent dwellings of his band, which were uninhabited at that time. This was a chance for me to penetrate more deeply into the unexplored Nambikuara territory and to meet groups too shy to venture forth on the outer fringe. The native band and my own group set out together on a journey supposed to be short; but, because of the animals I had taken, the chief had decided that the usual route through a dense forest could not be used. He led us through the open country, lost his way several times, and we did not reach our destination on the scheduled day. Supplies were exhausted and no game was in sight. The not unfamiliar prospect of a foodless day fell gloomily upon the natives. But, this time, it was the chief's responsibility. The whole project was his own, as well as the attempt to find an easier route. So, instead of trying to discover food, the hungry natives simply lay down in the shadow of the brush and waited for their leader to take them out of this most unpleasant situation. He did not wait or discuss; but, taking the incident as a matter of course, he simply left the camp accompanied by one of his wives. At the camp, the day was spent sleeping, gossiping, and complaining. There was no lunch or dinner. But, late at dusk, the chief and his wife reappeared, both heavily laden with baskets filled to the brim. They had hunted grasshoppers the entire day, and, although the expression "to eat grasshoppers" has approximately the same meaning in Nambikuara as the French *manger de la vache enragée,*[3] this food was enthusiastically received, shared, and consumed amidst restored good humor. The following morning, everybody armed himself or herself with a leafless twig and went grasshopper-hunting.

I have several times referred to the chief's wives. Polygamy, which is practically the chief's privilege, brings him a moral and sentimental reward

[3] Closest English equivalent: "to have a rough time of it," "to go through the mill."

for his heavy duties, together with the practical means of fulfilling them. In the Nambikuara band, apart from rare exceptions, only the chief and the sorcerer (when these functions are divided between two individuals) may have several wives. The chief's polygamy, however, presents special features. It does not constitute a plural marriage but rather a monogamous marriage to which relations of a different nature are added. I have already mentioned the fact that cross-cousin marriage is the usual pattern among the Nambikuara. Another type of marriage also exists, between a man and a woman belonging to the generation following his own, either a wife's "daughter" (true or classificatory) or a sister's niece. Both forms are not uncommon in South America, and, together or separately, they have been recorded among many tribes. Now, what do we find in the chief's case? There is first a monogamous marriage of the cross-cousin type, that is, where the wife belongs to the same generation as her husband. This first wife plays the same part as the monogamous wife in ordinary marriages. She follows the sexual pattern of the division of labor, taking care of the children, doing the cooking, and collecting and gathering wild food. To this marriage are added one or several unions, which, technically, are true marriages but of a different type. Usually, the secondary wives belong to a younger generation. The first wife calls them daughters or nieces. Besides, they do not follow the sexual pattern of the division of labor but share indifferently in men's or women's activities. At the camp, they disdain domestic tasks and remain idle, either playing with the children to whose generation they belong or flirting with their husband, while the first wife keeps busy with the food and the fire. On the contrary, when the chief leaves on an exploration, a hunt, or some other manly task, they will accompany him and bring him their moral and physical help. These somewhat "tomboy" girls, elected by the chief from among the prettiest and healthiest of the group, are to him rather "girl-friends" than spouses. They live on the basis of an amorous friendship that contrasts strongly with the more conjugal atmosphere of the first marriage.

This system exerts a tremendous influence upon the whole life of the group. The periodical withdrawal by the chief of young women from the regular cycle of marriages creates a permanent unbalance within the group, between the number of boys and girls of marriageable age. Young men are the chief victims of that situation and must either remain bachelors for several years or marry widows or old women discarded by their husbands. Thus, the right to plural marriages represents a concession of considerable importance made by the group to its leader. What does it mean from the latter's point of view? There is little doubt that access to young and pretty girls brings him a much appreciated gratification, not so much from the physical side (as the Nambikuara share in the quiet dispositions of most South American tribes) as from the psychological and sentimental one. But, above all, plural marriage, together with its distinctive features, constitutes the technical means and the functional device placed at the chief's disposal by the group to enable him to carry out his exacting duties. Left by himself, he could hardly do more than the others. His secondary wives, freed by their special status from the customary liabilities of their sex, are his helpers, comforters and assistants. They are, at the same time, leadership's prize and instrument. Can it be said, from the native point of view, that the prize is worth the trouble? To answer that question, I shall now have to consider the problem from a broader angle—namely, what does this elementary social structure, the Nambikuara band, teach us about leadership, its basis and its function?

There is a first point that does not require great elaboration. Nambikuara data contribute, with many others, to destroy the belief originated by early anthropologists, and temporarily revived by psychoanalysis, that the primitive chief could find his prototype in a symbolical father, and that the simpler forms of the state could progressively have grown out of the family. We have found at the root of the crudest forms of chieftainship a decisive step, which introduced something entirely new in respect to biological relations—and this step consists of *consent*. Consent, we have seen, is at the same time the origin and the limit of leadership. Unilateral relations, such as right of age, autocratic power, or others, may appear in groups having an already complex structure. In simple forms of social organization, such as the one I have tried to describe, they are inconceivable. Here, on the contrary, the relationship between the chief and the group can be seen as a perpetual process of arbitration, where the chief's talents and authority, on the one hand, and the group's size, cohesion, and willingness, on the other, constantly react on, and influence, each other. If I had the time, and if it were not so far removed from my topic, I would have liked to show what considerable support modern anthropological observations bring, in this respect, to the analysis of the eighteenth-century social philosophers. I am well aware of the fact that Rousseau's "social contract," which is the step by which individuals resign their autonomy in favor of the General Will, is entirely different from the nearly contractual relations existing between the chief and his followers. It remains true, however, that Rousseau and his contemporaries displayed a keen sociological feeling when they understood that cultural attitudes and elements such as "contract" and "consent" are not the result of secondary processes, as claimed by their opponents; they are culture's raw materials, and it is impossible to conceive a political or social organization in which they would not already be present. If I understand correctly, the recent analysis, by modern American anthropologists, of the state-growth significance of military societies among the Plains Indians leads to exactly the same conclusion.[4]

My second point is but an exemplification of the first: Consent is the psychological basis of leadership; but, in daily life, it expresses itself in, and is measured by, a game of give-and-take played by the chief and his followers, . . . which brings forth, as a basic attribute of leadership, the no-

[4] R. H. Lowie, *The Origin of the State* (reprint of 1927 edition; New York: Russell & Russell, 1962), pp. 76–107, and K. N. Llewellyn and E. A. Hoebbel, *The Cheyenne* pt. 2 (Norman: University of Oklahoma Press, 1941), chap. 5.

tion of reciprocity. The chief has power, but he must be generous. He has duties, but he is entitled to several wives. Between him and the group, there is a perpetual balance of prestations, privileges, services, and obligations. The notion of reciprocity, originated by Marcel Mauss, was brillantly analyzed by Malinowski in his "Crime and Custom in Savage Society." In respect to leadership, he says: "The claims of chief over commoners, husband over wife, parent over child and vice versa are not exercised arbitrarily and onesidedly, but according to definite rules, and arranged into well-balanced chains of reciprocal services."[5] This statement needs somewhat to be completed. Malinowski is right when he points out that the chief-commoner's relationship, as every relationship in primitive society, is based on reciprocity. In the first case, however, the reciprocity is not of the same type as in the others. In any human society, whether primitive or civilized, two different cycles of reciprocity are constantly at work: first, the chain of individual prestations linking the isolated members of the group; and, next, a relation of reciprocity binding the group considered as group (not as a collection of individuals) and its ruler. In the case we have studied, this is well illustrated by the rules of marriage. Taken in its broadest sense, the incest prohibition means that everybody in the group is obliged to deliver his sister or daughter to an individual; and, conversely, is entitled to receive his wife from the latter (whether from the same man, as in exchange-marriage, or from a different one). Thus, a continuous chain of reciprocal prestations is directly or indirectly set up between all the collective or individual members of the group.[6] This may be called qualitative reciprocity; but incest prohibition also provides the basis for a quantitative reciprocity. We may consider it as a "freezing" measure, which, while it forbids the appropriation of women who are at one's natural disposal, prepares the formulation of marriage rules allowing every man to get a wife. Therefore, a close relationship exists in a given society between the forbidden degrees and the extent to which polygamy is allowed. How does the preceding apply to the Nambikuara? If they had cross-cousin marriage associated exclusively with monogamy, there would be a perfectly simple system of reciprocity (from the individual's point of view), both qualitative and quantitative. This theoretical formula is, however, upset by the chief's privilege to polygamy. The withholding of the simpler rule, in a favor of the chief, creates for each individual an element of insecurity that would otherwise not exist. Let us state this in other terms: The granting of polygamous privilege to the chief means that the group has exchanged *individual elements of security* resulting from monogamous rule for *collective security* provided by leadership. Each man receives a wife from another man, but the chief receives several wives from the group. In exchange, he offers to guarantee against need and danger, not to the individuals whose sisters or daughters he marries; not to

[5] B. Malinowski, *Crime and Custom in Savage Society*: 46. New York, 1940. (Third Printing.)

[6] See the late F. E. Williams' remarkable analysis in *Papuans of the Trans-Fly* (Oxford: Clarendon Press, 1936), pp. 167–69.

those who will be deprived of a spouse by his polygamous right; but to the group, taken as a whole. For it is the group, taken as a whole, that has withheld the common law in his favor. The preceding considerations may have some bearing upon the theory of plural marriage; but, most of all, they remind us that the interpretation of the state, conceived as a security system, recently revived by discussions about a national insurance policy (such as the Beveridge plan and others), is not a modern development. It is a return to the basic nature of social and political organization.

So much for the group's point of view on leadership. What about the chief's own attitude in relation to his function? What is his incentive in assuming duties of which I have given a not too favorable account? We saw that the Nambikuara band leader has a tiresome and exacting role; that he must exert himself without pause to maintain his position. What is more, if he does not constantly improve it, he runs the risk of losing what he has taken months or years to achieve. This explains why many men, as I have already said, shun leadership. But why do others accept and even seek it? It is always difficult to appraise psychological motives; and the task is almost impossible when a culture totally alien to our own is considered. I venture to say, however, that the polygamous privilege, highly valued as it may be from the point of view of sexual gratification, sentimental appeal, and social prestige, would not suffice to determine a leader's vocation. Plural marriage is but a technical prerequisite of chieftainship; its individual value can only be residual. There must be something more; and, going over the moral and psychological features of the Nambikuara chiefs I knew, and trying to hold on to those fugitive and irreplaceable glimpses at their intimate selves (of which no scientific approach may certify the accuracy, but which gain, from a deep feeling of friendship and human communication, some sort of intuitive value), I feel imperiously led to this answer: There are chiefs because there are, in any human group, men who, unlike most of their companions, enjoy prestige for its own sake, feel a strong appeal to responsibility, and to whom the burden of public affairs brings its own reward. These individual differences are certainly emphasized and "played up" by the different cultures, and to unequal degrees. But their clear-cut existence in a society as little competitive as the Nambikuara strongly suggests to my mind that their origin itself is not cultural. They are rather part of those psychological raw materials out of which any given culture is made. Men are not all alike; and, in primitive societies, believed by early anthropologists to be overwhelmed by the crushing power of custom, these individual differences are as keenly perceived and worked out as in our so-called individualistic civilization.

It is remarkable how far the practical experience of colonial administrators has outgrown, in relation to the previous considerations, anthropologists' theoretical studies. During the past twenty years, Lowie's pessimistic appraisal of anthropological work in the field of political institutions[7] has certainly not lost its value. We have much to learn from the scientifically un-

[7] At the beginning of chapter 13 of *Primitive Society*.

trained who deal with native institutions. I shall not here record Lyautey's testimony without reservation: "In every society, there is a leading class born for leadership and without which nothing can be accomplished."[8] What may be true for the simpler structures cannot be considered equally valid when considering the complex ones, where the function of leadership does not manifest itself any more in a "pure" state. But let us listen to Eboué, who passed away a few months ago. Himself a full-blooded Negro, he wrote the following when he was Governor-General of French Equatorial Africa in special relation to those nomadic tribes that, as he put it, "live under a regime of organized anarchy." I quote: "Who is to be chief? I shall not answer, as was the custom in Athens, 'the best.' There is no best chief, there is just a chief"; and further, "the chief is not interchangeable . . . the chief pre-exists."[9] This is precisely what was suggested to us from the start of our analysis of Nambikuara society.

In conclusion, I submit that, when developing the study of political institutions, anthropologists will have to pay more and more attention to the idea of "natural leadership." I am well aware that this expression is almost contradictory. There is no possible form of leadership that does not receive its shape and specification inside of a given cultural context. But this expression can be taken as a borderline case, or as a limit—as say the mathematicians. While the limit can never be reached, simple social structures give us, in the order of their simplicity, an even closer approximation of it. In such studies, we may accordingly foresee a privileged field for close, cooperative work between anthropology and individual psychology.

The Supporters of Right-Wing Extremist Political Movements

The Wallace Whitelash*

Seymour Martin Lipset and Earl Raab

The American Independent Party of George C. Wallace brought together in 1968 almost every right-wing extremist group in the country and undoubtedly recruited many new activists for the rightist cause. Today, many of the state parties organized under his aegis have formal legal status and have announced that they intend to nominate candidates for state and local office

[8] Quoted in Governor-General Felix Eboué's memorandum on "Native Policy," issued on November 8, 1942.

[9] *Ibid.*

during the next few years in an effort to build the party. George Wallace himself has sent out a clear signal that he has plans for the future. He has begun to mail the *George Wallace Newsletter* monthly to a mailing list of over one million names that had been assembled during the election. The old address for Wallace activities was Box 1968, Montgomery, Alabama. It is now Box 1972.

The effort to maintain and build the party, however, faces the perennial problem of ideological extremist movements–splits among its supporters. Even during the 1968 campaign, sharp public divisions over local versus national control occurred in a number of states, usually because complete control over the finances and conduct of the party's work was kept in the hands of coordinators directly appointed by Wallace and responsible to the national headquarters in Montgomery. In some states, two separate organizations existed, both of which endorsed the Wallace candidacy but attacked each other as too radical. Since the 1968 election, two competing national organizations have been created, and again each is attacking the other as extremist.

The group directly linked to Wallace has had two national conventions. The first, held in Dallas in early February, attracted 250 delegates from 44 states and set up a group known as the Association of George C. Wallace Voters. The Dallas meeting was attended by a number of top Wallace aides, including Robert Walter, who represents Wallace in California; Tom Turnipseed, a major figure in the Wallace Presidential effort since it started; Dan Smoot, the right-wing radio commentator; and Kent Courtney, the editor of the *Conservative Journal*. The same group met again on May 3 and 4 in Cincinnati and formally established a new national party to be called the American Party. A Virginian, T. Coleman Andrews, long active on the ultraconservative front, was chosen as chairman. Wallace gave his personal blessing to the new party and its officers. One of his Montgomery aides, Taylor Hardin, who maintains a national office with twenty employees in Montgomery, indicated that the party would have a considerable degree of "central control."

The competing national group met in Louisville on February 22, 1969, and established a new national conservative party to be composed largely of autonomous state parties. As if to emphasize the extent to which it fostered local control, this organization called itself the "National Committee of the Autonomous State Parties, known as the American Independent Party, American Party, Independent Party, Conservative Party, Constitutional Party." This group, or constellation of groups, was united in its opposition to domination by Wallace and his Montgomery aides. Although the former candidate received compliments at the convention, the delegates were much more concerned with building a movement that was not limited to his supporters in 1968. The national chairman of the new group, William K. Shearer of California, editor of the *California Statesman,* had already broken with Wallace during the campaign on the issue of local autonomy. At the Louisville convention, Shearer said,

Governor Wallace has not shown any interest in a national party apart from a personal party. A candidate properly springs from the party and not the party from the candidate. The party should not be candidate-directed. While we have great respect for Mr. Wallace, we do not think there should be a candidate-directed situation. We want our party to survive regardless of what Mr. Wallace does.

The Shearer group also appears to be more conservative on economic issues than the Wallace-dominated one. During the convention, Wallace was criticized for being "too liberal" for his advocacy during the campaign of extended social security and farm parity prices.

The leaders of each faction claim that the other includes extremists. Robert Walters attacked Shearer's group as composed of "radicals and opportunists" and as having "a pretty high nut content." Shearer, on the other hand, has said that he finds many in the Wallace-dominated party "not too savory."

The publications of the competing groups indicate that each is supported by viable segments of the 1968 party. The Shearer National Committee, however, is clearly much weaker financially, since the Wallace national group retained a considerable sum from the 1968 campaign for future activities. It is also unlikely that they can attract many Wallace voters against the opposition of the candidate. The competition for support, however, does give each group an immediate function; and both national organizations appear to be busy holding state and local conventions designed to win over those who were involved in the Presidential campaign.

It is difficult to tell how much support the American Party retains. Early in 1969, the party ran a candidate in a special election for Congress in Tennessee's Eighth District. Wallace ran first in this district in the Presidential race, but the AIP congressional candidate, William Davis, ran a bad second to the Democrat. The AIP secured 16,319 votes (25 per cent) in the congressional race, compared to 32,666 for the Democrat and 15,604 for the Republican. Wallace himself took an active part in the campaign, making speeches for Davis, but he was clearly unable to transfer his Presidential support to his follower.

While Davis's showing in Tennessee was fairly respectable, another AIP by-election candidate, Victor Cherven, who ran for the state senate in Contra Costa County in California in late March, secured only 329 out of the 146,409 votes cast. Cherven even ran behind two other minor-party nominees. In mid-June, in a by-election for a seat in the California Assembly from Monterey, an AIP candidate, Alton F. Osborn, also secured an insignificant vote, 188 out of 46,602. The first effort to contest a congressional seat outside the South failed abysmally, when an American Party candidate in a Montana by-election received half of 1 per cent of the vote —509 out of 88,867 ballots on June 25. Election Day, November 4, 1969, produced the best evidence of the inability of the Wallace followers to develop viable local parties. In Virginia, a state in which Wallace had secured 322,203 votes, or 23.6 per cent, in 1968, both rightist parties ran candidates for governor. Dr. William Pennington, the gubernatorial nominee of the Andrews-Wallace American Independent Party, obtained 7,059 votes, or .8 per cent of the total; and Beverly McDowell, who ran on the Conservative Party ticket of the Shearer segment of the movement, did slightly better, with 9,821 votes, or 1.1 per cent of the electorate. Pennington's and McDowell's combined total in 1969 only equaled 5 per cent of Wallace's vote in Virginia.

But, if Wallace's strength cannot be transferred to local and state candidates, most of it still remains with him on the level of national politics. The Gallup Poll, which chronicled George Wallace's rise in popularity through 1967 and 1968, has continued to examine his possible strength in a future Presidential contest. In three national surveys in April, July, and September, samples of the electorate were asked how they would now vote in a contest between Nixon, Edward Kennedy, and Wallace. Nixon appeared to have gained from both parties, as compared with the 43 per cent he received in the 1968 election. His support remained consistently high–52 per cent in April, 52 in July, and 53 in September. Kennedy's backing fluctuated more–33, 36, 31–as contrasted with the 43 per cent that Humphrey had secured. Wallace also dropped, securing 10, 9, and 10 per cent in the same three polls. Thus, he lost about a quarter of his support during 1969, but still retains a respectable following for a new campaign. Wallace's social base remains comparable to that which backed him in the election, and he remains a major force in the South, where he pulls 25 per cent of the choices as compared with 5 per cent in the rest of the country.

Who *did* support George Wallace in 1968? A detailed answer to that question will perhaps tell us more than anything else about his chances for the future, as well as about the potentiality of right-wing extremism in America.

ELECTION RESULTS

Election Day results confirmed the basic predictions of the pre-election opinion polls. George Wallace secured almost 10 million votes, or about 13.5 per cent of the total voting electorate. He captured five states with 45 electoral votes, all of them in the Deep South–Mississippi, Georgia, Alabama, Louisiana, and Arkansas. With the exception of Arkansas, which had gone to Johnson in 1964, these were the same states Barry Goldwater won in that year. But Wallace lost two states carried by Goldwater–South Carolina, the home state of Nixon's Southern leader, the 1948 Dixiecrat candidate Strom Thurmond; and Arizona, Goldwater's home state.

Since the support for Wallace seemingly declined considerably between early October and Election Day, falling from about 21 per cent to 13 per cent, an analysis of his actual polling strength is obviously important. Fortunately, the Gallup Poll conducted a national survey immediately after the election, in which it inquired both how respondents voted and whether they had supported another candidate earlier in the campaign. The data of this survey were made available by the Gallup Poll for our analysis. They are particularly useful, since it would appear that most voters who had supported Wallace, but shifted to another candidate, did report this fact to Gallup interviewers. Thirteen per cent indicated they had voted for Wallace, while another 9 per cent stated that they had been for him at an earlier stage in the campaign.

From the national results among whites, it is clear that the data are heavily influenced by the pattern of support in the South. Wallace's voters were most likely to be persons who did not vote in 1964, or who backed Goldwater rather than Johnson. The pattern of an extremist party recruiting heavily from the ranks of nonvoters coincides with the evidence from previous extremist movements both in this country and abroad. Wallace also clearly appealed to those in smaller communities, and his strength was greatest among those with the least education. With respect to income, his backers were more likely to come from the poorer strata than from the more well-to-do, although he was slightly weaker among the lowest income class—under $3,000—than among the next highest. He was strongest among those in "service" jobs, a conglomerate that includes police, domestic servants, and the military. Of the regular urban occupational classes, his support was highest among the unskilled, followed by the skilled, white-collar workers, those in business and managerial pursuits, and professionals, in that order. The number of farmers voting for Wallace was relatively low, a phenomenon stemming from differences between farmers in the South and in the rest of the country. Among manual workers, Wallace was much weaker with union members than nonunionists.

VOTING PATTERNS

The vote behavior with respect to other factors also corresponds in general to pre-election predictions. Wallace was backed more heavily by men than by women, a pattern characteristically associated with radical movements, whether of the left or right. Surprisingly, young voters were more likely to prefer him than middle-aged and older ones, with the partial exception that voters in the twenty-five- to twenty-nine-year-old category were a bit more likely to prefer Wallace than the twenty-one- to twenty-four-year-old age group. Religion also served to differentiate: Wallace received a higher proportion of the votes of Protestants than Catholics, a product of his strength in the predominantly Protestant South.

Viewed nationally, however, the pattern of support for Wallace is a bit deceiving, since so much of his support was in the South. He carried five Southern states and received a substantial vote in all the others, plus the border states. To a considerable extent, his movement in the South took on the character of a "preservatist" defense of Southern institutions against the threat from the federal government. In most Southern states, it was a major-party candidacy. In the rest of the country, however, the Wallace movement was a small, radical third party, organized around various extreme right-wing groups. While it obviously gave expression to racial concerns, it also included a number of other varieties of the disaffected. One would expect, therefore, differences in the types of voters to whom he appealed in the different sections. . . .

The variations between the sections are apparent along a number of dimensions. Northern Wallace voters were more likely to come from the ranks of identified and committed Republicans than were those from the South. Thus, in the South, a much larger proportion of people who were identified as Democrats (37 per cent) than as Republicans (10 per cent) voted for him. Conversely, in the North, a slightly larger segment of the Republicans voted for him than did Democrats. This emphasis is reversed, however, with respect to the 1964 vote. In both sections, larger proportions of Goldwater voters opted for Wallace than did Johnson supporters. Relatively, however, he did better among the Southern Goldwater voters. The seeming contradiction may be explained by the fact that Wallace did best among "independents," and that there were proportionately many more independents in the South than in the North. Southern independents presumably are people who have opted out of the Democratic Party toward the right, many of whom voted for Goldwater in 1964 and Wallace in 1968. His greatest support, both North and South, of course, came from the ranks of those who did not vote in 1964. Almost half of the Southern nonvoters in the 1964 election who voted in 1968 chose Wallace.

The effect of the social stratification variables were relatively similar in both parts of the country. In general, the better educated, the more well-to-do, and those in middle-class occupations were less likely to vote for Wallace than [were] voters in the lower echelons.

As far as religion is concerned, nationally Wallace appeared to secure more support among Protestants than Catholics, but a sectional breakdown points up the fact that this was an artifact of the relatively small Catholic population in the South. Outside of the South, Wallace secured more support from Catholics than from Protestants. The pattern appears to be reversed in the South, but the number of Catholics in the sample is too small to sustain a reliable estimate. What is perhaps more significant than the Catholic-Protestant variation is the difference among the Protestant denominations. Wallace's greatest backing, North and South, came from Baptists, followed by "other," presumably mainly fundamentalist sects that have a history of disproportionately backing right-wing groups. Wallace, after all, became the protector of the "Southern way of life" and the status of those who bear it, not only for Southerners, but for Southern migrants to the North. This, apart from education, is one significance of the disproportionate support of Wallace by Northern Baptists.

As noted earlier, perhaps the most surprising finding of the polls was the consistent report by Gallup, Harris, and the Michigan Survey Research Center that youth, whether defined as twenty-one to twenty-four or twenty-one to twenty-nine years old, were more favorable to the third-party candidate than those in older age groups. Two special surveys of youth opinion also pointed in this direction. One was commissioned by *Fortune* and carried out by the Daniel Yankelovich organization among 718 young people aged eighteen to twenty-four in October, 1968. It revealed that, among employed youth, 25 per cent were for Wallace, as compared to 23 for Humphrey, 31 for Nixon, and 15 without a choice. Among college students, Wallace received 7 per cent of the vote. A secondary analysis of this survey indicated that class and educational level differentiated this youth group as well. Thus 31 per cent of young manual workers who were the sons of manual workers were for Wallace, as contrasted with but 6 per cent among nonmanuals whose fathers were on the same side of the dividing line. A pre-election survey by the Purdue Opinion Poll among a national sample of high school students reported that Wallace had considerable strength among them as well–22 per cent backing, which came heavily from members of Southern, and economically less affluent, families.

This "shift to the right" among youth had first been detected among young Southerners. Although various surveys had found a pattern of greater youth support for integration in the South during the 1940's and 1950's, by the 1960's this finding had been inverted, according to two NORC polls reported by Paul Sheatsley and Herbert Hyman. They suggested that Southern youth who grew up amid the tensions produced by the school integration battles reacted more negatively than the preceding generations who had not been exposed to such conflicts during their formative political years. And, as the issue of government-enforced integration in the schools and neighborhoods spread to the North, white opinion in central city areas, which are usually inhabited by workers, also took on an increased racist character.

What has happened is that increasing numbers of white young people in the South and in many working-class districts of the North have been exposed in recent years to repeated discussions of the supposed threats to their schools and communities posed by integration. They have been reared in homes and neighborhoods where anti-Negro sentiments became increasingly common. Hence, while the upper-middle-class scions of liberal parents were being radicalized to the left by civil-rights and Vietnam-war issues, a sizable segment of Southern and Northern working-class youth were being radicalized to the right. The consequence of such polarization can be seen in the very different behavior of the two groups in the 1968 election campaign.

The indications that the Wallace movement drew heavily among youth are congruent with the evidence from various studies of youth and student politics that suggests young people are disposed to support the more extreme or idealistic version of the politics dominant within their social strata. In Europe, extremist movements both of the right and left have been more likely to secure the support of the young than the democratic parties of the center. Being less committed to existing institutions and parties than older people, and being less inured to the need to compromise in order to attain political objectives, youth are disproportionately attracted to leaders and movements that promise to resolve basic problems quickly and in an absolute fashion.

So much for those who actually voted for Wallace. Equally significant are those who supported Wallace in the campaign but didn't vote for him. Presumably, many who shifted from Wallace did so because they thought he could not win, not because they would not have liked to see him as President. This is the uneasiness of the "lost vote." There is also the "expressive" factor—the votes in polls that do not count. Casting a straw vote for Wallace was clearly one method of striking a generalized note of dissatisfaction in certain directions. But, since total considerations take over in the voting booth, the nature of the defections becomes one way to measure these dissatisfactions in various quarters. On another level, there is the factor of the social reinforcements that may or may not exist in the voter's milieu and are important for the ability of a third-party candidate to hold his base of support under attack.

THE DEFECTORS

In general, Wallace lost most heavily among groups and in areas where he was weak to begin with. Individuals in these groups would find less support for their opinions among their acquaintances and also would be more likely to feel that a Wallace vote was wasted. In the South, however, almost four-fifths of all those who ever considered voting for Wallace did, in fact, vote for him. In the North, he lost over half of his initial support: only 43 per cent of his original supporters cast a ballot for him. Similarly, Baptists and the small "other" Protestant sects were more likely to remain in the Wallace camp than less pro-Wallace religious groups.

There were certain significant differences in the pattern of defections with respect to social stratification. In the South, middle-class supporters of Wallace were much more likely to move away from him as the campaign progressed. He wound up with 90 per cent of his pre-election support among Southern manual workers, and 61 per cent among those in nonmanual occupations. In the North, however, Wallace retained a larger proportion of his middle-class backers (52 per cent) than of his working-class followers (42 per cent).

The data from the Gallup survey suggest, then, that the very extensive campaign of trade-union leaders to reduce Wallace support among their membership actually had an effect in the North. Almost two-thirds (64 per cent) of Northern trade-union members who had backed Wallace initially *did not* vote for him, while over half of those Southern unionist workers (52 per cent) who had been for him earlier voted for him on Election Day. A similar pattern occurred with respect to the two other measures of stratification—education and income. Wallace retained more backing among the better educated and more affluent of his Northern supporters, while in the South these groups were much more likely to have defected by Election Day than the less educated and less privileged.

The variations in the class background of the defectors in the different sections of the country may be a function of varying exposures to reinforcing and cross-pressure stimuli in their respective environments. On the whole, we would guess that middle-class Wallace supporters in the North came disproportionately from persons previously committed to extreme rightist ideology and affiliations. Wallace's support among the Northern middle-class corresponds in size to that given to the John Birch Society in opinion polls. If we assume that most people who were pro-Birch were pro-Wallace, then presumably Wallace did not break out of this relatively small group. And this group, which was heavily involved in a reinforcing environment, could have been expected to stick with him. In the South, on the other hand, he began with considerable middle-class support gained from people who had been behind the effort to create a conservative Republican Party in that section. The majority of them had backed Barry Goldwater in 1964. This large group of affluent Southern Wallacites encompassed many who had not been involved in extremist activities. And it would seem that the efforts of the Southern conservative Republicans (headed by Strom Thurmond) to convince them that a vote for Wallace would help Humphrey were effective. Conversely, among Northern manual workers, an inclination to vote for Wallace placed men outside the dominant pattern within their class.

BACK TO THE HOME PARTY

Which of the other two candidates the Wallace defectors voted for clearly depended on background. Three-fifths of those who shifted away from Wallace during the campaign ended up voting for Nixon. But those Wallace backers who decided to vote for one of the major-party candidates almost invariably reverted to their traditional party affiliation. The pattern is even clearer when Southern Democrats are eliminated. Among the 29 Northern Democrats in our sample who defected from Wallace, 90 per cent voted for Hubert Humphrey. Humphrey recruited from among the less educated and poorer Wallace voters; Nixon, from the more affluent and better educated.

The pattern of shifting among the Wallace voters points up our assumption that Wallace appealed to two very different groups: economic conservatives concerned with repudiating the welfare state, and less affluent supporters of the welfare state who were affected by issues of racial integration and "law and order." As some individuals in each of these groups felt motivated to change their vote, they opted for the candidate who presumably stood closer to their basic economic concerns. The data also point up the difficulty of building a new movement encompassing people with highly disparate sentiments and interests.

After specifying what kinds of groups voted for whom, the most interesting question still remains, especially with respect to deviant and extremist political movements such as Wallace's: What creates the differentials within each of these groups? Why, in other words, do some members of a group vote for a particular candidate, but not others? Quite clearly, members of the same heuristic group or class may vary greatly in their perception of the world, and will therefore differ as to political choice. Since candidates do differ in their ideology and position on particular issues, we should expect that the values of the electorate should help determine which segments of a particular strata end up voting one way or another.

Data collected by the Louis Harris Poll permit us to analyze the connection between political attitudes and voter choice in 1968. The Harris data are derived from a special reanalysis of the results of a number of surveys conducted during the campaign that were prepared by the Harris organization for the American Jewish Committee. Based on 16,915 interviews, it points up consistent variations. The question that best indicated differing political attitudes among those voting for a given candidate was one in the Harris survey that asked, "Which groups are responsible for trouble in the country?" Choices ranged from the federal government to Communists, students, professors, Jews, and others.

The findings of the Harris organization clearly differentiate the supporters of the different candidates in 1968 and 1964: On most items, the rank order of opinions goes consistently from right to left, from Wallace to Goldwater to Nixon to Johnson to Humphrey. That is, the Wallace supporters show the most right-wing opinions, while the Humphrey ones are most left. As a group, those who voted for Goldwater in 1964 are somewhat more "perservatist" than the Nixon supporters in 1968. There is, of course, a considerable overlap. Since none of these items bear on attitudes toward the welfare state, what they attest to is the disdain that rightists feel toward groups identified with social changes they dislike.

The Wallace supporters differ most from the population as a whole with respect to their feelings toward the federal government, Negroes, the Ku Klux Klan, and, most surprisingly, "ministers and priests." Although Wallace himself did not devote much attention to attacking the liberal clergy, his followers were seemingly more bothered by their activities than by those of professors. Although the electorate as a whole was inclined to see "students" as a major source of trouble, Wallace backers hardly differed from the supporters of the two other candidates in their feelings. As far as we can judge from these results, they confirm the impression that Wallace appealed strongly to people who identified their distress with changes in race relations, with federal interference, and with changes in religious morality. It is of interest that the Wallace supporters in the South and those in the non-South project essentially the same pattern. The Southern differential is very slight with respect to blaming Negroes, still slight but higher in blaming clergymen, and higher yet in blaming the federal government.

Fears that Wallace would convert his following into an extraparliamentary influence on the government and terrorize opponents by taking to the streets—fears based on statements that Wallace himself made during the campaign—have thus far proved unwarranted. Wallace seems largely concerned with maintaining his electoral base for a possible Presidential campaign in 1972. The effort to continue control of the party from Montgomery seems to be dedicated to this end.

THE MOVEMENT IN '72

The existence of local electoral parties, even those willing to follow Wallace's lead completely, clearly poses a great problem for him. Wallace's electoral following is evidently much greater than can be mobilized behind the local unknown candidates of the American Party. To maintain the party organizations, they must nominate men for various offices. Yet, should such people continue to secure tiny votes, as is likely in most parts of the country, Wallace may find his image as a mass leader severely injured. He seems to recognize this, and, though concerned with keeping control over the party organization, he has also stressed the difference between the "movement" and the "party," describing the two as "separate entities" that agree on "purposes and aims." Wallace is emphatic about this: "The *movement* will be here in 1972. The *movement* is solvent and it will be active." Speaking at the Virginia convention of the American Party in mid-July of 1969, he said, "A new party ought to go very slow. It ought to crawl before it walks. It ought to nominate a candidate only if he has a chance to be elected." In Tulsa, he again warned his followers to move slowly, if at all, in nominating congressional and local candidates. He argued that, if he were elected President in the future, he "wouldn't have any trouble getting support from Congress, because most of its [major-party] members were for the things he's for."

One aspect of the nonparty "movement" may be the reported expansion of the Citizens Councils of America, whose national headquarters is in Jackson, Mississippi. Its administrator, William J. Simmons, helped direct Wallace's Presidential campaign in Mississippi, where he received 65 per cent of the vote. In June, 1969, Simmons said:

> There has been no erosion in Wallace strength. Wallace articulates the hopes and views of over 99 per cent of our members. This state is not enchanted with Nixon, and Wallace sentiment is very strong indeed.

He also reported that the Council, mainly concerned with the maintenance of segregation in the schools, had expanded "as a result of backlash generated by campus riots and better grassroots organizational work." The impetus of the Wallace campaign also had obviously helped. The Citizens Councils remain one reservoir of future organizational strength for Wallace.

Moreover, Wallace has attempted to maintain his ties to other groups whose members had backed him in 1968. The Birch Society's principal campaign during 1969 has been against sex education and pornography; Wallace has devoted a considerable part of his talks during the year to the subject. In addition, he publicly embraced for the first time the ultraconservative "Christian Crusade" of Billy James Hargis by attending its annual convention.

In his speeches and *Newsletter,* Wallace has retained the same combination of "preservatist" moralism and populist economic issues that characterized his Presidential campaign. On the one hand, he continues to emphasize the issues of "law and order," "campus radicalism," "military failures in Vietnam," and "the need for local control of schools." On the other hand, speaking in Tulsa, one of the principal centers of the oil industry, he called for tax reform that would benefit the little man, adding that "the 27½ per cent oil depletion allowance ought to be looked into." He argued that we must "shift the [tax] burden to the upper-class millionaires, billionaires, and tax-exempt foundations." Since this kind of rhetoric flies in the face of the deep-dyed economic conservatives among his supporters, such as the Birchers, it is clear that Wallace's cafeteria of appeals still suffers from the same sorts of contradictions that characterized it in 1968–contradictions, it might be added, that have characterized most other right-wing extremist movements in American history.

RIGHTEOUS RIGHTISTS

Another problem that Wallace faces comes from supporters who want to build an extremist movement, rather than an electoral organization for one man's candidacy. This can be seen in the activities of an autonomous youth organization, the National Youth Alliance, formed by those active in Youth for Wallace. As of September, 1969, the NYA claimed 3,000 dues-paying members recruited from the 15,000-person mailing list of the Youth for Wallace student organizations. The group has a more absolutist and militant character than either adult party, and it is much more unashamedly racist. Members wear an "inequality button" emblazoned with the mathematical symbol of inequality. Among other things, the Alliance advocates "white studies" curricula in colleges and universities. According to its national organizer, Louis T. Byers, "The purpose of these will be to demonstrate the nature of mankind. The equality myth will be exploded forever." In an article describing its objectives, the then national vice-president, Dennis C. McMahon, stated that NYA "is an organization with the determination to liquidate the enemies of the American people on the campus and in the community." The tone of this pro-Wallace youth group sounds closer to that of classic fascism than any statements previously made by Wallace's associates. As McMahon wrote:

> The National Youth Alliance is an organization that intends to bury the red front once and for all. . . . The NYA is made up of dedicated, self-sacrificing young people who are ready to fight, and die if necessary, for the sacred cause.
>
> . . . Now is the time for the Right Front terror to descend on the wretched liberals. In short, the terror of the Left will be met with the greater terror of the Right. . . .
>
> Tar and feathers will be our answer to the pot pusher and these animals will no longer be allowed to prowl and hunt for the minds of American students.

. . . A bright future full of conquest lies ahead of us . . . Soon the NYA will become a household word and the Left will be forced to cower in the sewers underground as they hear the marching steps of the NYA above them.

The racism of NYA leaders includes approval, if not advocacy, of virulent anti-Semitism. Its national headquarters in Washington distributes literature by Francis Parker Yockey, including his book *Imperium,* which defines Jews, Negroes, Indians, and other minorities as "parasites" on the Western world. The five members of its adult advisory board have all been involved in anti-Semitic activities. Two of them, Revilo P. Oliver and Richard B. Cotten, were forced out of the Birch Society because of their overt racist and anti-Semitic views. A third, retired Rear Admiral John Crommelein, ran for President on the anti-Semitic National States' Rights Party ticket in 1960; while a fourth, retired Marine Lieutenant General Pedro A. Del Valle, is an officer of the Christian Educational Association, which publishes the overtly anti-Semitic paper *Common Sense*. The fifth member of the board, Austin J. App, former English professor at LaSalle College, is a contributing editor to the anti-Semitic magazine *American Mercury*.

Perhaps most interesting of all the problems that Wallace will have to deal with is the fact that the national chairman of his American Party, T. Coleman Andrews, has publicly advocated the Birch Society's version of that hoary international conspiracy, the historic plot of the Illuminati. The Illuminati, which was an organization of Enlightenment intellectuals formed in Bavaria in 1776 and dissolved according to historical record in 1785, has figured in the conspiratorial theories of assorted American right-wing movements as the insiders behind every effort for religious liberalism [and] economic and social reform since the 1790's. In recent times, both Father Coughlin, the foremost right-wing extremist of the 1930's, and Robert Welch, the head of the Birch Society, have explained various threats to "the American way" from the French Revolution to the Communist movement, as well as the behavior of most key officials of the government, as reflecting the power of this secret cabal of satanically clever plotters. In a newspaper interview following the establishment of the American Party in May, Andrews bluntly announced:

I believe in the conspiratorial theory of History. . . . [The Birch Society has been] responsible, respectable. . . . [R]ecently, the Birch Society has begun to prosper. People are beginning to see that its original theories were right. . . . There is an international conspiracy.

Although George Wallace himself has never publicly stated a belief in the conspiracy of the Illuminati (he prefers to talk about the role of Communists, pseudo-intellectuals, and the Council on Foreign Relations), the formal organization of his personally controlled national party is headed by a man who has no such hesitation. On May 26, 1969, Wallace formally sanctioned the American Party as the political arm of the movement and said that, if he ran for President again, it would be under the American Party's banners.

However, while the pulls toward conspiracy theory and toward ideological racism are evident in the background, the logic of the Wallacite movement and its future as a mass movement obviously rest on other foundations. S. M. Miller points out that many had been shocked by the "attraction of George Wallace as a Presidential candidate to a large number of union members . . . racism appeared to be rampant in the working class." When the vote came, however, racism seemed to have receded before economic concerns. Their disaffection remains, nevertheless. As Miller writes, "About half of American families are above the poverty line but below the adequacy level. This group, neither poor nor affluent, composed not only of blue-collar workers but also of many white-collar workers, is hurting and neglected." It is the members of this group that the Wallacite movement must grow on if it is to grow, not out of their ideological racism as much as out of their general sense of neglected decline.

TEMPERED EXTREMISM

Whether the Wallace movement itself will have returned to full or fuller electoral vigor by 1972 depends on a number of factors that emerge from an examination of America's right-wing extremist past. Determinative–not just for the Wallace movement but for any extremist movement–will be the larger historical circumstances. The disaffection of the white working-class and lower middle-class has been noted; if that disaffection grows, and *at the same time* the pressures of an increasingly disaffected black population increase, the soil will, of course, be fertile for a George Wallace kind of movement. It is the pressure of the emergent black population that provides an essentially preservatist thrust to the social and economic strains of the vulnerable whites. Whether the major political parties can absorb these concomitant pressures in some pragmatic fashion, as they have in the past, is another conditional factor, which is also partly dependent on historical development.

Wallace, however, is clearly preparing to use another issue in 1972–the responsibility for American defeat in Vietnam. Like others on the right, he has repeatedly argued that if the U.S. Government really wanted to win the war, it could do so easily, given America's enormous superiority in resources and weapons technology. Consequently, the only reason we have not won is political: Those who have controlled our strategy consciously do not want to win. But, he argued recently, if it "should be that Washington has committed itself to a policy of American withdrawal, irrespective of reciprocal action on the part of the enemy, in effect acknowledging defeat for our forces, which is inconceivable, we feel that such withdrawal should be swiftly accomplished so that casualty losses may be held to a minimum." And he left on October 30 for a three-week tour of Vietnam and Southeast Asia, announcing that he would run in 1972 if Vietnam were turned over to the Communists "in effect or in substance." Clearly, Wallace hopes to run in 1972 on the issue that American boys have died needlessly, that they were stabbed in the back by Lyndon Johnson and Richard Nixon.

In order to do so, however, Wallace must keep his movement alive. As he well recognizes, it is subject to the traditional organizational hazards of such a movement, notably fragmentation, and the ascendancy of overt extremist tendencies that will alienate the more respectable leadership and support. During the year following the election, Wallace has performed as though he understood these hazards well. He has avoided expressions of overt extremism. He has attempted to keep his organization formally separated from the fringe groups and more rabid extremists, even those who were in open support of him. In a letter sent to key Wallace lieutenants around the country, asking about the local leadership that might be involved in the next Wallace campaign, James T. Hardin, administrative assistant to Wallace, carefully emphasized that "perhaps of greatest importance, we would like your opinion as to those who demonstrated neither ability nor capability to work with others and who were, in fact, a detriment to the campaign. . . ."

Whether Wallace can succeed in avoiding the organizational hazards of which he seems aware, and whether historical circumstances will be favorable, is, of course, problematical. But, whether his particular movement survives or not, George Wallace has put together and further revealed the nature of those basic elements that must comprise an effective right-wing extremist movement in America.

9. SUGGESTIONS FOR FURTHER READING

ALMOND, G., AND J. COLEMAN. *The Politics of Developing Areas* (Princeton, N.J.: Princeton University Press, 1960).*

BOTTOMORE, TOM. *Elites and Society* (New York: Basic Books, 1964).*

BRINTON, CRANE. *The Anatomy of Revolution* (New York: Vintage, 1960).*

CAMPBELL, ANGUS, *et al. The American Voter* (New York: John Wiley & Sons, 1960).*

DAHL, ROBERT. *Who Governs?* (New Haven, Conn.: Yale University Press, 1961).*

FROMM, ERICH. *Escape From Freedom* (New York: Holt, Rinehart & Winston, 1941).*

HOFFER, ERIC. *The True Believer* (New York: Harper & Row, 1951).*

HUNTER, FLOYD. *Community Power Structure* (Chapel Hill: University of North Carolina Press, 1953).*

KEY, V. O., JR. *Southern Politics* (New York: Vintage, 1949).*

KORNHAUSER, WILLIAM. *The Politics of Mass Society* (New York: The Free Press, 1959).

LIPSET, S. M. *Political Man: The Social Bases of Politics* (Garden City, N.Y.: Doubleday, 1960).*

MARCUSE, HERBERT. *One Dimensional Man: Studies in the Ideology of Advanced Industrial Society* (Boston: Beacon Press, 1964).*

MICHELS, ROBERT. *Political Parties* (New York: Collier Books, 1962).*

MILLS, C. WRIGHT. *Power, Politics, and People* (New York: Ballantine Books, 1963).*

MOORE, BARRINGTON, JR. *Social Origins of Dictatorship and Democracy* (Boston: Beacon Press, 1966).*

OPPENHEIMER, MARTIN. *The Urban Guerilla* (Chicago: Quadrangle Books, 1969).*

ROSE, ARNOLD. *The Power Structure: Political Process in American Society* (New York: Oxford University Press, 1967).*
ROSZAK, THEODORE. *The Making of a Counter Culture* (Garden City, N.Y.: Doubleday, 1969).*
SWARTZ, MARC, *et al. Political Anthropology* (Chicago: Aldine-Atherton, 1966).
TOCQUEVILLE, ALEXIS DE. *Democracy in America* (New York: Alfred A. Knopf, 1945).*
VIDICH, A., AND J. BENSMAN. *Small Town in Mass Society* (Garden City, N.Y.: Doubleday, 1960).*

* *Available in paperback.*

10. Social Change

INTRODUCTION

Social change may be defined as any transformation in the social structure, normative order, or behavior patterns typical of a given society. This definition embraces change in knowledge, beliefs, and values; in technology and material culture; in the various social institutions—e.g., the economy, government, the family, education, and religion; in the system of stratification and the patterns of intergroup relations; and in the conceptions members of society have of themselves.

Although the rate of change may vary considerably from one society to another, or from one time period to another within a given society, social change is inevitable and universal. Wilbert Moore has identified a number of the factors that account for this: movement through the life cycle, differing physiological potentialities and socialization experiences, variations in fertility and mortality rates, the changing physical and social environment, the ubiquity of nonconformity, and the failure to achieve ideal values.[1]

There has been a phenomenal acceleration of social change during the past several hundred years. Nowadays, novelty and upheaval characterize our everyday reality. Alvin Toffler articulately discusses the unparalleled rate of contemporary change:

> It has been observed, for example, that, if the last 50,000 years of man's existence were divided into lifetimes of approximately sixty-two years each, there have been about 800 such lifetimes. Of these 800, fully 650 were spent in caves.
>
> Only during the last seventy lifetimes has it been possible to

[1] Wilbert Moore, *Social Change* (Englewood Cliffs, N.J.: Prentice-Hall, 1963), pp. 11–21.

communicate effectively from one lifetime to another—as writing has made it possible to do. Only during the last six lifetimes did masses of men ever see a printed word. Only during the last four has it been possible to measure time with any precision. Only in the last two has anyone anywhere used an electric motor. And the overwhelming majority of all the material goods we use in daily life today have been developed within the present, the 800th, lifetime.

This 800th lifetime marks a sharp break with all past human experience, because during this lifetime man's relationship to resources has reversed itself. This is most evident in the field of economic development. Within a single lifetime, agriculture, the original basis of civilization, has lost its dominance in nation after nation. Today in a dozen major countries agriculture employs fewer than 15 per cent of the economically active population.[2]

This avalanche of social change is being experienced everywhere—in the peasant societies of the world that are becoming urbanized as well as in the modern industrial world that is being transformed into the little-understood postindustrial societies of the future.

Social change makes man uneasy; it uproots him from familiar surroundings, meanings, habits, and relationships, creating fear and anxiety. Toffler calls man's response to social change "future shock," akin to the phenomenon of culture shock—the sense of bewilderment, frustration, and disorientation that people experience when they confront an unfamiliar culture.

The ambiguity and psychologically threatening potential of change may spur many to resist innovation. Sometimes, resistance to change is based on the protection of vested interests. For example, the owners of barge canals and stagecoach lines were among the most active opponents of railroads. A century later, the shift from coal-burning engines to diesels was opposed by coal miners, who were threatened with reduction of work, and by railroad firemen, whose occupations were menaced with complete extinction.

Sociologists have observed that social change does not occur in a coordinated way. Frequently, changes take place at uneven rates throughout the different parts of the culture and social structure. About fifty years ago, W. F. Ogburn posited the theory of "cultural lag," which argues that material culture (technology and its artifacts) changes more readily than adaptive culture (customs, values, beliefs, and laws). He cited as an example the development of conservation laws in the United States, which has lagged behind the development of the technology that threatens to destroy most forest lands. We might also consider the development of nuclear weapons and the many other technical improvements in weaponry and warfare that appear to have far surpassed techniques of diplomacy and statesmanship.

[2] Alvin Toffler, *Future Shock* (New York: Random House, 1970), pp. 15–16.

Another element that determines whether change is opposed or welcomed within a society are the values shared by the social membership. In folk societies, where one usually finds greater endorsement of traditional authority, there tends to be a general resistance to social change. The time-honored way is considered to be the best way. By contrast, in urban-industrial societies, change is regarded as an everyday fact of life, socially desirable for its own sake, as well as an indication of progress. Perhaps this difference in resistance to change may reflect the fact that the peoples of folk societies are being exposed to substantially greater change than the peoples of the urban-industrial world. Those living in the folk societies of the world are facing the prospect of being catapulted from the Middle Ages to modernity in less than a generation —a change of the most colossal and staggering dimensions.

Space limitations require that we focus our examination on a selected few areas of social change. The demographic dimension—population—represents a most significant source of social change. The importance of the "population explosion" cannot be overemphasized.[3]

The total human population at the birth of Christ was approximately 250 million; it increased to 500 million by 1650, doubled to about 1 billion by 1850, and doubled again 80 years later, reaching two billion by 1930. At present, the world population is approximately 3.6 billion. If it continues to increase at the present rate, by 1975 it will have doubled again from 1930, reaching four billion. This represents an overwhelming rate of increase in population. It now takes approximately 45 years to double the world's population, compared to over 1,600 years at the dawn of the Christian era!

This growth has not occurred uniformly throughout the world. It has been most accelerated in the so-called underdeveloped societies. In the industrialized countries, the doubling time falls within the 50- to 200-year range; among underdeveloped nations, it falls between 20 and 35 years. For example, as of 1968, the population of Brazil was doubling every 22 years.

Rapid population growth is attributable not to any significant rise in the birth rate but to a dramatic drop in the number of early deaths. For example, in Ceylon the introduction of DDT, which controlled the malaria-carrying mosquito, resulted in a 34-per-cent drop in the death rate in the year following its wide-scale application.

Although estimates vary, many experts judge that at least half of the world's population today is improperly nourished. Even the most accelerated economic development imaginable for the next two generations probably would not result in a sufficient supply of food for our present population; and, by that time, the population will have more than doubled and perhaps even quadrupled.

[3] Perhaps the most authoritative and up-to-date assessment of the population problem can be found in Paul Ehrlich and Anne Ehrlich, *Population, Resources, Environment* (San Francisco: W. H. Freeman, 1970).

Calculations show that Asia, merely to maintain her present low level of living standards, must increase her aggregate product by 60 per cent between now and 1975, and by an additional 75 per cent between 1975 and 2000.[4]

If nothing is done to control the population explosion, alarming increases in the death rate appear to be inevitable. In "The Population Explosion: Facts and Fiction," Paul Ehrlich summarizes the most important aspects of the problem and demonstrates the fallacy of believing that population problems will not affect the peoples of the developed world. He examines several of the remedies proposed to rectify the population–food imbalance—e.g., the use of resources from the sea, outer space, and synthetic food—to underscore the staggering dimensions of the problem, as well as the need for immediate action.

Next to the threat posed by thermonuclear war, the problem of worldwide hunger represents today's most dramatic challenge. With half of the world population underfed, the need to increase mankind's productive capacity has great urgency. In the underdeveloped world, the revolution in transportation and communications has brought greater familiarity with the ways of urban-industrial society, awakening new desires for economic improvement and well-being. A revolution of rising expectations is beginning to eclipse the fatalistic resignation and traditionalism of folk-peasant societies. The question facing the student of social change, then, is how this tremendous economic transformation can be brought about most speedily and with the least disruption.

Robert Heilbroner has identified a number of factors that are necessary for economic development.[5] A nation must possess a sufficient number of natural resources. These assets are vital for the nation's own developmental needs as well as for attracting partners to provide whatever necessary materials may be lacking. Secondly, a nation needs funds for capital investment. Only by deferring consumption and increasing savings and investment can it create the necessary capital to bring about growth. Once acquired, machines, electrical power, factories, and the like present opportunities for revolutionizing productivity. The pace of industrialization depends heavily upon capital goods obtained from the developed world, whether by trade, investment, or aid. Vast changes in attitudes will be required to build and attract capital; the rich must refrain from conspicuous consumption and nepotism; peasant cultivators must be more amenable to innovation, the application of scientific farming, and the idea of producing beyond their family's daily living requirements; caste barriers will have to yield in order to create more fluidity in the system of stratification.

The population explosion presents an obvious handicap to economic

[4] Robert Heilbroner, *The Great Ascent: The Struggle for Economic Development in Our Time* (New York: Harper & Row, 1963), p. 56.

[5] *Ibid.*, pp. 33–141.

growth, not only because of the vastly increasing numbers of people who must be supported, but also because the fastest-growing societies are most likely to have high proportions of youthful members who can contribute very little to productivity and who are economically dependent. For example, in Costa Rica some 50 per cent of the population is under fifteen years of age.

A nationalistic spirit and leadership deeply committed to economic development are especially valuable elements for bringing about economic transformation. Yet, nationalist feeling among the members of society in itself is insufficient to carry the development along; social capital has to be created—schools and hospitals built, technicians and professionals trained—so as to set the course of development in a self-sustaining direction. In the past, many attempts to parlay social capital failed to yield results; young people sent abroad for specialized training all too often never return to deliver the benefits of their studies to their homelands.

Coordinated land reform is also necessary; in some cases, large land holdings will have to be broken up into smaller units; in other cases, small holdings will have to be consolidated into larger sectors. Central government authority must assume a pivotal role in planning and coordinating economic development. Forceful political leadership will be needed to inspire the sacrifices necessary to carry the economic development along.

William Pratt's "Anabaptist Explosion" is most instructive for our understanding of economic development. The Anabaptists are unique, in that their rate of population increase is possibly the fastest on earth. Although they by no means represent a "typical" Third World people, their phenomenal population growth highlights the fact that development is taking place in the context of a tremendous population explosion. Pratt's findings suggest that there may be advantages in centralized planning over a decentralized, laissez-faire economic system. The centrally coordinated Hutterite economy adequately supports the needs of its members. And the economic success of these people may contribute to the infrequently observed defections from the group and their high fertility, the highest of any Anabaptist sect. The less economically successful Amish, on the other hand, are sustaining more defections and appear to be less closely approximating the Anabaptist cultural ideal of large families. There are, however, a number of confounding factors that make this a less than satisfactory comparison of collective-versus-individual–based economies.

Another condition encouraging the economic-development process seems to be the existence of a stable political system. Political stability, it seems, helps to generate both a climate favorable for the growth of nationalism and the requisite altruistic behavior for developing national capital. It also attracts foreign capital, offering the prospect of greater security to would-be investors and benefactors. However, the reality of politics in the underdeveloped world falls far short of stability; revolution and political upheaval are very frequent events. Why is revolution apparently more common in transitional societies? What are the social factors associated with revolutionary political change?

James Davies, in "Toward a Theory of Revolution," addresses both questions. Drawing upon the events of Doar's Rebellion of 1842 in New England, the Russian Revolution of 1917, and the Egyptian Revolution of 1952, Davies posits a theory of rising expectations to account for revolutionary action. He maintains that revolutions are most likely to occur when a prolonged period of social and economic development is followed by a short period of deep reversal. Revolution is generated by the expectation that past progress, now blocked, can and must continue in the future. Underdeveloped societies, especially as they come into closer contact with the developed world, have become unusually susceptible to a climate of rising expectations. Societies that have recently thrown off the yoke of colonial status, that are experiencing rapid social change, and whose economic development is occurring at a phenomenal rate—conditions that describe many transitional societies—are very likely to generate rising expectations.

A closely related theory, originally presented by Alexis de Tocqueville and more recently by the late Crane Brinton, is the theory of "relative deprivation." Actual or objective deprivation is not so important in motivating revolutionary sentiment as subjective or relative deprivation—that is, how deprived a person feels himself to be in relation to others. Thus, the greatest support for the French Revolution came from the ranks of affluent farmers and urban merchants who were resentful because their political power and social prestige were not commensurate with their material wealth. Seemingly affluent, they felt deprived and envious. It was not that they opposed the feudal estate system as an inequitable and morally offensive institution so much as that they wished to enjoy the privileges and distinctions of the nobility.

This theory raises some important questions about what social types are likely to be among the revolutionaries, especially the revolutionary leadership. Davies suggests that the poorest and most oppressed are unlikely to be among the revolutionary forces, because they are so absorbed with the struggle for survival that they are unlikely to have energy left for politicizing. Examination of several revolutions shows that the revolutionary ranks have a rather broad and varied social base. Many studies, including the Kerner Commission Report on urban ghetto disorder in the United States, have found that revolutionary leaders are ordinarily drawn from relatively high social ranks, more affluent and more highly educated than their constituencies. Conceivably, this finding could be interpreted as evidence for the relative-deprivation theory. It also concurs with sociologists' findings regarding organized action in general; leaders usually possess more social skills, rank, and esteem than are found among their supporters.

In transitional societies, glaring social inequities also play a role in generating revolutionary sentiment. Bruce Russett finds that the higher the concentration of land ownership and the higher the rate of tenancy, the greater the likelihood of political instability.[6] The rapidity of change also affects the probability of revolution in underdeveloped societies. As rapid change liberates men from their traditional social statuses, it creates social dislocations that make men more susceptible to the revolution-initiating potential of rising expectations and relative deprivation.

Where do we go from here? What will be the direction of social change in postindustrial society? Fred Davis's "Why All of Us May Be Hippies Someday" raises some very important questions about dealing effectively with the problems of the future. As industrial society moves into an era of accelerated cybernation, increasing material abundance, and unprecedented leisure, we will have to grapple with, and resolve, a number of central life problems. Despite the real or imagined "perversions" that middle-class detractors assign to the "hippie" life-style, the hippie subculture represents an attempt to deal with some of the problems of the future. For example, its antimaterialistic focus presents an approach to the problem of overconsumption, which takes a heavy toll of the world's nonrenewable resources. The professionalization of art and leisure in modern society has created conditions whereby the average citizen is relegated to the role of passive spectator. Hippie spontaneity and expressiveness, with its democratization of art and leisure, try to renew a sense of active participation. Perhaps the most significant questions hippies pose are: What should be the purpose of our social institutions, if not to help realize man's happiness and satisfaction? Is human need-satisfaction always to be postponed to an indefinite future? These questions cannot be ignored if our society is to deal effectively with the environmental challenge, and if man is to have meaningful and satisfying relationships with his fellow beings.

The Demographic Dimension of Social Change

The Population Explosion: Facts and Fiction*

Paul R. Ehrlich

The facts of today's population crisis are appallingly simple. Mankind at first gradually, but recently with extreme rapidity, has intervened artificially

[6] Bruce Russett, "Inequality and Instability: The Relation of Land Tenure to Politics," *World Politics*, XVI, no. 3 (April, 1964), 442–54.

to lower the death rate in the human population. Simultaneously, we have not–repeat, *have not*–intervened to lower the birth rate. Since people are unable to flee from our rather small planet, the inevitable result of the wide discrepancy between birth and death rates has been a rapid increase in the numbers of people crowded onto the earth.

The growth of the population is now so rapid that the multitude of humans is doubling every 35 years. Indeed, in many undeveloped countries, the doubling time is between 20 and 25 years. Think of what it means for the population of a country like Colombia to double in the next 22 years. Throughout its history, the people of Colombia have managed to create a set of facilities for the maintenance of human beings: buildings, roads, farms, water systems, sewage systems, hospitals, schools, churches, and so forth. Remember that, just to remain even, just to maintain today's level of misery, Colombia would have to duplicate all of those facilities in the next 22 years. It would have to double its human resources as well–train enough doctors, lawyers, teachers, judges, and all the rest so that, in 22 years, the number of all these professionals would be twice that of today. Such a task would be impossible for a powerful, industrialized country with agricultural surpluses, high literacy rate, fine schools and communications, etc. The United States couldn't hope to accomplish it. For Colombia, with none of these things, with 30–40 per cent of its population illiterate, with 47 per cent of its population under fifteen years of age, it is inconceivable.

Yes, it will be impossible for Colombia to maintain its present level of misery for the next 22 years–and misery it is. Death control did not reach Colombia until after World War II. Before it arrived, a woman could expect to have two or three children survive to reproductive age if she went through ten pregnancies. Now, in spite of malnutrition, medical technology keeps seven or eight alive. Each child adds to the impossible financial burden of the family and to the despair of the mother. According to Dr. Sumner M. Kalman, the average Colombian mother goes through a progression of attempts to limit the size of her family. She starts with ineffective native forms of contraception and moves on to quack abortion, infanticide, frigidity, and all too often to suicide. The average family in Colombia, after its last child is born, has to spend 80 per cent of its income on food. And the per capita income of Colombians is $237 per year, less than one-tenth that of Americans. That's the kind of misery that's concealed behind the dry statistic of a population doubling every 22 years.

But it seems highly unlikely that, 22 years from now, Colombia will have doubled its present population of 20 million to 40 million. The reason is quite simple. The earth is a spaceship of limited carrying capacity. The 3.5 billion people who now live on our globe can do so only at the expense of the consumption of nonrenewable resources, especially coal and petroleum. Today's technology could not maintain 3.5 billion people without "living on capital," as we are now doing. Indeed, it is doubtful if any technology could permanently maintain that number. And note that, even living on capital, we are doing none too well. Somewhere between 1 and 2 billion people are *today* undernourished (have too few calories) or malnourished (suffer from various deficiencies, especially protein deficiencies). Somewhere between 4 and 10 million of our fellow human beings will starve to death this year. Consider that the average person among some 2 billion Asians has an annual income of $128, a life expectancy at birth of only 50 years, and is illiterate. A third of a billion Africans have an average life expectancy of only 43 years, and an average annual income of $123. Of Africans over fifteen years of age, 82 per cent are illiterate. Look at the situation in India, where Professor Georg Borgstrom estimates that only about one person in fifty has an adequate diet. For the vast majority, the calorie supply "is not sufficient for sustaining a normal workday. Physical exhaustion and apathy [are] the rule."

No, we're not doing a very good job of taking care of the people we have in 1968—and we are adding to the population of the earth 70 million people per year. Think of it—an equivalent of the 1968 population of the United States *added* to the world every three years! We have an inadequate loaf of bread to divide among today's multitudes, and we are quickly adding more billions to the bread line.

As I said at the beginning, the facts are indeed simple. We are faced by a most elementary choice. Either we find a way to bring the birth rate down or the death rate will soon go back up. Make no mistake about it—mankind has not freed itself on the tyranny of arithmetic! Anyone, including Pope Paul VI, who stands in the way of measures to bring down the birth rate is automatically working for a rise in the death rate.

The death rate could rise in several ways. Perhaps the most likely is through famine. The world has very nearly reached its maximum food production capacity—even with the expenditure of our nonrenewable resources. Agricultural experts, such as Professor Borgstrom and the Paddock brothers, present a dismal picture indeed. The Paddocks' best estimate of the onset of the "Time of Famines," the time when many tens of millions will starve to death annually, is 1975. How accurate their prediction is will depend on many factors, such as the weather, over which we have no control. It will also depend, in part, on what actions mankind takes to attempt an amelioration of the situation. I must, however, agree with the Paddocks that massive famines are now inevitable.

Plague presents another possibility for a "death rate solution" to the population problem. It is known that viruses may increase their virulence when they infect a large population. With viruses circulating in a weakened population of unprecedented size, and with modern transport capable of spreading infection to the far corners of the globe almost instantly, we could easily face an unparalleled epidemic. Indeed, if a man-made germ should escape from one of our biological warfare labs, we might see the extinction of *Homo sapiens.* It is now theoretically possible to develop organisms against which man would have no resistance—indeed, one Nobel laureate was so appalled at the possibility of an accidental escape that he quit research in this field.

Finally, of course, thermonuclear war could provide us with an instant death-rate solution. Nearly a billion people in China are pushing out of their biologically ruined country toward Siberia, India, and the Mekong rice bowl. The suffering millions of Latin America are moving toward revolution and Communist governments. An Arab population boom, especially among Palestinian refugees, adds to tensions. The competition to loot the sea of its fishes creates international incidents. As more and more people have less and less, as the rich get richer and the poor poorer, the probability of war increases. The poor of the world know what we have, and they want it. They have what is known as rising expectations. For this reason alone, a mere maintenance of current levels of living will be inadequate to maintain peace.

Unfortunately, we will not need to kill outright all human beings to drive mankind to extinction. Small groups of genetically and culturally impoverished survivors may well succumb to the inevitably harsh environment of a war-ravaged planet. War not only could end this population explosion, it has the potential for removing the possibility of any future population growth.

Faced with this dismal prospect, why haven't people, especially in an educated country like the United States, taken rational action to bring the birth rate down? Why haven't we led the way toward a world with an optimum population living in balance with its resources? Why, indeed, have most Americans remained unaware of the gravity of the entire problem? The answers to these questions are many and complex. In the rest of this talk, I'd like to discuss one major reason why we have not managed to defuse the population bomb. This reason is the perpetuation of a series of fictions that tend to discount the problem or present fantasy solutions to it. These fictions are eagerly believed by many people who show an all-too-human wish to avoid facing unpleasant realities. Let's look at some of the fictions, and some of the unpleasant realities.

FICTION: The population explosion is over, at least in the United States, because the birth rate is at an all-time low.

FACT: Although the birth rate of the United States has hit record lows (around 16 per thousand per year) for brief periods this year, it has not approached the death rate, which is down around 9 per thousand per year. Even at the record low rate (if it were to continue), the population of the United States would double in about 100 years. But the low birth rate will not persist, since the large group of women born in the post–World War II baby boom move into their peak reproductive period in the next few years. Birth rates are subject to short-term fluctuations, according to the number of women in their reproductive years, the condition of the economy, the occurrence of wars, etc. Viewing a temporary decline of the birth rate as a sign of the end of the population explosion is like considering a warm December 26th as a sign of spring. The ballyhooing of the temporary decline of birth rate (with, if you recall, no mention of death rate) has done great harm to the cause of humanity.

FICTION: The United States has no population problem—it is a problem of the undeveloped countries.

FACT: Considering the problems of air and water pollution, poverty, clogged highways, overcrowded schools, inadequate courts and jails, urban blight, and so on, it is clear that the United States has more people than it can adequately maintain. But, even if we were not overpopulated at home, we could not stand detached from the rest of the world. We are completely dependent on imports for our affluence. We use roughly one-half of all the raw materials consumed on the face of the earth each year. We need the ferroalloys, tin, bauxite, petroleum, rubber, food, and other materials we import. We, one-fifteenth of the population, grab one-half as our share. We can afford to raise beef for our own use in protein-starved Asia. We can afford to take fish from protein-starved South America and feed it to our chickens. We can afford to buy protein-rich peanuts from protein-starved Africans. Even if we are not engulfed in worldwide plague or war, we will suffer mightily as the "other world" slips into famine. We will suffer when they are no longer willing or able to supply our needs. It has been truly said that calling the population explosion a problem of undeveloped countries is like saying to a fellow passenger, "Your end of the boat is sinking."

FICTION: Much of the earth is empty land that can be put under cultivation in order to supply food for the burgeoning population of the planet.

FACT: Virtually all of the land that can be cultivated with known or easily foreseeable methods already is under cultivation. We would have to double our present agricultural production just to feed today's billions adequately—and the population of the earth is growing, I repeat, by some *70 million people* per year. No conceivable expansion of arable land could take care of these needs.

FICTION: Although land agriculture cannot possibly take care of our food needs, we still have "unmeasurable" resources of the sea that can be tapped so that we can populate the earth until people are jammed together like rabbits in a warren.

FACT: The resources of the sea have been measured and have been found wanting. Most of the sea is a biological desert. Our techniques for extracting what potential food there is in the sea are still very primitive. With a cessation of pollution, complete international cooperation, and ecologically intelligent management, we might manage to double our present yield from the sea or do even better on a sustained basis. But even such a miracle would be inadequate to meet the needs of the population growth. And there is no sign of such a miracle. Indeed, there is increasing pollution of the sea with massive amounts of pesticides and other biologically active compounds. In addition, a no-holds-barred race to harvest the fish of the sea has developed among China, Japan, Russia, the United States, and others. This race is resulting in the kind of overexploitation that led to the decline of the whaling industry. All the signs point to a *reduction* of the food yield of the sea in the near future—not to a bonanza from the sea.

FICTION: Science (with a capital S) will find a new way to feed everyone —perhaps by making food synthetically.

FACT: Perhaps, in the distant future, some foods will be produced synthetically in large quantity, but not in time to help mankind through the crisis it now faces. The most-discussed methods would involve the use of micro-organisms and fossil fuels. Since fossil fuels are limited in supply, and much in demand for other uses, their use as a food source would be a temporary measure, at best. Direct synthesis, even should it eventually prove possible, would inevitably present problems of energy supply and materials supply—it would be no simple "food for nothing" system. But, I repeat, science holds no hope of finding a synthetic solution to the food problem at this time.

FICTION: We can solve the crowding problem on our planet by migrating to other planets.

FACT: No other planet of the solar system appears to be habitable. But, if all of them were, we would have to export to them 70 million people a year to keep our population constant. With our current technology and that foreseeable in the next few decades, such an effort would be economically impossible—indeed, the drain on our mineral resources and fossil fuels would be unbelievable. Suppose that we built rockets immeasurably larger than any in existence today—capable of carrying 100 people and their baggage to another planet. Almost 2,000 of such monster ships would have to leave each day. The effects of their exhausts on the atmosphere would be spectacular, to say the least. And what if, through miracles, we did manage to export all those people and maintain them elsewhere in the solar system? In a mere 250 years, the entire system would be populated to the same density as the earth. Attempting to reach the planets of the stars raises the prospect of space ships taking generations to reach their destinations. Since population explosions could not be permitted on the star ships, the passengers would have to be willing to practice strict birth control. In other words, the responsible people will have to be the ones to leave, with the irresponsible staying at home to breed. On the cheery side, getting to the stars might not be so difficult. After all, in a few thousand years, at the current growth rate, all the material in the visible universe will have been converted into people, and the sphere of people will be expanding outward at better than the speed of light!

FICTION: Family planning is the answer to the population explosion. It has worked in places like Japan; it will work in places like India.

FACT: No country, including Japan, has managed to bring its population under rational control. After World War II, Japan employed abortion to reduce its birth rate, but it did not stop its growth. Indeed, in 1966, with its birth rate at a temporary low because it was the "Year of the Fiery Horse" (considered inauspicious for births), Japan's population was still growing at a rate that would double it in 63 years. Japan is in desperate straits. Today, it must import food equivalent to its entire agricultural production. In addition, it depends heavily on its fisheries, from which it gets food equivalent to more than one and one half times its agricultural production. Japan is so overpopulated that, *even if her population growth stopped,* she would succumb to disaster as her sources of food imports dry up and as her share of the yield from the sea shrinks. But, remember, grossly overpopulated Japan is continuing to grow at a rapid rate.

Family planning in India has had no discernible effect, even though it has had government support for some seventeen years. During those years, the population has increased by more than one half, and the growth rate itself has increased. The IUD (intrauterine device) was promoted by the professional optimists as the panacea for India, but the most recent news from that country indicates a recognition of the failure of the IUD campaign and a return to the promotion of condoms.

Most depressing of all is the point that family planning promotes the notion that people should have only the number of children they *want* and can support. It does not promote family sizes that will bring about population control. As Professor Kingsley Davis has often pointed out, people *want* too many children. Family planning has not controlled any population to date, and by itself it is not going to control *any* population.

These fictions are spread by a wide variety of people and organizations, and for a wide variety of reasons. Some have long-term emotional commitments to outmoded ideas, such as population control through family planning. Others wish to disguise the failure of the government agencies they run. Still others have simple economic interests in the sale of food or agricultural chemicals and equipment. Almost all also have genuine humanitarian motives. Most of these people have an incomplete view of the problem, at best. The less well informed simply have no grasp of the magnitude of the problem—these are the ones who propose solutions in outer space or under the sea. More sophisticated are those who hold out great hopes for agricultural changes (now often referred to as a "green revolution"), which will at least temporarily solve the problem. Such people are especially common in our government.

This sophisticated group tends to be ignorant of elementary biology. Our desperate attempts to increase food yields are promoting soil deterioration and contributing to the poisoning of the ecological systems on which our very survival depends. It is a long and complex story, but the conclusion is simple—the more we strive to obtain increased yields in the short run, the smaller the yields are likely to be in the long run. No attempt to increase food yields can solve the problem. How much, then, should we mortgage our future by such attempts?

I've concentrated, in my discussion, on the nature of the population explosion rather than attempting to detail ways of reaching a birth-rate solution. That is because the first step toward any solution involves a realistic facing of the problem. We must, as that first step, get a majority of Americans to recognize the simple choice: *Lower the birth rate or face a drastic rise in the death rate.* We must divert attention from the treatment of symptoms of the population explosion and start treating its cause. We have no more time; we must act now. Next year will not do. It is already too late for us to survive unscathed. Now we must make decisions designed to minimize the damage. America today reminds me of the fabled man who jumped off the top of a fifty-story building. As he passed the second floor, he was heard to say, "Things have gone pretty well so far."

The Economic Dimension of Social Change

The Anabaptist Explosion*

William F. Pratt

The survival of the Hutterites and the Amish, two religious sects whose communities are found in various parts of the United States and Canada, is a cultural anachronism. That these Anabaptist societies have persevered over several hundred years fraught with persecution and rejection is surprising enough. That they have maintained their medieval faith and their unsophisticated styles of life in a rapidly changing urban-industrial environment, is an ecological phenomenon of considerable moment. But of particular interest is their traditionally high level of fertility, which has persisted while their mortality rates have approximated that of the surrounding society. Consequently, they have experienced a phenomenal growth from natural increase, which has created portentous problems for them.

The Hutterites, settled in South Dakota, Montana, and the prairie provinces of Canada, and the Amish, formerly centered in Pennsylvania and Ohio, have birth rates of 46 and 33 per 1,000 population, respectively. A century and a half ago, the United States birth rate was a lofty 55—over three times higher than its present level; in 1967, it had dropped to an all-time low of 17.9 births per 1,000 population. It is against this shifting background that the continuing high fertility of the Hutterites and Amish is so startling.

Comparable fertility rates show that, from age twenty, Hutterite women have much higher birth rates than those of American women in general. Even in their late childbearing years (forty to forty-four), their birth rate

* Reprinted from *Natural History Magazine,* February, 1969.

exceeds that of American women in their peak childbearing years (twenty to twenty-four). (The Amish women, in a somewhat freer society, have birth rates about midway between those of Hutterites and of American women in general.) It may be that two centuries of high fertility, combined with the inbreeding brought about by the social isolation of the Hutterites, has created a unique strain of the human species—a strain distinct in its fertility from any other people. Indeed, the Hutterites, with an annual natural increase of about 4 per cent, are possibly the fastest-growing population on earth. Between 1950 and 1965, their numbers almost doubled, from 8,500 to 15,000. The United States growth rate, by contrast, is only .79. This would double the population in about 90 years, compared with a doubling among Hutterites about every 17 years.

The fertility of the two Anabaptist sects is one reflection of their rigidly theocratic cultures, which have managed to survive in an urban-industrial nation of 200 million that is wholly alien in outlook to the sects' own beliefs. At the same time, their rigid separatism, their being conscientious objectors, and their rapid growth have made these sects a focal point of hostility among their neighbors. The problems of the Amish families with respect to public education are familiar. As for Hutterite colonies, land laws have been proposed several times—and, in some cases passed—to restrict their spread. At their present growth rate, Hutterites would number 64,500 by the year 2000 and more than 55 million by 2168. Today, their colonies occupy about 1,000 square miles; by the year 2000, they would occupy an area almost equaling Connecticut.

The difference in birth rates of the two sects is intriguing. It undoubtedly reflects differences in social organization and comparative success in adapting to the secular milieu of modern America. Despite their common origins and life-style, they differ significantly in important respects.

HUTTERITES: A DISSIDENT SECT

The Anabaptists of the Reformation comprised several quite different sects, from the radical and violent Munsterites to the equally radical but wholly nonviolent Hutterites. What they shared was the label "Anabaptist"; it referred to their central belief in adult "rebaptism," baptism upon confession of faith. All these Protestant sects were religious responses of the socially disinherited of the Holy Roman Empire in the late fifteenth and sixteenth centuries.

Peasants, journeymen, and the landless were the most abject victims of that period's crises. Many turned from a cheerless reality to the comforts of a religion that made a virtue of their poverty and built a brotherhood on their passive suffering. But then Martin Luther and Huldrich Zwingli alike, having gained their patrimony from the state, turned upon the rabble. In 1527, the Swiss Anabaptists responded by formalizing many of the tenets that still characterize Hutterites and Amish. Among these are adult baptism, separation of church and state by the withdrawal of believers, and an emphatic rejection of violence. From the outset, then, Anabaptism was regarded as a threat to the established religious and secular authorities, both old and new.

Unsafe in Zurich, the Swiss Brethren–the main body of Swiss Anabaptists–found refuge in Nikolsburg, Moravia, where their mounting numbers undoubtedly created severe economic strains. These were soon reflected in doctrinal disputes between a liberal majority and a strict, radical minority. The radicals, proclaiming Christian communism, worshipping separately, holding fast to adult baptism, and rejecting military violence even to defend themselves, were expelled in 1528. At that time, they symbolically spread a cloak upon the ground to receive their worldly goods. This formally inaugurated the practice of "community of goods," which made them unique among sects descending from the Swiss Brethren. Under the organizational genius of Jacob Hutter (martyred in 1536), this radical group became known as Hutterites.

Although their communities flourished and increased through the first hundred years, they stood constantly in the shadow of persecution and dispersal. Between 1529 and 1622, an estimated 85 communal households, averaging from 300 to 400 members, had been established. But, by 1625, the sect had almost completely migrated to Hungary. There, the re-establishment of Catholic authority and the rise of the Jesuits overcame the reluctance of the nobility to persecute the Hutterites. Invasion by the Turks added to their troubles. Also, considerable internal discord arose, and, by the end of the seventeenth century, membership had been greatly reduced by apostasy to Catholicism.

Of the faithful, most migrated to Slovakia, Transylvania, and Walachia, and later to Russia. Here, unable to re-establish communal life, they accepted the individual family culture practiced by the Mennonites, an independent Anabaptist movement that also had set up some communities in Russia. In the 1870's, fearing Czarist persecution, most Hutterites migrated to the United States, where, returning to their former, communal order, they established three colonies, comprising about 440 persons.

HUTTERITES OF NORTH AMERICA

Thus began a demographic epic. As of January, 1965, there were 162 organized communities, averaging 94 "souls," in the United States and Canada. This growth to over 15,000 people is about a 33-fold increase, or over five doublings of population in less than a century.

These figures are the more remarkable because the Hutterites have been a "closed population" since arrival in America. Their growth has come entirely from natural increase, the excess of births over deaths.

Even when adjusted for differences in age distribution, the Hutterite death rate is only 85 per cent of the United States figure. The Hutterite rate for infant mortality in the past was above the national figure, but, with improving medical care and health practices, this, too, may now be equal to, or less than, for the nation as a whole.

Some practices, such as considerable reliance upon midwives, remain old-fashioned, but, in general, the Hutterites have adopted modern medical facilities. Although their anti-intellectualism and separation from the world have deprived them of the outstanding medical personnel they had in an earlier era, Hutterites do not hesitate to send ailing members to the Mayo Clinic and other medical centers. A recent study suggests that they may be spending more per capita on drugs and medical care than do most Americans. If their favorable mortality has been purchased at the cost of greater dependence upon the outside, it is nonetheless consistent with their historical emphasis on health and medical practice.

The exceptionally high fertility of Hutterite women is most sharply seen in their average completed fertility. It totals 10.4 live births, owing partly to the remarkably high rates of childbearing in the later fertile years. According to sociologists J. W. Eaton and A. J. Mayer, the fertility rate of over 425 per 1,000 for Hutterite women aged 35–39 exceeds that for women in any other culture now on record. Even at ages 40–44, Hutterites have a fertility rate higher than women in France, Sweden, and the United States during their years of maximum fertility, ages 20–29.

So striking a deviation suggests that something more than social or theocratic mores [is] involved. The inbreeding within the Hutterite population must be considerable. Since the 440 original brethren with only 15 patronyms among them (70 per cent had only five patronyms) came to America a century ago, they have attracted no "new blood." In view of the higher mortality of Hutterite women in the childbearing years and the continued reproduction of those women rugged enough to stay the course, genetic components favoring a superfecund strain in the species must have been added to the Hutterite gene pool. The degree to which inbreeding may have made this population genetically more uniform (homozygous) would depend on birth and marriage patterns within the colonies. Until a detailed genetic analysis of the Hutterite pedigree becomes available, it is impossible to derive accurate inbreeding coefficients and thereby add greatly to our knowledge of what inbreeding does to human populations.

At any rate, Hutterite fertility has few restrictions and strong positive encouragement from the culture. Hutterites take literally the Biblical injunction to "be fruitful and multiply": sex as pleasure is devalued and confined to marriage, the chief end of which is to beget children. Birth control, including the rhythm method, is prohibited. All but a very few Hutterites marry, divorce is unknown, and remarriage after the death of a spouse is frequent. The only major restraint upon fertility is the relatively late age at marriage, combined with prohibition of premarital sexual intercourse. Sociologist John A. Hostetler reports that, in 1965, the average age at marriage was 23.5 for men and 22.0 for women, compared with the national averages of 22.8 and 20.6 for men and women, respectively.

These direct factors are supported by the general cultural patterns of community life. Lack of privacy in one's household and possessions would make difficult the use of most mechanical or chemical contraceptive methods; and failure to bear children within a reasonably short time after marriage or the last birth starts gossip and insinuations about one's health and the health of one's marriage. The same lack of privacy makes premarital sexual adventures unlikely, not to mention the severe guilt and ostracism that a premarital pregnancy would bring.

In any case, there is little, if any, motivation for birth control. Unlike outsiders, the Hutterite family does not face the economic uncertainties that attend death and unemployment; it does not have the responsibilities of maintaining its own separate household and facilities; above all, it escapes "keeping up with the Joneses." The simplicity of Hutterite consumer needs, the economies of communal life, the low educational costs, and the early age at which youth enter the colony's productive enterprise all keep the costs of childbearing very low compared to the general population. This would seem to leave the state of the woman's health and the strains of childbearing as the only plausible focus for trying to limit the number of children, and, so far, these considerations have had no observable impact on fertility.

In view of its remarkably high fertility and rapid natural increase, the intriguing question is: How has this anti-intellectual, medieval communal order managed to adapt itself to a highly secular, urban-industrial environment and its rapidly changing technology? Other Anabaptist groups have clearly not resisted surrounding secular influences so well.

No longer subject to the whimsies of noble patrons, as in Europe, each Hutterite colony is an independent corporate enterprise integrated with the larger American economy. Hutterite economy is more specialized in agriculture today than when they were in Europe; they have sacrificed many of their former crafts and trades for modern mechanical skills and the economies of wholesale purchasing.

But their assimilation is exclusively at the economic and corporate level. Life within the contemporary colony is a revitalized communal order. Esthetic and individualizing interests are suppressed, as of old, by a common style in all things–a style marked by simplicity and sturdiness of materials. Thus, active economic choice does not intrude, and invidious status differences do not arise. Financial matters and control of funds are strictly communal. Although not motivated by profit, Hutterites are shrewd businessmen who must maintain a substantial level of savings for contingencies and for building new colonies every generation or less.

So far as possible, labor remains communal, and responsibilities are divided according to age, sex, and "election," as in former times. Cooking is done in a communal kitchen; eating is in a common dining hall. Although each family has one to two rooms in a communal apartment, toilet facilities are shared.

By isolating themselves socially, Hutterites sustain a strong sense of solidarity and a remarkable integrity of their communal life. Their rural location, the restrictions on working for outsiders, their language and quaint clothing, all help to separate them from the world. Information about the outside is primarily through the daily newspaper and farm journals, plus infrequent trips to town; but radios, TV, and movies are forbidden. Although bilingual and maintaining their level of literacy, they refuse state education beyond the legal required age, and maintain a parochial school in the colony to keep the children at home. The "English" teacher, certified by the state or province, generally lives in the colony but is as physically and socially isolated as Hutterite courtesy and hospitality will allow.

This social isolation of the Hutterite group itself is reinforced by a psychological turning inward. By constant reflection on their historical persecution and references to it, Hutterites maintain a fearful view of the outside world. The conditioning begins in earliest childhood, when Santa Claus is described as a bogeyman who kidnaps naughty children; consequently, the youngster shrinks from strangers. Also, the fundamentalist religious message stresses God's wrath and vengeance upon those who enter the world, or behave in worldly ways (against the community rules), and his forgiving love for those who repent. These teachings begin in the communal kindergarten and continue in the "German" school to age 15, where they are reinforced by the strict teacher. In sum, a somewhat paranoid fear of, and prejudice toward, the larger society is ritually induced from childhood, while the ascetic discipline of the community life comes to be viewed as the comforting, forgiving, God-given haven.

Contemporary Hutterites are keenly aware that colony size is also basically important. By limiting colonies to a maximum of about 150 members, they can preserve close interpersonal relations, with privacy nearly impossible and competing cliques seldom arising. When the colony population becomes too large, however, stresses do occur and feelings polarize along family and kinship lines.

This internal source of disruption is normally muted in several ways that characterize Hutterite communal life: The economic independence of the family is eliminated; family-centered activities are minimized; men and women are separated in labor, dining, and worship; and household privacy is limited.

North American society also fosters their internal solidarity. From time to time, their colonies have been harassed by neighbors and by attempted legislative restrictions; these, plus the jibes and prejudice of outsiders, suffice to keep their fears very much alive, even though their rights have been strongly protected.

Most significant, perhaps, is that the outside no longer offers a viable living alternative for the individual Hutterite or family. Neither by education, social skills, nor psychology is the Hutterite prepared to compete in the larger society. Since 1918, no more than 2 per cent of all Hutterites have ever forsaken their colonies. The young man who does "try the world" almost invariably feels a keen sense of loneliness and returns in short order, expressing a sense of guilt toward his parents.

STRESSES AND STRAINS

To the casual observer, Hutterite society may present the illusion of unchangeability over 400 years of history. A paradox is closer to the truth: They have changed, and in fundamental ways, in order to remain the same. A simple example is the principle of adult baptism. Although it is still observed in form, and plays a crucial part in Hutterite socialization, it has long since lost its original meaning. Today's young Hutterite adult does not "choose" the community life after having experienced and rejected the "world" on its own terms. He has been very successfully conditioned to fear the outside, to feel inadequate in the face of it, to cherish the psychological shelter of the community.

Will the adaptive processes that have so far preserved the Hutterite culture continue to operate in the indefinite future? This will depend on how much the stresses and strains are intensified by the phenomenal population growth.

The communal operation has an ideal or optimal labor demand that implies a population of about 100 persons in all ages. As sociologist Victor Peters observes: "A new colony with a population of about 100 persons will have an adult labor pool . . . of about 30 men and women. Approximately 15 . . . will be male, which means that almost all of them will be in charge of an office or enterprise. . . . As the population increases, there are duplications in the various enterprises (by a system of assistants)."

This is the stage at which invidious distinctions among equals arise and cause tensions; the basis for cliques and divisions along family lines now begins to emerge. The resulting tensions play upon the problem of esthetics and the adoption of consumer conveniences. In short, the intimate, primary relations of colony life begin to give way to more formal regulations and supervision. However, when colony size reaches about 150 members, the more informal, brotherly atmosphere of community life is re-established in Hutterite fashion. The oversize community splits, amoebalike, into two communities: one new and one old.

The rapid increase in colonies provides a classic illustration of ecological competition for territory and of population's role in intersocietal conflict. Hutterite aloofness is a source of prejudice; their economic efficiency is a source of envy; their refusal to bear arms can raise hostility to the boiling point. More direct and basic, the colonies, like corporate farms elsewhere, have reduced the population base that formerly provided support for the economies of local towns. The Hutterite ability to purchase wholesale from more distant centers further depresses the economy of these nearby towns. In some instances, Hutterite refusal to participate in local programs, such as rural electrification, has denied these services to other local farmers.

Against the resulting hostility, Hutterite protestations about contributing to the health of state and national economies, about paying school taxes from which they receive little benefit, about not drawing upon outside welfare funds to which they contribute, and about not contributing to problems of crime or mental illness are of little avail.

True, opposition so far has not blunted either their financial security in the general economy or their constitutional protections as citizens. Nonetheless, they have experienced outbreaks of vandalism against some of their colonies, especially in wartime, and there have been numerous proposals to restrict their land buying. A land law in Alberta requires that Hutterites purchase new colonies at least 40 miles away from any other and not exceeding 64,000 acres. To challenge such laws, Hutterites have been obliged to set up something hitherto alien to them–a national church. Although this secondary organization has had little effect on the daily operations of the colonies, it contains the seeds for wielding financial power and regulating communal life in a non-Hutterite way.

Given that this sect will number about 64,500 people in the year 2000, it is reasonable to expect that outside opposition will press harder for changes in Hutterite life. Moreover, given that Hutterites would number 55 million in another 168 years, it is clear that either their growth rate or their way of life, and probably both, must give way to change before that time. A fascinating experimental case study in the social consequences of demographic patterns appears to be rapidly unfolding before our eyes.

THE BELEAGUERED AMISH

Despite various similarities between the two sects, the story of the Amish is far more of a contrast with that of the Hutterites, especially in modern times.

The Amish arose as a branch from the Mennonites, an independent Anabaptist movement centering in the Netherlands. The Mennonites envisaged small, homogeneous, and self-sufficient communities living a scriptural way of life. Unlike Hutterites, they advocated no theocratic communism or any other economic mode of community life. In practice, like the majority of Swiss Brethren, they embraced the doctrine of Christian stewardship of private property and made the family the basic economic unit of their society.

However, the fanatical Mennonite preacher, Jakob Ammann, preached a harsher system of discipline. In 1693, angered by the refusal of a group of ministers to confer on this issue, he censured the lot of them and founded his own sect, the Amish. Thus was Amish life rigorously formalized and made more repressive.

Also for comparison: The migrations of the Amish–unlike those of Hutterites–have always occurred within the sphere of advancing Western culture rather than its backwash.

From communities widely scattered over Western Europe, the Amish emigrated to the United States over a long period of time, beginning with the first settlement, in Pennsylvania, in 1727. After the Napoleonic wars, large numbers of Amish fled Alsace and Bavaria, settling in Ontario, Illinois, and Ohio. Shortly, they were followed by others from central Germany, who settled in Ohio, Pennsylvania, and Maryland. By 1900, the Amish had either abandoned Europe or been reabsorbed by the Mennonites.

Through exceptional frugality, industry, and farming skill, the Amish prospered in their earlier years in America, compared with their neighbors. Today, the economic situation is reversed. The modern non-Amish farmer, utilizing farm machinery forbidden to the Old Order Amishman, is far more productive and also much less burdened by a large family. (Reference to the "Old Order Amish" reflects the fact that, over more recent times, the traditional order of Amish life has eroded and produced several schisms.)

By 1960, there were 258 loosely defined Amish "districts" in 19 states, with a total Amish population of about 43,000. Six years later, the population had grown to 49,370–an increase of just under 15 per cent, compared with 9 per cent for the United States as a whole. The Amish increase would be even greater were it not for their steady loss of members, who "emigrate" to the larger secular society.

In any case, the noticeably higher increase in the Amish population results almost exclusively from their higher fertility. Interestingly, the Amish apparently have a higher rate of twin births compared with the general population, suggesting the presence of a distinct genetic factor. Equally interesting is the lower fertility of the Amish compared with the Hutterites. Any superfecundity among the Hutterites might explain part of this difference. But, since the Amish have lower fertility than many other contemporary populations, a significant portion of the difference with the Hutterites must come from the spread of birth-control methods among the Amish.

Their higher fertility compared with that of the United States reflects a continuing influence of their fundamentalist views, but their lower fertility compared with Hutterites reflects the erosion of their large-family ideal. Although Amish couples marry somewhat younger than Hutterites, they produce fewer children per family. The median number of children in an Amish family is 6.7; it is 10.4 among the Hutterites. Yet, Amish doctrine, no less than that of the Hutterites, prohibits contraception and promotes the large-family ideal. Moreover, unlike Hutterites, they reject modern technology. This difference theoretically promotes the need for many farmhands, and these must come from the young. The Amish youth, like his Hutterite counterpart, enters the economic life of his community at about age fifteen.

In relations with the larger society, the Amish have probably been hurt less by population growth than the Hutterites. They have been less of a competitive threat to their neighbors, because their farming methods are less efficient and they do business in the local community rather than through their own communal organization, as Hutterites prefer to do. On the other hand, the simple mode of Amish life undoubtedly restricts the growth of local business, especially in farm equipment and through a wide range of consumer goods.

It is in relation to the internal life of their communities that population growth has undoubtedly been more distressing for the Amish than for the Hutterites. The family basis of Amish economy means that, as population increases, the community must spread geographically. This makes it increasingly difficult for each member to be equally well acquainted with all the others; consequently, those who see each other more often tend to form cliques. Moreover, the young people are forced to move away from the family home and seek new land when the family farm can no longer be subdivided. This development breaks down the positive controls with which kinship maintains conformity. In addition, high fertility increases the proportion of young dependents.

Actually, a population increase only creates pressure for change, and it is the type of community organization that determines the form of change. The small size of the Amish economy unit—the family—has severely restricted adaptability.

Unable to supply all its needs, either from its own resources or those of the Amish community, each family is compelled to operate directly in the larger market. Moreover, refusal to adopt fully modern farm technology restricts productivity and, therefore, family income. In turn, the income has to be spread among family members who include a higher proportion of nonproductive dependents.

Equally significant, the family system involves transmission of property through inheritance. With large numbers of children (an average of three or four sons), the size of an inheritance naturally decreases, providing a smaller income base for the next generation. The average size of an Amish farm has declined from several hundred acres in the eighteenth century to less than fifty acres today.

In turn, smaller home farms compel many unemployed young Amish to seek labor on other farms or in industry. Recent studies in Middlefield, Ohio, reveal that only 47 per cent of the Amish labor force was engaged in full-time agriculture. Employment outside the community exposes the Amish youth to worldly standards and friendships, and to more lucrative modes of livelihood. Even the young person who returns to farming brings an intense awareness of the advantages of modern methods.

It is the formation of cliques, combined with this exposure to outside influences, that generates considerable pressures for change, not only in farming methods but in all other areas of Amish life. This explains why, today, there are several different degrees of departure from standards of the Old Order Amish. In short, adaptation for the Amish has meant a progressive loss of members who have discarded many of the old ways, although many still call themselves Amish.

DOGMA IN A CHANGING WORLD

The story of the Hutterite and Amish offers a number of interesting things for contemporary man to think about. Two seem outstanding.

First, the impact of population on human affairs is dramatically demonstrated. Population movements do not enter human affairs only in the simplified Malthusian manner of too little food and too many people. Rather, the impact of population on human affairs is pre-eminently determined by social organization. For both the Hutterites and Amish, their very high levels of population increase have intensified competition with the larger society they prefer to avoid and have heightened intergroup conflict. Also for both, population increase has violated the primacy of informal, intimate social contact of each with all. This is most clearly seen among today's Amish; many of their people have spread geographically beyond the possibility of regular, daily interaction among all family members.

A similar process operated upon the Hutterites before their American adventure. Today, of course, Hutterites dull the effect of population growth by regularly dividing colonies when cliques arise and tensions become marked. But their conflict with the outside has sprouted the roots of a truly formalized secondary association: They have had to form a national church, with all its undesirable potential for regulation and control. This dynamic effect of population growth on social change seems everywhere unavoidable.

And this leads naturally to the second observation. Man does not live by ideology alone. Despite the rigid and unreflective character of their doctrines, these two groups have experienced fundamental changes in their social organization. It is this unreflective certainty in the rightness of their doctrines—and the blinders they place on the next generation—that blinds both sects to the dynamic causes of their tribulations and their successes. The Hutterites, for instance, do not attribute the successful revival of their life in America to the economic efficiency of corporate farming but to God's pleasure in their devotion. By the same token, they are unlikely to view their uncontrolled fertility as a principal factor in the probable unhappy course of future events. Perhaps they reflect a quite general human failing today: Our conventional ways of thinking no longer provide rational solutions for contemporary problems of human ecology, such as that of population pressure so well illustrated by the Hutterites and Amish.

The Political Dimension of Social Change

Toward a Theory of Revolution*

James C. Davies

In exhorting proletarians of all nations to unite in revolution, because they had nothing to lose but their chains, Marx and Engels most succinctly presented that theory of revolution that is recognized as their brain child. But

* From *American Sociological Review,* vol. 27, no. 1 (February, 1962). Reprinted by permission of The American Sociological Association.

this most famed thesis, that progressive degradation of the industrial working class would finally reach the point of despair and inevitable revolt, is not the only one that Marx fathered. In at least one essay, he gave life to a quite antithetical idea. He described, as a precondition of widespread unrest, not progressive degradation of the proletariat but rather an improvement in workers' economic condition that did not keep pace with the growing welfare of capitalists and, therefore, produced social tension.

> A noticeable increase in wages presupposes a rapid growth of productive capital. The rapid growth of productive capital brings about an equally rapid growth of wealth, luxury, social wants, social enjoyments. Thus, although the enjoyments of the workers have risen, the social satisfaction that they give has fallen in comparison with the increased enjoyments of the capitalist, which are inaccessible to the worker, in comparison with the state of development of society in general. Our desires and pleasures spring from society; we measure them, therefore, by society and not by the objects which serve for their satisfaction. Because they are of a social nature, they are of a relative nature.[1]

Marx's qualification here of his more frequent belief that degradation produces revolution is expressed as the main thesis by de Tocqueville in his study of the French Revolution. After a long review of economic and social decline in the seventeenth century and dynamic growth in the eighteenth, de Tocqueville concludes:

> So it would appear that the French found their condition the more unsupportable in proportion to its improvement. . . . Revolutions are not always brought about by a gradual decline from bad to worse. Nations that have endured patiently and almost unconsciously the most overwhelming oppression often burst into rebellion against the yoke the moment it begins to grow lighter. The regime which is destroyed by a revolution is almost always an improvement on its immediate predecessor. . . . Evils which are patiently endured when they seen inevitable become intolerable when once the idea of escape from them is suggested.[2]

On the basis of de Tocqueville and Marx, we can choose one of these ideas or the other, which makes it hard to decide just when revolutions are more likely to occur—when there has been social and economic progress, or when there has been regress. It appears that both ideas have explanatory

[1] The *Communist Manifesto* of 1848 evidently antedates the opposing idea by about a year. See Edmund Wilson, *To the Finland Station* (Garden City, N.Y.: Doubleday [Anchor Books ed.], n.d.), p. 157; Lewis S. Feuer, *Karl Marx and Friedrich Engels: Basic Writings on Politics and Philosophy,* (Garden City, N.Y.: Doubleday, 1959), p. 1. The above quotation is from Karl Marx and Frederick Engels, "Wage Labor and Capital," *Selected Works in Two Volumes* (Moscow: Foreign Languages Publishing House, 1955), vol. 1, p. 94.

[2] Alexis de Tocqueville, *The Old Regime and the French Revolution,* trans. by John Bonner (New York: Harper & Bros., 1856), p. 214. The Stuart Gilbert translation (Garden City, N.Y.: Doubleday, 1955), pp. 176–77, gives a somewhat less pungent version of the same comment. *L'Ancien régime* was first published in 1856.

and possibly predictive value, if they are juxtaposed and put in the proper time sequence.

Revolutions are most likely to occur when a prolonged period of objective economic and social development is followed by a short period of sharp reversal.[3] The all-important effect on the minds of people in a particular society is to produce, during the former period, an expectation of continued ability to satisfy needs—which continue to rise—and, during the latter, a mental state of anxiety and frustration when manifest reality breaks away from anticipated reality. The actual state of socio-economic development is less significant than the expectation that past progress, now blocked, can and must continue in the future.

Political stability and instability are ultimately dependent on a state of mind, a mood, in a society. Satisfied or apathetic people who are poor in goods, status, and power can remain politically quiet and their opposites can revolt, just as, correlatively and more probably, dissatisfied poor can revolt and satisfied rich oppose revolution. It is the dissatisfied state of mind, rather than the tangible provision of "adequate" or "inadequate" supplies of food, equality, or liberty, that produces the revolution. In actuality, there must be a joining of forces between dissatisfied, frustrated people who differ in their degree of objective, tangible welfare and status. Well-fed, well-educated, high-status individuals who rebel in the face of apathy among the objectively deprived can accomplish, at most, a coup d'état. The objectively deprived, when faced with solid opposition of people of wealth, status, and power, will be smashed in their rebellion as were peasants and Anabaptists by German noblemen in 1525 and East Germans by the Communist elite in 1953.

Before appraising this general notion in light of a series of revolutions, a word is in order as to why revolutions ordinarily do not occur when a society is generally impoverished—when, as de Tocqueville put it, evils that seem inevitable are patiently endured. They are endured in the extreme case because the physical and mental energies of people are totally employed in the process of merely staying alive. The Minnesota starvation studies conducted during World War II[4] indicate clearly the constant preoccupation of very hungry individuals with fantasies and thoughts of food. In extremis, as the Minnesota research poignantly demonstrates, the individual withdraws into a life of his own, withdraws from society, withdraws from any significant kind of activity unrelated to staying alive. Reports of behavior in Nazi concentration camps indicate the same preoccupation.[5] In less extreme and barbarous circumstances, where minimal survival

[3] Revolutions are here defined as violent civil disturbances that cause the displacement of one ruling group by another that has a broader popular basis for support.

[4] The full report is Ancel Keys *et al.*, *The Biology of Human Starvation* (Minneapolis: University of Minnesota Press, 1950). See J. Brozek, "Semi-Starvation and Nutritional Rehabilitation," *Journal of Clinical Nutrition,* 1 (January, 1953), pp. 107–118, for a brief analysis.

[5] E. A. Cohen, *Human Behavior in the Concentration Camp* (New York: W. W. Norton, 1953), pp. 123–25, 131–40.

is possible but little more, the preoccupation of individuals with staying alive is only mitigated. Social action takes place, for the most part, on a local, face-to-face basis. In such circumstances, the family is a—perhaps the major—solidary unit,[6] and even the local community exists primarily to the extent families need to act together to secure their separate survival. Such was life on the American frontier in the sixteenth through nineteenth centuries. In very much attenuated form, but with a substantial degree of social isolation persisting, such evidently is rural life even today. This is clearly related to a relatively low level of political participation in elections.[7] As Zawadzki and Lazarsfeld have indicated,[8] preoccupation with physical survival, even in industrial areas, is a force strongly militating against the establishment of the community-sense and consensus on joint political action that are necessary to induce a revolutionary state of mind. Far from making people into revolutionaries, enduring poverty makes for concern with one's solitary self or solitary family, at best, and resignation or mute despair, at worst. When it is a choice between losing their chains or their lives, people will mostly choose to keep their chains, a fact that Marx seems to have overlooked.[9]

It is when the chains have been loosened somewhat, so that they can be cast off without a high probability of losing life, that people are put in a condition of proto-rebelliousness. I use the term proto-rebelliousness because the mood of discontent may be dissipated before a violent outbreak occurs. The causes for such dissipation may be natural or social (including economic and political). A bad crop year that threatens a return to chronic hunger may be succeeded by a year of natural abundance. Recovery from sharp economic dislocation may take the steam from the boiler of rebellion.[10] The slow, grudging grant of reforms, which has been the political history of England since at least the Industrial Revolution, may effectively and continuously prevent the degree of frustration that produces revolt.

A revolutionary state of mind requires the continued, even habitual, but dynamic expectation of greater opportunity to satisfy basic needs, which may range from merely physical (food, clothing, shelter, health, and safety from bodily harm) to social (the affectional ties of family and friends) to

[6] For community life in such poverty, in Mezzogiorno Italy, see E. C. Banfield, *The Moral Basis of a Backward Society* (Glencoe, Ill.: The Free Press, 1958). The author emphasizes that the nuclear family is a solidary, consensual, moral unit (see p. 85), but, even within it, consensus appears to break down, in outbreaks of pure, individual amorality—notably between parents and children (see p. 117).

[7] See Angus Campbell *et al., The American Voter* (New York: John Wiley & Sons, 1960), chap. 15, "Agarian Political Behavior."

[8] B. Zawadzki and P. F. Lazarsfeld, "The Psychological Consequences of Unemployment," *Journal of Social Psychology,* 6 (May, 1935), pp. 224–51.

[9] A remarkable and awesome exception to this phenomenon occurred occasionally in some Nazi concentration camps—e.g., in a Buchenwald revolt against capricious rule by criminal prisoners. During this revolt, one hundred criminal prisoners were killed by political prisoners. See Cohen, *op. cit.,* p. 200.

[10] See W. W. Rostow, "Business Cycles, Harvests, and Politics: 1790–1850," *Journal of Economic History,* 1 (November, 1941), pp. 206–21, for the relation between economic fluctuation and the activities of the Chartists in the 1830's and 1840's.

the need for equal dignity and justice. But the necessary additional ingredient is a persistent, unrelenting threat to the satisfaction of these needs: not a threat that actually returns people to a state of sheer survival, but which puts them in the mental state where they believe they will not be able to satisfy one or more basic needs. Although physical deprivation in some degree may be threatened on the eve of all revolutions, it need not be the prime factor, as it surely was not in the American Revolution of 1775. The crucial factor is the vague or specific fear that ground gained over a long period of time will be quickly lost. This fear does not generate if there is continued opportunity to satisfy continually emerging needs; it generates when the existing government suppresses, or is blamed for suppressing, such opportunity.

Three rebellions or revolutions are given considerable attention in the sections that follow: Dorr's Rebellion of 1842, the Russian Revolution of 1917, and the Egyptian Revolution of 1952. Brief mention is then made of several other major civil disturbances, all of which appear to fit the J-curve pattern.[11] After considering these specific disturbances, some general theoretical and research problems are discussed.

No claim is made that all rebellions follow the pattern, but just that the ones here presented do. All of these are "progressive" revolutions in behalf of greater equality and liberty. The question is open whether the pattern occurs in such markedly retrogressive revolutions as Nazism in Germany or the 1861 Southern rebellion in the United States. It will surely be necessary to examine other progressive revolutions before one can judge how universal the J-curve is. And it will be necessary, in the interests of scientific validation, to examine cases of serious civil disturbance that fell short of producing profound revolution–such as the Sepoy Rebellion of 1857 in India, the Pullman Strike of 1894 in America, the Boxer Rebellion of 1900 in China, and the Great Depression of the 1920's and 1930's as it was experienced in Austria, France, Great Britain, and the United States. The explanation for such still-born rebellions–for revolutions that might have occurred–is inevitably more complicated than for those that come to term in the "normal" course of political gestation.

DORR'S REBELLION OF 1842

Dorr's Rebellion[12] in nineteenth-century America was perhaps the first of many civil disturbances to occur in America as a consequence, in part, of the Industrial Revolution. It followed by three years an outbreak in Eng-

[11] This curve is, of course, not to be confused with its prior and altogether different use by Floyd Allport in his study of social conformity. See F. H. Allport, "The J-Curve Hypothesis of Conforming Behavior," *Journal of Social Psychology,* 5 (May, 1934), pp. 141–83, reprinted in T. H. Newcomb and E. L. Hartley, *Readings in Social Psychology,* (New York: Henry Holt, 1947), pp. 55–67.

[12] I am indebted to Beryl L. Crowe for his extensive research on Dorr's Rebellion while he was a participant in my political-behavior seminar at the University of California, Berkeley, Spring, 1960.

land that had similar roots and a similar program—the Chartist agitation. A machine-operated textile industry was first established in Rhode Island in 1790 and grew rapidly as a consequence of domestic and international demand, notably during the Napoleonic wars. Jefferson's Embargo Act of 1807, the War of 1812, and a high tariff in 1816 further stimulated American industry.

Rapid industrial growth meant the movement of people from farms to cities. In Massachusetts, the practice developed of hiring mainly the wives and daughters of farmers, whose income was thereby supplemented but not displaced by wages. In Rhode Island, whole families moved to the cities and became committed to the factory system. When times were good, industrialized families earned two or three times what they got from the soil; when the mills were idle, there was not enough money for bread.[13] From 1807 to 1815, textiles enjoyed great prosperity; from 1834 to 1842, they suffered depression, most severely from 1835 to 1840. Prosperity raised expectations and depression frustrated them, particularly when accompanied by stubborn resistance to suffrage demands that first stirred in 1790 and recurred in a wave-like pattern in 1811 and then in 1818 and 1820, following suffrage extension in Connecticut and Massachusetts. The final crest was reached in 1841, when suffrage associations met and called for a constitutional convention.[14]

Against the will of the government, the suffragists held an election in which all adult males were eligible to vote, held a constitutional convention composed of delegates so elected, and, in December, 1841, submitted the People's Constitution to the same electorate, which approved it and the call for an election of state officers the following April, to form a new government under this unconstitutional constitution.[15]

These actions joined the conflict with the established government. When asked—by the dissidents—the state supreme court rendered its private judgment in March, 1842, that the new constitution was "of no binding force whatever," and [that, therefore,] any act "to carry it into effect by force will be treason against the state." The legislature passed what became known as the Algerian law, making it an offense punishable by a year in jail to vote in the April election and by life imprisonment to hold office under the People's Constitution.

[13] Joseph Brennan, *Social Conditions in Industrial Rhode Island: 1820–1860* (Washington, D.C.: Catholic University of America, 1940), p. 33.

[14] The persistent demand for suffrage may be understood in light of election data for 1828 and 1840. In the former year, only 3,600 votes were cast in Rhode Island, whose total population was about 94,000. (Of these votes, 23 per cent were cast for Jackson and 77 per cent for Adams, in contrast to a total national division of 56 per cent for Jackson and 44 per cent for Adams.) All votes cast in the 1828 election amount to 4 per cent of the total Rhode Island population and 11 per cent of the total U.S. population, excluding slaves. In 1840, with a total population of 109,000, only 8,300 votes—8 per cent—were cast in Rhode Island, in contrast to 17 per cent of the national population excluding slaves.

[15] A. M. Mowry, *The Dorr War* (Providence, R.I.: Preston & Rounds, 1901), p. 114.

The rebels went stoutly ahead with the election, and, on May 3, 1842, inaugurated the new government. The next day the People's legislature met and respectfully requested the sheriff to take possession of state buildings, which he failed to do. Violence broke out on the 17th of May in an attempt to take over a state arsenal with two British cannon left over from the Revolutionary War. When the cannon misfired, the People's Government resigned. Sporadic violence continued for another month, resulting in the arrest of over 500 men, mostly textile workers, mechanics, and laborers. The official legislature called for a new constitutional convention, chosen by universal manhood suffrage, and a new constitution went into effect in January, 1843. Altogether, only one person was killed in this little revolution, which experienced violence, failure, and then success within the space of nine months. . . .

THE RUSSIAN REVOLUTION OF 1917

In Russia's tangled history, it is hard to decide when began the final upsurge of expectations that, when frustrated, produced the cataclysmic events of 1917. One can truly say that the real beginning was the slow modernization process begun by Peter the Great over two hundred years before the revolution. And, surely, the rationalist currents from France that slowly penetrated Russian intellectual life during the reign of Catherine the Great a hundred years before the revolution were necessary, lineal antecedents of the 1917 revolution.

Without denying that there was an accumulation of forces over at least a two-hundred-year period,[16] we may nonetheless date the final upsurge as beginning with the 1861 emancipation of serfs and reaching a crest in the 1905 revolution.

The chronic and growing unrest of serfs before their emancipation in 1861 is an ironic commentary on the Marxian notion that human beings are what social institutions make them. Although serfdom had been shaping their personality since 1647, peasants became increasingly restive in the second quarter of the nineteenth century.[17] The continued discontent of peasants after emancipation is an equally ironic commentary on the belief that relieving one profound frustration produces enduring contentment. Peasants rather quickly got over their joy at being untied from the soil after two hundred years. Instead of declining, rural violence increased.[18] Having gained freedom but not much free land, peasants now had to rent or buy land to survive: Virtual personal slavery was exchanged for financial servi-

[16] There is an excellent summary in B. Brutzkus, "The Historical Peculiarities of the Social and Economic Development of Russia," in R. Bendix and S. M. Lipset, *Class, Status, and Power* (Glencoe, Ill.: The Free Press, 1953), pp. 517–40.

[17] Jacqueries rose from an average of 8 per year in 1826–30 to 34 per year in 1845–49. T. G. Masaryk, *The Spirit of Russia* (London: Allen and Unwin, 1919), vol. 1, p. 130. This long, careful, and rather neglected analysis was first published in German in 1913 under the title *Zur Russischen Geschichts– und Religionsphilosophie.*

[18] Jacqueries averaged 350 per year for the first three years after emancipation. *Ibid.*, pp. 140–41.

tude. Land pressure grew, reflected in a doubling of land prices between 1868 and 1897.

It is hard, thus, to tell whether the economic plight of peasants was much lessened after emancipation. A 1903 government study indicated that, even with a normal harvest, average food intake per peasant was 30 per cent below the minimum for health. The only sure contrary item of evidence is that the peasant population grew, indicating, at least, increased ability of the land to support life. . . .

The land-population pressure pushed people into towns and cities, where the rapid growth of industry truly afforded the chance for economic betterment. One estimate of net annual income for a peasant family of five in the rich blackearth area in the late nineteenth century was 82 rubles. In contrast, a "good" wage for a male factory worker was about 168 rubles per year. It was this difference in the degree of poverty that produced almost a doubling of the urban population between 1878 and 1897. The number of industrial workers increased almost as rapidly. The city and the factory gave new hope. Strikes in the 1880's were met with brutal suppression but also with the beginning of factory legislation, including the requirement that wages be paid regularly and the abolition of child labor. The burgeoning proletariat remained comparatively contented until the eve of the 1905 revolution.[19]

There is additional, noneconomic evidence to support the view that 1861–1905 was the period of rising expectations that preceded the 1917 revolution. The administration of justice before the emancipation had largely been carried out by noblemen and landowners, who embodied the law for their peasants. In 1864, justice was, in principle, no longer delegated to such private individuals. Trials became public, the jury system was introduced, and judges got tenure. Corporal punishment was alleviated by the elimination of running the gauntlet, lashing, and branding; caning persisted until 1904. Public joy at these reforms was widespread. For the intelligentsia, there was increased opportunity to think and write and to criticize established institutions, even sacrosanct absolutism itself.

But Tsarist autocracy had not quite abandoned the scene. Having inclined, but not bowed, in granting the inevitable emancipation as an act not of justice but grace, it sought to maintain its absolutist principle by conceding reform without accepting anything like democratic authority. Radical political and economic criticism surged higher. Some strong efforts to raise the somewhat lowered floodgates began as early as 1866, after an unsuccessful attempt was made on the life of Alexander II, in whose name serfs had just gained emancipation. When the attempt succeeded fifteen

[19] The proportion of workers who struck from 1895 through 1902 varied between 1.7 per cent and 4.0 per cent per year. In 1903 the proportion rose to 5.1 per cent but dropped a year later to 1.5 per cent. In 1905 the proportion rose to 163.8 per cent, indicating that the total working force struck, on the average, closer to twice than to once during that portentous year. In 1906 the proportion dropped to 65.8 per cent; in 1907 to 41.9 per cent; and by 1909 was down to a "normal" 3.5 per cent. *Ibid.*, p. 175n.

years later, there was increasing state action under Alexander III to limit constantly rising expectations. By suppression and concession, the last Alexander succeeded in dying naturally in 1894.

When it became apparent that Nicholas II shared his father's ideas but not his forcefulness, opposition of the intelligentsia to absolutism joined with the demands of peasants and workers, who remained loyal to the Tsar but demanded economic reforms. Starting in 1904, there developed a "League of Deliverance" that coordinated efforts of at least seventeen other revolutionary, proletarian, or nationalist groups within the empire. Consensus on the need for drastic reform, both political and economic, established a many-ringed circus of groups sharing the same tent. These groups were geographically distributed from Finland to Armenia and ideologically from liberal constitutionalists to revolutionaries made prudent by the contrast between their own small forces and the power of Tsardom.

Events of 1904–5 mark the general downward turning point of expectations, which people increasingly saw as frustrated by the continuation of Tsardom. Two major and related occurrences made 1905 the point of no return. The first took place on the Bloody Sunday of January 22, 1905, when peaceful proletarian petitioners marched on the St. Petersburg palace and were killed by the hundreds. The myth that the Tsar was the gracious protector of his subjects, however surrounded he might be by malicious advisers, was quite shattered. The reaction was immediate, bitter, and prolonged and was not at all confined to the working class. Employers, merchants, and white-collar officials joined in the burgeoning of strikes that brought the economy to a virtual standstill in October. Some employers even continued to pay wages to strikers. University students and faculties joined the revolution. After the great October strike, the peasants ominously sided with the workers and engaged in riots and assaults on landowners. Until peasants became involved, even some landowners had sided with the revolution.

The other major occurrence was the disastrous defeat of the Russian Army and Navy in the 1904–5 war with Japan. Fundamentally an imperialist venture aspiring to hegemony over the people of Asia, the war was not regarded as a people's but as a Tsar's war, to save and spread absolutism. The military defeat itself probably had less portent than the return of shattered soldiers from a fight that was not for them. Hundreds of thousands, wounded or not, returned from the war as a visible, vocal, and ugly reminder to the entire populace of the weakness and selfishness of Tsarist absolutism.

The years from 1905 to 1917 formed an almost relentless procession of increasing misery and despair. Promising, at last, a constitutional government, the Tsar, in October, 1905, issued from on high a proclamation renouncing absolutism, granting law-making power to a duma, and guaranteeing freedom of speech, assembly, and association. The first two dumas, of 1906 and 1907, were dissolved for recalcitrance. The third was made pliant by reduced representation of workers and peasants and by the prosecution and conviction of protestants in the first two. The brief period of a free press was succeeded in 1907 by a reinstatement of censorship and confiscation of prohibited publications. Trial of offenders against the Tsar was now conducted by courts-martial. Whereas there had been only 26 executions of the death sentence, in the thirteen years of Alexander II's firm rule (1881–94), there were 4,449 in the years 1905–10, in six years of Nicholas II's soft regimen.[20]

But this "white terror," which caused despair among the workers and intelligentsia in the cities, was not the only face of misery. For the peasants, there was a bad harvest in 1906, followed by continued crop failures in several areas in 1907. To forestall action by the dumas, [Premier] Stolypin decreed a series of agrarian reforms designed to break up the power of the rural communes by individualizing land ownership. Between these acts of God and government, peasants were so preoccupied with hunger or self-aggrandizement as to be dulled in their sensitivity to the revolutionary appeals of radical organizers.

After more than five years of degrading terror and misery, in 1910 the country appeared to have reached a condition of exhaustion. Political strikes had fallen off to a new low. As the economy recovered, the insouciance of hopelessness set in. Amongst the intelligentsia, the mood was hedonism or despair that often ended in suicide. Industrialists aligned themselves with the government. Workers worked. But an upturn of expectations, inadequately quashed by the police, was evidenced by a recrudescence of political strikes that, in the first half of 1914—on the eve of war—approached the peak of 1905. They sharply diminished during 1915 but grew again in 1916 and became a general strike in February, 1917.[21]

. . . The final . . . [event leading to revolution], after the first year of war, was a consequence of the dislocations of the German attack [World War I] on all kinds of concerted activities other than production for the prosecution of the war. Patriotism and governmental repression for a time smothered discontent. The inflation that developed in 1916 when goods, including food, became severely scarce began to make workers self-consciously discontented. The conduct of the war, including the growing brutality against reluctant, ill-provisioned troops, and the enormous loss of life, produced the same bitter frustration in the army.[22] When civilian discontent reached the breaking point in February, 1917, it did not take long for it to spread rapidly into the armed forces. Thus began the second phase of the revolution [which] started in 1905 and ended in death to the Tsar and Tsar-

[20] *Ibid.*, p. 189*n*.

[21] In his *History of the Russian Revolution,* Leon Trotsky presents data on political strikes from 1903 to 1917. In his *Spirit of Russia,* Masaryk presents comparable data from 1905 through 1912. The figures are not identical, but the reported yearly trends are consistent. Masaryk's figures are somewhat lower, except for 1912. Cf. Trotsky, *op. cit.,* (Doubleday Anchor Books ed., 1959), p. 32, and Masaryk, *op. cit., supra,* p. 197*n*.

[22] See Trotsky, *op. cit.,* pp. 18–21, for a vivid picture of rising discontent in the army.

dom—but not to absolutism—when the Bolsheviks gained ascendancy over the moderates in October. A centuries-long history of absolutism appears to have made this post-Tsarist phase of it tragically inevitable.

THE EGYPTIAN REVOLUTION OF 1952

The final slow upsurge of expectations in Egypt that culminated in the revolution began when the society became a nation in 1922, with the British grant of limited independence. British troops remained in Egypt not only to protect the Suez Canal but also, ostensibly, to prevent foreign aggression. The presence of foreign troops served only to heighten nationalist expectations, which were excited by the Wafd, the political organization that formed public opinion on national rather than religious grounds and helped establish a fairly unified community—in striking contrast to late-nineteenth century Russia.

But nationalist aspirations were not the only rising expectations in Egypt of the 1920's and 1930's. World War I had spurred industrialization, which opened opportunities for peasants to improve, somewhat, their way of life by working for wages in the cities and also opened great opportunities for entrepreneurs to get rich. The moderately wealthy got immoderately so in commodity market speculation, finance, and manufacture, and the uprooted peasants who were now employed, or at any rate living, in cities were relieved of at least the notion that poverty and boredom must be the will of Allah. But the incongruity of a money-based modern semifeudality that was like a chariot with a gasoline engine evidently escaped the attention of ordinary people. The generation of the 1930's could see more rapid progress, even for themselves, than their parents had even envisioned. If conditions remained poor, they could always be blamed on the British, whose economic and military power remained visible and strong.

Economic progress continued, though unevenly, during World War II. Conventional exports, mostly cotton, actually declined, not even reaching depression levels until 1945, but direct employment by Allied military forces reached a peak of over 200,000 during the most intense part of the African war. Exports after the war rose steadily until 1948, dipped, and then rose sharply to a peak in 1951 as a consequence of the Korean war. But, in 1945, over 250,000 wage earners[23]—probably over a third of the working force—became jobless. The cost of living by 1945 had risen to three times the index of 1937.[24] Manual laborers were hit by unemployment; white-collar workers and professionals, probably more by inflation

[23] C. Issawi, *Egypt at Mid-Century: An Economic Survey* (London: Oxford University Press, 1954), p. 262. J. and S. Lacouture in their *Egypt in Transition* (New York: Criterion Books, 1958), p. 100, give a figure of over 300,000. Sir R. Bullard, (ed.), *The Middle East: A Political and Economic Survey* (London: Oxford University Press, 1958), p. 221, estimates total employment in industry, transport, and commerce in 1957 to have been about 750,000.

[24] International Monetary Fund, *International Financial Statistics* (Washington, D.C.). See monthly issues of this report, 1950–53.

than unemployment. Meanwhile, the number of millionaires in pounds sterling had increased eight times during the war.[25]

Frustrations, exacerbated during the war by German and thereafter by Soviet propaganda, were at first deflected against the British[26] but gradually shifted closer to home. Egyptian agitators began quoting the Koran in favor of a just, equalitarian society and against great differences in individual wealth. There was an ominous series of strikes, mostly in the textile mills, from 1946 to 1948.

At least two factors stand out in the postponement of revolution. The first was the insatiable postwar world demand for cotton and textiles, and the second was the surge of solidarity with king and country that followed the 1948 invasion of the new state of Israel. Israel now supplemented England as an object of deflected frustration. The disastrous defeat a year later, by a new nation with but a fifteenth of Egypt's population, was the beginning of the end. This little war had struck the peasant at his hearth, when a shortage of wheat and of oil for stoves provided a daily reminder of a weak and corrupt government. The defeat frustrated popular hopes for national glory and–with even more portent–humiliated the army and solidified it against the bureaucracy and the palace, which had profiteered at the expense of national honor. In 1950 began, for the first time, a direct and open propaganda attack against the king himself. A series of peasant uprisings, even on the lands of the king, took place in 1951, along with some forty-nine strikes in the cities. The skyrocketing demand for cotton after the start of the Korean war in June, 1950, was followed by a collapse in March, 1952. The uncontrollable or uncontrolled riots in Cairo, on January 26, 1952, marked the fiery start of the revolution. The officers' coup in the early morning of July 23 only made it official.

* * *

SOME CONCLUSIONS

The notion that revolutions need both a period of rising expectations and a succeeding period in which they are frustrated qualifies substantially the main Marxian notion that revolutions occur after progressive degradation and the de Tocqueville notion that they occur when conditions are improving. By putting de Tocqueville before Marx, but without abandoning either theory, we are better able to plot the antecedents of at least the disturbances here described.

Half of the general, if not common, sense of this revised notion lies in the utter improbability of a revolution occurring in a society where there is the continued, unimpeded opportunity to satisfy new needs, new hopes, new expectations. Would Dorr's rebellion have become such if the estab-

[25] J. and S. Lacouture, *op. cit.*, p. 99.

[26] England threatened to depose Farouk in February, 1942, by force if necessary, if Egypt did not support the Allies. Capitulation by the government and the Wafd caused widespread popular disaffection. When Egypt finally declared war on the Axis in 1945, the prime minister was assassinated. See J. and S. Lacouture, *op. cit.*, pp. 97–98, and Issawi, *op. cit.*, p. 268.

lished electorate and government had readily acceded to the suffrage demands of the unpropertied? Would the Russian Revolution have taken place if the Tsarist autocracy had, quite out of character, truly granted the popular demands for constitutional democracy in 1905? Would the Cairo riots of January, 1952, and the subsequent coup actually have occurred if Britain had departed from Egypt, and if the Egyptian monarchy had established an equitable tax system and in other ways alleviated the poverty of urban masses and the shame of the military?

The other half of the sense of the notion has to do with the improbability of revolution taking place where there has been no hope, no period in which expectations have risen. Such a stability of expectations presupposes a static state of human aspirations that sometimes exists but is rare. Stability of expectations is not a stable social condition. Such was the case of American Indians (at least from our perspective) and perhaps Africans before white men with Bibles, guns, and other goods interrupted the stability of African society. Egypt was in such a condition, vis-à-vis modern aspiration, before Europe became interested in building a canal. Such stasis was the case in Nazi concentration camps, where conformism reached the point of inmates cooperating with guards even when the inmates were told to lie down so that they could be shot.[27] But, in the [last] case, there was a society with externally induced complete despair, and even in these camps there were occasional rebellions of sheer desperation. It is, of course, true that, in a society less regimented than concentration camps, the rise of expectations can be frustrated successfully, thereby defeating rebellion just as the satisfaction of expectations does. This, however, requires the uninhibited exercise of brute force as it was used in suppressing the Hungarian rebellion of 1956. Failing the continued ability and persistent will of a ruling power to use such force, there appears to be no sure way to avoid revolution short of an effective, affirmative, and continuous response on the part of established governments to the almost continuously emerging needs of the governed.

To be predictive, my notion requires the assessment of the state of mind —or, more precisely, the mood—of a people. This is always difficult, even by techniques of systematic public-opinion analysis. Respondents interviewed in a country with a repressive government are not likely to be responsive. But there has been considerable progress in gathering firsthand data about the state of mind of peoples in politically unstable circumstances. One instance of this involved interviewing in West Berlin, during and after the 1948 blockade, as reported by Buchanan and Cantril. They were able to ascertain, however crudely, the sense of security that people in Berlin felt. There was a significant increase in security after the blockade.[28]

[27] Eugen Kogon, *The Theory and Practice of Hell* (New York: Farrar, Straus, 1950), pp. 284–86.

[28] W. Buchanan, "Mass Communication in Reverse," *International Social Science Bulletin,* 5 (1953), pp. 577–83, at p. 578. The full study is W. Buchanan and H. Cantril, *How Nations See Each Other* (Urbana: University of Illinois Press, 1953), esp. pp. 85–90.

Another instance comes out of the Middle Eastern study conducted by the Columbia University Bureau of Applied Social Research and reported by Lerner.[29] By directly asking respondents whether they were happy or unhappy with the way things had turned out in their life, the interviewers turned up data indicating marked differences in the frequency of a sense of unhappiness between countries and between "traditional," "transitional," and "modern" individuals in these countries.[30] There is no technical reason why such comparisons could not be made chronologically as well as they have been geographically.

Other than interview data are available with which we can, from past experience, make reasonable inferences about the mood of a people. It was surely the sense for the relevance of such data that led Thomas Masaryk, before World War I, to gather facts about peasant uprisings and industrial strikes and about the writings and actions of the intelligentsia in nineteenth-century Russia. In the present report, I have used not only such data—in the collection of which other social scientists have been less assiduous than Masaryk—but also such indexes as comparative size of vote as between Rhode Island and the United States, employment, exports, and cost of living. Some such indexes, like strikes and cost of living, may be rather closely related to the mood of a people; others, like value of exports, are much cruder indications. Lest we shy away from the gathering of crude data, we should bear in mind that Durkheim developed his remarkable insights into modern society, in large part, by his analysis of suicide rates. He was unable to rely on the interviewing technique. We need not always ask people whether they are grievously frustrated by their government; their actions can tell us as well and sometimes better.

In his *Anatomy of Revolution,* Crane Brinton describes "some tentative uniformities" that he discovered in the Puritan, American, French, and Russian revolutions.[31] The uniformities were: an economically advancing society, class antagonism, desertion of intellectuals, inefficient government, a ruling class that has lost self-confidence, financial failure of government, and the inept use of force against rebels. All but the last two of these are long-range phenomena that lend themselves to studies over extended time periods. The first two lend themselves to statistical analysis. If they serve the purpose, techniques of content analysis could be used to ascertain trends in alienation of intellectuals. Less rigorous methods would perhaps serve better to ascertain the effectiveness of government and the self-confidence of rulers. Because tensions and frustrations are present at all times in every society, what is most seriously needed [is] data that cover an extended time period in a particular society, so that one can say there is

[29] Daniel Lerner, *The Passing of Traditional Society* (Glencoe, Ill.: The Free Press, 1958).

[30] *Ibid.,* pp. 101–103. See also F. P. Kilpatrick and H. Cantril, "Self-Anchoring Scaling: A Measure of Individuals' Unique Reality Words," *Journal of Individual Psychology,* 16 (November, 1960), pp. 158–73.

[31] See the revised edition of 1952, as reprinted by Vintage Books (1957), pp. 264–75.

evidence that tension is greater or less than it was *n* years or months previously.

We need also to know how long is a long cycle of rising expectations and how long is a brief cycle of frustration. We noted a brief period of frustration in Russia after the 1881 assassination of Alexander II and a longer period after the 1904 beginning of the Russo-Japanese War. Why did not the revolution occur at either of these times rather than in 1917? Had expectations before these two times not risen high enough? Had the subsequent decline not been sufficiently sharp and deep? Measuring techniques have not yet been devised to answer these questions. But their unavailability now does not forecast their eternal inaccessibility. Physicists devised useful temperature scales long before they came as close to absolute zero as they have recently in laboratory conditions. The far more complex problems of scaling in social science inescapably are harder to solve.

We therefore are still not at the point of being able to predict revolution, but the closer we can get to data indicating by inference the prevailing mood in a society, the closer we will be to understanding the change from gratification to frustration in people's minds. That is the part of the anatomy, we are forever being told with truth and futility, in which wars and revolutions always start. We should eventually be able to escape the embarrassment that may have come to Lenin six weeks after he made the statement in Switzerland, in January, 1917, that he doubted whether "we, the old, [will] live to see the decisive battles of the coming revolution."[32]

[32] Quoted in E. H. Carr, *A History of Soviet Russia,* vol. 1, *The Bolshevik Revolution: 1917–23* (London: Macmillan, 1950), p. 69.

Post-industrial Society: Its Future Prospects

Focus on the Flower Children: Why All of Us May Be Hippies Someday*

Fred Davis

> And thus in love we have declared the purpose of our hearts plainly, without flatterie, expecting love, and the same sincerity from you, without grumbling, or quarreling, being Creatures of your own image and mould, intending no other matter herein, but to observe the Law of righteous action, endeavoring to shut out of the Creation, the cursed thing, called Particular Propriety,

which is the cause of all wars, bloud-shed, theft, and enslaving Laws, that hold the people under miserie.

Signed for and in behalf of all the poor oppressed people of England, and the whole world.

—Gerrard Winstanley and others
June 1, 1649

This quotation is from the leader of the Diggers, a millenarian sect of communistic persuasion that arose in England at the time of Oliver Cromwell. Today, in San Francisco's hippie community, the Haight-Ashbury district, a group of hippies naming themselves after this sect distributes free food to fellow hippies (and all other takers, for that matter) who congregate at about four o'clock every afternoon in the district's Panhandle, an eight-block strip of urban green, shaded by towering eucalyptus trees, that leads into Golden Gate Park to the west. On the corner of a nearby street, the "Hashbury" Diggers operate their Free Store, where all—be they hip, straight, hostile, curious, or merely in need—can avail themselves (free of charge, no questions asked) of such used clothing, household articles, books, and secondhand furniture as find their way into the place on any particular day. The Diggers also maintained a large flat in the district, where newly arrived or freshly dispossessed hippies could stay without charge for a night, a week, or however long they wished—until some months ago, when the flat was condemned by the San Francisco Health Department. Currently, the Diggers are rehabilitating a condemned skid-row hotel for the same purpose.

Not all of Haight-Ashbury's 7,500 hippies are Diggers, although no formal qualifications bar them; nor, in one sense, are the several dozen Diggers hippies. What distinguishes the Diggers—an amorphous, shifting, and sometimes contentious amalgam of ex-political radicals, psychedelic mystics, Ghandians, and Brechtian avant-garde thespians—from the area's "ordinary" hippies is their ideological brio, articulateness, good works, and flair for the dramatic event. (Some are even rumored to be over thirty.) In the eyes of many Hashbury hippies, therefore, the Diggers symbolize what is best, what is most persuasive and purposive, about the surrounding, more variegated hippie subculture—just as, for certain radical social critics of the American scene, the hippies are expressing, albeit elliptically, what is best about a seemingly ever broader segment of American youth: its openness to new experience, puncturing of cant, rejection of bureaucratic regimentation, aversion to violence, and identification with the exploited and disadvantaged. That this is not the whole story barely needs saying. Along with the poetry and flowers, the melancholy smile at passing and ecstatic clasp at greeting, there is also the panicky incoherence of the bad LSD trip, the malnutrition, a startling rise in VD and hepatitis, a seemingly phobic reaction to elementary practices of hygiene and sanitation, and—perhaps most disturbing in the long run—a casualness about the comings and goings of human relationships that must verge on the grossly irresponsible.

But, then, social movements—particularly of this expressive-religious variety—are rarely of a piece, and it would be unfortunate if social scientists, rather than inquiring into the genesis, meaning, and future of the hippie movement, too soon joined ranks (as many are likely to, in any case) with solid burghers in an orgy of research into the "pathology" of it all: the ubiquitous drug use (mainly marihuana and LSD, often amphetamines, rarely heroin or other opiates), the easy attitudes toward sex ("If two people are attracted to each other, what better way of showing it than to make love?"), and the mocking hostility toward the middle-class values of pleasure-deferral, material success, and—ultimately—the whole mass-media–glamorized round of chic, deodorized, appliance-glutted suburban existence.

THE HIP SCENE IS THE MESSAGE

Clearly, despite whatever real or imagined "pathology" middle-class spokesmen are ready to assign to the hippies, it is the middle-class scheme of life that young hippies are reacting against, even though in their ranks are to be found some youth of working-class origin who have never enjoyed the affluence that their peers now so heartily decry. To adulterate somewhat the slogan of Marshall McLuhan—one of the few nonorientalized intellectuals whom hippies bother to read at all—*the hip scene is the message,* not the elements whence it derives or the meanings that can be assigned to it verbally. (Interestingly, this fusion of disparate classes does not appear to include any significant number of the Negro youths who reside with their families in the integrated Haight-Ashbury district or in the adjoining Negro ghetto, the Fillmore district. By and large, Negroes view with bewilderment and ridicule the white hippies who flaunt, to the extent of begging on the streets, their rejection of what the Negroes have had scant opportunity to attain. What more revealing symbol of the Negro riots in our nation's cities than the carting off of looted TV sets, refrigerators, and washing machines? After all, aren't these things what America is all about?)

But granting that the hippie scene is a reaction to middle-class values, can the understanding of any social movement—particularly one that just in the process of its formation is so fecund of new art forms, new styles of dress and demeanor, and (most of all) new ethical bases for human relationships—ever be wholly reduced to its reactive aspect? As Ralph Ellison has eloquently observed in his critique of the standard sociological explanation of the American Negro's situation, a people's distinctive way of life is never solely a reaction to the dominant social forces that have oppressed, excluded, or alienated them from the larger society. The cumulative process of reaction and counterreaction, in its historical unfolding, creates its own ground for the emergence of new symbols, meanings, purposes, and social discoveries, none of which are ever wholly contained in embryo, as it were, in the conditions that elicited the reaction. It is, therefore, less with an eye toward explaining "how it came to be" than toward explaining what it may betoken of life in the future society that I now want to examine certain facets of the Hashbury hippie subculture. (Of course, very similar youth movements, subcultures, and settlements are found nowadays in many parts of the affluent Western world—Berkeley's Telegraph Avenue teeny-boppers; Los Angeles' Sunset Strippers; New York's East Village hippies; London's mods; Amsterdam's Provos; and the summer *Wandervögel* from all over Europe who chalk the pavement of Copenhagen's main shopping street, the Strøget, and sun themselves on the steps of Stockholm's Philharmonic Hall. What is culturally significant about the Haight-Ashbury hippies is, I would hazard, in general significant about these others as well, with—to be sure—certain qualifications. Indeed, a certain marvelous irony attaches itself to the fact that perhaps the only genuine cross-national culture found in the world today builds on the rag-tag of beards, bare feet, bedrolls, and beads, not on the cultural-exchange programs of governments and universities, or tourism, or—least of all—ladies' clubs' invocations for sympathetic understanding of one's foreign neighbors.)

What I wish to suggest here is that there is, as Max Weber would have put it, an *elective affinity* between prominent styles and themes in the hippie subculture and certain incipient problems of identity, work, and leisure that loom ominously as Western industrial society moves into an epoch of accelerated cybernation, staggering material abundance, and historically unprecedented mass opportunities for creative leisure and enrichment of the human personality. This is not to say that the latter are the *hidden causes* or tangible *motivating forces* of the former. Rather, the point is that the hippies, in their collective, yet radical, break with the constraints of our present society, are—whether they know it or not (some clearly do intuit a connection)—already rehearsing *in vivo* a number of possible cultural solutions to central life problems posed by the emerging society of the future. While other students of contemporary youth culture could no doubt cite many additional emerging problems to which the hippie subculture is, willy-nilly, addressing itself (marriage and family organization, the character of friendship and personal loyalties, the forms of political participation), space and the kinds of observations I have been able to make require that I confine myself to three: the problems of *compulsive consumption,* of *passive spectatorship,* and of the *time-scale of experience.*

COMPULSIVE CONSUMPTION

What working attitude is man to adopt toward the potential glut of consumer goods that the new technology will make available to virtually all members of the future society? Until now, modern capitalist society's traditional response to short-term conditions of overproduction has been to generate—through government manipulation of fiscal devices—greater purchasing power for discretionary consumption. At the same time, the aim has been to cultivate the acquisitive impulse—largely through mass advertising, annual styling changes, and planned obsolescence—so that, in the economist's terminology, a high level of aggregate demand could be sustained.

Fortunately, given the great backlog of old material wants and the technologically based creation of new wants, these means have, for the most part, worked comparatively well–both for advancing (albeit unequally) the mass standard of living and ensuring a reasonably high rate of return to capital.

But, as Walter Weisskopf, Robert Heilbroner, and other economists have wondered, will these means prove adequate for an automated future society in which the mere production of goods and services might easily outstrip man's desire for them or his capacity to consume them in satisfying ways? Massive problems of air pollution, traffic congestion, and waste disposal aside, is there no psychological limit to the number of automobiles, TV sets, freezers, and dishwashers that even a zealous consumer can aspire to, much less make psychic room for in his life space? The specter that haunts postindustrial man is that of a near worker-less economy in which most men are constrained, through a variety of economic and political sanctions, to frantically purchase and assiduously use up the cornucopia of consumer goods that a robot-staffed factory system (but one still harnessed to capitalism's rationale of pecuniary profit) regurgitates upon the populace. As far back as the late 1940's, sociologists like David Riesman were already pointing to the many moral paradoxes of work, leisure, and interpersonal relations posed by a then only nascent society of capitalist mass abundance. How much more perplexing the paradoxes if, using current technological trends, we extrapolate to the year 2000?

Hippies, originating mainly in the middle classes, have been nurtured at the boards of consumer abundance. Spared their parents' vivid memories of economic depression and material want, however, they now, with what to their elders seems like insulting abandon, declare unshamefacedly that the very quest for "the good things of life" and all that this entails–the latest model, the third car, the monthly credit payments, the right house in the right neighborhood–are a "bad bag." In phrases redolent of nearly all utopian thought of the past, they proclaim that happiness and a meaningful life are not to be found in things but in the cultivation of the self and by an intensive exploration of inner sensibilities with likeminded others.

Extreme as this antimaterialistic stance may seem, and despite its probable tempering should hippie communities develop as a stable feature on the American landscape, it nonetheless points a way to a solution of the problem of material glut; to wit, the simple demonstration of the ability to live on less, thereby calming the acquisitive frenzy that would have to be sustained, and even accelerated, if the present scheme of capitalist production and distribution were to remain unchanged. Besides such establishments as the Diggers' Free Store, gleanings of this attitude are even evident in the street panhandling that so many hippies engage in. Unlike the street beggars of old, there is little that is obsequious or deferential about their manner. On the contrary, their approach is one of easy, sometimes condescending casualness, as if to say, "You've got more than enough to spare; I need it; so let's not make a degrading charity scene out of my asking you." The story is told in the Haight-Ashbury of the patronizing tourist who, upon being approached for a dime by a hippie girl in her late teens, took the occasion to deliver a small speech on how delighted he would be to give it to her—provided she first told him what she needed it for. Without blinking an eye, she replied, "It's my menstrual period, and that's how much a sanitary napkin costs."

PASSIVE SPECTATORSHIP

As social historians are forever reminding us, modern man has—since the beginnings of the industrial revolution—become increasingly a spectator and less a participant. Less and less does he, for example, create or play music, engage in sports, dance, or sing; instead, he watches professionally trained others, vastly more accomplished than himself, perform their acts, while he, perhaps, indulges in Mitty-like fantasies of hidden graces and talents. Although this bald statement of the spectator thesis has been challenged in recent years by certain social researchers—statistics are cited of the growing numbers taking guitar lessons, buying fishing equipment, and painting on Sunday—there can be little doubt that "doing" kinds of expressive pursuits, particularly of the collective type, no longer bear the same *integral* relationship to daily life that they once did, or still do in primitive societies. The mere change in how they come to be perceived, from what one does in the ordinary course of life to one's "hobbies," is in itself of profound historical significance. Along with this, the virtuoso standards that once were the exclusive property of small aristocratic elites, rather than being undermined by the oft-cited revolutions in mass communications and mass education, have so diffused through the class structure as to even cause the gifted amateur *at play* to apologize for his efforts with some such remark as, "I only play at it." In short, the cult of professionalism, in the arts as elsewhere, has been institutionalized so intensively in Western society that the ordinary man's sense of expressive adequacy and competence has progressively atrophied. This is especially true of the college-educated, urban middle classes, which—newly exposed to the lofty aesthetic standards of high culture—stand in reverent, if passive, awe of them.

Again, the problem of excessive spectatorship has not proved particularly acute until now, inasmuch as most men have had other time-consuming demands to fill their lives with, chiefly work and family life, leavened by occasional vacations and mass-produced amusements. But what of the future, when, according to such social prognosticators as Robert Theobald and Donald Michael, all (except a relatively small cadre of professionals and managers) will be faced with a surfeit of leisure time? Will the mere extension of passive spectatorship and the professional's monopoly of expressive pursuits be a satisfactory solution?

Here, too, hippies are opening up new avenues of collective response to life issues posed by a changing sociotechnological environment. They are doing so by rejecting those virtuoso standards that stifle participation in high culture; by substituting an extravagantly eclectic (and, according to traditional aestheticians, reckless) admixture of materials, styles, and motifs from a great diversity of past and present human cultures; and, most of all, by insisting that every man can find immediate expressive fulfillment, provided he lets the socially suppressed spirit within him ascend into vibrant consciousness. The manifesto is: "All men are artists–and who cares that some are better at it than others? We can all have fun!" Hence the deceptively crude antisophistication of hippie art forms, which are, perhaps, only an apparent reversion to primitivism. One has only to encounter the lurid *art nouveau* contortions of the hippie posters and their Beardsleyan exoticism, or the mad mélange of hippie street costume–Greek-sandaled feet peeking beneath harem pantaloons encased in a fringed American Indian suede jacket, topped by pastel floral decorations about the face–or the sitar-whining cacophony of the folk-rock band, to know immediately that one is in the presence of *expressiveness* for its own sake.

In more mundane ways, too, the same readiness to let go, to participate, to create and perform without script or forethought is everywhere evident in the Hashbury. Two youths seat themselves on the sidewalk or in a store entranceway; bent beer can in hand, one begins scratching a bongo-like rhythm on the pavement, while the other tattoos a bell-like accompaniment by striking a stick on an empty bottle. Soon, they are joined, one by one, by a tambourinist, a harmonica player, a penny-whistler or recorder player, and, of course, the ubiquitous guitarist. A small crowd collects, and, at the fringes, some blanket-bedecked boys and girls begin twirling about in movements vaguely resembling a Hindu dance. The wailing, rhythmic beating and dancing, alternately rising to peaks of intensity and subsiding, may last for as little as five minutes or as long as an hour, players and dancers joining in and dropping out as whim moves them. At some point–almost any–a mood takes hold that "the happening is over"; participants and onlookers disperse as casually as they had collected.

Analogous scenes of "participation unbound" are to be observed almost every night of the week (twice on Sunday) at the hippies' Parnassus, the Fillmore Auditorium, where a succession of name folk-rock bands, each more deafening than the one before, follow one another in hour-long sessions. Here, amidst the electric guitars, the electric organs, and the constantly metamorphizing show of lights, one can see the gainly and the graceless, the sylph bodies and rude stompers, the crooked and straight–all, of whatever condition or talent, *dance* as the flickering of a strobe light reduces their figures in silhouette to egalitarian spastic bursts. The recognition dawns that this, at last, is dancing of utterly free form, devoid of fixed sequence or step, open to all and calling for no Friday after-school classes at Miss Martha's or expensive lessons from Arthur Murray. The sole requisite is to tune in, take heart, and let go. What follows must be "beautiful" (a favorite hippie word), because it is *you* who are doing and feeling, not another to whom you have surrendered the muse.

As with folk-rock dancing, so (theoretically, at least) with music, poetry, painting, pottery, and the other arts and crafts: expression over performance, impulse over product. Whether the "straight world" will, in time, heed this message of the hippies is, to be sure, problematical. Also, given the lavish financial rewards and prestige heaped upon more talented hippie artists by a youth-dominated entertainment market, it is conceivable that high standards of professional performance will develop here as well (listen to the more recent Beatles' recordings), thus engendering perhaps as great a participative gulf between artist and audience as already exists in the established arts. Despite the vagaries of forecasting, however, the hippies—as of now, at least—are responding to the incipient plenitude of leisure in ways far removed from the baleful visions of a Huxley or an Orwell.

THE TIME-SCALE OF EXPERIENCE

In every society, certain activities are required to complete various tasks and to achieve various goals. These activities form a sequence—they may be of short duration and simple linkage (boiling an egg); long duration and complex linkage (preparing for a profession); or a variety of intermediate combinations (planting and harvesting a crop). And the activity sequences needed to complete valued tasks and to achieve valued goals in a society largely determine how the people in that society will subjectively experience *time*.

The distinctive temporal bent of industrial society has been toward the second of these arrangements—long duration and complex linkage. As regards the subjective experience of time, this has meant what the anthropologist Florence Kluckhohn has termed a strong "future orientation" on the part of Western man, a quality of sensibility that radically distinguishes him from his peasant and tribal forebears. The major activities that fill the better part of his life acquire their meaning less from the pleasure they may or may not give at the moment than from their perceived relevance to some imagined future state of being or affairs, be it salvation, career achievement, material success, or the realization of a more perfect social order. Deprived of the pursuit of these temporally distant, complexly modulated goals, we would feel that life, as the man in the street puts it, is without meaning.

This subjective conception of time and experience is, of course, admirably suited to the needs of post–eighteenth-century industrial society, needs that include a stable labor force; work discipline; slow and regular accumulation of capital with which to plan and launch new investments and to expand; and long, arduous years of training to provide certain people with the high levels of skill necessary in so many professions and technical fields. If Western man had proved unable to defer present gratifications for future rewards (that is, if he had not been a future-oriented being), nothing resembling our present civilization, as Freud noted, could have come to pass.

Yet, paradoxically, it is the advanced technology of computers and servomechanisms, not to overlook nuclear warfare, that industrial civilization has carried us to that is raising grave doubts concerning this temporal ordering of affairs, this optimistic, pleasure-deferring, and magically rationalistic faith in converting present effort to future payoff. Why prepare, if there will be so few satisfying jobs to prepare for? Why defer, if there will be a superabundance of inexpensively produced goods to choose from? Why plan, if all plans can disintegrate into nuclear dust?

Premature or exaggerated as these questions may seem, they are being asked, especially by young people. And merely to ask them is to prompt a radical shift in time-perspective—from what *will be* to what *is,* from future promise to present fulfillment, from the mundane discounting of present feeling and mood to a sharpened awareness of their contours and their possibilities for instant alteration. Broadly, it is to invest present experience with a new cognitive status and importance: a lust to extract from the living moment its full sensory and emotional potential. For, if the present is no longer to hold hostage to the future, what other course than to ravish it at the very instant of its apprehension?

There is much about the hippie subculture that already betokens this alteration of time-perspective and concomitant reconstitution of the experienced self. Hippie argot—some of it new, much of it borrowed, with slight connotative changes, from the Negro, jazz, homosexual, and addict subcultures—is markedly skewed toward words and phrases in the active present tense: "happening," "where it's at," "turn on," "freak out," "grooving," "mind-blowing," "be-in," "cop out," "split," "drop acid" (take LSD), "put on," "uptight" (anxious and tense), "trip out" (experience the far-out effects of a hallucinogenic drug). The very concept of a happening signifies immediacy: Events are to be actively engaged in, improvised upon, and dramatically exploited for their own sake, with little thought about their origins, duration, or consequences. Thus, almost anything—from a massive be-in in Golden Gate Park to ingesting LSD to a casual street conversation to sitting solitarily under a tree—is approached with a heightened awareness of its happening potential. Similarly, the vogue among Hashbury hippies for astrology, tarot cards, I Ching, and other forms of thaumaturgic prophecy (a hippie conversation is as likely to begin with "What's your birthday?" as "What's your name?") seems to be an attempt to denude the future of its temporal integrity—its unknowability and slow unfoldingness—by fusing it indiscriminately with present dispositions and sensations. The hippie's structureless round-of-day ("hanging loose"), his disdain for appointments, schedules, and straight society's compulsive parceling out of minutes and hours, are all implicated in his intense reverence for the possibilities of the present and uninterest in the future. Few wear watches, and, as a colleague who has made a close participant-observer study of one group of hippies remarked, "None of them ever seems to know what time it is."

It is, perhaps, from this vantage point that the widespread use of drugs by hippies acquires its cultural significance, above and beyond the fact that drugs are easily available in the subculture, or that their use (especially LSD) has come to symbolize a distinctive badge of membership in that culture. Denied by our Protestant-Judaic heritage the psychological means for experiencing the moment intensively, for parlaying sensation and exoticizing mundane consciousness, the hippie uses drugs where untutored imagination fails. Drugs impart to the present—or so it is alleged by the hippie psychedelic religionists—an aura of aliveness, a sense of union with fellow man and nature, that—we have been taught—can be apprehended, if not in the afterlife that few modern men still believe in, then only after the deepest reflection and self-knowledge induced by protracted experience.

A topic of lively debate among hippie intellectuals is whether drugs represent but a transitory phase of the hippie subculture to be discarded once other, more self-generating means are discovered by its members for extracting consummatory meaning from present time, or whether drugs are the *sine qua non* of the subculture. Whatever the case, the hippies' experiment with ways to recast our notions of time and experience is deserving of close attention.

THE HIPPIES' FUTURE

As of this writing, it is by no means certain that Haight-Ashbury's "new community," as hippie spokesmen like to call it, can survive much beyond early 1968. Although the "great summer invasion" of émigré hippies fell far short of the 100,000 to 500,000 forecast, the influx of youth from California's and the nation's metropolitan suburbs was, despite considerable turnover, large enough to place a severe strain on the new community's meager resources. "Crash pads" for the night were simply not available in sufficient quantity; the one daily meal of soup or stew served free by the Diggers could hardly appease youthful appetites; and even the lure of free love, which to young minds might be construed as a substitute for food, tarnished for many—boys outnumbered girls by at least three to one, if not more. Besides, summer is San Francisco's most inclement season, the city being shrouded in a chilling, wind-blown fog much of the time. The result was hundreds of youths leading a hand-to-mouth existence, wandering aimlessly on the streets, panhandling, munching stale doughnuts, sleeping in parks and autos, and contracting virulent upper-respiratory infections. In this milieu, cases of drug abuse, notably involving Methedrine and other "body-wrecking" amphetamines, have shown an alarming increase, beginning about mid-summer and continuing up to the present. And, while the city fathers were not at first nearly so repressive as many had feared, they barely lifted a finger to ameliorate the situation in the Haight-Ashbury. Recently, however, with the upcoming city elections for mayor and members of the Board of Supervisors, they have given evidence of taking a "firmer" attitude toward the hippies: Drug arrests are on the increase; many more minors in the area are being stopped for questioning and referral to juvenile authorities; and a leading Haight Street hippie cultural establishment, the Straight Theatre, has been denied a dance permit.

It has not, therefore, been solely the impact of sheer numbers that has subjected the new community to a difficult struggle for survival. A variety of forces, internal and external, appear to have conjoined to crush it. To begin with, there is the hippies' notorious, near-anarchic aversion to sustained and organized effort toward reaching some goal. Every man "does his own thing for as long as he likes" until another thing comes along to distract or delight him, whereupon the hippie ethos enjoins him to drop the first thing. (Shades of the early, utopian Karl Marx: ". . . in the communist society it [will be] possible for me to do this today and that tomorrow, to hunt in the morning, to fish in the afternoon, to raise cattle in the evening, to be a critic after dinner, just as I feel at the moment; without ever being a hunter, fisherman, herdsman, or critic." From *The German Ideology.*) Even with such groups as the Diggers, projects are abandoned almost as soon as they are begun. One of the more prominent examples: An ongoing pastoral idyll of summer cultural happenings, proclaimed with great fanfare in May by a group calling itself the Council for the Summer of Love, was abandoned in June when the Council's leader decided one morning to leave town. Add to this the stalling and ordinance-juggling of a city bureaucracy reluctant to grant hippies permits and licenses for their pet enterprises, and very little manages to get off the ground. With only a few notable exceptions, therefore, like the Haight-Ashbury Free Medical Clinic, which—though closed temporarily—managed, through its volunteer staff, to look after the medical needs of thousands of hippies during the summer, the new community badly failed to provide for the hordes of youth drawn by its paeans of freedom, love, and the new life. Perhaps there is some ultimate wisdom to "doing one's own thing"; it was, however, hardly a practical way to receive a flock of kinsmen.

Exacerbating the "uptightness" of the hippies is a swelling stream of encounters with the police and courts, ranging from panhandling misdemeanors to harboring runaway minors ("contributing to the delinquency of a minor") to what is most unnerving for hip inhabitants, a growing pattern of sudden mass arrests for marihuana use and possession in which as many as 25 youths may be hauled off in a single raid on a flat. (Some hippies console themselves with the thought that, if enough middle-class youths get "busted for grass," such a hue and cry will be generated in respectable quarters that the marihuana laws will soon be repealed or greatly liberalized.) And, as if the internal problems of the new community were not enough, apocalyptic rumors sprung up, in the wake of the Newark and Detroit riots, that "the Haight is going to be burned to the ground," along with the adjoining Fillmore Negro ghetto. There followed a series of ugly street incidents between blacks and whites—assaults, sexual attacks, window smashings—that palpably heightened racial tensions and fed the credibility of the rumors.

Finally, the area's traffic-choked main thoroughfare, Haight Street, acquired in the space of a few months so carnival and Dantesque an atmosphere as to defy description. Hippies, tourists, drug peddlers, Hell's Angels, drunks, speed freaks (people high on Methedrine), panhandlers, pamphleteers, street musicians, crackpot evangelists, photographers, TV camera crews, reporters (domestic and foreign), researchers, ambulatory schizophrenics, and hawkers of the underground press (at least four such papers are produced in the Haight-Ashbury alone) jostled, put-on, and taunted one another through a din worthy of the Tower of Babel. The street-milling was incessant, and all heads remained cocked for "something to happen" to crystallize the disarray. By early summer, so repugnant had this atmosphere become for the "old" hippies (those residing there before—the origins of Hashbury's new community barely go back two years) that many departed; those who remained did so in the rapidly fading hope that the area might revert to its normal state of abnormality following the expected post–Labor Day exodus of college and high-school hippies. And, while the exodus of summer hippies has, indeed, been considerable, the consensus among knowledgeable observers of the area is that it has not regained its former, less frenetic, and less disorganized ambience. The transformations wrought by the summer influx—the growing shift to Methedrine as *the* drug of choice, the more general drift toward a wholly drug-oriented subculture, the appearance of hoodlum and thrill-seeking elements, the sleazy tourist shops, the racial tensions—persist, only on a lesser scale.

But, although Haight-Ashbury's hippie community may be destined to soon pass from the scene, the roots upon which it feeds run deep in our culture. These are not only of the long-term sociohistoric kind I have touched on here, but of a distinctly contemporary character as well, the pain and moral duplicity of our Vietnam involvement being a prominent wellspring of hippie alienation. As the pressures mount on middle-class youth for ever greater scholastic achievement (soon a graduate degree may be mandatory for middle-class status, as a high-school diploma was in the 1940's), as the years of adolescent dependence are further prolonged, and as the accelerated pace of technological change aggravates the normal social tendency to intergenerational conflict, an increasing number of young people can be expected to drop out, or opt out, and drift into the hippie subculture. It is difficult to foresee how long they will remain there and what the consequences for later stages of their careers will be, inasmuch as insufficient time has passed for even a single age cohort of hippies to make the transition from early to middle adulthood. However, even among those youths who "remain in" conventional society in some formal sense, a very large number can be expected to hover so close to the margins of hippie subculture as to have their attitudes and outlooks substantially modified. Indeed, it is probably through some such muted, gradual, and indirect process of social conversion that the hippie subculture will make a lasting impact on American society, if it is to have any at all.

At the same time, the hippie rebellion gives partial, as yet ambiguous, evidence of a massiveness, a universality, and a density of existential texture—all of which promise to transcend the narrowly segregrated confines of age, occupation, and residence that characterized most bohemias of the past (Greenwich Village, Bloomsbury, the Left Bank). Some hippie visionaries already compare the movement to Christianity sweeping the Roman Empire. We cannot predict how far the movement can go toward enveloping the larger society, and whether, as it develops, it will—as have nearly all successful social movements—significantly compromise the visions that animate it with the practices of the reigning institutional system. Much depends on the state of future social discontent, particularly within the middle classes, and on the viable political options governments have for assuaging this discontent. Judging, however, from the social upheavals and mass violence of recent decades, such options are, perhaps inevitably, scarce indeed. Just possibly, then, by opting out and making their own kind of cultural waves, the hippies are telling us more than we can now imagine about our future selves.

10. SUGGESTIONS FOR FURTHER READING

APPLEBAUM, RICHARD. *Theories of Social Change* (Chicago: Markham, 1970).

BOULDING, KENNETH. *A Primer on Social Dynamics* (New York: The Free Press, 1970).*

DALTON, GEORGE (ed.). *Economic Development and Social Change* (Garden City, N.Y.: Natural History Press, 1971).*

EHRLICH, PAUL. *The Population Bomb* (New York: Ballantine Books, 1968).*

EISENSTADT, S. N. (ed.). *Comparative Perspectives on Social Change* (Boston: Little Brown, 1968).*

——— (ed.). *Readings in Social Evolution and Development* (London: Pergamon Press, 1970).*

ETZIONI, A., AND E. ETZIONI. (eds.). *Social Change* (New York: Basic Books, 1964).

FOSTER, GEORGE. *Tzintzuntzan: Mexican Peasants in a Changing World* (Boston: Little Brown, 1967).*

HAGEN, EVERETT. *On the Theory of Social Change* (Homewood, Ill.: Dorsey Press, 1962).

HEILBRONER, ROBERT. *The Great Ascent: The Struggle for Economic Development in Our Time* (New York: Harper & Row, 1963).*

KERR, CLARK, *et al. Industrialism and Industrial Man* (New York: Oxford University Press, 1964).*

LERNER, DANIEL. *The Passing of Traditional Society* (New York: The Free Press, 1958).*

LOPREATO, JOSEPH. *Peasants No More* (San Francisco: Chandler, 1967).

MACK, RAYMOND. *Transforming America* (New York: Random House, 1967).*

MILLIKAN, M., AND D. BLACKMER (eds.). *The Emerging Nations* (Boston: Little Brown, 1961).*

MOORE, BARRINGTON, Jr. *Political Power and Social Theory* (Cambridge, Mass.: Harvard University Press, 1958).*

MOORE, WILBERT. *Social Change* (Englewood Cliffs, N.J.: Prentice-Hall, 1963).*

NASH, MANNING. *Machine Age Maya* (Chicago: University of Chicago Press, 1958).*

POWDERMAKER, HORTENSE. *Coppertown: Changing Africa* (New York: Harper & Row, 1962).*

SLATER, PHILIP. *The Pursuit of Loneliness* (Boston: Beacon Press, 1970).*

TOFFLER, ALVIN. *Future Shock* (New York: Bantam Books, 1971).*

* *Available in paperback.*